LIVES OF THE MASTERS

Tsongkhapa

A BUDDHA IN THE LAND OF SNOWS

Thupten Jinpa

FOREWORD BY

The Dalai Lama

Shambhala
BOULDER · 2019

Shambhala Publications, Inc.
4720 Walnut Street
Boulder, Colorado 80301
www.shambhala.com

9 8 7 6 5 4 3 2 1

FIRST EDITION
Printed in Canada

♾ This edition is printed on acid-free paper that meets the
American National Standards Institute z39.48 Standard.
♻ This book is printed on 100% postconsumer recycled paper.
For more information please visit www.shambhala.com.

Shambhala Publications is distributed worldwide by
Penguin Random House, Inc., and its subsidiaries.

LIBRARY OF CONGRESS CATALOGING-IN-PUBLICATION DATA
Names: Thupten Jinpa, author.
Title: Tsongkhapa: a Buddha in the Land of Snows/Thupten Jinpa.
Description: First edition. | Boulder: Shambhala, 2019. |
Series: Lives of the Masters | Includes bibliographical references and index.
Identifiers: LCCN 2019007663 | ISBN 9781611806465 (pbk.: alk. paper)
Subjects: LCSH: Tsong-kha-pa Blo-bzang-grags-pa, 1357–1419. |
Dge-lugs-pa lamas—Tibet region—Biography.
Classification: LCC BQ7950.T757 T585 2019 |
DDC 294.3/923092 [B]—dc23
LC record available at
https://lccn.loc.gov/2019007663

Contents

Series Introduction

BUDDHIST TRADITIONS are heir to some of the most creative thinkers in world history. The Lives of the Masters series offers lively and reliable introductions to the lives, works, and legacies of key Buddhist teachers, philosophers, contemplatives, and writers. Each volume in the Lives series tells the story of an innovator who embodied the ideals of Buddhism, crafted a dynamic living tradition during his or her lifetime, and bequeathed a vibrant legacy of knowledge and practice to future generations.

Lives books rely on primary sources in the original languages to describe the extraordinary achievements of Buddhist thinkers and illuminate these achievements by vividly setting them within their historical contexts. Each volume offers a concise yet comprehensive summary of the master's life and an account of how they came to hold a central place in Buddhist traditions. Each contribution also contains a broad selection of the master's writings.

This series makes it possible for all readers to imagine Buddhist masters as deeply creative and inspired people whose work was animated by the rich complexity of their time and place and how these inspiring figures continue to engage our quest for knowledge and understanding today.

KURTIS SCHAEFFER, *series editor*

Series Introduction

THE DALAI LAMA

I WELCOME THE PUBLICATION of this new biography of the great Tibetan scholar-yogi Jé Tsongkhapa compiled by Dr. Thupten Jinpa Langri.

Born in 1357 in Amdo, northeastern Tibet, and educated in central Tibet, Tsongkhapa led a life that exemplified the importance of study, critical reflection, and meditative practice. In an autobiographical poem he declared:

> First I sought wide and extensive learning,
> Second I perceived all teachings as personal instructions,
> Finally, I engaged in meditative practice day and night;
> All these I dedicated to the flourishing of the Buddha's
> teaching.

By the end of his life, 600 years ago, Tsongkhapa was widely revered across Tibet. He had studied and corresponded with the most renowned teachers of his time, from all the major traditions, and had spent years in meditative retreat. His collected writings fill eighteen volumes and cover a wide range of topics.

His teachings have been crucial to my own education. As a young boy I memorized his verses in praise of the Buddha for his explanation of dependent arising. My scholarly training entailed studying his works elucidating the great Indian classics of Nāgārjuna, Asaṅga, Maitreya, and Candrakīrti. My respect for his *Great Treatise on the Stages of the Path to Enlightenment* was such that when I fled Lhasa in March 1959, I made sure I took my own copy with me. Later, in the 1960s in India, reading his *Elucidation of the Thought* I came upon lines that stated that the "I" is merely designated on the basis of the psycho-physical aggregates, and I felt as if I'd been struck by lightning. Subsequently, I realized that what I had understood at that moment was the coarse selflessness of a person.

An important part of Tsongkhapa's legacy is the emphasis he placed on critical analysis as essential to the attainment of enlightenment. He revitalized the approach, typical of the Nalanda tradition, that takes reasoned philosophical scrutiny as essential to understanding the nature of reality. In preparing *The Golden Rosary*, his commentary on Maitreya's *Ornament for Realizations*, he analyzed and critically compared the positions of twenty-one treatises by Indian masters before determining his own interpretation. He went out of his way to clarify the most difficult points. When I asked an eminent Indian scholar of Sanskrit literature how Jé Rinpoché's treatises compared with the works of the great Indian masters of Nālandā, he replied that even in such illustrious company, Tsongkhapa would have been considered outstanding.

Tsongkhapa's meticulous approach, when interpreting crucial philosophical issues, of going back to the authentic Indian sources rather than relying solely on Tibetan commentaries, has inspired me too to delve into the great Indian treatises. Consequently, I regularly read the works of great masters like Nāgārjuna, Āryadeva, and Candrakīrti. Whenever the opportunity arises, I receive the oral transmission of such texts to pass on to others in the hope that they too will read and study these books rather than letting them merely gather dust on the shelf.

Tsongkhapa had a far-reaching impact on Tibetan tradition. In terms of the three higher trainings in ethics, concentration, and wisdom, he wrote, "Those who wish to discipline others have first to discipline themselves." His strict adherence to the culture and practice of *vinaya*, or monastic discipline, set a widely admired standard. His thorough and illuminating writings about Madhyamaka philosophy profoundly enriched Tibetan understanding of Nāgārjuna's school of thought, stimulating critical thinking about the deeper implications of the view of emptiness. Moreover, his systematic exploration of Buddhist tantra, especially the highest yoga systems of Guhyasamāja and Cakrasaṃvara, has ensured not only that their practice has flourished but also that they have been more clearly understood.

I continue to study Tsongkhapa's writings, particularly his *Essence of Eloquence* that explores which of the Buddha's teachings can be regarded as definitive and which are provisional, as well as *Ocean of Reasoning*, his consummate exposition of Nāgārjuna's *Treatise on the Middle Way*. While remaining a life-long student, I have also been fortunate to explain many of Tsongkhapa's texts to others in the hope of keeping alive the tradition of study, teaching, and practice based on his writing and thought.

I congratulate Thupten Jinpa, my translator of many years, for preparing this fresh biography of Jé Tsongkhapa. I am confident that it will enable a broader readership to appreciate the life, thought, and legacy of this exceptional Tibetan philosopher and teacher.

Ganden Monastery, founded by Tsongkhapa in 1409.
© Hugh Richardson/Tibet Images

Preface

One cold spring morning in 1969, a small group of Tibetan monks left their monastery in hushed silence, moving quickly under cover of darkness before the day broke. They were carrying with them something that had been a sacred object of worship at their monastery for centuries. It was the embalmed body of a Tibetan lama that had remained, for over five hundred years, encased within a stūpa, a reliquary monument. The body belonged to Tsongkhapa—arguably the most influential figure in Tibetan Buddhist history—and the monks were members of Ganden Monastery, which Tsongkhapa had founded in 1409.

The body was brought to a quiet location away from the monastery, and the monks, with their hearts heavy, conflicted, and terrified, burned it to ashes. They did this at the urging of a sympathetic Tibetan Communist party cadre so that the sacred body would not suffer public desecration at the hands of the Red Guards, the young Communists who, at the urging of Mao Zedong and in the name of the Cultural Revolution, were destroying "the four olds"—old ideas, old culture, old customs, and old habits. Rumor has it one of the monks sliced off a piece of Tsongkhapa's body and successfully kept it for posterity.

Beginning just a few days after this secretive cremation and continuing over a period of some two and a half weeks, a horde of Red Guards picked Ganden apart using picks, crowbars, shovels, spades, and daggers. "Tons of loot were carried off in trucks," reported a

New York Times journalist who later collected eyewitness accounts of the destruction. "Then the monastery was dynamited."[1] Today, Ganden has been mostly rebuilt, and Tsongkhapa's stūpa, known as the "Golden Reliquary at Ganden," has been once again installed at the monastery, albeit minus its most important contents—Tsongkhapa's embalmed body.

My first conscious memory connected with Tsongkhapa goes back to my years as a Tibetan refugee child at a Tibetan Children's Home in Shimla, India. I remember celebrating the Tibetan Light Festival; what made this particular celebration memorable was the unique custom of placing rows of butter lamps on windowsills on the outside at night. The occasion is called Ganden Ngachö Chenmo, "the Great Ganden Festival of the Twenty-Fifth," a date referring to the passing of Tsongkhapa in 1419.

Even as a child, thanks to two monk teachers at the children's home, I knew by heart the following lines from Tsongkhapa:

> Good and bad karma are functions of your intention;
> When your intention is good, everything becomes good;
> When your intention is bad, everything becomes bad;
> So everything depends on your intention.

After I became a monk at Dzongkar Chödé Monastery at the age of eleven, I had more explicit exposure to Tsongkhapa—participating in elaborate celebrations of his nirvāṇa, listening to his life story told by older monks, and memorizing texts he had composed. I learned to chant hymns written by him in praise of the Buddha as well as hymns to him composed by his own disciples. In the spring of 1971, as a young monk, I heard His Holiness the Dalai Lama teach Tsongkhapa's *Great Treatise on the Stages of the Path to Enlightenment*. The teaching went on, two sessions a day, for nearly two months. Little did I realize then how my own life would later revolve so much around the writings and legacy of this great Tibetan master.

In 1978, I joined Tsongkhapa's Ganden Monastery, by then reestablished in Mundgod in southern India. There, I had the chance to formally study Tsongkhapa's great texts, memorize his hermeneutic work *The Essence of True Eloquence*, debate the intricate meanings of his treatises, critically engage with his thought, and undertake meditative practices based on his instructions. Even as I plunged into contemporary academic scholarship at Cambridge University, studying Western philosophy, I ended up writing my PhD thesis on Tsongkhapa's philosophy, focusing on his views of self, reality, and reason. As I write this biography, I am in the final stages of editing my English translation of Tsongkhapa's last major, and possibly most influential, philosophical work, *Elucidation of the Intent*.

Tsongkhapa was a monk, a poet, a philosopher, a teacher, and a student of the Buddha. To his devout followers, he came to be known as none other than "the second Buddha." Personally, what I find most compelling in Tsongkhapa's life and work is the journey of a clear intellect that earnestly sought to develop a truly integrated worldview. Tsongkhapa strove to articulate a kind of Buddhist path wherein the demands of rational inquiry support, rather than undermine, a robust spiritual vision of enlightenment. He believed and demonstrated that the application of analysis and reason to understanding reality and our human existence could underpin a profound quest for meaning. Not all contemporary readers will share my enthusiasm for what Tsongkhapa proposes as a worldview integrating intellect and spirit. But I contend that there are substantive lessons we can learn from engaging with his thought even in this postmodern, digital, global age. I, for one, cannot imagine my own philosophical outlook, moral sensibility, and personal spiritual path without my exposure to Tsongkhapa.

It gives me great joy to have this opportunity to introduce the larger world to Tsongkhapa, one of Tibet's greatest minds, whose life and thought have remained a source of profound inspiration and meaning for so many Tibetans and others over the past six centuries.

Acknowledgments

ONE OF THE JOYS of writing a book is to have the chance to offer heartfelt gratitude to others. First and foremost, I would like express profound gratitude to my root guru, His Holiness the Fourteenth Dalai Lama. Through his life and teaching, His Holiness powerfully demonstrates what Tsongkhapa's life, thought, and teachings represent. I also thank His Holiness also for honoring this volume with a foreword. I acknowledge my deep indebtedness to my two personal teachers at Ganden Monastery, Kyabjé Zemey Rinpoché and Khensur Lati Rinpoché, who educated me in the classical Buddhist disciplines of knowledge, especially through introducing me to Tsongkhapa's great treatises.

I would like to thank my colleagues Alexander Norman, Donald Lopez Jr., Elizabeth Napper, Geshe Ngawang Samten, Jas Elsner, Robert Thurman, and Roger Jackson, who all offered critical feedback on my first draft of the book. I am especially indebted to Donald Lopez and Roger Jackson, who each independently devoted substantive time to help improve the manuscript through careful line editing, correcting spelling of Sanskrit terms, and ensuring consistency of translation terms across the entire text. That said, whatever errors still remain are all mine. I would like to thank the BDRC (Buddhist Digital Resource Center) and its research associate Lobsang Shastri for giving me access to scanned Tibetan texts, including especially those that are still in development stages. Without the BDRC's online resources, this book would have been quite impoverished. I thank Gelong Thupten Yarphel of Namgyal

Monastery for obtaining for me the entire set of the recent four-volume *Anthology of the Biographies of Jé Tsongkhapa*, published in Tibet, as well as my colleague Geshe Lobsang Choedar for assisting me in examining some of the obscure references in the Tibetan sources. My gratitude to Jane Moore for helping me obtain permission to reprint the beautiful photograph of Ganden Monastery taken by Hugh Richardson and to Don Larson for creating the map of the Tibetan Plateau. I thank Kurtis Schaeffer, the editor of The Lives of the Masters series, and Nikko Odiseos, Shambhala's president, for inviting me to be part of the series. To my two editors at Shambhala, Matt Zepelin and Emily Coughlin, I am grateful for their careful copyediting of this book. Matt, in particular, I owe deeply for his kindness in undertaking a critical review of the first draft and offering insightful counsel on how best to frame and present complex ideas of Tibetan Buddhist thought and practice in ways that might resonate more easily with my reader.

I thank my family: my wife, Sophie Boyer-Langri, and our two daughters, Khando and Tara, for their patience in enduring my frequent passionate outbursts about Tsongkhapa's life and thought during the period of writing. I might have abused them as my sounding boards whenever I was trying to articulate some intricate ideas in plain English. Last but not least, I would like to express my deep gratitude to the Ing Foundation for its patronage of the Institute of Tibetan Classics, and I would also like to thank the Scully Peretsman Foundation for its generous support of my own work. These sources of support together enabled me to find the time to initiate, undertake, and implement this important project and to bring it to successful completion.

Tsongkhapa

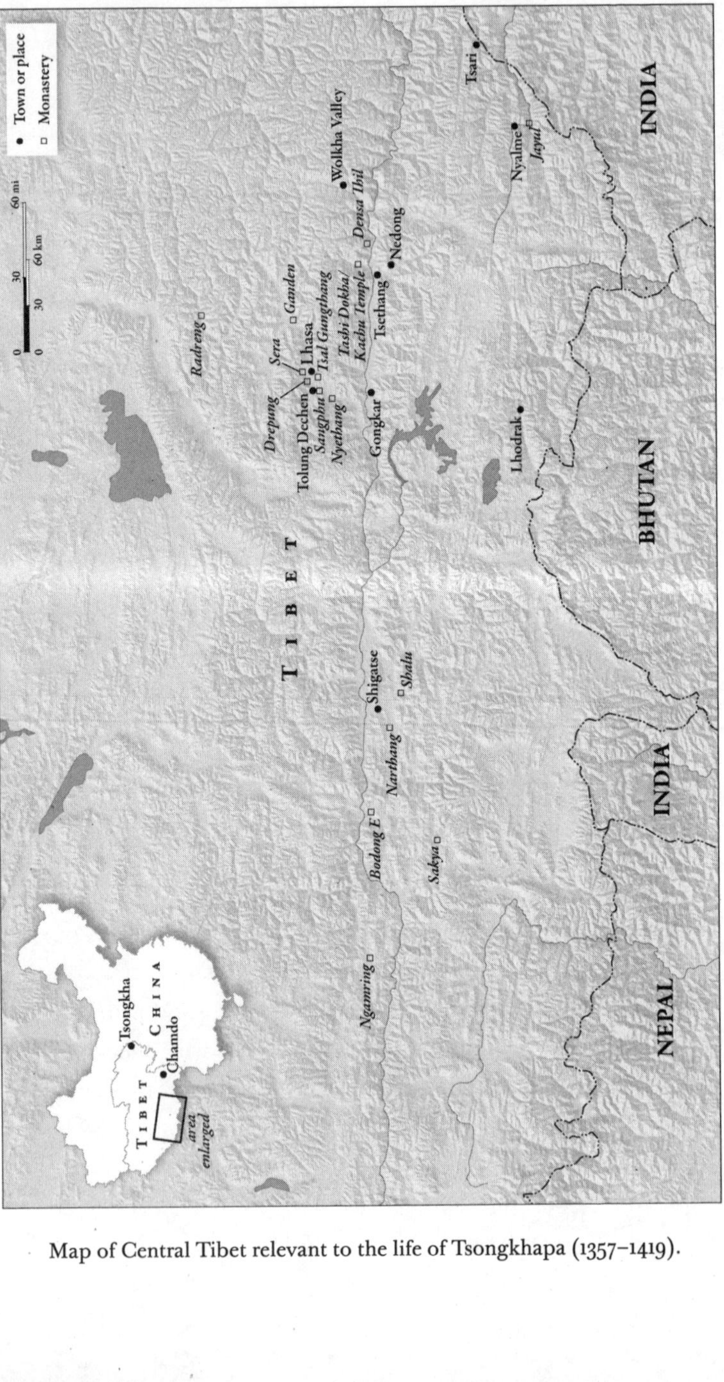

Map of Central Tibet relevant to the life of Tsongkhapa (1357–1419).

Introduction

On March 18, 1716, an Italian Jesuit priest named Ippolito Desideri reached Tibet's holy city of Lhasa, completing a months-long journey from the Portuguese colony of Goa in southern India. Desideri had come to Tibet as a missionary, intent on converting the population to Catholicism. He soon came to understand that the Tibetans had an advanced intellectual culture of dialectics and reason. Preaching the Gospel alone, on the assumption of its unquestioned truth, would not be adequate to convince Tibetans of the truth of Christianity. If he were to succeed in missionizing Tibet, he would first have to demonstrate the falsity of the Tibetan people's own Buddhist faith. To this end, he plunged into the study of the Tibetan language and Buddhist philosophy.

A brilliant individual, Desideri made quick progress in his education. He studied at Sera Monastery, one of the three great monastic universities of central Tibet. The Italian debated with scholars from Drepung, the largest monastic university in central Tibet (and possibly in the world at the time). While he retained his determination to convert his hosts, Desideri wrote admiringly that "although the Tibetans are quite amenable to listening with good will, they are not superficial or credulous; they want to see, weigh, and discuss everything in great detail, with logical reasoning; they want to be convinced and not to be instructed."[2]

More and more, Desideri saw the extent of the task he had taken on in attempting to missionize the Tibetans. He recognized the centrality of the role of critical inquiry in Tibet's spiritual and intellectual tradition; he witnessed the great monastic universities—Sera, Drepung, and Ganden—thriving with study, debate, and meditative contemplations; and he saw the profound devotion with which the institution of the Dalai Lama (whom he called the "grand lama") was held by the Tibetan people. Most important, from his missionary point of view, he saw that the Tibetan monks' resilience against missionizing was grounded in a deep sense of confidence in their own worldview.

Desideri first focused on mastering the Tibetan language as well as the Tibetan tradition's unique dialectic debate system.[3] He also came to see that he needed to find the right text, a key to unlock the mystery of the Tibetans and their confidence. Soon he believed he had found just such a key. It became clear to him that there existed a text so esteemed by Tibetan scholars that if he could decisively refute it, it would be akin to destroying one of the central pillars of the religion. That text was *The Great Treatise on the Stages of the Path to Enlightenment* (popularly known in Tibetan by its shorter name *Lamrim Chenmo*), a monumental work written by the great fourteenth-century teacher Tsongkhapa.

Desideri took extensive notes from the work, copied its entire topical outline, and read the Indian canonical sources cited in Tsongkhapa's text. The Jesuit priest described his chosen Tibetan text as "a virtual compendium of the 115 volumes of the Kangyur [the Tibetan Buddhist canon]." He wrote that Tsongkhapa "sets forth with wonderful organization, style, and clarity all the principles and false beliefs of this sect, and in particular, summarizes the abstruse treatises on *tongpanyi* (emptiness)."[4] Later, when he wrote his "Tibet Missionary Manual," Desideri would insist that those who wish to missionize Tibet must furnish themselves with a personal copy of Tsongkhapa's *Great Treatise*, "which is [a] profuse, admirable, clear, elegant, subtle, clever, methodical, and most accurate compendium of everything pertaining to that sect."[5]

Although Desideri did eventually compose the grand refutation of *The Great Treatise*—and thereby, he hoped, of the Tibetan Buddhist tradition at large—that he had set out to write, his work got caught up in the power struggles between rival orders of the Catholic Church.[6] In 1732, the Vatican's Sacred Congregation for the Propagation of the Faith confirmed its grant of the Tibet mission to the Capuchin order and barred the publication of any writings from the Jesuit mission. This meant that the four works Desideri had written in Tibetan—most notably, his *Inquiry Concerning the Doctrines of Previous Lives and Emptiness*—would sit unread, gathering dust in the archives of the Society of Jesus in Rome. Following his return to Europe, Desideri would translate Tsongkhapa's great work into Italian, making it the first major Tibetan work to be translated into a European language—but that too sat virtually unnoticed for centuries.

Desideri's engagement with *The Great Treatise* powerfully captures how Tsongkhapa and his legacy appeared to a discerning outsider at the turn of the eighteenth century. It is no surprise that Desideri chose this work of Tsongkhapa to help open the secrets of Tibetan Buddhism. Imagining the roles reversed, it would be as if a discerning Tibetan of that era were to select St. Thomas Aquinas's *Summa Theologica* to help develop a more systematic understanding of Catholic theology.

Who Was Tsongkhapa?

Assessing the depth of his thought and the breadth of his legacy, traditional Tibetan historians and modern scholars alike rank Tsongkhapa among the most important figures in the history of Tibetan

Buddhism. Who was Tsongkhapa? There is no simple answer to this question. For his followers, especially the most devout, Tsongkhapa was "the second Buddha," "the regent of the Buddha," "Guru Mañjuśrī, the buddha of wisdom," "the Sovereign Lord of the Dharma Kingdom," and the "Light of the Buddha's Doctrine." For members of other Tibetan Buddhist schools, including even his critics, he was still "the Great Tsongkhapa from the East," "the Teacher, the Great Tsongkhapa," or "the Precious Guru Lobsang Drakpa," Lobsang Drakpa being his monastic ordination name.

Tsongkhapa (1357–1419) was the founder of the Geluk school of Tibetan Buddhism. Although Geluk is the youngest of the four major Tibetan traditions (the other three being Nyingma, Sakya, and Kagyü), it rose to prominence on the strength of Tsongkhapa's innovative, rigorous, and comprehensive interpretations of Buddhist thought and practice. Through his close critical reading and insightful interpretation of the major Indian Buddhist classics, extensive meditative cultivation over prolonged periods in various hermitages, and composition of highly influential works, Tsongkhapa created a remarkable integration of the vast Indian Buddhist heritage that the Tibetans had received in preceding centuries. His interpretation of Nāgārjuna's philosophy of emptiness, read especially through Candrakīrti and combined with epistemological insights from Dignāga and Dharmakīrti, led to an entirely new school of Madhyamaka thought in Tibet. His emphasis on the role of analysis and reasoned knowledge as essential elements of the path to enlightenment challenged the assumptions of many in Tibet about the nature and function of meditative practice and ethical conduct. Tsongkhapa's teachings helped stimulate a sophisticated appreciation of the important trio of view, meditation, and conduct. In particular, Tsongkhapa's two syntheses—his *Great Treatise on the Stages of the Path to Enlightenment* and a treatise on the stages of the Vajrayāna path—powerfully brought home the importance of having the "big picture" while one is engaged in specific aspects of the Buddhist path. They also helped forge a cogent and clear understanding of the relationship between the Mahāyāna path of the six perfections (generosity, morality, forbearance, diligence, concentration, and wisdom) and the "esoteric" Vajrayāna path constituted by the twin stages of generation and completion (as described below). In modern parlance, what Tsongkhapa offered his fellow Tibetan Buddhists was a complete, philosophically rigorous worldview integrating all the important insights of Buddhist thought and practice.

When, in the seventeenth century, the Dalai Lama rose to become the central figure of Tibetan Buddhism and the Tibetan nation, the Geluk tradition became the politically dominant school and has remained so to this day. Tsongkhapa's importance as the inspirational founder of the Geluks continued into the twentieth century. In 1959, when His Holiness the Fourteenth Dalai Lama fled Lhasa, in disguise, to escape Communist Chinese persecution, he carried among his few possessions a copy of Tsongkhapa's *Great Treatise*.

Tibetan Buddhist History Prior to Tsongkhapa

To appreciate who Tsongkhapa was and his importance to Tibetan Buddhism requires some understanding of his background, including the history of Buddhism in Tibet prior to his lifetime.

Buddhism first came to Tibet in the seventh century, during the reign of the powerful emperor Songtsen Gampo (ca. 605–50).[7] According to traditional accounts, the emperor married, in addition to his Tibetan queen, princesses from Nepal and China, Tibet's two neighboring kingdoms with strong Buddhist presence. It was during Songtsen Gampo's reign that the current Tibetan writing system, based on a version of the Indian Devanagari script, was developed; the first translations of Indian Buddhist texts were undertaken; and the great Jokhang Temple of Lhasa was built.

The next major epoch occurred in the eighth century under Emperor Trisong Detsen. During Trisong's forty-two-year reign (755–97), the famed Indian philosopher Śāntarakṣita was successfully invited to Tibet, where he helped found Samyé Monastery, instituted monastic ordination, and introduced the literature of philosophical scholarship as it was then being practiced at India's great Nālandā University. He also urged the king, according to traditional Tibetan sources, to invite the great tantric master Padmasambhava to Tibet. Most important, it was at this time that the systematic project of translating the Indian Buddhist texts into Tibetan began.

It was also during Trisong's reign that the struggle for dominance between the Indian and Chinese forms of Buddhism in Tibet, which had been going on for several decades, was finally resolved, with the Indian side prevailing. While politics and power may have been at play, especially with respect to attracting allegiances of powerful ruling families at the Tibetan imperial court, there was a serious philosophical dispute at the heart of the struggle. This concerned the role of reasoning and discursive inquiry on the path to enlightenment, with the Chinese side rejecting the need for it, and also whether the attainment of enlightenment is a matter of progressive stages of development or instantaneous, with the Chinese side advocating the latter.

Although subsequent Tibetan emperors continued their support of Buddhism in the country, the Tibetan tradition recognizes especially the contributions of Songtsen, Trisong, and the ninth-century emperor Tri Ralpa Chen (r. 815–38). Thus, these three emperors are honored in traditional sources as Tibet's "three ancestral religious kings" (*chögyal mewön namsum*), and this period between the seventh and mid-ninth centuries is described as the first diffusion of Buddhism in Tibet.

In 838, Emperor Tri Ralpa Chen was deposed in a coup d'état by Udumtsen, popularly known as Lang Darma, who began to rein in what he perceived to be excesses of the Tibetan emperor's patronage of Buddhism and its institutions. Lang Darma was assassinated in 842. Coinciding with a decline of the military power of the Tibetan empire, Lang Darma's assassination began a period of major disruption and strife, eventually leading to the empire's collapse in the latter half of the ninth century. With the political fragmentation of Tibet into smaller regional kingdoms, and with no centralized imperial patronage, Buddhist institutions struggled. Monasteries shrank or closed, and systematic translation and scholarship projects decreased.[8] According to traditional sources, even the monastic ordination lineage came to an end, and no monastics were seen in central Tibet for almost a century.[9]

Systematic attempts to revive Buddhism in Tibet began in several regions around the end of the tenth century. Monastic ordination was revived in central Tibet by a group of ten men who were sent to Amdo (northeastern Tibet) by the ruler of Samyé to receive formal ordination from the elder Lachen Gongpa Rapsel (b. 953).[10] Around this time, the great Indian scholar Smṛti Jñānakīrti, who later wrote a major grammar of the Tibetan language, also happened to visit Tibet. The most influential initiative in reviving Buddhism in Tibet took place through the efforts of the Gugé rulers of western Tibet, who were seeking to "reinstitute the Tibetan empire within their own domains."[11] They founded temples, including Tholing Monastery; sent young monastics to be trained in India; and sponsored translations of major Buddhist texts, especially under the leadership of the great translator Rinchen Sangpo (958–1055). Thanks to their efforts and sacrifice, the Indian Bengali teacher Atiśa (982–1054) agreed to come to Tibet, where he helped greatly in the systematic revival of Buddhism in Tibet. This period, the early to mid-eleventh century, is known as the start of the second diffusion of Buddhism in Tibet.[12]

Atiśa's mission in western and central Tibet, over the course of twelve years' stay in the country—with support from his spiritual heir Dromtönpa (1005–64)—led to the emergence of the Kadam school, effectively Tibet's first formal Buddhist school. Retroactively, the tradition that continued to focus on the teachings of the early imperial period, especially the esoteric Vajrayāna instructions, would come to be known as Nyingma, the "Old School." Around the same time, the independent efforts of Drokmi Shākya Yeshé (993–1074) and Marpa Chökyi Lodrö (1012–97), two Tibetan translators, eventually led to the emergence of two new schools of Tibetan Buddhism. From Drokmi, whose disciples included Khön Könchok Gyalpo (1034–1102), the founder of Sakya Monastery and the grandfather of Sachen Künga Nyingpo (1092–1158), emerged the Sakya school. From Marpa and his most famous disciple, Tibet's beloved poet-saint Milarepa (1052–1135), as well as Milarepa's own principal student, Gampopa (1079–1153), emerged the Kagyü school. (Over time, especially after the founding of Ganden Monastery by Tsongkhapa in 1409, Atiśa and Dromtönpa's Kadam school evolved into Tsongkhapa's Geluk school, later known also as the New Kadam school.)

Unlike the classical schools of Indian Buddhism, these Tibetan schools of the new translation period—Kadam, Sakya, and Kagyü—were distinguished not so much by their doctrinal or philosophical differences; rather, the distinctions emerged based on primary allegiances to specific instruction lineages. The Kadam school traces its lineage to the Indian master Atiśa. Similarly, the Sakya school emphasizes the lineage of translator Drogmi and his successors, especially Khön Könchok Gyalpo and his grandson Sachen Künga Nyingpo. The Kagyü school focuses on the lineage stemming from the translator Marpa, his chief disciple Milarepa, and the latter's student Gampopa.

These "new" Tibetan traditions also trace their lineages back to India, and especially to the great Indian monastic universities of Nālandā and Vikramalaśīla. Although the Indian monastic universities were later destroyed by central Asian Turkic Muslim invaders, they would continue to serve as the model for many Tibetan monasteries, beginning with Sangphu Monastery, founded in 1072 by Atiśa's disciple Ngok Lekpai Sherap. From Sangphu hailed two of Tibet's great intellectual giants: the translator Ngok Loden Sherap (1059–1109) and the logician Chapa Chökyi Sengé (1109–69). The first was, effectively, the founder of the Tibetan scholastic tradition. In addition to translating major Indian Buddhist classics, especially on *pramāṇa* (logic and epistemology), Loden Sherap is accredited with the invention of the multilayered topical outline system (*sapché*) that became a central feature of Tibetan textual composition and interpretation. He wrote summaries of major Indian Buddhist classics and also composed authoritative commentaries on key texts. Chapa is remembered for his original views on logic and epistemology and for inventing the Tibetan system of dialectical debate.

In 1153, Narthang Monastery, the Kadam's second major scholastic center of learning, was established by Tumtön Lodrö Drak. This monastery would become a major center for scholarship on Abhidharma (Buddhist psychology and metaphysics), producing two of Tibet's greatest Abhidharma authorities: Chim Namkha Drak (1210–85) and Chim Jampel Yang (thirteenth century). It was key Narthang figures, especially Chomden Rikrel (1297–1305) and his students Üpa Losel and others, who initiated the task of systematic compilation of the canon of translated Indian Buddhist texts, classifying them into the well-known collections of Kangyur (translated sūtras and tantras) and Tengyur (translated treatises).

This project of the canonization of Indian Buddhist texts would be finalized later by Butön Rinchen Drup (1290–1364),[13] who would also compose what became the "official" catalog of these two canonical collections. (It was the young Tsongkhapa's immersive reading, over a period of some four years, of the two canons finalized by Butön and housed at Tsal Gungthang Monastery that would revolutionize his take on the Indian Buddhist heritage of his Tibetan tradition.)

Another noteworthy Tibetan figure from this period is the brilliant Künga Gyaltsen (1182–1251), known popularly by his epithet Sakya Paṇḍita or its abbreviated form Sapaṇ. If Loden Sherap is the father of the Tibetan scholastic tradition, Sapaṇ must be recognized as the father of Tibet's high literary culture. It was Sapaṇ who formalized in Tibet the classification of knowledge into what are known as the five major fields (arts and crafts, medicine, linguistics, logic and epistemology, and the inner science of Buddhist thought) and the five minor fields (poetics, synonyms, prosody, plays, and astronomy). Sapaṇ also introduced classical Sanskrit poetics in Tibetan, wrote a treatise on music, and single-handedly invented the Tibetan literary genre of "wise sayings" (*lekshé*)—aphorisms that convey cultural and commonsense wisdom in evocative poetry with the aid of an analogy, often through an embedded story with a moral. He also wrote *Gateway to Becoming a Learned* (*Khejuk*), a handbook intended for anyone who aspires to be a scholar, outlining the three most important pursuits of a learned person: exposition, debate, and composition. For Tsongkhapa personally, perhaps the most important legacy of Sapaṇ was his role as "the gatekeeper of Dharma," engaging in critical examination of the Indian sources of many of the instructional lineages that had proliferated in Tibet.[14] In his *Clear Differentiation of the Three Codes*,[15] for instance, Sapaṇ subjected some of the Tibetan lineages that he deemed problematic to a sustained critique, questioning their authenticity.

In brief, by the second half of the fourteenth century, the stage was set in Tibet for the emergence of a grand synthesizer who could help bring together the vast and at times conflicting heritage of Indian Buddhist texts, knowledge, and practices into a truly integrated Tibetan tradition. Although the parallels aren't exact, Tsongkhapa's role as such a grand synthesizer could be compared to that of Thomas Aquinas in medieval European Christianity or Dogen in Japanese Zen.

Tibetan Understanding of Its Indian Buddhist Heritage

Thanks largely to historical coincidence, the tradition of Indian Buddhism that finally took root in Tibet happened to be the one dominant during the Pala dynasty in central India from the eighth century. This is a tradition that differentiated between the three vehicles (*yāna*) within Buddhism: Hīnayāna (literally, "lesser vehicle"), Mahāyāna ("great vehicle"), and Vajrayāna ("diamond vehicle"). Roughly put, the first refers to what could be called the foundational teachings of the Buddha—the four noble truths, the threefold training, the eightfold path, the thirty-seven aspects of the path to enlightenment, and so on—as embodied in the three scriptural baskets (*tripiṭaka*) of today's Theravāda tradition of countries such as Thailand, Sri Lanka, and Burma. Within this first vehicle are also the teachings of monastic discipline, or *vinaya*. The primary goal of an aspirant within this vehicle is personal liberation, the attainment of nirvāṇa, or lasting freedom from suffering and its origin.

The second vehicle, Mahāyāna, is based on a collection of scriptures—including the famed *Heart Sūtra*—attributed to the Buddha that present, among others, two key themes: universal compassion and the wisdom of emptiness, that is, that the ultimate nature of things is their lack of existence as independent, definable, and discrete entities with intrinsic natures. The heart of the Mahāyāna path consists of the development and practice of six perfections: generosity, morality, forbearance, diligence, concentration, and wisdom. The primary goal of an aspirant within this vehicle is the attainment of buddhahood for the sake of all beings.

Finally, the third vehicle, Vajrayāna, refers to a unique system of teachings and associated meditative practices that involve, in addition to the methods that are part of general Mahāyāna, the use of imagination, emotions, and the manipulation of psychophysical elements within the body. A characteristic of Vajrayāna practice, which is known also as Buddhist tantra, is "deity yoga," a meditative cultivation that involves visualizing a meditation deity, including imaginatively adopting the form and identity of that deity. Roughly, these meditation deities can be seen as anthropomorphic representations of enlightened attributes—for example, compassion, wisdom, energy, transmutation of passions—and their specific forms are often the results of yogis' visions. Each of these meditation deities is associated with a *maṇḍala* (a celestial mansion), the various aspects of which symbolize the attributes of the enlightened mind. Based on progressive stages of the ability to transmute emotions, especially sexual desire, into the path of awakening, Buddhist tantra is divided into four classes: Kriya (performance), Cārya (action), Yoga, and Highest Yoga. In Tibetan Buddhism, the teaching and practice of Highest Yoga tantra became both widespread and dominant. The heart of the practice of Highest Yoga tantra consists of the two stages of generation and completion. The generation stage involves imaginatively generating oneself into the meditation deity through various steps of cultivation, while the second stage, completion, focuses on applying yogic methods centered on visualization and manipulation of channels, winds, and drops within the human body.

For the Tibetans, in Tsongkhapa's time and still today, the three vehicles are not seen as mutually exclusive forms of Buddhism.[16] All lineages of Tibetan Buddhism share the view that Tibet's inherited Buddhist tradition represents the integration of all three vehicles and that Vajrayāna or Tantra represents the highest and also the swiftest path to buddhahood. For the Tibetans, Vajrayāna is not a vehicle separate from Mahāyāna. Mahāyāna itself is composed of the Sūtra path (sometimes referred to also as the Perfection Vehicle) and the path of Tantra or Vajrayāna. Thus, the Tibetans would characterize their Buddhist tradition's path to enlightenment as the "union of Sūtra and Tantra" (*dongak zungdrel*).[17] Tsongkhapa too shared this basic understanding of the Buddhist vehicles and their interrelationship.

The Political Context of Tibet during Tsongkhapa's Lifetime

As we move into the fourteenth century, we arrive at Tsongkhapa's own period, and it therefore becomes appropriate to consider the historical context of Tibet in finer detail.

In 1354, three years before Tsongkhapa's birth, Tai Situ Jangchup Gyaltsen (1302–64) founded the Phagdru dynasty in central and western Tibet. Jangchup Gyaltsen toppled the Sakya rulers who, with the help of their Mongol Yuan dynasty patrons, had been in power since the second half of the thirteenth century. Jangchup Gyaltsen established a unique system in which the actual ruler would remain a celibate monastic, with selected sons of his siblings groomed to be future rulers—a process that required extensive monastic education as well as assuming the abbotship of Densa Thil Monastery. This was the principal monastic seat of Phagdru Kagyü, the tradition allied with the Phagdru rulers.[18]

The reign of the longest-serving Phagdru ruler, Miwang Drakpa Gyaltsen (r. 1385–1432), coincided exactly with Tsongkhapa's rise as one of the foremost intellectual and religious figures in Tibet.

This ruler, who first met Tsongkhapa when the latter was a young monk, became his most important patron. Drakpa Gyaltsen sponsored major teachings from Tsongkhapa and supported his initiatives, such as the staging of the Great Prayer Festival in Lhasa and the founding of Ganden Monastery, both in 1409, as well as the founding of Drepung Monastery in 1416 by Tsongkhapa's disciple Jamyang Chöjé and the establishment of Sera Monastery in 1419 by another disciple, Jamchen Chöjé. In brief, the stable political climate in central Tibet created by the lengthy rule of the Phagdru dynasty, especially its fifth ruler Miwang Drakpa Gyaltsen, provided a most favorable environment for the success of Tsongkhapa's mission in Tibet.

In interpreting Tsongkhapa's life and legacy, the traditional Tibetan biographies tend to adopt what Thomas Carlyle called the Great Man theory, which emphasizes a focus on the individual heroic leader. This view is summed up by Carlyle's famous statement, "The history of the world is but the biography of great men."[19] For Tsongkhapa's Tibetan biographers, their master was destined to be who he became—in fact, some would assert that he was an enlightened being who chose to be born as a human to serve a specific need in the world. Even as a child, according to this view, he was no ordinary infant; he was an emanation of Mañjuśrī, the buddha of wisdom.

An alternative view of history, sometimes described as the zeitgeist theory, was articulated by Carlyle's contemporary Herbert Spencer. In that view, the life of a leader, even an extraordinary one, is best viewed in terms of social circumstances, with the individual leader seen primarily as a product of their circumstances.

As is often the case, the truth probably lies somewhere in between. There is no doubt that Tsongkhapa was an extraordinary man of destiny, but he was also the beneficiary of his circumstances, including a favorable political climate in central Tibet and patronage from the most powerful political figure of his time.

No Tibetan historical figure has been the subject of such extensive biographical writing in Tibetan as Tsongkhapa. Over forty biographical works of varying length are known to have appeared in the six centuries since his death. Of these, three are quite extensive, each running to over four hundred pages in the codex format.[20] These and the shorter accounts were written in the traditional style of hagiography, reflecting the Tibetan conception of the biographies of lamas as "liberating stories" (*namthar*), whose primary purpose is to inspire the faithful so that they may emulate the liberating life of their master. With a few exceptions, all of the biographies of Tsongkhapa were authored by ardent followers of his Geluk school. Understandably, these Tibetan accounts focus on the spiritual and "liberating" aspects of their master's life, including especially his extensive scholarship, meditation practice, and public deeds. The aim of these biographies is to portray the master as a perfect embodiment of the union of learning and spiritual realization (*khedrup nyidan*) and, ultimately, nothing less than a truly enlightened being.[21]

This new biography of Tsongkhapa, in contrast, is intended for the contemporary reader. It seeks to answer the following key questions: Who was or is Tsongkhapa? How is he important to Tibetan Buddhism? How did he help to create, and to attain such exalted status for, the Geluk school of Tibetan Buddhism? What relevance do his thought and legacy have in the contemporary world?

The first aim of this book is to tell the story of Tsongkhapa's life, from his birth through his gradual emergence as arguably the most influential figure in the history of Tibetan Buddhism. Drawing on the traditional biographies, the goal here is to depict an individual person whose life is both embedded in and shaped by the larger environment: the society, culture, and the beliefs he shared with other Tibetans.[22] As a biography in the contemporary sense, the book seeks to portray a complex person: his character, his drives, his relationships with key figures in his life, the influences that shaped him, and his trials and triumphs. I, for one, find the life of a master much more inspiring when it relates the journey of an ordinary human being like you and me. The challenge for me, as the narrator of the story, is to extract the human Tsongkhapa from the mythical narrative sustained over six centuries and to tell the simple story of a mortal, with all his struggles, against the backdrop of the long namthar tradition of portraying his life as enlightened deeds displayed out of compassion for the benefit of us unenlightened beings.

A second aspiration I hold for this book is to offer an accessible introduction to Tibet's rich classical philosophical, intellectual, and spiritual heritage. In telling Tsongkhapa's story—especially his early education, years of intensive meditative practice, prolonged quest for the correct view of emptiness, and spiritual attainments—my hope is to afford readers a view of the fascinating world of premodern Tibet. Furthermore, since one of my aims is to help guide the reader through Tsongkhapa's own life journey, as much as possible I attempt to outline what Tsongkhapa himself took to be the central issues of concern, both for himself and for Tibetan Buddhism at large. I also provide substantive summaries of important work he wrote on specific subjects. This way, in addition to knowing the story of Tsongkhapa's life, the reader also has an opportunity to learn something about his contributions and importance to the history of Tibetan Buddhist thought, practice, and culture.

Although I have not written this book in the traditional vein—for devout readers to help deepen their faith in a revered teacher—

Western readers should be prepared for a journey in a language and a conceptual framework quite different from those of their own culture. The reader I have foremost in mind is someone who is curious yet discerning, open to the possibilities of human experience, and interested in engaging with fundamental questions of human existence.

I have attempted to write a modern biography of Tsongkhapa, yet it would be disingenuous of me to pretend that I am approaching my subject purely as an impartial biographer with no prior biases. I am a former monk from Tsongkhapa's Ganden Monastery and continue to be a practitioner in his Geluk tradition. I undertake daily guru yoga meditation, which involves viewing the master as a truly enlightened being, renewing my emotional and spiritual connection to him.

In effect, my hope is to find a middle way between the devotional approach of earlier Tibetan writers and the objectivity demanded by the norms of modern biographical writing. I want to render Tsongkhapa as a real human figure and, in doing so, perhaps to convey to some readers the sense of enlightening potential that I and so many others have found in his writings and the example of his life.

Another middle way I have tried to find, perhaps not entirely successfully, is to write primarily for the general, educated reader while keeping in mind the specialized readership of the scholarly world of Tibetan and Buddhist studies. For the general reader, I have chosen to keep the body of the text driven mainly by the narrative of Tsongkhapa's life, focusing on chronology as well as thematic issues important for appreciating his biography and the times in which he lived. For the specialists, I have offered, primarily in the form of various endnotes, information that could shed light on issues in the intellectual history of Tsongkhapa's era: important concepts, practices, and people, as well as the formation of sectarian identities, interlineage relationships, and the larger social and political contexts of medieval Tibet. I expect that, for the specialist reader, some of the matter in the endnotes will be of greater interest than the more straightforward biography in the body of the text.

In writing this biography, I have chosen to develop the story by unfolding the events in Tsongkhapa's life in chronological order. Important to this process are the choices I have made with regard to the voluminous traditional biographical material. In the traditional sources, a distinction is drawn between public or conventional biographies (*thunmong wai namthar*), which present the life of the subject in terms of its ordinary, commonplace details, and so-called secret biographies (*sangwai namthar*), a special genre that records the more mystical and esoteric aspects of the subject's life, including especially his or her various visions. Since these stories will understandably challenge the credulity of contemporary readers, in my endnotes I clearly identify these as coming from the "secret biographies."

Visionary encounter is a theme common across many religious traditions, with St. Paul's vision of Jesus on the road to Damascus being a well-known example in the Christian tradition. In the Tibetan tradition, vision is widely recognized as both a mystical phenomenon and a source of important transmission of esoteric instructions. The Nyingma school, for example, speaks of three types of transmission: long lineage of scriptures (*ringgyü kama*), close lineage of revealed treasure texts (*nyegyü terma*), and profound lineage of pure vision (*sabmo daknang*). As for the question of what precisely occurred to Tsongkhapa with respect to these visionary accounts and what they might mean, I leave it to readers to make their own judgments. But in order to understand his life as closely as possible, to know how he and his contemporaries understood it, and to appreciate his significance to subsequent generations of Tibetan Buddhists, it is important to take seriously the extent and profound effect of visionary encounters on Tsongkhapa's development.

CHAPTER 1

Birth and Early Years

TSONGKHAPA was born in the tenth month of the Fire Bird year in the sixth Rabjung (sixty-year cycle) of the traditional Tibetan calendar. According to an alternative calendar system, based on the dating of the coronation of the first known Tibetan king, Nyatri Tsenpo, it was Tibetan Royal Year 1484. Using the Roman calendar, Tsongkhapa's birth falls sometime in October 1357.[23]

According to a biography by one of his earliest disciples, Tokden Jampel Gyatso (1356–1428), his birth is said to have occurred when the Morning Star was shining bright and clear in the sky and as the crisp fall night was giving way to the dawning of a new day.[24] Some 302 years had passed since the death of Atiśa, the Bengali missionary who spent his final years in Tibet and whose life and teachings on the Tibetan plateau would come to powerfully shape Tsongkhapa's own mission. The year 1357 was also the seventeenth year of the reign of Toghan Temür, the Mongolian ruler of Yuan dynasty China. Temür, the last ruler of the Yuan, was overthrown in 1368, thus ushering in the Han Chinese–led Ming dynasty.

Tsongkhapa was born in Tsongkha, "the Land of Onions," from which he acquired the name Tsongkhapa, "the man from Tsongkha." The area is part of a larger region known as Amdo, which lies in the northeastern part of Tibet. Amdo was one of the three provinces that made up old Tibet, the other two being Ü-Tsang (central, southern, and western Tibet) and Kham (eastern Tibet). Today Amdo falls mainly in Qinghai Province of the People's Republic of China, though a small part lies in Gansu Province—a historical legacy of the Kuomintang Nationalist period in China. Amdo has a long and complex history and comprises numerous tribes and regions. The regions of Amdo—Tsongkha, Asha, Sumpa, and so on—had been formally incorporated into the Tibetan kingdom in the seventh century by Emperor Songtsen Gampo, subsequently falling under the rule of the Gar clan. The members of this clan were the successors of a famed minister of Songtsen known as Gar Dongtsen. Even after the collapse of the Tibetan empire and the fragmentation of Tibet into smaller polities in the second half of the ninth century, Amdo—like its southerly counterpart, Kham—remained culturally, linguistically, and religiously close to central Tibet. At the time of Tsongkhapa's birth in 1357, Tibet had effectively thrown off the yoke of Mongol rule (executed through the proxy of Sakya rulers) following Jangchup Gyaltsen's successful coup in 1354. Thus, describing the birthplace of Tsongkhapa, his biographer and principal student Khedrup Gelek Palsang writes:

> First, as for the place where this great being was born, it lies in the east and is known as Tsongkha, which is part of the lower areas of Dokham—a region that once belonged to the kingdom of the powerful emperors [of Tibet]. That Tsongkha is a place of excellent attributes is proclaimed through the words emitted from the mouths of successive generations of elders.[25]

Tsongkhapa was the fourth of six children—one daughter and five sons—born to Lumbum Gé and his wife Shingsa Achö.[26] His mother was a devout Buddhist known for her compassion toward the needy and for her devotion to circumambulating temples and reciting the six-syllable mantra of the buddha of compassion, OṂ

MAṆI PADME HŪṂ. While Tsongkhapa's mother belonged to the Shing clan, his father was from the well-known ancient Tibetan Mal clan, which had a tradition of sons entering the monastery. His paternal relatives belonging to the Mal clan are said to have numbered a thousand people at the time of Tsongkhapa's birth.

The day after Tsongkhapa was born, the family received a visit from a monk bearing gifts from the nearby Jakhyung Monastery. He was sent by the monastery's founder, the well-known teacher and mystic Chöjé Dhöndrup Rinchen—Chöjé being a title meaning "Dharma master." The gifts included some blessed pills; a red protection string; a *thangka*, or scroll painting, of Vajrabhairava (an important meditation deity in Tibetan Vajrayāna tradition); and a letter containing some advice on the need to raise this child with special care and cleanliness. For both parents, the visit and the gifts from Chöjé Dhöndrup Rinchen were a confirmation of their intuition that they had become the vehicle for the appearance of a special child in the world.

Toward the end of the Fire Monkey year (1356), the year before Tsongkhapa's birth, his father, Lumbum Gé, had a prophetic dream: He dreamed of a monk wearing robes made of flower garlands who said he had come from Wutai Shan, the five-peaked mountain in northern China considered to be the abode of Mañjuśrī, the buddha of wisdom. The monk, carrying a text wrapped in a cloth, asked for shelter. He then entered and disappeared into a shrine room that was on the rooftop of the house. Since Tsongkhapa's father, Lumbum Gé, regularly recited the well-known prayer *Chanting the Names of Mañjuśrī*, he felt that he was somehow being blessed by Mañjuśrī. A few months later, Tsongkhapa's mother dreamed of a procession of people playing drums and carrying banners while awaiting the arrival of Avalokiteśvara, the buddha of compassion. There was a large, radiant golden icon in the sky, surrounded by celestial beings. As they descended to the earth, at one point the icon dissolved into her body, and the gods and goddesses circled around her while chanting auspicious verses.[27]

Later, when the parents met Chöjé Dhöndrup Rinchen, Tsongkhapa's father asked the master why he had sent an attendant bearing those gifts immediately after the child's birth. Chöjé replied that he himself was a longtime yogi of Vajrabhairava and had dreamed an unusual dream in which he was making fervent supplications to that meditation deity, asking for blessings and to be honored with a vision of him. In response, the meditation deity turned his face toward their region and told him that around the same time tomorrow he would appear in that valley. "Till then," the deity said, "you should remain joyful."[28]

Sources tell us that Tsongkhapa's father buried the afterbirth at a nearby site. Soon after, a white sandalwood tree is said to have grown on the spot. An alternative version of the story speaks of the tree growing where drops of blood from the infant's umbilical cord had fallen on the ground. This tree, which came to be revered as the Great Tree of Merit (*tshokshing chenmo*), is reputed to have had leaves that bore impressions of the Buddha and patterns that resembled Tibetan characters. Sometime in the late 1370s, Tsongkhapa's mother built a small temple with a stūpa on that same site to honor the birth of her very special son. Today, the well-known Kumbum Monastery stands at this sacred site, the name Kumbum (literally, "hundred thousand sacred images") alluding to the mysterious patterns found on the leaves of the tree.[29]

Kumbum Monastery grew from an earlier, smaller monastery called Gönpalung, which was founded in 1560 by Rinchen Tsöndrü Gyaltsen as a retreat for intensive meditative practice. Everything would change when, in 1577, the third Dalai Lama, Sönam Gyatso, stopped at the retreat on his way to meet the Mongolian chieftain Altan Khan near Lake Kokonor. The third Dalai Lama requested

Rinchen Tsöndrü Gyaltsen to build a larger monastery on the site so that Tsongkhapa's birthplace could be honored in a way that would allow it to be visited by more devotees. The construction of the new monastery was completed in 1583, and, as the Indian emperor Ashoka had done with the sacred Bodhi Tree in Bodhgayā some eighteen hundred years earlier, a fence was built around the Great Tree of Merit.

Today this mysterious tree is no longer standing. However, we have an eyewitness account from two Catholic missionaries, Huc and Gabet, who happened to visit Kumbum Monastery in the 1840s and saw the tree when it was still alive. Having earlier heard of this special tree, the two missionaries were ready to dismiss the story as a fanciful tale of the Tibetan pagans. When they finally came face to face with the tree, they were unprepared for what they saw. Evariste Huc, one of the two missionaries, recorded his experience as follows:

> We were filled with an absolute consternation of astonishment, at finding that, in point of fact, there were upon each of the leaves well-formed Tibetan characters.... Our first impression was suspicion of fraud on the part of the lamas; but after a minute examination of every detail, we could not discover the least deception.[30]

To return to our story, Chöjé Dhöndrup Rinchen paid regular visits to the family and began instructing the young boy. By age three, the toddler Tsongkhapa had learned how to recite the mantras of Mañjuśrī and goddess Sarasvatī, the two meditation deities in the Tibetan Buddhist pantheon associated with knowledge, wisdom, and poetic eloquence. When the child turned three, during one of these frequent visits, Chöjé brought with him offerings to the family consisting of yaks, horses, and sheep, as well as other material gifts.

Chöjé then asked the family that he be given custodianship of the boy, to which the father consented with delight.

Soon after it was decided that Chöjé would take custody of the young child Tsongkhapa, the patriarch of the Tibetan Karma Kagyü lineage, Karmapa Rolpai Dorjé (1340–83), the fourth Karmapa, happened to stop in the region on his way back from China, where he had visited the court of Emperor Temür.[31] This was 1360, the year of the Earth Ox. The Karmapa blessed the boy and bestowed on him the *upāsaka* (lay Buddhist precept) vows. Ceremonially cutting the tip of the boy's hair, he gave him a new name, Künga Nyingpo. He also instructed that the child be sent to central Tibet and predicted that he would grow up to serve the Buddha's doctrine in a way comparable to that of the Buddha himself.[32]

Around the age of six, the young Tsongkhapa apparently moved to Dhöndrup Rinchen's residence and began learning how to read, write, and memorize liturgical texts. Born in Repkong, Chöjé Dhöndrup Rinchen was himself a native of Amdo and had studied with several great teachers in the major learning centers of the Kadam school in central Tibet. He had engaged in single-pointed meditative practice and is reputed to have attained advanced levels of tranquility (*śamatha*). Following his sojourn in central Tibet, Chöjé returned to Amdo, where he founded two major monasteries: Jakhyung and Shadrang Gön. Assigning the abbotship of Shadrang Gön to his student Shākya Sangpo, Chöjé himself remained in single-pointed meditative practice at Jakhyung Monastery and is reputed to have experienced visions of meditation deities.[33] It was this great teacher, meditator, and mystic who had taken charge of bringing up the young Tsongkhapa.

Built in 1349 at the site where the second Karmapa, Karma Pakshi (1204–83), had founded a small monastery in the twelfth century, Jakhyung Monastery lies on a ridge providing an impressive view of the great Machu (the Yellow River) snaking through a vast valley below. Located in a small forested area on a ridge, some parts of the monastery hug the slopes of the mountain. It was at this breathtaking mountaintop site, with its broad vistas, that Tsongkhapa began his formal monastic education. For the next ten years, he studied, received various tantric initiations, and joined his master in meditation retreats. Chöjé took good care of the young child and loved him deeply; he is said to have nursed him personally when Tsongkhapa once fell gravely ill.[34]

Even before he received his novice vows, Tsongkhapa was initiated into Vajrayāna and was conferred the tantric name Dönyö Dorjé. Vajrayāna refers to a unique system of practice within Mahāyāna Buddhism that originated in India and flourished in Tibet. A key element of its practice involves focusing on a "meditation deity" through visualizing his or her form, adopting its enlightened identity, and reciting a specific mantra (incantation) associated with the deity. This entire process of meditative cultivation is known as *sādhana*, "method of cultivation," indicating its main purpose, which is to cultivate the state of the deity's enlightened form. Tsongkhapa received initiations into the sādhanas of Vajrabhairava, Cakrasaṃvara, Hevajra, and Vajrapāṇi, and around age seven the boy began to have frequent dreams about the meditation deity Vajrapāṇi and an Indian monk who claimed to be Atiśa. These were later seen as early portents of the special connection that Tsongkhapa would have with Vajrapāṇi (through a yogi by the name of Lhodrak Namkha Gyaltsen) and with the instruction lineage of the Indian master Atiśa.

It was also at age six (seven according to the Tibetan system, which counts the period in utero) that the young Tsongkhapa received his novice vows at Jakhyung Monastery, with Chöjé serving as the officiating abbot of the ordination ceremony.[35] As was customary, Tsongkhapa received his monastic name at this novitiate ceremony. It was Lobsang Drakpa, the personal name he would use throughout his life. The usual custom is for the officiating lama to give the novice the first part of his own name as the first part of the ordination name. In this system, the monastic name Tsongkhapa received should have been Dhöndrup X. It is said, however, that when Chöjé Dhöndrup Rinchen was in central Tibet, he had met with the great Narthang scholar Chim Lobsang Drakpa, who predicted that sometime in the future Chöjé would meet with an excellent student from Amdo, to whom he should give the name Lobsang Drakpa. Hence, the young boy received the monastic name Lobsang Drakpa, literally, "Excellent Intellect and Repute."

Because of the care, love, and wise counsel with which he was raised by Chöjé from such an early age, Tsongkhapa deeply revered the memory of his first teacher. As a grown man, whenever he would mention Chöjé's name, he would instinctively fold his palms together in a gesture of respect and shed tears. Following Chöjé's death, Tsongkhapa unfailingly observed the annual commemoration of his teacher's passing.[36]

Chöjé took great care to expose the young monk to everything he knew, instructing him in both scholastic tradition and meditative practice. Yet he never forgot the Karmapa's advice that the boy be sent to central Tibet to fulfill his destiny. By sixteen, Tsongkhapa had mastered much of what Chöjé had to teach. The young monk had proven to be a quick learner with a sharp and penetrating intellect, someone with an impressive capacity for comprehension and memorization as well as a natural feel for the mystical—especially Vajrayāna yogic meditative practice. He had memorized key texts inherited from the great Indian monastic centers of Nālandā, Vikramalaśīla, and Jagaddala. Chöjé had ensured particularly that Tsongkhapa memorize and receive classes on two essential Buddhist works—*Ornament of Realizations* (*Abhisamayālaṃkāra*) and *Ornament of Mahāyāna Sūtras* (*Mahāyānasūtrālaṃkāra*)—two of the so-called

Five Works of Maitreya.[37] He had received numerous Vajrayāna initiations, undertaken retreats associated with them, and recited the mantras connected with the sādhanas of the Vajrayāna meditation deities. The young Tsongkhapa had chosen Mañjuśrī to be his principal meditation deity and had recited his mantra OṂ ARAPACANA DHĪH over a hundred million times.[38]

When Tsongkhapa was sixteen, Chöjé formally started preparing for the next phase in the young monk's life, the journey to central Tibet. Just as in ancient India the more promising students traveled to central India to study at the great Buddhist monastic centers like Nālandā and Vikramaśīla, in Tibet too the brightest students from different parts of the land would aspire to study in central Tibet. In fact, among the three provinces that composed old Tibet, Ü-Tsang (central, southern, and western Tibet) was known as the land of Dharma study and practice (*chökyi shingsa*) and has been the center of gravity for Buddhism since it first took root in Tibet in the seventh century.

Chöjé himself had spoken to Tsongkhapa at length about the great learning centers of central Tibet where the young monastic would have the chance to study. Decades earlier, Chöjé himself had studied at some of these great centers. As the master and his beloved disciple spoke of what lay ahead—the long journey and the years of rigorous study—Chöjé told Tsongkhapa that he would like to give him a special teaching and asked him what he desired. "I would love to receive some advice that would benefit my heart," Tsongkhapa replied. Moved by this request, Chöjé gave him a lengthy piece of advice with specific details as to, for instance, what texts he should study and in which order, how to apply the knowledge gained from these texts to his personal practice and meditative cultivation, how later to teach and fulfill the needs and aspirations of students, and so on. He then composed these points into a long verse so that Tsongkhapa would remember them easily. It began with the following lines:

> O young Lobsang Drakpa,
> You possess the virtuous karma born of past deeds.
> Certain it is that you bear imprints of the past experience
> Of having savored the sweet nectar of the sublime Dharma.[39]

Years later, Tsongkhapa's own students came to ask him about his early life with his first teacher, Chöjé. Although he had lost the page on which he had written down the verses, he could still recall many of the lines by heart.

On the day of Tsongkhapa's departure for central Tibet, Chöjé prepared a ceremony of *tsok*, a ritual offering of food and drink that serves as a celebratory feast. He prayed for the young monk's protection by the *dharmapāla*s (the protectors) and the *ḍākinīs* (female deities). As part of the ritual, when making the maṇḍala offering—a symbolic offering of the entire universe to the buddhas—Chöjé grabbed a handful of barley grains and threw them into the air. He saw patterns of shining jewels on the tossed grains, which he interpreted as an auspicious sign. Deeply pleased, Chöjé declared that his young protégé would indeed become a master of the Dharma.

For his part, Tsongkhapa felt torn; while excited by the unknown prospects that lay ahead in central Tibet, he also found it hard to bid farewell to his beloved teacher Chöjé, who had cared for him as both a teacher and a father as long as he could remember. As he was about to embark on this long journey, he knew that he would not see his dear teacher for a long time, if ever again. He was going to travel with a caravan of Amdo traders, joined by two of his uncles as well as a Drigung official by the name of Denma Rinchen Pal, who was bringing various material offerings to Drigung Thil Monastery.[40]

Once on the road, as was his habit, the young Tsongkhapa immediately began reciting *Chanting the Names of Mañjuśrī*, a text he used to recite every day with his teacher. The recitation of this text made his knowledge of the long separation from Chöjé most acute, and tears came to his eyes. He looked back to see his beloved teacher and the monastery that had been his home receding farther into the horizon.[41]

CHAPTER 2

Education in Central Tibet

ON A CLEAR DAY in the Water Rat year—sometime in the second half of 1372—the eager sixteen-year-old Tsongkhapa left Amdo for central Tibet. Having bidden farewell to his beloved teacher, he embarked on a journey of almost thirteen hundred miles through a vast swath of the Tibetan plateau. The caravan he joined traveled by the southern route, as opposed to the northern route, which would have taken them through the vast empty plains of the Tibetan nomadic region known as the Jangthang (literally, "northern plain"). We know little of what transpired during this trek to central Tibet, other than a brief mention of a respite in Chamdo in eastern Tibet, at the place where two major rivers, the Ngomchu and Dzachu (Mekong), intersect. There the young Tsongkhapa had a vision of the protector Mahākāla and a vivid dream about the sixteen arhats—mythic disciples of the Buddha whose invocation is part of a popular rite in Tibet. Tsongkhapa predicted that one day a monastery would be built at the site. Indeed, in 1437, eighteen years after Tsongkhapa's death, one of his own disciples from Amdo, Sherap Sangpo, would establish Jampa Ling Monastery at the site, thus fulfilling the prophecy.[42]

Landing at Drigung Thil Monastery

In the fall of 1373, the Water Ox year, Tsongkhapa's caravan reached central Tibet. It had been almost a year since the young monk had departed Amdo, leaving behind his family and his beloved teacher Chöjé. The caravan ended its long journey at the famous monastery of Drigung Thil. Founded in 1179 by Kyobpa Jikten Gönpo (1143–1217), the founder of the Drigung Kagyü lineage of Tibetan Buddhism, the monastery is located in the slopes of a long mountain range and stands at an elevation of about 13,600 feet overlooking the scenic Shorong Valley. This is where the principal northeast tributary of the Kyichu River flows southwest toward the holy city of Lhasa, eventually merging into the great river of Yarlung Tsangpo, which in South Asia is known as the Brahmapūtra.

Located on the slopes of a long mountain range, Drigung Thil is some seventy-five miles northeast of Lhasa. There Tsongkhapa met with the Drigung patriarch Chenga Chökyi Gyalpo (1335–1407), who at that time was residing at the secluded hermitage known as the Glorious Forest (*Palgyi Naktrö*). Tsongkhapa received from Chökyi Gyalpo various teachings, such as the ceremony of generating *bodhicitta*—the altruistic aspiration to attain enlightenment for the benefit of all beings—and instructions on the five-branch Mahāmudrā and the six yogas of Nāropa, the latter two being part of the core instructions of the Kagyü school of Tibetan Buddhism.[43] (Decades later, Tsongkhapa would himself compose a major work on the instructions and practice of the six yogas of Nāropa.) He also received oral transmissions of the reading of the collected works of the great Drigung patriarchs, including those of the revered founder Jikten Gönpo.[44] These were the first formal teachings the young Tsongkhapa received from a teacher other than his beloved Chöjé, who had been inseparable from him for as long as he could remember. As we shall see, the fact that Tsongkhapa's introduction to the complex world of Tibetan Buddhism in Ü-Tsang came through the Kagyü tradition would have far-reaching implications for his own understanding, practice, and exposition of advanced Vajrayāna teachings.

Although, as advised by his childhood teacher Chöjé, Tsongkhapa was set on pursuing the study of the great Indian Buddhist classics, at the urging of friends he joined a small group that went to learn Tibetan medicine from the well-known physician Könchok Kyap. For several months, Tsongkhapa studied with this physician, memorizing the *Aṣṭaṅgahṛdayasaṁhitā* (*Summary of the Essence of the Eight Branches*), an ancient Indian text on Ayurvedic medicine by Vāgbhaṭa. The students received expositions of this text as well as practical instructions on diagnostic methods. Years later, on occasions when Tsongkhapa became ill, his knowledge of medicine would prove useful to him for taking an active role in both diagnosing and treating his own illness.[45] Realizing, however, that his medical studies could become a diversion, Tsongkhapa soon left his companions to seek out a rigorous environment to deepen his Buddhist study and practice. Before long, he arrived at one of the major centers of learning in central Tibet—the Dewachen Monastery in Nyethang.

Initial Studies at Nyethang Dewachen

Nyethang Monastery was founded in 1209 by the Kadam master Gya Chingruwa and is located to the southwest of Lhasa (in present-day Chushul District). Nyethang was one of what were known as the six major learning centers of central Tibet at the time, the others being Sangphu, Kyormolung, Gadong, Zulphu, and Tsal Gungthang.[46] The Nyethang region, where Nyethang Dewachen is located, is famous as the site of one of the holiest temples of Tibet, the Tārā Temple of Atiśa, the Indian Bengali master who came to Tibet in 1042. Although little is known of Nyethang before Tsongkhapa's time, during his student years the monastery was a major center for learning, especially for the Perfection of Wisdom studies based on Maitreya's *Ornament of Realizations* (*Abhisamayālaṃkāra*).

Tsongkhapa's education in central Tibet revolved primarily around a set of key Indian Buddhist texts and the four scholarly disciplines they cover: (1) Perfection of Wisdom (*parchin*) studies, based on the *Ornament of Realizations* attributed to Maitreya; (2) logic and epistemology (*pramāṇa*), based on the works of Dignāga and Dharmakīrti; (3) Abhidharma (Buddhist psychology and metaphysics), based on the texts of Asaṅga and Vasubandhu; and (4) vinaya (ethics and monastic discipline), based on the texts of Guṇaprabha and Śākyaprabha. Monastic students would memorize the root texts, receive exposition of their meaning with the aid of authoritative commentaries, engage in careful comparative reading of diverse sources, and undertake regular debates with fellow students on the difficult points (a pedagogical method that continues to this day in the Tibetan monastic colleges). Those who completed the formal study of these four disciplines and successfully sat for their debates were conferred the title *kashipa*, "master of four treatises." (For a more detailed description of the scholastic curriculum of Tsongkhapa's day, see the appendix.)[47]

During Tsongkhapa's student years, Madhyamaka studies on Nāgārjuna's philosophy of emptiness apparently had not yet become formalized as an independent discipline of scholarship in the monastic centers.[48] As we shall see, Madhyamaka would be an important area of classical Indian Buddhist scholarship that Tsongkhapa pursued, and he emerged as a major Tibetan authority on the subject.

At Nyethang Dewachen, Tsongkhapa, now seventeen or eighteen years old, first studied with Rinpoché Tashi Sengé and was assisted in his studies by two other senior monks, Yönten Gyatso and Ogyenpa. His primary focus initially was the influential Indian Buddhist text *Ornament of Realizations*, which had become the root text in the formal study of a class of Mahāyāna scriptures known as the Perfection of Wisdom sūtras (*prajñāpāramita*, the *Heart Sūtra* being a well-known example). Although Tsongkhapa had already memorized this root text as a child, he was now challenged to explore its meaning such that he could call forth salient points from the text, even in the midst of debate. "Within about eighteen days," according to one account, "he had gained command of the broad outline of the text."[49]

Attributed to Maitreya (ca. fourth century) and written entirely in verse as an "instruction on the Perfection of Wisdom," the *Ornament* is a dense work aimed at summarizing the entire contents of the three-volume *Perfection of Wisdom in Twenty-Five Thousand Lines*. While the explicit subject matter of the Perfection of Wisdom scriptures, namely, the doctrine of emptiness, is expounded in Nāgārjuna's philosophical writings, the implicit subject matter of these scriptures, namely, the many stages of the path and their cultivation, is the principal topic of the *Ornament*.[50] It is an encyclopedia and a fundamental text on all important topics of Mahāyāna Buddhism, including preparing the mind to enter the path, the cultivation of universal compassion and bodhicitta, the four noble truths and the twelve links of dependent origination, the two truths, the cultivation of tranquility and insight, the attainment of meditative absorptions, the thirty-seven aspects of the path to enlightenment according to Mahāyāna, the six perfections, the five levels of the path, the ten bodhisattva grounds, and the resultant state of buddhahood defined in terms of the three bodies (*kāya*). In contemporary terms, the subject matter of the *Ornament* can be characterized as "religious studies" according to classical Indian Mahāyāna Buddhism. In brief, the *Ornament* serves as an exhaustive table of contents for the voluminous Perfection of Wisdom scriptures.

Initially, Tsongkhapa's study of the *Ornament* seems to have been based on the Tibetan commentary composed by Jamkya Namkha Pal, a teacher of the great Butön and a student of Shang Dodé-Pal (the author of the earliest biography of Sakya Paṇḍita).[51] In residence at the monastery was also a known expert on the Five Works of Maitreya by the name of Jamyang Rinchen, from whom Tsongkhapa received lessons on the remaining four Maitreya texts. By the end of his two years of study of the *Ornament*, Tsongkhapa had "become versed in the words and meaning of 'the perfection of wisdom'" such that "everyone, his teachers as well as his fellow students, came to see him as a great wonder, considering his intellect to be unfathomable."[52]

At some point during his two years at Nyethang, Tsongkhapa heard about the visit of Lama Dhampa Sönam Gyaltsen to the nearby Chözong Hermitage. Lama Dhampa was a senior master in the Sakya school who, in addition to once having been the ruling patriarch of Sakya, was also the author of the Tibetan historical work *Clear Mirror on Royal Genealogy*. Upon hearing that this illustrious master was nearby, Tsongkhapa went to see him there, receiving from him various teachings, including blessings of Mañjuśrī, the empowerment of Cakrasaṃvara according to the Indian mystic Ghaṇṭapa's lineage, and the special Sakya blessings of the protector Mahākāla in his form known as the Lord of the Tent (*Gönpo Gur*).[53] Lama Dhampa recognized Tsongkhapa's destiny, giving him his ceremonial hat and telling him that he would become a custodian of the lineages of the great Butön.[54] About a year later, in 1375, Lama Dhampa would pass away.

After nearly two years of study at Nyethang, in the Wood Rabbit year (1375), at the age of nineteen, Tsongkhapa sat for his first formal debate. Known as *drakor* (literally, "doing the rounds of the debating courtyards"), formal debate in Tsongkhapa's time involved making a request to the heads of the monastery, sitting in an assembly of learned scholars, and responding to questions posed by them in the form of a series of debates.[55] Tsongkhapa's first drakor would naturally be on the subject he had been studying, the Perfection of Wisdom scriptures, and the debates would be held at the two great centers of learning in the Lhasa area: Sangphu Monastery and Nyethang Dewachen. He chose Sangphu first, possibly because of its significance as the birthplace of scholastic and philosophical studies in Tibet.[56] The full name of the monastery was Sangphu Neutok; it had been founded in 1071 by Ngok Lekpai Sherap, who was a senior disciple of Atiśa and the paternal uncle of Ngok Loden Sherap (1059–1105), one of Tibet's greatest translators of Indian Buddhist texts, esteemed especially for his masterly translations of Indian texts on pramāṇa.

At both Sangphu and Nyethang Dewachen, the monastic scholars were deeply impressed by the breadth of knowledge and the depth of understanding that Tsongkhapa displayed during his first formal debate session. As they observed the clarity of his mind, his sharp and penetrating intellect, and his humility, his fame spread quickly across central Tibet. Thus, it appears that by the end of his two years of study at Nyethang, Tsongkhapa had gained sufficient confidence in his scholarship to write his earliest texts. Both were short works addressing important topics in the *Ornament of Realizations*: one about the twenty *saṃghas*, or twenty persons (a classification of persons characterized by progressive levels of attainment on the path), and the other concerning the levels of meditative concentration.[57]

From One Monastery to Another

Having successfully sat for his formal debates on Perfection of Wisdom studies at Sangphu and Nyethang Dewachen in 1375, Tsongkhapa set out for the next center of learning. His plan was to go to the great monastery of Sakya next, but upon meeting some monks from Joden on the road, he decided to travel with them over the pass of Gyangkhar. Taking this route meant that Tsongkhapa arrived first at Shalu Monastery, instead of Sakya as was his original plan.

Shalu Monastery was founded in 1040 by Chetön Sherap Jungné at a site some thirteen miles south of the town of Shigatse in the province of Tsang. Though small in size, Shalu came to prominence thanks to the activities of the great Butön. With financial support from the Mongol Yuan ruler Toghan Temür, Butön had the monastery rebuilt in 1333 following its destruction by a massive earthquake in 1329. Butön's contributions included writing an authoritative history of Buddhism in India and Tibet; finalizing the compilation and cataloging of the complete Tibetan Buddhist canons of the Kangyur (translated scriptures) and Tengyur (translated treatises); organizing the entries according to a coherent structure; writing expositions of many Indian Buddhist texts; and being the custodian of many Vajrayāna lineages, notably Guhyasamāja, Kālacakra, and the Yoga tantras.[58] During Tsongkhapa's student years, Shalu was famed as the seat of the great Butön's lineage, especially of Vajrayāna study and practice.

At Shalu Monastery Tsongkhapa met with Dratsepa Rinchen Namgyal (1318–88), the foremost student of Butön and his successor at Shalu. Tsongkhapa took the opportunity to receive from this master important Vajrayāna transmissions connected with the meditation deity Cakrasaṃvara.

From Shalu, traveling through Narthang Pass, Tsongkhapa finally arrived at the great monastic center at Sakya. Founded in 1073 by Khön Könchok Gyalpo (1034–1102), the monastery served as the official seat of the Sakya school of Tibetan Buddhism and was the base for all five patriarchs of the Sakya tradition: Sachen Künga Nyingpo (1092–1158), Jetsün Sönam Tsemo (1142–82), Jetsün Drakpa Gyaltsen (1147–1216), Sakya Paṇḍita (1182–1251), and Drogön Chögyal Phakpa (1235–80), the last of whom served also as the imperial priest of Kublai Khan. Located around eighty miles west of the town of Shigatse, the monastery became a major center for scholarship on Indian Buddhist classics in large part due to the great Sakya Paṇḍita. During Tsongkhapa's student years, Sakya was a major center for scholarship, hosting renowned scholars such as Nyawön Künga Pal (1285–1379), Sasang Mati Panchen (1294–1376), and Rendawa Shönu Lodrö (1349–1412). The last of these would become Tsongkhapa's principal teacher.

The tradition at Sakya during Tsongkhapa's student years was to have a clear delineation between active semesters (*chöthok*), during which both classes and debates were held, and interval breaks (*chötsam*), during which students and scholars pursued their own reading, studies, and practice. Tsongkhapa happened to arrive at Sakya during a break, so until the start of the next semester, he went to Sasang Monastery.[59] There, he received various teachings from Sasang Mati Panchen (1294–1376), a senior Sakya master who was also a key figure in the dissemination of the Kālacakra tantra according to the lineage of the Jonang school.

When the next semester began at Sakya, Tsongkhapa returned there and sat for another formal debate on Perfection of Wisdom studies. During Tsongkhapa's time, in the fourteenth century, it appears to have been customary for aspiring students to go on a debate circuit, visiting selected monasteries. Following this formal debate, Tsongkhapa journeyed farther north to other monasteries, such as Dharsangden, Ngamring Chödé (a Sakya monastery founded in the thirteenth century and later converted to Geluk), and Garong Chödé (a Sakya monastery in central Tsang). As he traveled in this way, visiting different monastic centers, his fame as an emerging scholar kept growing.

He next went to Jonang Monastery, the seat of the esteemed Jonang master Dolpopa (1292–1361), where he received instructions on the six yogas of Kālacakra tantra for the first time. From Jonang, on his way to the great Bodong É Monastery (founded in 1049 by the Kadam master Geshe Mudrakpa Chenpo),[60] Tsongkhapa stopped at Chiwo Lhé Monastery, founded by Chiwo Lhepa

Jangchup Wö, the ordination master of Sakya Paṇḍita. There, Tsongkhapa received from the abbot of that monastery an oral transmission on Kadam instruction of *lamrim* (stages of the path), possibly based on Atiśa's seminal text on the genre, the *Lamp for the Path to Enlightenment*.

After reaching Bodong É Monastery and sitting for formal debate there, Tsongkhapa continued to Narthang Monastery. There, he hoped to undertake the formal study of Vasubandhu's *Treasury of Abhidharma* (*Abhidharmakośa*), having seen it cited often in various texts he had studied at Nyethang. Founded in 1153 by the Kadam teacher Tumtön Lodrö Drakpa and located nine miles west of the town of Shigatse in Tsang Province, Narthang became, after Sangphu, the second most important academic center of Atiśa's Kadam school. Its luminaries included Sangye Gompa (1179–1250), the author of a major work known as *Public Explication of Mind Training*; Chim Namkha Drak (1210–1285), the great Abhidharma scholar and the author of Atiśa's "official" biography; Chomden Rikral (1227–1305), a well-known author on epistemology and the initiator of the project to compile the first Tibetan canonical collections; and Khenchen Nyima Gyaltsen (1223–1305), the compiler of *The Book of Kadam*. During Tsongkhapa's student years, Narthang was particularly admired as a center for the study of Abhidharma and vinaya (monastic discipline and ethics).[61]

Tsongkhapa first took classes on Vasubandhu's classic from the Narthang scholar Lotsawa Dhönsang, but these did not meet with his satisfaction. In the meantime, Tsongkhapa learned that one of the Narthang monks possessed a copy of the commentary on Maitreya's *Ornament* by Nyawön Künga Pal (1285–1379), which impressed him deeply. Compared with the earlier Tibetan commentary he had studied at Nyethang, Nyawön's exposition of the Indian classic was written with far greater clarity and an authoritative command of the topics. Elated by this discovery, Tsongkhapa felt a strong desire to study the commentary with Nyawön himself. So he left Narthang for Tsechen Monastery, the monastery Nyawön had founded and made his primary residence.[62]

So it was that in the Fire Dragon year of 1376, when Tsongkhapa was twenty years old, he spent the summer semester at Tsechen Monastery receiving a complete exposition of Nyawön's commentary on Maitreya's *Ornament*. The young student was deeply impressed: he found Nyawön's exposition to be lucid, penetrating, and eloquent, displaying all the hallmarks of a deeply learned mind. Tsongkhapa then requested master Nyawön to give an exposition of Vasubandhu's *Treasury*. Nyawön, being already quite old, responded, "Yes, I can expound this text well, but lately there haven't been that many students who were interested in studying it. So I would need to refresh my memory and do some preparations in order to do justice to the text. Furthermore, my health isn't in the best state right now, and given that I need to continue to teach Perfection of Wisdom and pramāṇa in the immediate terms, it will be not possible for me to teach Vasubandhu's Abhidharma text." Seeing that these conditions would delay Tsongkhapa's progression, Nyawön did something that would have a radical impact on the young monk's future studies. He continued, "However, I have a most discerning student by the name of Rendawa who is extremely learned in Abhidharma. It might be better if you study Abhidharma with him."

Meeting Rendawa, Tsongkhapa's Most Important Teacher

It so happened that the man whom Nyawön recommended to Tsongkhapa, Rendawa Shönu Lodrö (1349–1412), was visiting Tsechen Monastery at the same time and was scheduled to spend the summer semester there. With the help of some of Nyawön's senior students, the young Tsongkhapa approached Rendawa and asked him to teach him Vasubandhu's *Treasury.* Rendawa gladly agreed. Tsongkhapa soon noticed that, in addition to Rendawa's ability to explain every verse with great clarity, every now and then he would relate his explanation of a specific point to an overall understanding of the text. Tsongkhapa took a keen interest in Rendawa's ability and choice to maintain the big picture so that his students did not get lost in the details. During these classes Tsongkhapa frequently asked questions, which deeply impressed and pleased the teacher. Later, Rendawa would tell Tsongkhapa, "I need to remain sharp when expounding on a text for you."

In Rendawa, Tsongkhapa had finally found a teacher who could occupy that special place formerly held by his childhood teacher, Chöjé Dhöndup Rinchen. In one sense, during his three years of wandering from one monastery to another, studying at the feet of different teachers and sitting for formal debates, Tsongkhapa was in fact searching for a personal teacher, someone with whom he had a special karmic connection. Once he had found such a teacher in Rendawa, Tsongkhapa forged a relationship with the master that would come to define his life, not just during his student years but also later, when he became a great master of Dharma in his own right. Speaking of Rendawa's singular importance to Tsongkhapa as the latter's teacher, Tsongkhapa's official biographer Khedrup would later write:

> With respect to our own precious master [Tsongkhapa] too, it was from this most venerable Rendawa that he first discovered the systems of the great charioteers [Nāgārjuna and Asaṅga] as well as found the doors to the reasoning of Madhyamaka philosophy and pramāṇa. Therefore, Tsongkhapa considered Rendawa to be his unrivaled principal teacher.[63]

Rendawa and Tsongkhapa would remain close throughout their lives, meeting on numerous occasions and keeping up a constant correspondence, even after Rendawa retired to his favorite retreats, such as in Kyirong in western Tibet. The age difference between the two was relatively small—only about eight years. This was certainly one of the reasons, as we shall see later, that their relationship would eventually evolve into a collegial one, with Rendawa sometimes even receiving teachings from his former student. Rendawa and Tsongkhapa would not always see eye to eye, especially when it came to the Kālacakra tantra. Tsongkhapa would practice and later teach this hugely popular Indian and Tibetan Buddhist system, while Rendawa would critique it as being a corrupt form of Buddhist tantra.[64] Nonetheless, given the mature and collegial nature of their bond, their relationship would come to deeply enrich each one's understanding and practice on their path to enlightenment.

Following the end of the summer semester at Tsechen Monastery, Tsongkhapa accompanied his new teacher to spend the interval break at Nyangtö Samten Ling Monastery. There Tsongkhapa received an exposition of *Entering the Middle Way* (*Madhyamakāvatāra*), a classic on Madhyamaka philosophy composed by the seventh-century Indian philosopher Candrakīrti—a text that would later serve as the subject of one of Tsongkhapa's most influential works. This was, in fact, the first time Rendawa had taught this important text. While the two were at Nyangtö Samten Ling, they heard that the revered yogi, scholar, and translator Jangchup Tsemo (1303–80) would be teaching Asaṅga's *Compendium of Abhidharma* (*Abhidharmasamuccāya*) at Potala in Lhasa.[65] Enticed by this prospect, both Rendawa and Tsongkhapa went to the Lhasa area in the late fall of 1376. Arriving in Lhasa, they found out that although the master Jangchup Tsemo was indeed planning to teach the text, because of his advanced age he had been requested to return to his home monastery in Tsang Province. Instead of teaching in Lhasa, the master was scheduled to leave for Tsang with a brief stop at Chözong retreat in Nyethang to see the newly built statue of the late lama Dhampa Sönam Gyaltsen.

Although Tsongkhapa was thus not able to receive Jangchup Tsemo's teaching on Asaṅga's Abhidharma text, he did receive some shorter teachings from the master before his departure to Tsang. Tsongkhapa next returned to Nyethang Dewachen and stayed there for the winter semester of 1376. Then, wanting to engage in the formal study of monastic discipline, he traveled to Kyormolung Monastery, where the renowned authority on the subject Kashipa Lodrö Sangpo was in residence.[66] Founded in the eleventh century by the Kadam master Balti Drachompa, Kyormolung at its height had three colleges and was a major center for learning, especially on the subject of monastic discipline. There Tsongkhapa studied Guṇaprabha's *Root Lines on Vinaya* (*Vinayasūtra*), the primer on monastic discipline, at some length.

During his stay at Kyormolung Monastery, as he focused on the study of vinaya, Tsongkhapa joined the monastic community for their prayer sessions. Often, during these sessions, when the congregation would recite the *Heart Sūtra*, Tsongkhapa would enter into deep meditation and remain in single-pointed absorption in states characterized by clarity, emptiness, and subjectlessness, as well as nonconceptuality.[67] At times he would remain so deeply absorbed that he would be left alone in the hall, the rest of the congregation having completed the prayer session and left. The particular pillar near where Tsongkhapa sat during these sessions later came to be revered as "the meditation pillar."[68]

While deeply immersed in the study of Guṇaprabha's extensive autocommentary on his *Root Lines on Vinaya*, Tsongkhapa suffered acute pain in the upper back, a malady that would recur later in his life.[69] Tsongkhapa first sought the help of a yogi in Tölung who was learned in special healing rites, and then he tried out other treatments at Nyethang Dewachen Monastery; neither proved helpful.

In the winter of 1377, wishing to see his teacher Rendawa again, Tsongkhapa took to the road to travel to Sakya from Nyethang. Although only twenty-one years old, the young monk had already started to attract a small following of his own, and so he traveled with several attendants.[70] That winter was particularly cold, and making the long journey by foot proved too difficult. So he and his companions settled instead for Nenying, a much closer monastery, and spent the winter there. Founded in the eighth century during the first diffusion of Buddhism in Tibet, Nenying is one of the oldest monasteries in central Tibet.[71] Encamped at this ancient monastery for the winter, at the request of the resident monks as well as the attendants traveling with him, Tsongkhapa gave what was effectively his first formal teaching: an exposition of Asaṅga's *Compendium of Abhidharma*, a text he had studied with Rendawa only a year earlier.[72]

As the cold winter gave way to the spring of 1378, the Earth Horse year, Tsongkhapa and his group were finally able to travel to Sakya Monastery. At that time Rendawa was in residence there attending a special series of teachings on the Sakya instruction of "path and fruits" (*lamdré*). This time Tsongkhapa stayed at Sakya with Rendawa for over eleven months. In this period, during the intervals between the formal teachings Rendawa was attending, Tsongkhapa received from him a detailed exposition of Asaṅga's *Compendium of Abhidharma* but focused much of his own study on an in-depth reading of Dharmakīrti's classic on logic and epistemology, the *Exposition of Valid Cognition* (*Pramāṇavārttika*). Tsongkhapa also received oral transmissions of other important texts from Rendawa. It was during this sojourn at Sakya that Tsongkhapa received his first teachings on the Hevajra tantra, a Vajrayāna teaching of special importance for the Sakya school.

Seeing that Tsongkhapa continued to suffer back pain, Rendawa arranged for him to meet with an experienced yogi in order to learn a special breath-based therapeutic yogic technique known as "Letting Out the Neutral Syllable Ha" (*maning gi hadönpa*). Tsongkhapa engaged in intensive practice of this breath yoga for several days, and this helped relieve the persistent pain in his upper back.[73]

During the semester breaks in both spring and summer of 1378, Rendawa and Tsongkhapa went to Ngamring Monastery, north of Sakya. There Tsongkhapa formed an important relationship with Namkha Pal, often referred to as Machik Wönpo, who was the son of the local ruler Jangdak. Namkha Pal would later serve as one of Tsongkhapa's scribes, helping him render his cursive manuscripts into the formal *uchen* script for distribution to others. Tsongkhapa would maintain a constant correspondence with him as well.

At Ngamring, at Tsongkhapa's request, Rendawa composed his authoritative commentary on Asaṅga's *Compendium of Abhidharma* and read it out first to his protégé. Tsongkhapa also requested and received a detailed explanation of Dharmakīrti's autocommentary on the first chapter of the *Exposition of Valid Cognition*. Inspired by Rendawa's instructions on Asaṅga's text, Tsongkhapa himself composed his first substantive philosophical work, *Ocean of Eloquence*, which consists of a root text in verse and a prose autocommentary. It provides a detailed exposition of the Yogācāra theory of mind, including especially its concept of the "store consciousness" (*ālayavijñāna*).[74] In its concluding verses, one can already detect a certain level of scholarly confidence in the young Tsongkhapa. In his colophon, after acknowledging his debts to his two principal teachers, Chöjé and Rendawa, he refers to himself as "Lobsang Drakpa, one from Amdo who is the upholder of the 'three baskets'"—referring to the three scriptural categories of vinaya, sūtra, and Abhidharma, which together constitute the entirety of the Buddha's teachings.

A Letter from Home

In the fall of that year, Tsongkhapa received the news that his family had sent several packages through a caravan of traders traveling from Amdo to central Tibet and that they had been delivered to Drigung Thil, the monastery where he first landed nearly six years earlier in 1372. He also received a letter from his aged mother pleading with him to return to Amdo. His mother's letter read, in part, "I am an old woman. It has now been several years since you, my son, left for studies. You must return now. I would like to see you before I die." Tsongkhapa's mother had enclosed a tuft of her white hair in her letter, to show her age.[75]

Clearly moved by this letter from his mother, and wishing to see her before she died, Tsongkhapa decided to return to Amdo for a short visit. Thus, leaving Ngamring Monastery and traveling via Sakya, he headed toward Lhasa. He stopped in the Maldro area with the intention to learn some useful rituals that he could perform for the laypeople back home. There, however, he had a sudden change of heart. He asked himself why he wanted to learn these rituals and what it would mean to take on performing them at the request of laypeople back in Amdo. He realized that were he to go to Amdo, he might never return to central Tibet to complete his studies and fulfill whatever destiny he might have in service to the Dharma. He then made the difficult decision to not return home. Aware that not returning home at that time could mean that he would never see his mother again, Tsongkhapa felt deeply saddened, but he had made his decision and felt certain it was the right one.

Now that he had decided against returning home, he needed to send something to his mother that would be meaningful. A letter alone would not be enough. He came up with a unique idea: he would draw a portrait of himself and send it to his mother so that she could have something to remember him by. Thus, one source tells us, Tsongkhapa drew a self-portrait using ink mixed with a bit of his own blood from a nosebleed. He sent this portrait, along with a thangka of the Buddha. In his letter, Tsongkhapa suggested that his mother build a stūpa at the site of his birth made of one hundred thousand clay imprints (*tsatsa*) of this particular Buddha. Such a marker would serve as a substitute for his presence and would be a source of benefit for the Dharma and many beings.[76] Though deeply saddened, Tsongkhapa's mother was touched to receive this letter and the accompanying gifts from her son, especially the precious self-portrait, which when unfurled is said to have uttered the word "Mother!" Tsongkhapa's mother then took it upon herself to have a stūpa built at the site of her son's birth.

There is an intriguing twist to the story of Tsongkhapa's self-portrait. A later source writes that the Amdo merchant with whom the portrait was sent, one Norbu Sangpo, had received teachings from Tsongkhapa and developed deep devotion toward him. Feeling that such a precious self-portrait should not be in the home of an ordinary layperson—never mind that she was Tsongkhapa's own mother—the merchant had a copy made of the portrait scroll and gave that to Tsongkhapa's mother. He kept the original himself and later offered it to Khatika Monastery, one of the five monasteries to be founded in Amdo by Jang Lama, an early student of Tsongkhapa. This portrait thangka has remained ever since, according to this source, as the principal sacred icon of this monastery.[77]

Preparing for the Debate Tours on the Remaining Disciplines

Having decided against returning home to Amdo, Tsongkhapa spent some time in the Maldro area receiving numerous oral transmissions from a lama named Sönam Drakpa. At some point during that fall of 1378, Tsongkhapa went into a strict solitary retreat.

Between meditation sessions, he engaged once again in a careful study of Dharmakīrti's text on logic and epistemology, the *Exposition of Valid Cognition*, based on a close reading of Uyukpa's *Treasury of Reasoning*, an extensive analytic commentary on it. Tsongkhapa was particularly struck by the second chapter of this Indian classic. He saw it as a beautiful application of the principles of logic to the presentation of the path to enlightenment, from the beginner's stage of mental training through insight into the truth of the Buddha's teaching on no-self (*anātman*) and to the eventual eradication of all the pollutants that obscure the mind. This awakened in him so profound and powerful a faith in the Buddha and his teaching—a faith grounded in reason—that he would often feel moved to tears and get goose bumps.[78] As we shall see, this special experience with Dharmakīrti's text, especially its second chapter, would have a lasting impact on Tsongkhapa's understanding of the role of reason on the Buddhist path to enlightenment.

Tsongkhapa spent the winter of 1378–79 at Nyethang Dewachen, returning to the very monastery where he had sat for one of his first formal debates. He found the Nyethang community divided into two opposing factions that were caught up in intractable disputes. Seeing this, the young Tsongkhapa wrote the following lines of lament:

> The sun of the correct view appears to have set now.
> The learned ones who used to show the truth have passed away.
> Everyone seems to honor the ignorant who lead the wrong way.
> Alas! Who can uphold the Buddha's doctrine now?
> If one speaks the truth, he is viewed as pretending to be learned.
> If one speaks distortedly, false views will proliferate.
> If one remains silent, no aims are accomplished.
> Alas! How is one supposed to uphold the Buddha's
> doctrine?[79]

These verses appear as part of the colophon of Tsongkhapa's second major work, *Staircase for the Intelligent*. The text is a detailed exposition on the topic of "twenty persons," persons characterized by their specific attainments on the various levels of the path. Composed at the behest of others, it is a remarkably original work based on a comparative analysis of the topic of the twenty persons in three principal classical Indian sources: Maitreya's *Ornament*, Asaṅga's *Compendium of Abhidharma*, and Vasubandhu's *Treasury of Abhidharma*. One can see that Tsongkhapa's confidence in his scholarship had soared even higher since he wrote *Ocean of Eloquence*. In the colophon, he describes himself as one who, thanks to the kindness of Rendawa, "has gained the light of intelligence with regard to the subject matter of all of upper and lower Abhidharma, and who, due to his confidence in Sūtra and the vinaya as well as in the modes of reasoning, has the capacity to examine what is correct and what is incorrect."[80] With his two earliest substantive works, Tsongkhapa not only demonstrated his originality, but in fact established his chosen topics—the Yogācāra theory of mind and the "twenty persons"—as constituting important subjects in themselves.

While at Nyethang, Tsongkhapa also wrote a reply to a letter he had received from one of the princes of the Mongol Khanate that had until 1370 ruled all of China as the Yuan dynasty.[81] Although the Yuan dynasty no longer remained, it appears the descendants of Toghan Temür continued to seek out connections with important religious personalities in central Tibet.

In the spring of 1379, at age twenty-two, intent on preparing for formal debates on the remaining disciplines—logic and epistemology, Abhidharma, and vinaya—Tsongkhapa went to Narthang Monastery. There, the Narthang master, Lotsawa Dhönsang, showed him a commentary he had composed on Dharmakīrti's *Exposition of Valid Cognition* and suggested that Tsongkhapa listen to a reading of this new text, which Tsongkhapa did. Having prepared himself throughout the spring, Tsongkhapa finally sat during the summer semester for his formal debates on the three remaining disciplines. Passing all three, he was now considered a master of the four primary disciplines of Buddhist scholarship. It is said that this was the first time that successive formal debates on multiple disciplines had been held at Narthang Monastery in one stretch.[82]

Around the same time that Tsongkhapa undertook his formal debates at Narthang, he had begun to formally accept students of his own. Tsakho Ngawang Drakpa, a young monk from the Gyalrong area in eastern Tibet, became Tsongkhapa's student as well as his principal attendant at the time. Tsakho would remain with Tsongkhapa, accompanying him everywhere, until returning to his native eastern Tibet, after which the two would maintain a constant correspondence. Years later, it was for the benefit of Tsakho that Tsongkhapa would compose his much admired *Three Principal Elements of the Path*, an important verse work on the stages of the path to enlightenment.

In the fall of 1379, hearing that Rendawa was at Bodong É Monastery, Tsongkhapa went there to further his study with the master. Although he had already completed his formal drakor debates on the four classical subject areas of Tibetan monastic scholarship, Tsongkhapa earnestly wanted to deepen his formal studies with Rendawa. More specifically, he wanted to further his study of Madhyamaka, the Middle Way philosophy of Nāgārjuna, a discipline that was not then part of the formal curriculum.[83]

Under Rendawa's guidance, he studied Madhyamaka and received lessons also on pramāṇa epistemology (based principally on Dharmakīrti's *Exposition of Valid Cognition*) and Abhidharma as well. Tsongkhapa also requested Rendawa to read with him the root texts of vinaya as well as Perfection of Wisdom studies, the subject of the very first debate he had passed. In choosing to return to these topics with his primary teacher, Tsongkhapa demonstrated his genuine dedication to gaining a deep mastery of the key Indian Buddhist classics so seminal to the Tibetan tradition.

Even in the setting of formal teaching, it appears that, during Tsongkhapa's time, the study of the Madhyamaka philosophy of emptiness was limited to Candrakīrti's *Entering the Middle Way.* Tsongkhapa had to look beyond the teachers he had already met, including Rendawa, even for the reading transmissions (*lung*) of certain Madhyamaka texts in which he was interested. (A reading transmission is the simple reading aloud of a text performed by a teacher who has, in turn, received a reading from his or her own predecessor, and so on through an uninterrupted lineage.) Tsongkhapa thus received readings of the other seminal Madhyamaka texts, including the works of Nāgārjuna himself, from the thirteenth Narthang abbot, Künga Gyaltsen (1338–1400), in a transmission lineage traceable to Sherap Sengé, also of Narthang Monastery.[84]

While at Bodong É Monastery, Tsongkhapa also took classes from Lochen Namkha Sangpo (a student of the famous translator Pangtön and of Lochen Jangchup Tsemo) on the influential Sanskrit work on poetics entitled *The Mirror of Poetry* (*Kāvyādarśa*), as well as other Sanskrit literary works.[85] *The Mirror of Poetry*, a verse text by the seventh-century Indian literary figure Daṇḍin, was introduced to Tibet by the great Sakya Paṇḍita in the twelfth century, and the text itself was translated into Tibetan by Shongtön Lotsawa Dorjé Gyaltsen in the thirteenth century. This work represents one of the earliest-known systematic treatments of poetics in Sanskrit. Based on the proposition that a poem's beauty derives primarily from its use of rhetorical devices, especially metaphors, the main part of the text defines and explores thirty-six types of such devices. Over time, *Mirror of Poetry* became the foundational work not only for Sanskrit poetics in Tibet but, more important, for the study and practice of Tibetan poetry itself.[86] Tsongkhapa would later be recognized as one of the greatest poets of the Tibetan language, with his poetic retelling of the story of the bodhisattva Sadāprarudita especially recognized as a literary masterpiece.[87]

Following their sojourn at Bodong É Monastery, Rendawa and Tsongkhapa went to Sakya Monastery. There, as he had done earlier at Narthang Monastery, Tsongkhapa sat for formal debates on logic and epistemology (based on Dharmakīrti's *Pramāṇavārttika*), the upper and lower Abhidharma (based respectively on Asaṅga's *Abhidharmasamuccāya* and Vasubandhu's *Abhidharmakośa*), and vinaya (based on Guṇaprabha's *Root Lines on Vinaya* and its autocommentary). If at that time there had existed the tradition, that was formalized later, of sitting for debates to qualify as a "master of ten treatises" (*kachupa*), Tsongkhapa would have been ready to do it.[88] Following his debates at Sakya, he left immediately for central Tibet to formally sit for debates at Sangphu, Tsethang,[89] and other central Tibetan monastic centers. Following the completion of these formal debates, Tsongkhapa acquired the title kashipa, "master of four disciplines." By all accounts, it appears that the young Tsongkhapa did excellently at the formal debates in all the major monastic centers of learning in central Tibet. He had already begun to make a name for himself as an emerging scholar, and his performance at the debates in these important monastic centers further impressed the community of scholars, adding momentum to the ascendance of his reputation across Ü-Tsang Province.

Contacting Sarasvatī and Taking Full Ordination

There is an important footnote to Tsongkhapa's formal education in central Tibet. Soon after his debates at Sangphu in 1379, Tsongkhapa undertook an intensive solitary retreat focused on Sarasvatī, the goddess of wisdom and poetry, reciting her mantra more than fifty million times. Sources speak of Tsongkhapa experiencing a vision of Sarasvatī. Deeply inspired by his experience of the long retreat, he composed a poetic hymn to the goddess, which includes these lines:

> With eyes like darting bees on a lotus-like face;
> Sporting a glowing moon atop your hair arranged in a bun;
> You assume the playful pose of a dancer, O Sarasvatī;
> Pray continue to grant me proficiency in words.[90]

As a result of this retreat, Tsongkhapa's reputation for having a special connection with the goddess Sarasvatī spread widely. Within a matter of months, monastics and laypeople alike began flocking to Tsongkhapa to receive the blessings of Sarasvatī. And, coincidentally, Tsongkhapa's writings began to acquire, from this point on, a new degree of eloquence.[91]

At the age of twenty-three, following his final formal debate at Tsethang Monastery, Tsongkhapa received his full ordination vows as a *bhikṣu*. This took place in 1380, the Iron Monkey year, at Joden Monastery in Yarlung. The ceremony was officiated by the monastery's abbot, Tsultrim Rinchen, who was himself a recipient of the vows from a lineage of ordination going back to the thirteenth-century Kashmiri paṇḍita Śākyaśribhadra. The ceremony was assisted by a special assembly of over twenty senior monks.[92] As we have seen, Tsongkhapa had devoted long study to the *Root Lines on Vinaya*, the primer on monastic discipline according to the Mūlasarvāstivāda tradition, which had been the mainstream lineage in Tibet since its introduction in the eighth century by the Indian master Śāntarakṣita. Now, having received the full ordination vows, he was ready to fully appreciate all the implications of what it meant to join a community of monastics living according to guidelines established by the Buddha himself nearly nineteen centuries earlier in India. As we shall see, the systematic institution of the monastic rules, including strict adherence to celibacy, would come to define the life of monks belonging to the Geluk tradition that would emerge from Tsongkhapa's legacy.

Meeting with the Phagdru Ruler Drakpa Jangchup

Soon after his full ordination, Tsongkhapa visited Densa Thil Monastery, the principal seat of the Phagdru Kagyü tradition. Founded in the second half of the twelfth century by Phagmo Drupa Dorjé Gyalpo (1110–1170), the founder of the Phagdru Kagyü lineage and an important student of Gampopa (1079–1159), Densa Thil became closely associated with the Phagdru dynasty established by Tai Situ Jangchup Gyaltsen (1302–64). Jangchup Gyaltsen had wrested political power from his overlords, the Sakyapas, and since that time the locus of political power in Tibet had moved from Sakya to Nedong, a region in the Yarlung Valley where the Phagdru historically had been based. In establishing his Phagdru rule, Jangchup Gyaltsen initiated a system whereby the actual ruler would be a monastic and would assume the abbotship of Densa Thil Monastery. He probably made this choice because of what he witnessed at the Sakya court, where different factions allied with specific branches of the family competed against each other. By setting the precedent that the dynastic ruler would be a celibate monk, Jangchup Gyaltsen hoped to prevent the family infighting he had seen undermine the Sakya rule. In any case, the next four successors of Jangchup Gyaltsen—Shākya Gyaltsen (r. 1365–73), Drakpa Jangchup (r. 1374–81), Sönam Drakpa (r. 1381–85), and Drakpa Gyaltsen (r. 1385–1432)—maintained this tradition, opting to rule while remaining monks.

Understandably, by Tsongkhapa's time, the monastery of Densa Thil had become a major center of political power in central Tibet. During his visit, he met with the patriarch of Densa Thil as well as the Phagdru ruler Chenga Drakpa Jangchup (1356–85). During several audiences, Drakpa Jangchup asked the young scholar numerous questions concerning the Dharma, its practice, the view, and their profound significance. Drakpa Jangchup was deeply impressed by Tsongkhapa and is reported to have remarked to others around him, "Such a great mine of knowledge is found in this youth. It's my bad fortune that I am too frail now."[93]

Clearly, the young Tsongkhapa had left a powerful impression on Drakpa Jangchup, who was, in fact, only a year older but destined for a short life. It is said that Drakpa Jangchup, when speaking of his meeting with Tsongkhapa, would often have tears in his eyes. And Tsongkhapa had been similarly inspired by his meeting with Drakpa Jangchup. During his stay at Densa Thil, Tsongkhapa received a series of important teachings from Drakpa Jangchup, including the six yogas of Nāropa, reading transmissions of the collected works of Phagmo Drupa and Drigung Jikten Gönpo, and "instructions on path and result," possibly a reference to some instruction belonging to the Sakya lamdré cycle of teaching.[94] During this stay, Tsongkhapa also composed an alphabetical poem in praise of Drakpa Jangchup, extolling his virtues. This was not an ordinary alphabetical poem; it was written in such a way that not only does every line begin with a specific consonant in its respective order in the Tibetan alphabet, but many of the lines end with the next letter in the alphabet, thus anticipating its appearance in the next line. This literary feat had never been attempted before in the Tibetan language.[95]

In 1381, barely a year after his last meeting with Tsongkhapa, Drakpa Jangchup retired from his throne to remain only the abbot of Densa Thil Monastery. His successor, Sönam Drakpa, was a reluctant ruler, committed more to his role as a spiritual teacher and practitioner than to the exercise of political power. He would rule for only five years and choose to remain only as the abbot of Densa

Thil Monastery. So, in 1385, Sönam Drakpa transferred his political power to the young Drakpa Gyaltsen. Although Drakpa Gyaltsen was then barely twelve years old, he would later become one of the most successful rulers of the Phagdru dynasty.[96] In one of those rare coincidences that often shape history, Drakpa Gyaltsen's long and stable reign, lasting for forty-seven years, happened to be the exact time when Tsongkhapa was emerging as a major intellectual and religious force in Tibet. Tsongkhapa's early, successful interactions with one of the Phagdru dynasty's revered figures, Drakpa Jangchup, would have important ramifications in his life. As we shall see, Tsongkhapa's close personal relationship with Densa Thil and, by extension, its patrons, the Phagdru rulers of Tibet, would prove critically important both for the success of his own mission and for the fortunes of the Geluk school that would emerge from his legacy.

CHAPTER 3

Coming of Age

By the fall of 1380, Tsongkhapa had completed his formal studies in central Tibet. It was thus that, at the age of twenty-five, at the Keru Temple of the Wön Valley in the ancient territory of Drakmar, he first taught as a kashipa. Known also as Kachu Temple, Keru is believed to have been built in the eighth century, during the reign of King Tridé Tsukten, making it one of the oldest temples in central Tibet.[97] There Tsongkhapa gave an extensive series of classes to a group of students, including his attendant Tsakho, on the topics of the Perfection of Wisdom, logic and epistemology, and the Madhyamaka philosophy.

Inspired by the two syllables of the name of the temple, *ke* and *ru*, Tsongkhapa composed two alphabetical poems of advice, in which the first syllable in each line begins with a new consonant affixed with the vowel *e* in the first poem and the vowel *o* (in place of *u*) in the second poem, a challenging literary task. The poem opens with these lines:

> Those of us who are here at this famed Keru site,
> Let's shun profit and wealth but strive in the Dharma;
> Just as the rising sun dignifies the flower stamens,
> Let's pierce our ears by the light of the scriptures.[98]

What Was Tsongkhapa Like?

Thanks to Neringpa Chimé Rapgyé, a fifteenth-century Nyingma teacher and a profound admirer of Tsongkhapa, we have some idea of what Tsongkhapa looked like in person. As someone from northeastern Tibet, he was quite tall. He was also said to have a largish nose such that, in his student years, his nickname was Big-Nosed Amdo (*Amdo nawoché*). According to Neringpa, Tsongkhapa cut a rather imposing figure, and everyone within his vicinity would feel his presence. Yet he had a gentle personality and was easy to be with, so that those around him enjoyed his company. Whoever met him immediately felt his naturally compassionate nature.

When others, including his own students, asked him questions—whether concerning doubts they might have, difficult points of Buddhist thought, or challenges related to an interpretation of a passage of a text—Tsongkhapa would treat those questions with respect and patience. Before offering his own views, he would delve into the questions with the interlocutor so that they could gain a better grasp of the points they were asking about. When addressing someone, he was always polite, rarely addressing them by their name alone but using their title, such as Kashipa So-and-so, Chengapa (senior tutor) So-and-so, or Khenchen (great abbot) So-and-So. Although he spoke with a hint of an Amdo accent, he was perfectly fluent in the central Tibetan dialect; in fact, this faint accent made his speech melodious. He had a rich voice that projected quite far, so that even those sitting at the edge of a crowd could hear him clearly. Listening to Tsongkhapa teach, with eloquence and a natural melody, monks would remark, "Even days after the end of the teaching sessions, we would have the feeling of hearing the melody of Tsongkhapa's voice."[99] He would retain this humble and gentle personality throughout his life, even after his emergence as one of the most important religious figures in Tibet.

Chenga Sönam Gyaltsen (1386–1433), a younger brother of Tibet's Phagdru ruler and a close student of Tsongkhapa's, who was also an important figure in the Kagyü tradition, offers this personal portrait:

> This great being, having gained meditatively derived realization of the twin seals of Mahāmudrā—the nature of reality and the seal of [the union of] bliss and emptiness—possessed an intimate mastery of the scriptures. As a result, he had an intellect that resembled the penetrating power of a spear flying through the air. When others read a portion of a text, he could explain the meaning of [the] passage without having to ponder and without any hesitation, stating, "It means this and that," and he would offer his explanation together with its underlying rationale. Even spiritual mentors whose intellect had been well exposed to the scriptures would remark that one gains more insight from spending a period of [time] drinking tea at the feet of Tsongkhapa and asking him questions than from personal contemplation of a given text for months and years. Many speak of how nothing compares to the joy brought by Tsongkhapa's visit or by being in his presence. Whenever those around him see the master, they feel as if they cannot take their gaze away from him, that seeing him brings much joy and peace. There were numerous instances when simply being in his presence would trigger growth in one's spiritual practice and progress in realization. These things are quite well known and remain fresh in the minds of students who are still alive.[100]

Among the Texts of the Tibetan Canon at Tsal Gungthang Monastery, 1381–85

From Wön, Tsongkhapa went to the region of Kyishö to Tsal Gungthang Monastery, located in the region of the lower Kyichu

River, a center that at the time was famed for its possession of the entire collection of the Tsalpa edition of the Kangyur and Tengyur. Tsongkhapa would spend the next four years—from 1381 (the Iron Bird year) to 1385 (the Wood Ox year), from age twenty-five to twenty-eight—at Tsal Gungthang Monastery, deeply immersed in reading many important Indian Buddhist treatises.

Fortunately for Tsongkhapa, the two canons of the Kangyur and Tengyur had been revised, finalized, and categorized sometime around 1351, a few years before his birth, by Butön. This major undertaking had been sponsored by Tsalpa Künga Dorjé, himself a noted scholar and the author of the historical work *The Red Annals*. Located about six miles east of Lhasa, the monastery where these two canons were housed had been founded in 1187 by Lama Shang (Shang Yudrakpa, 1123–93). Shang was a disciple of Gampopa and later came to be recognized as the founder of the Tsalpa branch of the Kagyü school of Tibetan Buddhism. In commenting on Lama Shang's place in Tibetan history, a modern-day historian remarks, "Shang was himself important to Tibetan history because it was arguably he who set the precedent for sectarian (as distinguished from royalist) polity, which became the predominating form of government in Tibet down until the 1950s."[101] Shang was known for his advocacy of a unique perspective on Mahāmudrā, emphasizing the rhetoric and language of immediacy and approaching enlightenment through a subitist, or instantaneous, path. Shang's Mahāmudrā teachings would later become an object of critique by Sakya Paṇḍita in his *Clear Differentiation of the Three Codes*.[102]

None of the biographies of Tsongkhapa offers any details on how he spent his time during the four-year sojourn at Tsal Gungthang Monastery, nor do we have access to any notes Tsongkhapa himself took during this period. One thing that emerges clearly, though, is that this was primarily a solitary period, during which he devoted himself to close and careful reading of the key Indian Buddhist texts that are part of the Tibetan Buddhist canon. Judging by *The Golden Rosary*, the lengthy work he began composing toward the end of his reading period, Tsongkhapa clearly was taking extensive notes from his reading to be able to engage in in-depth comparative analysis across multiple texts. As someone with a disciplined mind, Tsongkhapa must have followed a strict routine combining prolonged sessions of reading with critical reflection, while maintaining and deepening his personal meditative practice.

Tsongkhapa's four-year immersion in the careful reading of key Indian texts left a powerful impression on him. The experience completely changed the way he viewed the existing Tibetan understandings of the Indian source texts and their associated practice traditions. It gave him the chance to critically appreciate the plurality of views among the great Indian Buddhist masters, gave rise to a confidence in developing his own views, and helped raise crucial doubts about many of the Tibetan interpretations that had become orthodox. Not unlike a methodologically sophisticated doctoral researcher in contemporary academia, Tsongkhapa began to develop his own "original" critical understanding of the key Indian Buddhist source texts.

Toward the end of this long period of reading and contemplation, at the age of twenty-nine, he began the composition of his first major work, *The Golden Rosary*, an extensive two-volume exposition of Maitreya's *Ornament of Realizations*. The choice to write about a text he had already studied in depth at Nyethang Dewachen Monastery years earlier makes sense, as it gave Tsongkhapa the chance to test out his new critical apparatus on a body of teachings with which he had deep and long-standing familiarity and on which extensive Tibetan commentarial literature already existed. It also joined him to a commentarial tradition, as this particular Indian Buddhist text had inspired a huge number of commentaries, both in India and in Tibet; it remains to this day a key text in Tibetan monastic centers of all traditions.

During these four years at Tsal Gungthang, Tsongkhapa paid short visits to important nearby sites. Accompanied by his attendant Tsakho, he traveled to Lhasa where he performed repeated *nyungné* fasting rites in the presence of the sacred image of Avalokiteśvara (the buddha of compassion) at the Jokhang Temple.[103] Known as Thukjé Chenpo Rangjön Ngaden ("Five-Aspected Self-Originated Great Compassion"), this is one of the most sacred images in the Tibetan Buddhist world. As its name indicates, this icon is believed not to have been made by a human sculptor, but to have arisen naturally. This image, and the Jokhang Temple more generally, came to occupy a special place in Tsongkhapa's heart, and he would repeatedly return for subsequent visits. (Years later, as we shall see, Tsongkhapa's devotion to the Jokhang Temple would culminate in his major restoration of the temple and his hosting the first Great Prayer Festival of Lhasa there.)

One night during Tsongkhapa's nyungné fasting rites in the presence of the sacred image of Avalokiteśvara, after days of fervent prayers, he and his attendant Tsakho both had significant dreams. Tsakho dreamed of two large white conches in the sky that fell into his lap and merged into a single conch. He dreamed of picking up this conch and blowing it loudly. Later, this dream came to be interpreted as a portent that in the future Tsakho would make important contributions to the Dharma in his native Gyalrong area, in eastern Tibet.

Tsongkhapa dreamed of climbing a steep, rocky mountain cliff and finding at the top a large, beautiful blue flower, attached to a living stem, lying on a smooth white slab at the summit. In the dream, he picked it up, thinking that the blue lotus was in fact a hand implement of the goddess Tārā. This dream would come to be imbued with all manner of special meaning by his biographers.[104]

According to Khedrup, in his dream Tsongkhapa first thought that picking up the blue flower was a sign of a special blessing from Tārā, but he was subsequently told in the same dream that it had more to do with his life span.[105]

The Rise of Drakpa Gyaltsen as the Fifth Phagdru Ruler

As mentioned earlier, Drakpa Jangchup was succeeded by Sönam Drakpa (1359–1408), who assumed the throne at the age of twelve as the fourth ruler of the Phagdru dynasty. The five-year period of Sönam Drakpa's reign coincided almost exactly with Tsongkhapa's long immersion in the canonical texts held at Tsal Gungthang Monastery. It was also during this period of intense reading that, in 1383, Karmapa Rolpai Dorjé, who had blessed the infant Tsongkhapa, passed away.

In 1385, Drakpa Gyaltsen assumed the throne of the Phagdru dynasty. Barely twelve, at the beginning he was little more than a figurehead. The real power was exerted by his uncle Dzongchi Drakpa Rinchen, who would later be assassinated by some of the court officials dissatisfied with his autocratic rule.[106] In any case, Drakpa Gyaltsen's rise as the new ruler would come to have a lasting effect on Tsongkhapa's fortune. The new Phagdru ruler shared with Tsongkhapa a deep affection for the senior Phagdru religious patriarch Drakpa Jangchup. In 1385, this revered Phagdru figure passed away. So, while visiting Lhasa, at the request of an official named Rinchen Gyalpo, Tsongkhapa composed a supplication prayer to Drakpa Jangchup containing the following lines:

> O refuge of beings, whether you have departed
> To Maitreya's presence [in Tuṣita] or Amitābha's pure land,
> Whatever pure realm you may have gone to,
> May we, too, be reborn there, as part of your retinue.[107]

Having seen Tsongkhapa's alphabetical poem in praise of Drakpa Jangchup, as well as his supplication prayer, the new Phagdru ruler formally requested him to compose the "official" poetic rendering (*avadāna*; *tokjö*) of the life of Chenga Drakpa Jangchup. Entitled "Mount Meru of Blessings: A Poem Narrating the Life of the Great Bodhisattva Drakpa Jangchup," this composition would attract deep admiration as a great work of poetry in Tibetan. Tsongkhapa wrote it in a combination of prose and verse, at the Samantabhadra Forest Retreat near the monastery of Drigung Thil, sometime around 1386. His authorship of the official biographical poem of the deeply revered Phagdru figure sealed the close bond between Tsongkhapa and the new Phagdru ruler, Miwang Drakpa Gyaltsen, a relationship that would remain strong until Tsongkhapa's death. According to the colophon of another text, Tsongkhapa also wrote a textbook on logic and epistemology, *A Gateway to the Seven Texts of Dharmakīrti*, at the behest of the new Phagdru ruler.[108]

As we shall see later, sometime between 1393 and 1394, in the midst of a long period of solitude in the Wölkha Valley, Tsongkhapa would write a lengthy letter of advice to the young Phagdru ruler. The letter begins by acknowledging receipt of it, written in poetic form, from Miwang, and replies that he would have loved to visit him and spend time discussing various topics of Dharma interest. Tsongkhapa then goes on to relate how, the year before, he had made "a firm pledge to immerse myself in the yoga of not visiting the towns," so that he is not able to visit the palace at this time.[109] The body of Tsongkhapa's advice letter consists of twenty four-line stanzas interspersed with sections in prose, covering a wide range of topics including the values, norms, and deeds appropriate to a ruler of the land. The letter refers to the Indian genre of treatises on governance (*nītiśāstra*), which can be a useful resource, but he also warns the young ruler to differentiate between good and bad treatises of this kind. Tsongkhapa writes that if Miwang, as the ruler, upholds the path, reigns over the kingdom with skillful means, and leads his subjects to the Dharma, his well-being in both this life and future lives will be assured.

Over time, two of the Phagdru ruler's brothers (Sönam Sangpo and Sönam Gyaltsen) would become close disciples of Tsongkhapa's, and most of Phagdru's trusted ministers, including the Neu governor Namkha Sangpo, became his disciples as well. As we shall see later, the close relationship that Tsongkhapa enjoyed with Phagdru ruling families would have a major influence in many areas of his mission.

Completion of *The Golden Rosary*

In the winter of 1385 (the Wood Ox year), Tsongkhapa returned to Nyethang Dewachen Monastery from Tsal Gungthang. Then, in the spring of 1386 (the Fire Tiger year), when he was twenty-nine, Tsongkhapa visited Jayül, the monastery associated with the important Kadam master Jayülwa Shönu Wö (1075–1138). There, he taught an assembly of over seventy monks the following texts: Maitreya's *Ornament*, Dharmakīrti's *Exposition of Valid Cognition*, Candrakīrti's *Entering the Middle Way*, and Asaṅga's *Compendium of Abhidharma*. He then returned to Tsal Gungthang once again to resume writing *The Golden Rosary*.

During this stay at Tsal Gungthang, he met a well-known expert on Kālacakra, Tokden Yeshé Gyaltsen,[110] and requested teachings on that tantra. Thus, during an interval, Tsongkhapa left with Tokden Yeshé Gyaltsen for Kyormolung Monastery, where, over a period of several months, he received a detailed reading and explanation of a famous commentary on the Kālacakra tantra entitled *Stainless Light* (*Vimalaprabhā*).[111] While receiving this teaching, Tsongkhapa also learned all the important facets of this tantra, including astronomy and the calculation of celestial movements. While at Kyormolung,

Tsongkhapa also taught classes on selected key Indian Buddhist classics and composed texts, including a hymn to Maitreya. It was also around this time that Tsongkhapa composed his twenty-three-stanza hymn to Goddess Tārā, which contains the following lines:

> A kind mother never loses her love for her infant child,
> Even when she sees him doing something wrong;
> So what need is there to speak of the chance
> Of us losing your love, O mother of all beings.
> ....
> Never disheartened by our countless wrongs,
> Us childish beings falsely pursuing our own interests,
> You carry the burden to free all sentient beings;
> I admire your enlightened deeds, vast and expansive.[112]

The next year, the Fire Rabbit year of 1387, Tsongkhapa returned once more to Nyethang Dewachen for the summer semester. It was here that Tsongkhapa met Tokden Jampel Gyatso (1356–1428), who had come to attend Tsongkhapa's teaching on *The Sublime Continuum* (*Ratnagotravibhāga*), Maitreya's key work on buddha nature.[113] Tokden became Tsongkhapa's disciple at the time, and later he came to play a crucial role in the more mystical dimension of Tsongkhapa's spiritual life.

It was also at Nyethang Dewachen, as noted in his colophon, that he completed the final sections of his two-volume *Golden Rosary*, bringing this major writing project to completion in the summer (the fifth month of the Tibetan calendar). Tsongkhapa was thirty-one when *The Golden Rosary* finally came out; it had taken him three years to complete. The text immediately attracted the attention of many Tibetan scholars and students. Over time, this work would transform Tibetan monastic academia and set a new standard for critical, rigorous, and comprehensive Buddhist scholarship.[114]

Tsongkhapa's *Golden Rosary* is a masterpiece by any measure. Judged even by today's standards of critical scholarship, it is a remarkable work. Through a careful comparison of some twenty-one Indian commentaries on the root text, highlighting their commonalities and, more important, their differences, Tsongkhapa initiated a new scholarly method comparable to a modern literature review of the primary and secondary sources on a given topic. Ostensibly a commentary on Maitreya's *Ornament of Clear Realizations* as well as on Haribhadra's influential eighth-century short commentary *The Clear Meaning* (*Sphuṭārthā*), Tsongkhapa's *Golden Rosary* offers a sophisticated critical reading of this important Indian root text. Maitreya's work is a verse summary of the voluminous Perfection of Wisdom sūtras, especially the *Twenty-Five Thousand Lines* and *Eight Thousand Lines*, respectively the medium and short versions of the Perfection of Wisdom scripture. Ngok Lotsawa translated the root text into Tibetan in the eleventh century and established its formal study in Tibet through writing his own topical outline—a kind of map of the text as well as his own commentary. His was the first Tibetan exegesis of this Indian text. From that time on, the careful and detailed study of this Indian text was a major academic focus in the various Tibetan monasteries.

The Golden Rosary skillfully disentangles the complex, multilayered relationship of Maitreya's root text with its own source, the Perfection of Wisdom scriptures, and with the subsequent commentaries it inspired. Distinguishing between two influential Indian readings of the root text, one by Vimuktisena and the other by Haribhadra, Tsongkhapa demonstrates many elements of the scholarly method typical of the modern humanities, which many assume to be recent Western developments. His methods include a text-critical approach, philological analysis, hermeneutics, and contextualization, as well as consideration of the commentators' philosophical positions and scholastic alliances—all of which he accomplishes without ever losing sight of the larger perspective, something he had learned from Rendawa in his student years.

The Golden Rosary explores each of the important topics covered in the root text in a sophisticated framework of four elements: (1) transitional comments (*tsamjar*) linking the current topic to the preceding one; (2) general points (*chidön*) related to the relevant topic, presenting the overall terrain and tracing the topic to the original source in the Perfection of Wisdom scripture; (3) word-by-word exposition (*tsikdön*), composed of two layers, one of the root text and the other of Haribhadra's commentary; and, finally, (4) critical analysis (*thachö*) of the key questions relevant to the topic, both in terms of the divergent standpoints of important Indian authors and, as the culmination, Tsongkhapa's own understanding. To read and study *The Golden Rosary* is, therefore, to be treated to an intellectual feast seasoned with rigor, clarity, and depth of understanding.

Unlike the mature works of his later period, *The Golden Rosary* brims with youthful energy. Tsongkhapa did not resist the occasional urge to revel in rhetorical flourish, both in style and in poetic eloquence. At the end of the customary opening salutation verse, for example, Tsongkhapa writes:

> This *Golden Rosary* of wondrous and eloquent words
> May not delight the foolish whose eyes are assailed
> By the prickly thorns of the demon of envy;
> Yet if it were to be seen by one with a clear and unbiased
>   mind,
> Whose beautiful intellect body is clothed in diligence,
> And, who wishes to be adorned by the jewel mother of the
>   buddhas,
> At that moment, the round orb of their face will light up
> Brightly, with the radiance of their cheerful smile.[115]

From this point onward, an important hallmark of Tsongkhapa's writing, especially on scholarly topics of philosophy, epistemology, and Abhidharma, would be the near absence of citations from Tibetan thinkers as source authorities. The sources he would cite as authorities on a given topic or question would be almost exclusively Indian, giving the impression that he was embarking on developing an entirely fresh reading of the Indian Buddhist sources. As we shall see later, this would be seen by some as arrogance, a lack of respect for the contributions of Tibetan thinkers of the past. Also, from then on, Tsongkhapa would attach the phrase "someone who has read widely" to his name Lobsang Drakpa in the colophons of his works.[116] *The Golden Rosary* sealed Tsongkhapa's reputation as a scholar of highest note excelling in the mastery of the great Indian Buddhist classics. Among Tibetan commentaries on Maitreya's *Ornament*, Tsongkhapa's *Golden Rosary* remains unrivaled in both scope and depth.[117]

Furthering His Quest for Vajrayāna Teachings

After the completion of *The Golden Rosary*, Tsongkhapa's main focus for the next few years would be to deepen his study, understanding, and practice of Vajrayāna teachings. As a young boy he had been exposed to many aspects of Vajrayāna: his childhood teacher Chöjé had conferred on him numerous initiations, especially of Vajrabhairava, Mañjuśrī, Tārā, and Vajrapāṇi; he had done several intensive meditation retreats and had recited a huge number of mantras. After arriving in central Tibet, Tsongkhapa continued his daily sādhana practice, especially of Vajrabhairava. He also expanded his repertoire of Vajrayāna transmissions by receiving the six yogas of Nāropa according to the Kagyü lineage, a set of teachings associated with the so-called mother tantra, Sakya transmissions of the Hevajra tantra, the Cakrasaṃvara tantra according to the lineage of Butön, and the transmissions of the six-branch yoga of the completion stage of the Kālacakra tantra according to the Jonang lineage. What he wished to do now was to take a more systematic approach to the Vajrayāna teachings. He was particularly keen to deepen his knowledge and practice of the Kālacakra tantra. Thus, he spent the entire winter of the Fire Rabbit year (1387–88) at Tölung Monastery—founded by the great Kadam master Tölungpa Rinchen Nyingpo (1032–1116)—and Ngangkar Monastery (located in the lower region of Tölung) immersed in the study and practice of the Kālacakra. While residing at these monasteries, he also gave teachings on selected texts to the assemblies of monks at each.[118]

Earlier, Tsongkhapa had received repeated requests from Dzongchi Drakpa Rinchen to visit his region, the Yarlung Valley. At this time, he decided to accept the invitation. He left Tölung and headed toward Sinpori (the westernmost ridge of the Yartö mountain range that divides the Tsangpo River from the Kyichu),[119] accompanied by a number of monks. On the way, he stopped at Gongkar, where the local ruler of that region was a devotee. He stayed at the Riknga Temple (a Kagyü monastery founded in 1325) and gave a series of teachings to over seventy monks on such texts as Maitreya's *Ornament*, Dharmakīrti's primer on logic and epistemology, the two Abhidharma texts of Asaṅga and Vasubandhu, Guṇaprabha's *Root Lines on Vinaya*, and Candrakīrti's *Entering the Middle Way*. During this period of teachings, the Gongkar ruler served as the host, providing for all needs of the group.[120]

The Great Teaching Session at Mönkhar Tashi Dong

After Gongkar, Tsongkhapa and his group journeyed to Yarlung and took up residence at Mönkhar Tashi Dong Monastery, where both hospitality and food were provided by Dzongchi Drakpa Rinchen. Fulfilling requests from devotees, Tsongkhapa taught various Indian Buddhist classics and also conducted several Vajrayana empowerment ceremonies (*wang*), authorization blessings (*jenang*), and reading transmissions (*lung*). In particular, given his widespread fame as someone who had had visions of Sarasvatī, the goddess of wisdom and poetry, many devotees came to seek jenang blessings of the goddess of wisdom and poetry from him.

One evening that winter, while resting in his room in the company of some close disciples sitting around a fire, Tsongkhapa told them the life stories of some of Tibet's great past masters—Ngok Lotsawa, Chapa Chökyi Sengé, Sakya Paṇḍita, Butön, and so on. Someone brought up the story of how Kashipa Sherap Sengé had once given a series of lectures on eleven Indian Buddhist texts during a single period—the greatest number of Indian texts ever taught in one continuous stretch. A monk by the name of Geshe Shatön asked Tsongkhapa if he would consider conducting a similar lecture series, teaching multiple texts in one go. "If I make an effort, yes, I could possibly do it," he replied. Everyone leaped up and made fervent appeals for him to do so. Tsongkhapa agreed.[121]

Having accepted the challenge, Tsongkhapa went into retreat from the tenth of that month until the end of the month. On the thirtieth, the day of the new moon, he had all the texts he had chosen to teach wrapped in cloth, intending to start the teaching the next day, the first day of the new month. As word spread of Tsongkhapa's plan to teach a number of Indian Buddhist texts in a single stretch, however, requests came from many monks at neighboring monasteries to delay the start of the teachings so that they could attend. In response, Tsongkhapa postponed the formal teachings, but he still began on the first day of the month by spending a few days teaching on selected verses of advice, as well as on life stories of Kagyü masters, including Milarepa and his teacher Marpa.[122]

On the fifth day of the Tibetan month, Tsongkhapa finally began his teaching series, reading the titles of fifteen Indian Buddhist texts, one immediately after the other. Typically, translated Indian texts in Tibetan begin with the phrase "In the Indian language this work is entitled. . . ." After he had completed teaching on two of the shorter texts, Tsongkhapa decided to add two more short works to the list. Thus, over a period of three months, Tsongkhapa gave expositions on a total of seventeen Indian Buddhist texts, with special attention to more substantive philosophical works, such as Dharmakīrti's primer on logic and epistemology. Where necessary, Tsongkhapa brought into the discussion divergent interpretations of specific texts by past Tibetan authors, though for the most part he remained close to the commentaries by the Indian authors themselves (where they existed). The seventeen texts he taught in this single series were these:

1. Dharmakīrti's *Exposition of Valid Cognition*
2. Maitreya's *Ornament of Realizations*
3. Asaṅga's *Compendium of Abhidharma*
4. Vasubandhu's *Treasury of Abhidharma*
5. Guṇaprabha's *Root Lines on Vinaya*
6. Maitreya's *Ornament of Mahāyāna Sūtras*
7. Maitreya's *Differentiation of the Middle and Extremes*
8. Maitreya's *Differentiation of Phenomena and Their Nature*
9. Maitreya's *Sublime Continuum*
10. Nāgārjuna's *Treatise on the Middle Way*
11. Nāgārjuna's *Sixty Stanzas of Reasoning*
12. Nāgārjuna's *Seventy Stanzas on Emptiness*
13. Nāgārjuna's *Repelling the Arguments*
14. Nāgārjuna's *Grinding the Postulations to Dust*
15. Candrakīrti's *Entering the Middle Way*
16. Āryadeva's *Four Hundred Stanzas*
17. Śāntideva's *Way of the Bodhisattva*[123]

Everyone in attendance at these teachings was deeply inspired. It is said that many of those who were present started to chant the following praise:

When teaching the tantras he is Vajradhara himself;
When teaching the sūtras he is the savior Śākyamuni;
Tsongkhapa, the all-knowing Dharma king,
Unrivaled and supreme indeed he is among the learned.[124]

While at Mönkhar Tashi Dong Monastery, Tsongkhapa composed a poetic hymn to Sakya Paṇḍita. In this short piece of twelve stanzas, he honors Sakya Paṇḍita as a manifestation of Mañjuśrī in the Land of Snows and praises him for his unique contributions. Tsongkhapa especially highlights Sakya Paṇḍita's dedication to ensuring the authenticity of the Buddhist teachings in Tibet (possibly a reference to his writing of *Clear Differentiation of the Three Codes*) and his pioneering role in establishing the various literary disciplines in the country. He concludes the praise with the following two stanzas, which nicely capture the tone:

Dharma master unrivaled on this earth;
Mañjuśrī unimpeded in all fields of knowledge;
Paṇḍita who has mastered all five sciences—
O Sakyapa, sole refuge of this Land of Snows,

Day and night I offer supplications:
"In life after life, may I see your buddha body
Resplendent with the major and minor marks,
And may I hear your speech without disruption."[125]

In his colophon, Tsongkhapa writes, "This was composed at the glorious Mönkhar Tashi Dong at the request of Sengé Gyaltsen of

Yarlung, an upholder of the tantras. It was written by the easterner Tsongkhapa Lobsang Drakpa, someone who has indestructible reverence for this Dharma master."

A Solitary Retreat on Okar Mountain

That summer of the Earth Snake year (1389), when Tsongkhapa was thirty-three, he spent some time in solitary retreat on Okar, a rocky mountain in the Yarlung Valley. He focused his practice on the Cakrasaṃvara tantra, following a strict discipline of sitting for four sessions per day, as well as performing the self-empowerment rites of the tantra. He also practiced the six yogas of Niguma, an important instruction of the Shangpa Kagyü tradition stemming from the Indian yogini Niguma. In between the formal sessions, Tsongkhapa engaged in intensive breath-based yogic exercises connected with *tummo* (psychic heat) practice, performing this exercise up to one hundred times a session.[126] The experiences Tsongkhapa gained, especially of tummo, during this retreat would deeply affect his understanding of the key meditative practices associated with the mother tantra—Cakrasaṃrava and Hevajra being the two important ones in the class—including their unique methods of engendering bliss and applying it to meditative practice.

That fall, Tsongkhapa had a reunion with his teacher Rendawa, who happened to be visiting the Lhasa area during a semester break at Sakya Monastery. Both stayed at the Potala and had the chance to engage in a series of dialogues, sharing their growing understanding and practice. While with his teacher, Tsongkhapa also gave teachings to the students who were following him on his travels from place to place. After a while, Rendawa returned to Sakya, and Tsongkhapa spent the rest of the year at the rocky caves of Kyormolung. There, in addition to continuing his meditative practice, he taught many students and scholars Kālacakra, the Perfection of Wisdom,

Abhidharma, and Dharmakīrti's *Exposition of Valid Cognition*. However, in the spring of the Iron Horse year (1390), seeking further transmissions of Vajrayāna teachings and also eager for another round of dialogue with Rendawa, Tsongkhapa left for Tsang Province, taking up residence at Nup Chölung (known also as Rong Chölung) retreat. There he was able to receive oral transmissions from the abbot of the monastery, Rinpoché Drakpa Shenyen, on the cycle of teachings connected with the five stages of Guhyasamāja.

Meeting with the Mystic Umapa

Around this time, two of Tsongkhapa's students—Sönam Drak and Geshé Sherap Drak—went to see the mystic Umapa Pawo Dorjé (whose personal name was Tsöndrü Sengé), who was staying at a nearby hermitage. This mystic was famed for having constant visions of Mañjuśrī. The students met with Umapa and received some transmissions from him. During their conversation, Umapa said he wanted to receive the blessings of the goddess Sarasvatī from their teacher. Upon their return, the two students passed on the message to Tsongkhapa, who soon visited Umapa and conferred the desired Sarasvatī blessing on him.

During their conversation, Umapa told Tsongkhapa that even from his early years as a young yak herder in eastern Tibet, he would have occasional visions of Mañjuśrī and would receive teachings. He confided, "Although I have tried my best to examine whether or not this is a genuine visionary encounter, I still haven't been able to gain full conviction. In fact it was Mañjuśrī who urged me this time to go and receive the Sarasvatī blessing from you." Then, while Umapa was experiencing visions of Mañjuśrī, Tsongkhapa asked him some important questions concerning the view of emptiness and other points of Dharma practice. After considering his answers, Tsongkhapa told Umapa that the visions that he had were credible and that he should not have any further doubt about their authenticity. He then advised the mystic, "You should fervently pray to Mañjuśrī, but you must remember that the form that one sees with the eyes is not actually Mañjuśrī himself. The genuine form of a meditation deity appears only at the level of mental cognition, not sensory perception." Tsongkhapa then went on to say that, for his part, he would like to receive teachings from Mañjuśrī, with Umapa as the medium, but "for the moment, I need to go to Taktsang to be with my teacher Rendawa, so let's arrange to meet again in the near future."[127] As we shall see in chapter 5, Umapa would play a crucial role in Tsongkhapa's mystical life, especially in his personal relationship with Mañjuśrī.

Before leaving Rong Chölung retreat for Taktsang (a Sakya monastery and the main base of Lochen Kyapchok Palsang) to meet Rendawa, Tsongkhapa wrote a letter to Rinpungpa Namkha Gyaltsen, who was living in the Nedong area as a minister at the Phagdru court. Rinpungpa had sent a formal invitation to Tsongkhapa requesting that he visit his home. Replying in poetic verse, Tsongkhapa compared Namkha Gyaltsen to the merchant Anāthapiṇḍika, who generously donated the Jetavana Grove to the Buddha and his monastic community for their residence. Tsongkhapa then spoke of the news he had received from his teacher Rendawa, to the effect that Rendawa had arrived at Taktsang Monastery and that he was eager to see him there, making it impossible to accept Rinpungpa's invitation just then.[128] Judging by the tone of this letter, it appears that by this time Tsongkhapa already had a close relationship with this important member of the Phagdru ruling elite.

A Rare Gathering at Taktsang Monastery

At Taktsang Monastery, possibly in the summer of 1390, a rare gathering occurred. It was a convergence, in a single place, of five of Tibet's greatest minds: Khenchen Drakpa Gyaltsen (possibly the translator of Dignāga's *Ñyāyapraveśa* into Tibetan), Narthang Lotsawa Dhönsang, Lochen Kyapchok Palsang (d. 1412),[129] Rendawa, and Tsongkhapa. This was in fact part of a larger gathering, since some of these masters were accompanied by many of their students as well.

Taktsang Monastery being his home, Lochen Kyapchok Palsang served as the host, taking charge of the needs of his august visitors and their students. Lochen had invited his colleagues to be part of several days of dialogue on various aspects of philosophy, logic and epistemology, Abhidharma, and meditative practice. The host, Lochen, although considerably older than Tsongkhapa, was deeply impressed by him; he would later be the key person to request Tsongkhapa to compose some of his most influential works, including the two great syntheses *The Great Treatise on the Stages of the Path to Enlightenment* and *The Great Treatise on the Stages of the Path of Tantra*.

During their stay at Taktsang, three more senior masters also conducted specific teachings concurrently. Khenchen Drakpa Gyaltsen taught Maitreya's *Ornament of Realizations,* Lochen himself taught the Hevajra tantra,[130] and Rendawa taught his own work on Prajñākāragupta's *Ornament of the Pramāṇavārttika*, itself a detailed analytic commentary on Dharmakīrti's influential work on logic and epistemology. Tsongkhapa attended Rendawa's classes and received the entire teaching on his teacher's newly completed commentary on this important work.[131] During these classes, as Rendawa was reading from his text, the teacher and his brilliant student discussed and debated a range of important issues of logic and epistemology.

Following this memorable gathering at Taktsang Monastery, Rendawa and Tsongkhapa departed for Ba'u Banyer. There, Tsongkhapa received from Rendawa an explanation of the Guhyasamāja root tantra in its entirety. Having conceived a desire to receive teachings on the Kālacakra tantra from Chökyi Palwa (1316–97), a direct student of Butön, Tsongkhapa had a dream one night in which Chökyi Palwa told him that he had received the Kālacakra teachings seventeen times from Butön. Later, when Tsongkhapa actually met Chökyi Palwa and asked him how many times the master had received the Kālacakra teachings from Butön, he replied, "Seventeen times!"[132]

Rendawa had noticed that his protégé Tsongkhapa was increasingly focused on the Vajrayāna—seeking ever more teachings and transmissions, and in turn giving empowerments and teachings to his students. It had been around six years since Rendawa had urged Tsongkhapa to start teaching the great Indian classics to others. Seeing him now focused on searching for more tantric instructions, Rendawa observed: "Spending this much time seeking the Vajrayāna teachings could delay everything. Wouldn't it be more beneficial right now to be spending more time teaching the Buddhist classics instead?" Tsongkhapa replied, "I have always had a keen interest in Tantra even from my youth, so, for the time being, I would like to dedicate some time to the search for instructions."[133]

It is not that Rendawa himself did not take Tantra seriously. Rendawa too shared the view that Tantra represents the highest teachings within Buddhism and also presents the swiftest and the most advanced path to buddhahood; in fact, Rendawa would himself later write a major work on the Guhyasamāja tantra. Even so, it appears that at that time what the mainstream monastic community in Tibet admired most was mastery of the great Indian Buddhist classics, especially those that constituted the key texts in the formal monastic curriculum. In suggesting that Tsongkhapa delay his more focused quest for the transmissions of the various tantric teachings, it appears Rendawa was simply expressing his concerns as a teacher who cared deeply about the developing career of his protégé.

Years later, recounting this somewhat difficult exchange with his teacher, Tsongkhapa would tell his student and biographer Khedrup: "When it comes to Tantra, I have never had the need for others to encourage me. From a young age I had a keen desire to learn about it. Right from start I had the aspiration to study the entire corpus of the tantras."[134]

By this time, Rendawa and Tsongkhapa had developed a strong teacher-student bond. Not only had Tsongkhapa come to consider Rendawa his foremost teacher, on Sūtra as well as Tantra, but Rendawa had come to see Tsongkhapa as his principal student. Rendawa's biography tells a story that succinctly captures how he felt about his protégé, including Tsongkhapa's sharp intellect, his vast knowledge, and his prospect as an important figure in Tibet. Once at Ngamring Monastery, according to this source, Rendawa was sitting with seventeen of his students, engaged in a casual conversation. At that time, elsewhere in the monastery, Khenchen Tengyalwa was conducting a teaching session attended by around seven hundred monks. Rendawa wondered aloud: between that large group of monks and their small group of seventeen, which might have a greater impact on the Buddha's doctrine? Reflecting, Rendawa told the group, "In the future, those seven hundred combined will not be able to rival the impact of Lobsang Drakpa [Tsongkhapa] alone."[135] Among Rendawa's seven principal students, Tsongkhapa would be described as "foremost among all disciples," "foremost in learning," "foremost in vinaya discipline," and "foremost in impact."[136]

In any case, in the fall of 1390, following the rare gathering at Taktsang Monastery, Rendawa returned to Sakya, while Tsongkhapa went back to Rong Chölung to spend some time with the mystic Umapa. There, he engaged in a series of dialogues on important points of Buddhist thought and practice. Also, availing himself of the service of Umapa as the medium, Tsongkhapa was able to ask Mañjuśrī a series of questions pertaining to Dharma practice.

At this time, Umapa also received a teaching from Tsongkhapa on Candrakīrti's *Entering the Middle Way*. Although planning to go to Nyangtö (upper Nyang) to study Kālacakra with Chökyi Palwa, Tsongkhapa had to delay his departure as word spread that Phagdru soldiers who had gone to take part in a military campaign in northwestern Tibet (Latö) were on their way back, and best avoided.[137] As a result, Tsongkhapa spent that fall in a mountain cave in the Rong area.

Receiving the Vajrayāna Instructions of Butön's Lineage

Toward the end of the fall of 1390, Tsongkhapa was finally able to travel to Gongsum Dechen, where Chökyi Palwa was in residence. (Because of his close association with this place, Chökyi Palwa came to be known as Gongsum Dechenpa, literally "the man from Gongsum Dechen.") The evening when Tsongkhapa met Chökyi Palwa for the first time, he offered him a yellow silk scarf. The next day, when Tsongkhapa made a ceremonial tea offering to the master, he offered a yard of blue silk cloth and formally asked him to teach him the great commentary on the Kālacakra tantra known as *Stainless Light* (*Vimalaprabhā*). The master replied, "The yellow silk scarf you gave me yesterday, which is a symbol of the dissolution of the earth element, indicates that you will attain the completion stage of Kālacakra, while this morning's blue silk—blue being the color of sky—indicates that you will attain the realization of the generation stage." He continued, "When you arrived here, I had in fact finished the first chapter and was reading from the opening section of chapter two where there is the phrase, 'Now, in order to help mature the great beings . . .' so I see a sign of great auspiciousness."[138] Thus, master Chökyi Palwa accepted Tsongkhapa's request. After he completed his teaching of chapter two, he returned to chapter one and retaught it so that Tsongkhapa would receive the entire teaching of the great Kālacakra commentary. The teaching lasted from late fall 1390 to the early spring of 1391. During this period, Tsongkhapa received not only an exposition of the *Stainless Light* commentary according to the tradition of Butön but also a set of practical instructions on the sādhana rites and the six yogas of Kālacakra.

Wishing to further his familiarity with the Yoga tantra, Tsongkhapa was able to connect with Butön's personal ritual assistant, Gönsang, who was still alive at Butön's Shalu Monastery. Tsongkhapa and the ritual master met, and the two of them stayed together for some time at a place called Tri Tsakhang, located at the junction of the upper and lower regions of Nyang. Tsongkhapa learned from this ritual master many of the practical and artistic aspects of the various tantras—how to draw and construct the maṇḍalas, performance of ritual dances, rites of initiation, complex hand gestures (*mudrā*), and so on.

One night, Tsongkhapa dreamed of an old monk seated on a high throne, wearing a diadem and holding a vajra and bell in his hands, who said he was Khyungpo Lhepa. In the dream, Tsongkhapa was seated in front of the master and, at one point, the master descended from the throne and walked around Tsongkhapa three times, placed his hand implements on Tsongkhapa's head, and said, "Karmavajra." Tsongkhapa woke up wondering what this dream might mean and realized that Karmavajra could be associated with the tantric initiation name he had received earlier, Amoghasiddhi Vajra (the Amogha Buddha family being associated with karma, or action). Later, Tsongkhapa would have another prophetic dream about the same master, this time involving a long string of mantras that appeared at the master's heart, which Tsongkhapa was reading aloud. When Tsongkhapa actually met Khyunpo Lhepa in person, his physical appearance was almost exactly as he had dreamed![139] At this time, however, Tsongkhapa returned to master Chökyi Palwa for further teachings, now focused on the Vajramāla cycle, a collection of tantric maṇḍalas and their associated sādhana practices. Tsongkhapa also received from Chökyi Palwa the empowerment of Great Wheel Vajrapāṇi (Mahācakra Vajrapāṇi), a special aspect of that well-known meditation deity.[140]

In the late fall of 1391, Tsongkhapa was able to go to Shalu to meet with master Khyungpo Lhepa Shönu Sönam, a principal student of Butön as well as the author of one of his biographies. Residing there for the rest of that fall until the summer of 1392, Tsongkhapa received from this master many of the empowerments, explanatory guidance, and oral instructions connected with a vast collection of Vajrayāna teachings and practices established and transmitted by Butön. It is said that every time Khyungpo Lhepa would complete an empowerment, he would say, "Now I have passed on the teaching to its rightful owner, so I have no regret."[141]

Having received all the teachings from Khyungpo Lhepa, Tsongkhapa returned once again to Butön's other disciple, Chökyi Palwa, who was at that time residing at Phakpa Ri in Panam, in order to continue with the remaining transmissions of Vajrayāna teachings. Thus, by end of 1392, Tsongkhapa had received all the transmissions of Vajrayāna teachings possessed by the great Butön, becoming the principal custodian of Butön's Vajrayāna lineage.

By this time, Tsongkhapa had received the transmissions of all the great tantras and their associated instructions and practices. These comprise what are known as the New Tantras—Indian Buddhist tantric teachings introduced to Tibet during the so-called second diffusion of Buddhism that began with the career of the great translator Lotsawa Rinchen Sangpo in the eleventh century. Tsongkhapa had received the entire cycle of teachings connected with the Guhyasamāja tantra, stemming from the two great eleventh-century Tibetan transmitters of that cycle of teaching—Gö Khukpa Lhatsé and Marpa Chökyi Lodrö—later synthesized and fused into a single transmission lineage by Butön. He had received transmissions associated with the so-called mother tantras—Cakrakasaṃvara, Vajrayoginī, and so on—transmitted into Tibet by Marpa and other great Tibetan translators. He had received transmissions of the Hevajra tantra, so revered and emphasized in the Sakya tradition of Tibetan Buddhism. He had also received transmissions of the Kālacakra tantra according to the lineage of Butön as well as that of the Jonang tradition. As for Vajrabhairava of the Yamāntaka family of tantras, given that this was the principal practice of his childhood teacher Chöjé, Tsongkhapa had been familiar with the transmissions and practices of this tantra from his childhood.[142] Thus, at age thirty-four, Tsongkhapa was not only a master of the sūtras but also a master and a lineage holder of the great tantras of the Vajrayāna tradition as well.

CHAPTER 4

Queries from a Sincere Heart

EARLIER, we learned how, in the spring of 1390 (the Iron Horse year), Tsongkhapa met with Umapa, a mystic blessed with constant visions of Mañjuśrī, the meditation deity who would become a personal guru for Tsongkhapa. This relationship with a mysterious guru—a meditation deity communicating first through a medium and later through visions—would transform Tsongkhapa's destiny. For his disciples and his future followers, the members of the Geluk school, this special relationship with Mañjuśrī would serve as the "proof" that theirs was a unique teacher and that the tradition he set forth was a revelation of Mañjuśrī's enlightened mind. For some of Tsongkhapa's detractors and future critics, this mysterious relationship would become a reason to be suspicious of the brilliant but maverick Tsongkhapa.

Before we delve into the details of Tsongkhapa's relationship with Umapa and, through him, with Mañjuśrī, there is another important strand to examine in the story of Tsongkhapa's emergence as a dominant voice in the Tibetan Buddhist world toward the end of the fourteenth century. I speak here of a series of questions Tsongkhapa openly raised about various Tibetan views on key aspects of Buddhist thought and practice.

First, the Appeal

Although the exact chronology is difficult to determine, sometime around 1390–91, after Tsongkhapa had met Lama Umapa and had his first encounter with Mañjuśrī through him, he composed a short prose work entitled *Queries from a Sincere Heart*. Written in the form of an open letter, it is addressed to "the meditators of Tibet" and those who "abide in the single-pointed experience of savoring the tasteful nectar essence of the Buddha's teaching and are keen to lead others to that experience."[143] Using the well-known tripartite framework of view, meditation, and conduct for Buddhist thought and practice in the Tibetan tradition, the letter is divided into two parts: (1) queries pertaining to conduct and (2) queries pertaining to the view and meditation.

Though written with youthful zest and an informal tone, *Queries* powerfully captures Tsongkhapa's fundamental quest for a more integrated understanding of Buddhist thought and practice. The open letter calls for the need for a coherent understanding of how the combinations of view, meditation, and conduct, and study, critical reflection, and meditative cultivation are supposed to lead to perfect enlightenment. As we shall see later, the questions Tsongkhapa raised at the time would continue to motivate his own quest with respect to his understanding and practice and to formulating these in his writings.

According to the Tibetan historian Pawo Tsuklak Trengwa, the occasion that spurred Tsongkhapa to write his *Queries* was a retreat at which he met a number of longtime meditators who were immersed in intensive practice.[144] Though clearly moved by their dedication to practice, Tsongkhapa was also saddened by what he perceived to be their limited knowledge and understanding of the Dharma, including the very practices in which they themselves were engaged.

For Tsongkhapa, genuine transformation—"attainment of realization," in technical Buddhist terminology—arises from a combination of knowledge, meditation, and insight and their expressions in everyday conduct. It is through acquiring knowledge of the truths of our existence as revealed by the Buddha—impermanence, no-self, and emptiness—and internalizing them through meditative cultivation that one gains profound insight into these truths. And it is through embodying these truths in our everyday life that our very being will come to be transformed. In contemporary parlance, Tsongkhapa is saying that lasting change has to begin with a change in our mind-set, in the way we see ourselves and the world, which then begins to shape our feelings, behavior, and way of being in the world. For Tsongkhapa, this is the fundamental insight at the heart of the Tibetan Buddhist framework of view, meditation, and conduct (*ta gom chö sum*). In this understanding, there is an intimate and dynamic connection between knowledge, insights, and meditative practice. Encountering meditators who had very little understanding of the Dharma seemed to have raised in Tsongkhapa a deep feeling of concern. Most probably, what Sakya Paṇḍita had written more than a century earlier must have come to Tsongkhapa's mind:

> Meditation that is without learning
> May bring temporary attainments, but those soon fade.[145]

Aware that this kind of critical querying could cause offense to some, Tsongkhapa cites the precedent of Sakya Paṇḍita's similar questioning in his *Clear Differentiation of the Three Codes*, and explains himself as follows:

> I raise the following queries not to display my own learning or to belittle others, nor out of desire for honor, material gain, or fame. In general, Sakya Paṇḍita, who was an emanation of Mañjuśrī, says the following in his *Treasury of Reasoning*:

Though people strive to practice meditation with
constant effort,
They deviate from the path that would please the
buddhas;
O people of the degenerate era who are so easily
content,
Think well and rely on a learned teacher.

He also made similar observations in his *Clear Differentiation of the Three Codes*. Furthermore, both in India as well as here in Tibet, there have been countless who had erred in view, meditation, and conduct. In particular, Nāgārjuna says that if one were to err in the view and meditation of emptiness, it would lead to serious downfall. For example, in his *Treatise on the Middle Way*, Nāgārjuna says: "If they wrongly view emptiness, / Those of feeble mind will be ruined."[146] We also see in the writings of numerous Indian and Tibetan masters statements such as "It is difficult at first to find without error what is to be meditated upon." In view of these statements—and motivated by my concern that some who strive in meditation practice, as it were from the bottom of their heart, should not end up in a pursuit that could result in wasting their life and leading others to such a course—I offer here the following queries in the form of an appeal.[147]

Presaging what he would later come to define as the "the principal elements of the path," Tsongkhapa's queries revolve around the themes of renunciation, bodhicitta, and the correct view of emptiness, as well as their place in overall meditative cultivation. In this chapter I shall focus on Tsongkhapa's queries pertaining to the view of emptiness and, more specifically, its related meditation practice, since it was his questions pertaining to the view and meditation on emptiness that posed the greatest challenges to the received understandings of some of the Tibetan traditions of his time.[148]

On Meditation and Its Object

The first series of questions Tsongkhapa raises about meditation concern the nature and function of two faculties that the Buddhist tradition regards as central to meditation practice—mindfulness (*smṛti*) and meta-awareness (*saṃprajanya*)—and the two principal hindrances: mental laxity (*laya*) and mental excitement (*auddhatya*). Tsongkhapa asks:

> Is mindfulness the simple fact of nondistraction, and is meta-awareness the monitoring of whether or not one is distracted? If so, what is meant by distraction here? Is it to be defined in terms of whether or not one has been distracted from a chosen object of focus? Or is it the case that what is meant by distraction here has nothing to do with the object of focus but is defined in terms of whether the state of mind itself is scattered or not; and, similarly, does the term *meta-awareness* refer to the awareness that monitors whether or not the mind is scattered?[149]

Tsongkhapa acknowledges the widespread opinion in Tibet that the highest form of meditation is a state characterized by three qualities—bliss, clarity, and nonconceptuality (sometimes translated as "nonthought" or "nondiscursivity")[150]—echoing the language one finds often in some Mahāmudrā texts. Leaving bliss aside, Tsongkhapa raises questions about what is meant, respectively, by clarity and nonconceptuality as attributes of a meditative state in this context. Once again, his question concerns whether one should understand these attributes in relation to the object of meditation or whether one is speaking purely about the subjective character of the meditative state itself. If the attributes of clarity and nonconceptuality are to be understood in terms of the mind's relation to its object, Tsongkhapa asks, how would one respond to the assertion that, given that it has an object, albeit an empty one, a meditative state of tranquility (*śamatha*) focused on emptiness characterized by clarity and nonconceptuality cannot be an objectless meditation?[151]

Fearing this consequence, Tsongkhapa suggests that some people might maintain that all these attributes of the meditative state—mindfulness, meta-awareness, clarity, and nonconceptuality—have nothing to do with the mind's relation to the object of meditation. They are purely subjective attributes of the experience of meditation. In this view, the mind, not engaging with anything, remains undistracted, unscattered, and nondiscursive, and as long as one's mind abides within such a state that is vivid and clear, then the five attributes (mindfulness, awareness, bliss, clarity, and nonconceptuality) would all be present. Such meditation, some suggest, constitutes the union of tranquility (*śamatha*) and insight (*vipaśyanā*) as well as the meditation on the ultimate truth, namely, emptiness. They hold that this is the heart of Mahāmudrā practice and that this also is the attainment of "the yoga of individual withdrawal" (*pratyāhara*), the first of the six yogas of the completion stage according to Kālacakra.[152]

To these possible responses, Tsongkhapa simply asks whether this way of defining the attributes of meditation accords with the understanding of the great Indian Buddhist masters, especially Nāgārjuna and Asaṅga, or of the tantras. In particular, he recommends reading Kamalaśila's three books on *The Stages of Meditation*, in which the Indian master refutes the notion of nonmentation (*amanasikāra*) as interpreted by the Chinese teacher Hoshang.[153] In other words, Tsongkhapa is warning that to define the attributes of the meditative state in terms of total absence of thought or mental engagement, independent of its relation to the object of meditation, could be tantamount to upholding the already discredited views of the Chinese monk Hoshang.[154]

Must Meditation Necessarily Be Nondiscursive?

Next, Tsongkhapa takes up the question of whether meditation should be necessarily nondiscursive or, as stated by authoritative Indian Buddhist masters, one needs to recognize two kinds of meditation: analytic or discursive meditation (*chegom*) and resting or placement meditation (*jokgom*).[155] If there is indeed a discursive form of meditation, how does one square this with the statement made by some Tibetans that in meditation one's mind should not engage in any activity? If mental engagement is to be shunned in meditation, how does one understand the statement found in Asaṅga's *Compendium of Abhidharma* to the effect that no genuine meditatively derived insight is possible without learning and reflection?[156] Cognizant of statements such as this, some maintain that the suggestion that mental engagement is a hindrance in meditation is meant to be read in the context of meditation on the ultimate truth, emptiness. "In that case," Tsongkhapa asks, "is it not essential to employ discriminative wisdom when meditating on emptiness?" If not, he suggests, "such emptiness meditation would be contrary to the cultivation of insight on emptiness according to master Nāgārjuna and must be shunned."[157]

Tsongkhapa's teacher Rendawa too appeared to have been quite concerned about the dismissal of discursive meditation by some Tibetan meditators. Referring to some of "today's proponents of Mahāmudrā," Rendawa speaks of how "they view the meditative practice of ultimate truth based on discursive analysis to be a flaw and regard meditating simply without any thought through the cessation of all mental engagement to be flawless meditation. However, such an approach has been stated by the *King of Meditations Sūtra* as being outside the Buddhist doctrine."[158] Rendawa then goes on to cite two verses from the sūtra that explicitly state that meditation (*dhyana*) alone does not lead to liberation, and that it is only with the help of discursive analysis that one gains insight into no-self and opens the door to liberation.[159] "In brief," Rendawa concludes, "those who stop their thought and mental activity and, keeping their eyes open in the dark, meditate with their mind in a state of wonderment, as well as those who do not take anything as a focus of their mind but seize upon whatever thoughts happen to arise in the mind, are, in fact, unmistakably upholding the position of the Chinese monk Hoshang."[160]

Later, in a long letter to Tsongkhapa, Rendawa would speak about how "today's instruction holders do not appear to have meditative practice dedicated to cultivating insight as opposed to tranquility. Because of this, many appear to focus only on tranquility attained through the stopping of thoughts and highly regard the experience of stillness attained from such meditation."[161] Rendawa then goes on to ask, "If, without the wisdom analyzing the ultimate nature of reality, nonconceptuality alone could lead to liberation, why wouldn't non-Buddhists attain liberation? Why then would the Chinese monk Hoshang be wrong?"[162]

To return to Tsongkhapa's *Queries*, the letter then turns to the topic of the second kind of meditation, the nondiscursive resting meditation (*jokgom*), and asks, "When one is engaged in this type of meditation, is the mind placed or resting on the single chosen object or not? If this is not how resting meditation is defined, how is it that this form of meditation is called resting or placement meditation?" If, on the other hand, it is maintained that resting does not mean placing the mind on a chosen object but simply resting the mind without any engagement, he then asks, "Where is this state of wonderment or astonishment (*hedewa*), with nothing at all as content, described as resting meditation?" One might claim that it comes from the oral tradition, so there is no need to ground it in any authoritative sūtra or tantric source. Hence, when engaged in this kind of meditation, one might maintain that there is no need for learning; in fact, one might contend that engaging in this practice alone is sufficient. "Of course," Tsongkhapa concedes, "if this kind of practice does indeed lead to the attainment of buddhahood, this is absolutely fine." But he, for one, does not see how this kind of meditative practice differs from that of the discredited Chinese master Hoshang.[163]

It is not sufficient, Tsongkhapa argues, to say that one's meditation practice is different from Hoshang's because, unlike the Chinese master, one does not reject the importance of virtuous deeds like generosity. Now one might assert that their meditation is not a form of total nonmentation, for they take Mahāmudrā to be the focus of their attention. To this, Tsongkhapa responds simply by asking them if what they propose as meditation accords with the view and meditation described by the master Nāgārjuna.

On the View of Emptiness

In the next section, Tsongkhapa turns more specifically to the topic of the view of emptiness. He begins by asking how we understand Nāgārjuna's Middle Way view, which is characterized as being free from all extremes. He asks how one ensures that their understanding of this Middle Way view—not tending to "is," "is not," "both is and is not," and "neither is nor is not"—does not collapse into a quietism akin to the notorious nonmentation of the Chinese master Hoshang? Tsongkhapa then asks, "What exactly is this emptiness the meditation on which is described as unexcelled meditation?" Here, too, Tsongkhapa warns against adopting an understanding of emptiness that is nothing but a form of mystical obscurantism, subscribing to some sort of indeterminate, ineffable truth.

Next, Tsongkhapa takes up the question of what in the teaching of emptiness is meant by the assertion that nothing possesses real existence. Presaging his later, mature view that emphasizes the critical importance of identifying *the object that is to be negated* in the context of emptiness, Tsongkhapa speaks of the need to have a sense of what that hypothetical "real existence" should look like, if it were to exist. Only then, Tsongkhapa suggests, can one negate it in relation to one's identity and existence. Tsongkhapa suggests that a distinction must be drawn between, on the one hand, not grasping at real existence, which is a form of disengagement, and, on the other, a more active process of negating or dismantling such real existence.[164]

Queries about the "Guide to the Nature of Mind" Meditations

Tsongkhapa next considers the form of meditation instruction known as the guide to the nature of mind (*semtri*).[165] He questions the position, held by some, that when the mind is examined in terms of whether it has color, shape, and so on, and it is thus found to be devoid of these properties, then this constitutes finding the mind's true nature. Tsongkhapa then turns to one specific form of nature-of-mind instruction. In this instruction, it is said that if one is able to simply look, in the present moment, at the mind itself—"the mind's own face," as it were—then immediately after, in the next instant, one will be able to recognize the mind's empty nature. Thus, whatever thought arises, it is crucial simply to observe that momentary mental event and not lose one's mindfulness—for if one can sustain this kind of mindfulness, then for as long as it lasts, whatever thoughts arise during that period will dissolve into the mind, just as bubbles arise and dissolve into the same water. In brief, some advocates of this type of nature-of-mind meditation maintain that although arising thoughts are conceptual in the first instant, when sustained with mindfulness, these conceptual thoughts will arise as *dharmakāya* (ultimate truth of buddhahood) in the second instant. For this reason, whether thoughts are good or bad, there is no need to cease them. There is no need to seek dharmakāya and wisdom elsewhere; all conceptual thoughts that arise are transformed into dharmakāya. In this way, and through this meditation practice, they maintain, one will be able to see the face of dharmakāya. Furthermore, it is held, this is a practice to be undertaken whether in formal meditation sessions or during intervals. It is also the practice that should be applied at the point of death and during the intermediate state. So, it is said, there is no practice more profound than this; it is a practice that equalizes the tastes of all conceptual thoughts into the single taste of dharmakāya. "So some maintain," Tsongkhapa writes.[166]

In response, he asks, "Is this practice of looking at the mind's nature the same as the one that involves applying discriminative wisdom, as taught by Nāgārjuna? Or is it a different approach that involves simply leaving the mind as it is and resting in it?" If it is the latter, Tsongkhapa contends, such an approach would not even lead to the realization of emptiness, let alone the realization of dharmakāya. Tsongkhapa then observes that the awareness of the mind's absence in the moment immediately after its arising is, in fact, more an awareness of its impermanence than of its emptiness.[167] Furthermore, he questions the language of equating emptiness and dharmakāya, since in the great Indian sources a clear distinction is made between dharmakāya and emptiness (*śūnyatā*).

The final point he raises about this particular form of introducing the nature of mind involves reinforcing the importance of distinguishing between two levels or categories of analysis and discourse:

the relative or conventional level and the ultimate. He underscores the important point that, other than analysis or discourse pertaining to the ultimate nature of things—that is, emptiness—all other forms of analysis and discourse fall within the domain of conventional truth. This means that the realization of emptiness—let alone the attainment of dharmakāya—cannot be affected through perspectives that remain within the relative or conventional domain. In brief, Tsongkhapa asks, "How would one respond if I were to say that any view that is contrary to Nāgārjuna is bound to be erroneous, even if one were to speak about it a hundred times?"[168]

Tsongkhapa is not, in fact, questioning the legitimacy of these "introduction to the nature of mind" meditations. His point is that the states these meditation practices lead to—nondiscursive bare awareness with no specific attentional focus—do not represent the genuine meditative experience of emptiness, the ultimate nature of reality, as understood in Nāgārjuna's tradition.

A Plethora of Standpoints

Before concluding his *Queries*, Tsongkhapa identifies some twelve views current in Tibet, grouping these into six sets of two opposite or contrasting standpoints. He writes:

> In general there seem to be a variety of ways in which the view arises in people. (1) There is one camp that asserts that, regardless of their good or bad moral character, all forms of conceptualization must be stopped. (2) Some maintain that all conceptual thoughts, both good and bad, should not be stopped because the greater the proliferation of conceptual thoughts, the greater the enhancement of experience and realizations—just as, for example, the greater the amount of fuel the bigger the blaze of the fire.[169] These two positions

directly oppose each other. (3) Again some, citing the line "conceptualization is the great ignorance,"[170] assert that conceptuality is ignorance, while (4) others maintain that conceptuality is the dharmakāya. These two are directly contradictory. (5) Some say that when this very mind abides naturally, without any activity, it is buddhahood, or nirvāṇa, and the instant it engages in activity, this is the ordinary state, or saṃsāra.[171] (6) In contrast, others say that when conceptualization occurs, regardless of how long this occurs, looking at it nakedly leads to the spontaneous arising of dharmakāya. These two are contradictory. (7) There is one set of opinions that maintain that dharmakāya is the perception of an absence-like state that comes from being in a dark room, or through yogic postures, or stopping of thoughts. It is the "emptiness endowed with all attributes." Thus, even ordinary beings can, through direct pointing out, perceive dharmakāya. (8) In contrast, some say that such an experience does not constitute seeing dharmakāya in its completeness, but seeing only a tip or a part of dharmakāya. These two contradict each other. (9) Some say that, in fact, this does not constitute seeing dharmakāya at all, either fully or in part; it is merely the seeing of emptiness. Further, with respect to emptiness, they say that this is not the inferior intrinsic emptiness (*rangtong*) asserted by Candrakīrti and Haribhadra, but rather it is the extrinsic emptiness (*shentong*) accepted by the Great Middle Way (*uma chenpo*) master Asaṅga. (10) Some, while accepting the bulk of this position, assert that this is the seeing not of extrinsic emptiness but of intrinsic emptiness. These two views contradict each other. (11) Some assert that what is seen is not actual emptiness but merely the form or reflection of emptiness; it is not dharmakāya itself but its signs, just as, for example, one sees smoke as a

> sign of fire's presence.[172] (12) Others assert that the actual view of Mahāmudrā is in fact that of intrinsic emptiness and is equivalent to the *withdrawal yoga* stage within the six yogas of the completion stage of Kālacakra. However, one must then move on to the more advanced view of extrinsic emptiness, which is the view of the *concentration yoga* stage from among the six yogas. Therefore, the view of emptiness of the six yogas of the Kālacakra completion stage is superior to that of Mahāmudrā.[173]

Tsongkhapa then briefly notes the divergence of opinions that seem to exist among his Tibetan peers on the understanding of important Vajrayāna practices, such as the remaining stages of the six yogas of Kālacakra, the six yogas of Nāropa, and the six yogas of Niguma, and in particular the method of tummo practice. Strictly speaking, Tsongkhapa does not offer any specific refutations of these divergent views. Rather, he makes a general appeal to the proponents of these views to examine if what they propound is in accord with the authoritative sūtras and the tantras. For the view of emptiness, in particular, Tsongkhapa underlines the critical importance of relating one's views to the writings of Nāgārjuna and his authoritative commentators.

Concluding Remarks

Before concluding his *Queries*, Tsongkhapa identifies two principal causes that lead to the dilution of what are in fact authentic instructions. One is that some who are dedicated to a single-pointed pursuit of meditative practice view study and critical reflection as obstacles. In contrast, others, keen to engage in study and critical reflection, have no interest in relating their knowledge to their own mind through meditation, instead remaining immersed in the pursuit of an outwardly focused scholarship motivated by empty fame. The need to avoid these two extremes, Tsongkhapa says, is the key reason that it is necessary to practice the Buddha's doctrine through the combination of learning, critical reflection, and meditative cultivation.[174]

Tsongkhapa acknowledges that his *Queries* might attract criticism from some but states that the benefits far outweigh the drawbacks entailed by possibly offending a few. He lists three main benefits of writing the piece: (1) The work could delight those who engage in Dharma practice through the perfect union of study, critical reflection, and meditative practice; (2) it could open the eyes of some who otherwise would not have thought about these important questions; and (3) it could encourage beginners keen to engage in meditation not to do so blindly but to seek the guidance of learned teachers to cultivate their understanding of Dharma.[175] The *Queries* ends with the following colophon:

> This work has been composed by a meditator (*samtenpa*), one who, having read the sūtras and the tantras extensively, is immersed in single-pointed contemplation of their meaning, one who is known to be sustained by Guru Mañjuśrī. May these few queries offered from the mountain of a special meditation retreat, a place of solitude, be of great benefit to the Buddha's doctrine.[176]

CHAPTER 5

The Mystery of Guru Mañjuśrī

ONE OF THE MOST intriguing aspects of Tsongkhapa's life and, for some, perhaps the most controversial was the enduring "presence" of a mysterious teacher whom he referred to as Guru Mañjuśrī (*Jamyang Lama*). All traditional sources, including the earliest biographical works composed by his contemporaries, assume this to be an experience of Tsongkhapa's mystical life wherein he was somehow able to communicate with Mañjuśrī, the buddha of wisdom.

In Tibetan Buddhism, the status of Mañjuśrī—as well as similar figures such as Avalokiteśvara (the buddha of compassion), Tārā (the buddha of enlightened action), and Vajrapāṇi (the buddha of enlightened energy)—is multidimensional. In the Mahāyāna sūtras (sacred to all Tibetan traditions) such as the *Lotus Sūtra* and *Vimalakīrti Sūtra*, Mañjuśrī is recognized as an advanced bodhisattva. In contemporary Western works on Buddhism, such a figure is sometimes referred to as a "celestial bodhisattva," an almost primordial being who predates the Buddha and yet is his disciple.

When viewed from the perspective of general Mahāyāna Buddhism, Mañjuśrī would be considered a bodhisattva—someone on the path toward becoming a buddha and whose life embodies the powerful ideal of the union of wisdom and compassion. When the context shifts to Vajrayāna or Tantra, however, Mañjuśrī would be recognized as a fully enlightened buddha. Indeed, at the deepest level, Mañjuśrī then is no longer an individual being; rather, he is the embodiment of the wisdom of all the buddhas—a kind of archetype, an aspect of the enlightened mind of all the buddhas. When we speak of Mañjuśrī as Tsongkhapa's guru, we refer to this buddha of wisdom appearing in the form of a meditation deity.

In attempting to understand Tsongkhapa's relationship with Guru Mañjuśrī, we are confronted with a dimension of reality that challenges the limits of what one might call our contemporary sensibility, wherein our notion of truth is shaped by scientific concern for verifiable facts. My aim is not to challenge this demand or to "prove" this aspect of Tsongkhapa's life to be factually true, which clearly would be impossible. My interest is to tell the story as it has been handed down and leave it up to the reader to decide how to relate to it.[177]

But before we plunge into the story itself, it might be worth knowing that the understanding that Tsongkhapa had a unique relationship with Mañjuśrī appeared to be widely acknowledged during his lifetime. We read, for example, in the biography of Tsongkhapa's own teacher Rendawa, "These days, all the learned monks in central Tibet speak of Lobsang Drakpa having experienced the vision of Mañjuśrī. Wherever he travels, he brings with him four *dzo* [an animal that is a cross between a yak and a cow] loads of texts, which he reads both day and night."[178] It is perhaps due to this widespread belief that in his official "conventional" biography of Tsongkhapa, Khedrup includes the story of how Tsongkhapa formed this unique relationship with Mañjuśrī, with Umapa as the medium—a matter typically more appropriate for a "secret" biography.

We have textual evidence in the form of letters that Tsongkhapa's own teacher, Rendawa, believed in Tsongkhapa's unique access to the deity to such a degree that he would request Tsongkhapa to consult Mañjuśrī on his behalf and ask him for specific instruction.[179] Tsongkhapa himself on several occasions speaks explicitly of his communication with Mañjuśrī. In a letter to Umapa, he relates how the instructions he had received from the deity with Umapa's help had been profoundly beneficial. In that same letter, Tsongkhapa speaks about how one of his own students, Tokden Jampel Gyatso, was also experiencing visions of the deity.[180] Finally, as we shall see later, Tsongkhapa's writings contain a set of important notes he made from instructions he had received from Mañjuśrī, which he later sent to Rendawa in the form of a scroll.

In brief, the evidence is compelling that the key figures here—Tsongkhapa himself, Rendawa, Umapa, and later Tokden Jampel Gyatso—as well as many of their contemporaries fully believed in Tsongkhapa's special communication with Mañjuśrī. And so, although I do not attempt to establish whether Tsongkhapa's contact with Mañjuśrī was "real" in any scientific or objective sense, there is no denying that it was experientially and socially real for him, for his closest teachers and students, and for the broader milieu in which he lived and practiced the Buddhist path.

The Story of Umapa

We saw in chapter 1 that Tsongkhapa's childhood teacher Chöjé had made the invocation of Mañjuśrī a special focus for his protégé, with the young boy reciting Mañjuśrī's mantra around a hundred million times in a meditation hut at Jakhyung Monastery. Throughout the years of his arduous study in Ü-Tsang Province, moving from one monastery to the next, Tsongkhapa never slackened in his daily Mañjuśrī practice. In the spring of 1390 (the Iron Monkey year), when he was thirty-three, Tsongkhapa experienced a great breakthrough in his relationship with Mañjuśrī. That spring, as noted in chapter 3, Tsongkhapa met with the mystic Lama Umapa, renowned for having constant visitations from Mañjuśrī. For the next two years, according to the sources, Tsongkhapa and Umapa would meet regularly, have numerous consultations, and receive teachings from each other.

Who was this mystic called Lama Umapa, whose name literally means "Middle Way Lama"? Umapa, whose personal name was Tsöndru Sengé, was born in the eastern Tibetan province of Kham.[181] Because of his deep fondness for the Middle Way view of emptiness, he acquired the nickname Umapa, "Mādhyamika" in Sanskrit, or "the Middle Way man." In his youth, as he was herding animals one day, a thunderous noise, which sounded like the mantra ARAPACANA DHĪH, struck from nowhere, causing him to faint. When he regained consciousness he was face to face with a form that resembled Mañjuśrī, with a black-colored body. Later, the boy received initiations of Mañjuśrī and undertook his sādhana practice, which led to his experiencing constant visions of the deity. He did not, however, take these too seriously but went to central Tibet to study, staying first at Sangphu Monastery. There, having studied Maitreya's *Ornament of Realizations*, he was planning to sit for formal debates on the text. But Mañjuśrī dissuaded him from continuing his studies and urged him instead to dispose of all his material possessions and make an offering to the monastic assembly. He was advised to devote himself to meditative practice as a hermit.

Deciding to follow this advice, Umapa traveled to the Kongpo area, where he received Mahāmudrā instructions according to the Karma Kagyü lineage. He practiced these assiduously, and this further enhanced his visions of the deity. Upon his return to central Tibet, at Samyé Monastery he received from Tokden Tsokarwa the instructions on the six yogas of the completion stage of Kālacakra. Umapa then met with one Shöngyalwa, who demonstrated some part of the code language associated with the four empowerment rites of the Sakya lamdré cycle of instructions, to which Umapa, serving as the medium for Mañjuśrī, responded without error. This latter experience gave him some assurance that the visions he was experiencing might be authentic.

Some time later, Umapa went to Tsang Province, where he met Barawa Gyaltsen Palsang (1310–91), an important Kagyü master, and received from him further instructions on Mahāmudrā. Barawa, a famed renunciant, was an inspiration to Umapa. At the urging of Mañjuśrī, Umapa then went to Sakya Monastery and received teachings from Rendawa, especially on the Middle Way philosophy and vinaya. Again at the urging of Mañjuśrī, he met Tsongkhapa at Rong Chölung. As noted earlier, during this first meeting with Tsongkhapa, Umapa received Sarasvatī's blessing and also an explanation of the entire autocommentary of Candrakīrti's *Entering the Middle Way*.

Umapa Becomes the Medium

When Tsongkhapa met with Lama Umapa for the second time, both came prepared to spend an extended period together. This was in the Iron Monkey year (1392), when Tsongkhapa was thirty-four. The two men met up at Gadong Monastery, founded in the eleventh century by the Kadam master Zingpo Sherap and located in Lower Tölung, close to Lhasa.[182] After their arrival at Gadong, Tsongkhapa and Umapa went to Lhasa to pray in the presence of the sacred Buddha image in the Jokhang Temple. They then went into an intensive retreat at Gadong Monastery, during which the masters prayed fervently to Mañjuśrī and undertook his invocation practice with great intensity. Each master had his own room, but they took their breakfast and lunch together; as observant Buddhist monks, neither of them ate supper. These shared meals proved to be critically significant, for it was during these occasions that Mañjuśrī would sometimes spontaneously come to life for Tsongkhapa, with Umapa as the medium.[183] For Tsongkhapa this was a dream come true, a chance finally to attain some clarity on critical questions with which he had been struggling. As for questions, he had no shortage of them!

Tsongkhapa had studied and read widely. He had been blessed with a great teacher in Rendawa, and he had also undertaken a series of intensive meditative retreats. Yet questions persisted, particularly on two important topics. One had to do with arriving at a final understanding of Nāgārjuna's philosophy of emptiness and fully appreciating its profound implications; the other concerned the five stages of the completion stage of the Guhyasamāja tantra, especially the theory and practice of the illusory body (*māyādeha*), which was immensely challenging and could have profound consequences if realized. Tsongkhapa was keen to ensure that his understanding of these important topics did not remain confined to the theoretical level or to an understanding of merely the words. He wanted to make them real in personal experience. To this end he was willing to commit everything to find a teacher, wherever he might be—Tibet or even India or Nepal—who could reveal the entirety of the intention of Nāgārjuna and his heirs, both on the philosophy of emptiness and on the advanced tantric practices.

Years later, Tsongkhapa would tell Khedrup, who would become his official biographer, that, of course, like other great Tibetan minds of the time, he had the ability to grasp the essential points of any important Indian Buddhist text he would read. He also had the skill to teach these texts in a way that led to clear comprehension on the part of his students. "But," Tsongkhapa continued, "I never remained content with these, for I realized quite early that sometimes you might think you had grasped something well, but when you subject that understanding to careful scrutiny, then what initially seemed like a solid understanding tends to collapse." As a result, Tsongkhapa would urge Khedrup, too, to never be hasty in arriving at conclusions on any important point of doctrine.[184]

Now seizing the opportunity, Tsongkhapa asked Mañjuśrī questions about the following themes: the view of emptiness, differences between Sūtra and Tantra, key points of the path of the Highest Yoga tantra, the sequence of the five stages of the completion stage of tantra and the significance of their number being five, and so on. Instead of requesting a special oral instruction, Tsongkhapa chose to ask Mañjuśrī a series of questions. It appears that Tsongkhapa's own philosophical inclination concerning the view of emptiness at the time was somewhat similar to the view held by many of his Tibetan contemporaries. On this view, insofar as one's own position is concerned, no standpoint is to be held, and statements and standpoints can only be articulated from the point of view of one's opponents—representing a kind of agnosticism or quietism with no commitment to any proposition. Tsongkhapa therefore asked Mañjuśrī whether the view of emptiness he espoused at the time was that of the Prāsaṅgika Madhyamaka (of Candrakīrti) or that of the Svātantrika Madhyamaka (of Bhāviveka). To his surprise, Mañjuśrī replied, "It is neither."[185] Speaking of the need for a fine balance in one's understanding of the two truths, the ultimate truth and the conventional truth, the deity advised, "It is inappropriate to be partial either to emptiness or to appearance. In particular, you need to take the appearance aspect seriously."[186]

Mañjuśrī then gave Tsongkhapa a series of teachings on the distinction between the views of Prāsaṅgika Madhyamaka and the Svātantrika; the differences between innate versus intellectually acquired forms of grasping at self-existence; the levels of subtlety involved in understanding what is being negated in the context of emptiness; the criteria of finding the correct view of emptiness; and how the reality of conventional truths needs to be understood according to Prāsaṅgika Madhyamaka. Mañjuśrī also gave instructions based on questions Tsongkhapa asked on important topics of Highest Yoga tantra. As Mañjuśrī gave these teachings, at one point Tsongkhapa remarked, "I do not comprehend what you are saying," to which the deity responded,

> Do not forget what I have taught you, and commit these to notes. You should (1) continue to supplicate the gurus and meditation deities and engage in sādhana practice; (2) strive in the dual practice of accumulating merit and purifying negative karma; and (3) reflect deeply on the meaning of the great treatises. Engage in your practice by combining these three things. Do not be easily satisfied but continue with your inquiry with sustained critical reflection. A time will come when what I have offered you here will act as the seed giving rise to a thorough understanding.[187]

As he had a keen desire to deepen his understanding of emptiness and the Highest Yoga tantra connected with Nāgārjuna and his immediate disciples,[188] Tsongkhapa then asked Mañjuśrī who in Tibet he should approach. Mañjuśrī said that there was no one better than Rendawa. "However," the deity continued,

> even he would not be able to engender full understanding in you. The best would be for Umapa to be our medium so that I can continue to guide you. However, it seems that Umapa has to leave for eastern Tibet. So now you should stop teaching, seek solitude as a hermit, and engage in meditative practice combining the three things I have mentioned, striving in meditative visualizations, and so on. Before long, the meaning of these teachings will dawn upon you.[189]

Tsongkhapa then raised the problem about the diversity of understandings found even in the writings of authoritative Indian

Buddhist masters. With his own strong affinity for the work of Candrakīrti in mind, he asked Mañjuśrī, "Can I rely on Candrakīrti and consider him flawless when it comes to interpreting the thought of Nāgārjuna?" Mañjuśrī replied, "Indeed. There is not an iota of error in Candrakīrti's interpretation of Nāgārjuna. By all means, you can rely on his writings."[190]

Aware of Mañjuśrī's advice that Tsongkhapa drop everything and go into solitary retreat, and knowing what this could mean, Umapa asked the deity if it wouldn't be more beneficial to the Buddha's doctrine at present for Tsongkhapa to continue his teaching career. "Furthermore," he said, "if Tsongkhapa interrupts his teaching career and seeks the life of a hermit, I will be criticized for being responsible for this. Can Tsongkhapa, for the time being, continue with his teaching instead?" Mañjuśrī replied, "I know what would benefit the Buddha's doctrine and sentient beings, not you. As for people's criticism, just practice forbearance. In fact," the deity continued, "if Tsongkhapa does not go into solitude, he will not have a long life. Furthermore, even though, without this intensive retreat, his teaching will benefit others, it will have only a limited impact. So it is best that he go to a place of solitude."[191] Thus, on this strict advice from Mañjuśrī, Tsongkhapa made the decision to take up the life of a meditator and seek a place of solitude.

According to two early sources, it was also during this stay at Gadong Monastery that Mañjuśrī, with Umapa as the medium, revealed some specific details about Tsongkhapa's previous lives. These included the story of how, as a young Brahmin boy, he had generated the altruistic awakening mind in the presence of the Buddha, and how by offering a crystal rosary the young boy had made aspirations that planted the seed to later attain the view of emptiness.[192] As we shall see in chapter 15, this story would become part of a larger narrative mythology surrounding Tsongkhapa.

Initially, during his stay at Gadong Monastery, Tsongkhapa focused, in his own personal practice, mainly on cultivating tranquility (śamatha), based on a special instruction from Umapa. One day, Tsongkhapa felt that it might in fact be more beneficial to concentrate on Mañjuśrī practice, so he shifted the focus of his practice. He made fervent supplications to Mañjuśrī, visualized the deity, and recited his mantra. A few days later, Tsongkhapa had his first direct vision of the deity. Mañjuśrī sat resplendent at the center of a ring of light emitting rainbow-colored light rays. The deity was seated cross-legged, his body an orange hue. Before Tsongkhapa had the chance to share this exciting news with Umapa, the mystic remarked, "It seems you too have the vision of the deity's form."[193] It was also during this sojourn at Gadong Monastery that Tsongkhapa received from Mañjuśrī, through the medium of Umapa, a series of important oral transmissions, which later came to be known as the Mañjuśrī cycle of teachings.[194] Tsongkhapa's student Tokden Jampel Gyatso, who would himself later experience visions of Mañjuśrī, was present at some of these oral teachings.[195] In fact, according to one source, Mañjuśrī instructed Tokden to be the first one to try out the oral instructions he had just given.[196] Also while at Gadong Monastery, Tsongkhapa composed a hymn to Mañjuśrī at the request of one Drakpa Wangchuk.[197]

Mañjuśrī's Guide to the View Instruction

One important legacy of Umapa's early encounters with Tsongkhapa was the transmission of a brief oral instruction Umapa passed on from Mañjuśrī known as "Vajra Lines on the View of the Equality of Saṃsāra and Nirvāṇa." The following is the full text of this oral instruction:

Through various examples of dependent origination
I reveal here the truth of ultimate nature just as it is.
Preceded by taking refuge, gather the accumulations and purify negative karma.
Contemplate dependent origination, forward and in reverse.
Through profound instructions touching upon
The nature of the Buddha's body, speech, and mind,
O fortunate ones who seek enlightenment,
Abide in equipoise in concentrative states.
This host of aggregates—body, speech, and mind—
None of these exists as the self,
Nor is there a self apart from these.
O fortunate ones who seek enlightenment,
Know the truth of this no-self.
Aggregates, elements, and sense bases,
Appearance and emptiness, saṃsāra and nirvāṇa, and so on,
Nothing in this dependent world possesses intrinsic reality.
Devoid of arising, cessation, or persistence,
They transcend words like *exists*, *doesn't exist*, *is*, and *is not*.
The one who knows this profound undifferentiated peace,
Which is free of elaborations, will attain nirvāṇa.[198]

In addition to writing these instructions in verse, Tsongkhapa compiled a prose commentary on them. He divides the instruction into three main parts: the opening, followed by preliminary practice (lines 1–3); the main instruction (4–18); and a concluding affirmation (19–20). The main instruction, in turn, consists of two parts: A "common" practice of contemplating the twelve links of dependent origination, both in their forward order and reverse order (line 4), is aimed at generating a genuine desire to attain freedom from saṃsāric existence. The uncommon part of the main instruction is composed of cultivating tranquility (lines 5–8) and insight (9–18). Here, tranquility is cultivated by taking the enlightened body, speech (mantra), and mind (symbolized by the visual image of the syllable HŪṂ) as the focus of attention. Cultivation of insight consists of contemplating emptiness in relation to one's own self (9–13) and the factors of one's existence, such as the physical and mental constituents that make up our existence (14–18). The last two lines (19–20) conclude the instruction by stating that someone who understands emptiness attains the true peace of nirvāṇa.[199]

Final Meeting with Umapa

In that same fall of 1392, with Umapa having decided to return to his native Kham, Tsongkhapa traveled with the mystic up to Lhasa to see him off. When they reached the holy city, aware that they might not see each other again, they decided to pray to Mañjuśrī together, requesting a special teaching containing essential points of practice.

So, on a fine day, they went to the rooftop of the Jokhang Temple and found a shaded place under the golden roof on the south side. They arranged an altar there and laid out various offerings. Both made fervent supplications to Mañjuśrī. Then, with Umapa as the medium, Tsongkhapa requested an instruction distilling the essential elements of Dharma practice. Mañjuśrī then gave several verses of instruction, which Tsongkhapa wrote down on the spot.[200] On the same day, in return, Tsongkhapa conducted the empowerment of Guhyasamāja for the benefit of Umapa. With the teachings over and their stay in Lhasa at an end, Tsongkhapa bade his companion farewell; Umapa began his long journey back to eastern Tibet, and Tsongkhapa returned to Kyormolung Monastery, where he imparted various teachings to the resident monks.

Though Tsongkhapa and Umapa corresponded, the two would never meet again. Tsongkhapa later composed a lengthy hymn to Mañjuśrī entitled *Ocean of Clouds of Praises*, which contains the following lines:

> Even if I were to search across all the realms,
> I would find no refuge better than you.
> So, like a sun-scorched elephant that thinks only of a
> watering hole,
> My mind naturally turns toward you alone.
> When I come to speak of your enlightened attributes,
> I become like the impoverished beggar
> Who has just seen a benefactor known for his generosity,
> Who he knows will help fulfill his wish.[201]

CHAPTER 6

Intensive Retreats in the Wölkha Valley

WITH MAÑJUŚRĪ'S exhortation to seek solitude fresh in his mind, Tsongkhapa started making preparations for a long retreat. In early November 1392 (the Water Monkey year), at the age of thirty-five, he left Kyormolung Monastery accompanied by eight students, each of whom had been carefully selected for this long period of intensive meditative practice. They were four disciples from central Tibet (Rinpoché Jamkarwa, Jangsengwa, Neten Sangkyongwa, and Neten Rinchen Gyaltsen) and four from his native Amdo (Tokden Jampel Gyatso, Geshé Sherap Drak, Geshé Jampel Tashi, and Geshé Palkyong). All eight had been recommended by Mañjuśrī through the mystic Umapa before the latter returned to eastern Tibet.[202]

Accompanied by these eight disciples, who later came to be referred to as the eight attendants of perfect karma (*'khor dakpa namgyé*), Tsongkhapa left for the beautiful Wölkha (also spelled Wöka) Valley region, which lies to the east of the Yarlung Tsangpo River. From Kyormolung, the group walked the riverbank and took a boat in the direction of the Dakpo area; they got off near Khartak la, walking the rest of the way to Wölkha.[203] As one moves farther away from the river, the valley opens to reveal a wide space with the sacred Odé Gungyal Mountain in the background. Named after the mountain god Odé Gungyal, who is thought to be the father of another mountain god, Nyenchen Thangla, Odé Gungyal is a towering mountain that is part of a range demarcating the boundary between central Tibet and the Jangthang, Tibet's barren northern plains.

On the Slopes of Odé Gungyal Mountain

Namkha Sangpo, the governor of Neu district, adjacent to the Wölkha Valley, was already a devotee of Tsongkhapa, so he initially provided the necessary provisions to the master and his eight disciples. The governor also offered to help support the small group of meditators during their stay in the region. At first, the group chose as their base the small Wölkha Samten Ling Retreat, a cave hermitage once used by Gampopa. This small hermitage, affiliated with Densa Thil Monastery, is said to have been built by the "seven meditators."[204] During a later sojourn at Samten Ling, Tsongkhapa would also spend time meditating at Garphuk, another hermitage where Gampopa had meditated and which later would be recognized as an important site of a treasure text attributed to Padmasambhava.

Sometime in 1393, Namkha Sangpo had a new hermitage built for Tsongkhapa and his students. Named Wölkha Chölung, this retreat site is situated on the western slopes of Odé Gungyal Mountain and commands an impressive panoramic view of the vast Wölkha Valley. So taken was Tsongkhapa by the beauty of the site and the vast expanse below that he would describe one of his Wölkha retreats as a perfect place of solitude, "just as the Buddha on numerous occasions exhorted his followers to seek."

> Gloriously snow-capped, with healing medicinal herbs growing in the lower slopes, this site is adorned with the rich foliage of thick-leafed flowering trees, as well as bushes of various kinds. As for the row of snow-capped summits, they seem like a latticed white curtain hanging down from the

> top, with mists hovering below, as if these snowy peaks were wearing a sash around them like a belt. The numerous hills and valleys of the mountain look as if they were deliberately crafted. With the humming sounds of hovering bees, this is the ideal place for a monk yogi who is dedicated to meditative practice.[205]

Despite his fondness for Wölkha Chölung Hermitage, Tsongkhapa was always reluctant to stay too long in one place. In a short letter of advice to one Yönten Gyatso, written during his initial retreat in the Wölkha Valley, Tsongkhapa describes himself as "a vagabond wandering around in indeterminate places."[206]

Tsongkhapa had insisted that during this long retreat, everyone in the small group would initially follow the tradition of the great Kadam masters, starting with building a solid foundation of training their minds in the practices of the common path. Thus, at the start, the focus for everyone, Tsongkhapa included, would be the "foundational practices of the common path," namely nontantric practices like the *ngöndro* (preliminary) practices of going for refuge to the three jewels; repeated prostrations; contemplation of impermanence; cultivation of mindfulness, awareness, and regulation of emotions; generation of bodhicitta; and deepening one's view and experience of no-self and emptiness. Everyone was discouraged from bringing any advanced tantric texts or iconography, with the exception of Tokden Jampel Gyatso, who, as a longtime mystic, brought a small image of Mañjuśrī. Tokden was also allowed to bring a text on lamdré—a cycle of instructions connected with Hevajra tantra—the transmission of which he had just recently received.[207]

So the retreatants, each in his own cell, first undertook the preliminary practices dedicated to gathering merit and purifying negative karma. Observing a strict regimen of four sessions a day, they performed the seven-limb worship: (1) prostrations; (2) making offerings to the buddhas; (3) purifying negative karma; (4) rejoicing in the good deeds; (5) supplicating the buddhas to turn the wheel of Dharma; (6) appealing to the buddhas not to enter nirvāṇa; and (7) dedicating the merit of one's practice to the well-being of all sentient beings.[208] As is customary for purification practice, Tsongkhapa recited the invocation of the thirty-five confessional buddhas and performed hundreds of full-body prostrations on a daily basis. At the end of his period of preliminary practice, the stone floor on which Tsongkhapa performed these prostrations bore visible signs where his hands and head had touched. Similarly, a flat rock Tsongkhapa used during this retreat for the performance of the maṇḍala offering (symbolically offering the entire universe to the buddhas and bodhisattvas)—wiping the surface with the inside of one's right arm and pouring grains over it repeatedly—had been wiped so much that it came to resemble the surface of a mirror![209]

Each of the eight disciples took turns attending Tsongkhapa, serving him the water and simple meals of cold cereal they all were eating. After some time, when it became clear that this ascetic diet was taking its toll on the master's health, his students implored him to eat at least one hot meal a day. Tsongkhapa and one other retreatant, Palden Sangpo, did so, while the remaining seven still maintained their severe diet.

One day, when it was Tokden's turn to attend the master, Tsongkhapa had a special altar of offerings arranged and called in the other disciples. He then shared with his eight disciples some of the communications he had had with Mañjuśrī through Umapa. Hearing this and learning how, in fact, each of them had been recommended by Mañjuśrī himself to accompany Tsongkhapa on the retreat, all the disciples were deeply inspired. It turns out that, at Tsongkhapa's urging, Tokden had been undertaking the special Mañjuśrī meditation practice the deity himself had earlier given him and Tsongkhapa, through Umapa as the medium. As a result, Tokden had started experiencing visions of Mañjuśrī and receiving verbal communications from him. Tsongkhapa examined Tokden's visions by asking specific questions pertaining to various aspects of Dharma practice and thus determined his visions were authentic.[210] In a letter Tsongkhapa later wrote to Umapa, he spoke of this: "The cycle of Mañjuśrī teachings you gave me proved extremely beneficial. There have been several cases where a few within my circle had encounters with Mañjuśrī's body and speech. Among them there is one where all the pronouncements have proven to be definitive."[211]

Remembering Umapa's kindness, especially his singular role in opening the door to Mañjuśrī, Tsongkhapa composed the following prayer, which he called "A Prayer to the Lineage Gurus of the Immediate Transmission:"

Through wisdom you have cast away saṃsāric bondage;
Through compassion you have thrown off love for nirvāṇic peace;
Abiding beyond saṃsāra and nirvāṇa, you are the lord of both;
Buddha Vajradhara, I pray to you.
You are the wisdom body distilled into one,
The wisdom minds of all the countless buddhas,
Beyond the count of particles in the countless realms;
Savior Mañjuśrī, I pray to you.
Through the force of your noble aspirations,
Revered Mañjuśrī himself in actual form
Eliminates the whole network of your doubts;
Umapa Pawo Dorjé, I pray at your feet.

The root of all virtuous qualities,
Both worldly and transmundane, is the kind teacher.
Bless me so that even simple recollection of him
Effortlessly gives rise to admiration and respect.

May I live with few wants, contented, peaceful, and disciplined;
Seeking liberation from my heart, may I always speak the truth;
May I be with good friends who promote conscientiousness;
Bless me so that I see everyone as friends, with no biases.

Death is certain, but we cannot predict when it might strike;
Contemplating it, not just in words, I realize that there is no
time;
Bless me so that I feel repulsed from deep within
By wealth and honor, and know that they have no meaning.

Recognizing all beings as my kind mothers, and
Contemplating the sufferings of these desperate beings,
May I turn away from the desire to seek my welfare alone;
Bless me so that compassion arises in me without effort.

The single medicine to cure the illness of all extreme views
Is the profound truth of dependent origination beyond extremes.
Bless me so that I may comprehend this truth,
In exact accord with the intent of Nāgārjuna and his sons.

As exemplified by this present virtuous deed,
Whatever roots of virtue I and others may have amassed in all
three times,
May none of it turn into a cause, even for an instant,
In all my births, life after life,
For things contrary to the pursuit of enlightenment:
Seeking material gain through teaching dharma, becoming
famous,
Having followers, possessing wealth, or receiving honor,
All of which are contrary to the pursuit of enlightenment.
May these virtues become causes for enlightenment alone.

Through the blessings of the wondrous buddhas and
bodhisattvas,
Through the infallible truth of the laws of dependent
origination,
And through the power of the purity of my aspirations,
May the aims of my prayer be fulfilled without hindrance.[212]

Tsongkhapa describes this piece as a prayer to the lineage gurus of the immediate transmission lineage (*nyé gyu*) as opposed to the long transmission lineage (*ring gyu*). As such, the first three stanzas (lines 1–12) pay homage to Vajradhara (the Buddha in his form as the origin of Vajrayāna teachings), to the meditation deity Mañjuśrī, and finally to Umapa, the teacher who served as the medium between Tsongkhapa and the deity. This kind of immediate transmission lineage is typical of oral instructions that have their origin in pure visons. The next five stanzas present, in order, the contemplation of the kindness of one's spiritual teacher (lines 13–16), cultivating the appropriate attitudes for Dharma practice (17–20), true renunciation inspired by awareness of death (21–24), compassion for all beings (25–28), and comprehension of profound emptiness (29–32). The final three stanzas entail dedication of merit, with the final verse especially invoking the power of truth to help realize the author's aspirations. Over time, this final verse would come to be used as a stand-alone prayer or attached to the end of other liturgical texts.

Restoring the Maitreya Statue at Dzingchi

A few months into the retreat, Tsongkhapa had an unexpected vision of Maitreya, the future Buddha. It was a massive image of Maitreya, gold in color, attired in the garb of a celestial bodhisattva, with jewel ornaments and his right hand in the gesture of teaching while holding the stems of two flowers. He was seated on a jeweled throne. Then, at another time, Tsongkhapa had a different vision of Maitreya, this time in the form of a monk seated with his feet touching the ground and attired in saffron robes, holding his usual hand implement, a water jar atop a small tree branch. Tsongkhapa did not dwell on these visions, thinking that they might just be fleeting experiences. However, through Tokden, Mañjuśrī informed Tsongkhapa that these were signs indicative of certain events that would later have great significance for the Dharma.[213]

During these months of purification practice at Wölkha, Tsongkhapa made special efforts to read many of the sūtras connected with Mahāyāna teachings on universal compassion, bodhicitta, and the bodhisattva's altruistic deeds for the welfare of all sentient beings. He read an important set of Mahāyāna scriptures from the canonical collection known as the *Avatamsaka Sūtra* (*Flower Ornament Scripture*), of which Drolungpa, the author of the influential Tibetan work *Great Exposition of the Stages of the Doctrine* (*Tenrim Chenmo*) once remarked: "Had this *Avatamsaka Sūtra* not been translated into Tibetan, how would we Tibetans learn about the noble deeds of the bodhisattva at all?"[214] (Drolungpa's text would later play a crucial role in inspiring Tsongkhapa to compose his own synthesis of the Buddhist path.) Beginning with cultivating the bodhisattva's courageous altruistic intention, Tsongkhapa endeavored in the cultivation of the specific attitudes, attributes, and deeds of the bodhisattva. Years later, he would tell his students that at first these practices proved quite challenging; however, as time went by, he was able to arrive at a point where the perspectives, attitudes, and intentions of a bodhisattva would come effortlessly, accompanied by great joy and enthusiasm.[215]

Inspired by the bodhisattva ideal and its practices, Tsongkhapa wanted to teach others about it, and he asked Mañjuśrī's permission. The deity replied:

Sentient beings' nature is wild and difficult to tame;
To give explanations to them would not be much use.
It is better to concentrate on your meditative practice.
You will soon find a path to benefit both self and others.[216]

So, for the time being, Tsongkhapa abandoned the idea of teaching and continued with his intensive meditative practice. That summer of 1393, as part of their preliminary practice of purifying negative karma and gathering virtue, Tsongkhapa and his companions visited the Dzingchi Temple, where they made offerings to the famed Maitreya image. This temple had been built sometime in the tenth century by Garmi Yönten Yungdrung, a disciple of Lachen Gongpa Rapsel, the latter credited by Tibetan historians with reviving monastic ordination in Tibet at the end of the tenth century. Legend has it that this alloyed Maitreya statue once belonged to a Khotanese king named Dhammika Candragarbha, and the icon is, in fact, triple-layered: at the heart of the large statue is a sandalwood statue of Maitreya, within whose heart is another smaller crystal statue. Following his full ordination, Garmi was given this Maitreya statue by his master Lachen and told to go to central Tibet, where his personal destiny lay.[217]

Although it was a historically important temple and the statue itself—made of gold and copper alloy and standing a little taller than life-size—was an impressive work of art, Tsongkhapa and his group found the temple in a derelict state. With visitors making butter-lamp offerings inside the temple, and with hardly any caretakers to keep the place up, the paintings on the walls had crumbled away, and the statue itself was covered in layers of dust and bird droppings. Seeing the temple and its revered central image in such a dire state, Tsongkhapa could not control his tears.[218] He resolved that somehow he would find a way to restore this important temple.

It became clear to Tsongkhapa that he had a special destiny to restore the Maitreya statue and its temple at Dzingchi to their former glory. He asked the local Wölkha ruler, Taktsewa, to sponsor the renovation of the temple; Taktsewa gladly agreed, and the work soon began. Once the renovation of the temple was complete, Tsongkhapa determined that the murals on the interior walls should be restored to their original state where it was possible, and new murals painted where it was not. However, hiring professional artists would prove expensive. He and his companions (twelve of them by this time) tried to raise some funds by selling anything they could spare from their own meager possessions. After they disposed of most of their spare ritual implements—vases, copper vessels, and so on—their funds amounted to far too little for the task at hand.

Tsongkhapa and his companions performed the rites of Vaiśravaṇa, an important god of wealth in the Buddhist pantheon. That very day, a young monk came to offer them a chunk of butter, which they used as part of the ritual offering. Strangely, the next day, a group of nomads came to offer the small community of meditators a multitude of wrapped bundles of butter. Then, as if floodgates had been opened, many people came to make offerings of various gifts, and within a short time they had the necessary funds to pay the artists. In fact, many artists came from the Yarlung area to volunteer their services to this restoration project. Being devout Dharma practitioners themselves, a number of them observed special precepts during the restoration work. Even the ordinary laborers recited mantras and chanted prayers during their work instead of singing the work songs typical of Tibetan laborers.[219]

Among the murals, the first to be completed was the depiction of the buddha realm of Mañjuśrī. Tsongkhapa performed the consecration rites for this new mural; the next morning, the small butter lamp that was lit as part of the ceremony was still burning, a good omen in his mind. As new murals were completed, Tsongkhapa and his companions would consecrate them. When all the murals were finished, a sand maṇḍala connected to Mañjuśrī was created to consecrate the entire temple and its images. As word of the upcoming ceremony spread, more and more devotees came to pay homage and make offerings at the temple. Following a brief retreat, Tsongkhapa and his companions performed the grand ceremony of the reconsecration of the temple.

Everyone gathered felt that they were part of a special event, with some claiming that the day itself lasted longer than usual. Some dreamed of ḍākinīs drawing some of the murals, and the famed Vajrapāṇi mystic Lhodrak Namkha Gyaltsen, whom we will meet in the next chapter, claimed to have experienced a vision in which buddhas were flying through the sky, saying that they had been invited to the consecration of Dzingchi Temple.[220] Deeply moved by this entire experience, Tsongkhapa composed the following extemporaneous hymn to Maitreya:

Your refined golden body is wrapped in a mass of great light;
Your eyes resemble the long petals of a lotus in full bloom;
You are seated on a beautiful throne in the *bhadra* posture;
I prostrate at your feet, O Conqueror Maitreya.
I see a towering pipal known as the Nāga Tree.
Its height reaches into the sky up to a league,
Its massive branches extend outward,
Reaching all the way out to six leagues.
Sitting at the foot of this tree, you grant the supreme nectar
To someone who encounters you the very same night.
I prostrate to you, Maitreya, treasure of great compassion.
Your body is eighty cubits tall
And twenty cubits in width and breadth.
Half of this is the size of your face.
I bow to you who are most majestic, like a roaring lion.

Through this effort [of ours], may all beings and I,
The instant we die, be reborn in Tuṣita heaven,
Inside the celestial mansion elevated by the Dharma;
May we become chief disciples of you, Lord Maitreya.
When you, the Buddha's regent, the master of the ten
bodhisattva grounds,
Attain the status of the Buddha endowed with ten powers,
May I be among the first ones to savor the nectar of your
speech,
And may I be able to perfect all the deeds of the enlightened
buddhas.
Here at Dzingchi Ganden Ling, the sacred residence of Maitreya,
May all be filled with the presence of Buddha Śākyamuni's heirs,
Upholders of vinaya, striving in their precepts,
All adopting the life of celibacy praised by the Buddha;
May they strive in the great Buddhist treatises,
Without any distractions by the eight worldly concerns;
And with the thought of shouldering the great task
Of serving the doctrine and sentient beings,
May they perfect the threefold activity of learning.[221]

This restoration of the statue of Maitreya at Dzingchi would be later recognized as the first of "the four great deeds of Tsongkhapa."[222] Later, at another retreat, this time in a part of the Lhodrak area called Töri Nyishar (literally, "Summit of Sunrise"), Tsongkhapa would compose a longer hymn to Maitreya entitled "Brahmā's Diadem," a moving invocation of Maitreya as well as a declaration of the heartfelt aspirations to be sustained by Maitreya throughout all his lives until the attainment of enlightenment. This long hymn opens with the following verse, which juxtaposes two apparent contradictions in the first three lines:

Though always moistened by loving-kindness, you burn the forces of darkness;
Though you have cut fetters so hard to cut, you are tightly bound by compassion;
Though you possess tranquil equanimity, you care more for others than yourself;
O Mañjuśrī, reverently I bow to you and offer these praises to Lord Maitreya.[223]

Although it cannot be dated exactly, sometime during this long retreat in the Wölkha Valley, Tsongkhapa composed verses of praise to his teacher Rendawa. Clearly, they were missing each other and did manage to communicate occasionally, mostly through mutual students bringing messages. In his verses of praise, Tsongkhapa speaks of how Rendawa's wisdom is incomparable, how his commitment to reason never slackens, and how he reveals to others the essence of the Buddha's teaching based on his own insights. The text also speaks of how he, Tsongkhapa, recalls his teacher's enlightened qualities and kindness while meditating on the slopes of a mountain.[224] Later, Rendawa's biographer would use key verses from this praise to highlight the master's attributes and accomplishments.

A Grand Vision of Mañjuśrī at Gya Sokphu Hermitage

In the winter of 1393, Tsongkhapa and his companions moved their retreat base to Gya Sokphu, located in the Menlung (Valley of Medicinal Herbs) region of Dakpo, still in the vicinity of Wölkha Valley.[225] There, Tsongkhapa made great progress in his meditative practice. One day he experienced a vision of Mañjuśrī surrounded by a large retinue of buddhas, bodhisattvas, and the great Indian Buddhist masters of the past—Nāgārjuna, Āryadeva, Buddhapālita, Nāgabodhi,[226] and Candrakīrti, as well as Asaṅga, Vasubandhu, Dignāga, Dharmakīrti, Guṇaprabha and Śākyaprabha, Devandrabuddhi, Prajñākāragupta, Śāntideva, Śāntarakṣita, Kamalaśīla, and "Abhyākaragupta"—and numerous mahāsiddhas such as King Indrabhuti, the great Brahmin Sarāha, and the mystics Lūipa, Ghaṇṭapa, and Kṛṣnācārya. According to the sources, Tsongkhapa not only had visions of these figures but also received blessings from them. As before, Tsongkhapa did not take these visions seriously, thinking that they might be just fleeting experiences. However, through Tokden, Mañjuśrī communicated that these visions were significant, for they were indications of how on the basis of these masters' writings Tsongkhapa would bring great benefit to many people in the future.[227]

Another vision Tsongkhapa experienced at the time involved seeing Vajrabhairava, a wrathful form of Mañjuśrī, a meditation deity dear to Tsongkhapa's childhood teacher Chöjé. After this vision of the deity, each day Tsongkhapa performed the self-empowerment rite of the deity. The personalities of Mañjuśrī that appeared to Tsongkhapa and his student Tokden could not have been more different. The form that appeared to Tsongkhapa was reserved and uttered few words, while the one that appeared to Tokden was approachable and loquacious.[228]

One day Tsongkhapa had another vision of Mañjuśrī, again surrounded by a host of many figures. This time, however, something different occurred. Tsongkhapa saw a sword of light extending from the deity's heart to touch his own heart. Along the blade, a stream of silver nectar flowed into his heart. As Tsongkhapa experienced this vision, his body was pervaded with great bliss, and his mind became absorbed in a state of rapture. It is said that when this vision occurred, a few of those sitting near Tsongkhapa felt as if they too were tasting the nectar.[229] Deeply inspired by his vision, Tsongkhapa wrote the following spontaneous hymn to Mañjuśrī:

In this city of Katara,
Attracted by flowers of its garden,
Swarms of honeybees frolic about,
Busily sucking the honey.[230]

There, at Gya Sokphu Hermitage, Tsongkhapa also received from the deity these verses of instruction on the essence of Dharma practice, which he wrote down at that time:

Without abiding anywhere,
Contemplate your mind as space-like.
Strive in all complementary practices.

Remaining alone like a rhinoceros,
Discard all distractions
And, abiding within equipoise,
Approach the great awakening.

The fruition of karma is never in doubt.
Cultivate renunciation and bodhicitta.
Keeping ablaze the great fire of mindfulness,
The fuel of six objects will definitely be consumed.

No phenomena, of either saṃsāra or nirvāṇa,
Ever were nor will be perceived;
Like space they transcend all boundaries.
The appearance of objects resembles sky flowers;
As for mind, the subject, which buddha has found such a thing?

The oneness of space and awareness is proven by the son of a
barren woman;
These truths constitute the path of the conquerors.[231]

In addition to recording these eighteen lines, Tsongkhapa wrote the following summary of their meaning:

> There are two aspects of the path that leads to enlightenment: the method aspect and the wisdom aspect. With respect to the method, there are the common practices and the uncommon practices, with the latter presented in terms of three points: the actual point, how to practice it, and the benefit of such practice. With respect to the wisdom, there is the summary presentation and its detailed exposition, with the latter presented in terms of four points: (1) the negation of the object; (2) the negation of the subject; (3) the negation of reflexive awareness that is the identity of space and awareness; and (4) the greatness of the path.[232]

In brief, these eighteen lines—four and a half stanzas—present the essence of the entire Mahāyāna path to enlightenment. The first two stanzas offer a brief summary, with the first two lines presenting the practice of the *profound view* through cultivating insight into emptiness, followed in the third line by a description of *vast practice*, covering the entire terrain from relying on a spiritual mentor up to cultivation of tranquility, and with lines 4 to 5 explaining how to engage in meditative cultivation. Starting with the third stanza, the teaching is elaborated further in terms of the path of the three scopes—the initial, medium, and advanced scopes as defined in Atiśa's lamrim instruction (lines 8–9); the generation and completion stages of tantra (lines 10–11); and presentation of emptiness in a more specific way, with respect to the object, the subject, and their union (lines 12–18).

Moving the Base Next to the Maitreya Temple

Although the sources are not clear, sometime in 1394 Tsongkhapa and his small group of meditators appeared to have moved their retreat base to the newly renovated Jampa Ling Hermitage attached to the Dzingchi Maitreya Temple at the base of Odé Gungyal Mountain. Throughout this year Tsongkhapa and his disciples continued their personal meditative practices, for the most part individually in their own cells, although Tsongkhapa would occasionally give brief instructions to the group and advise the meditators individually as well. With the prelimary and foundational practices of the common path completed, Tsongkhapa seems to have focused more on deepening his experience of bodhicitta, his expertise in the view of emptiness, and his engagement with meditative practice based on the special oral instructions that he had received from Umapa as part of the Mañjuśrī cycle of teachings.

It was also here at Dzingchi Temple that, at the urging of Mañjuśrī, Tsongkhapa composed a lengthy prayer for rebirth in Sukhāvatī, the pure land of Amitābha, entitled *Opening the Doors to the Buddha Realms.* It contains a detailed and evocative description of the pure land of Buddha Amitābha.[233] (An abridged version of this prayer would later become an important liturgical text in the main afternoon session at the Great Prayer Festival [*Mönlam*] at Lhasa, a tradition maintained to this day.)

As news of Tsongkhapa's restoration of the Maitreya Temple spread, many devotees—feeling deeply grateful to Tsongkhapa and his small community of wandering monks—came from various parts of Tibet to pay homage to the ancient temple and marvel at its renewed state. But for Tsongkhapa and his students, this was an indication that they needed to move on. So, sometime in 1395 (the Wood Pig year), they left the Wölkha Valley.

All in all, Tsongkhapa spent around three years in retreat in the Wölkha Valley. Never staying too long in one place, he and his small group of disciples had meditated at Wölkha Samten Ling, at the purposely built Wölkha Chölung Hermitage, at Garphuk, at Dzingchi Jampa Ling Hermitage, and at Gya Sokphu in the Dakpo Menlung region.

For Tsongkhapa, this three-year period, from the winter of 1392 to 1395, stood in marked contrast to the period immediately before it, which had been characterized by intensive scholarship, writing, and teaching. In the Wölkha Valley, the pace Tsongkhapa chose was that of a typical hermit or a true *jadrelwa* (literally, "one who has nothing to do"), as Tibetans put it. With no fixed plans, everything slowed down for Tsongkhapa. For the most part, he and his small band shunned public interaction and remained in solitude. For Tsongkhapa, this was a period not only of deep meditative silence but also of profound devotion, which was particularly amplified by the visions he experienced and by the privilege of restoring the Dzingchi Maitreya Temple. His attainment of meditative tranquility and stillness had been profoundly enhanced. His compassion, undifferentiated and universal, no longer required any effort for its arising; it came spontaneously whenever he invoked it. His realization of bodhicitta had been deeply enriched by the mythic portrayal and passionate exhortation of the bodhisattva ideal that he had read in the *Flower Ornament Scripture*. And his deity yoga practice, especially of Mañjuśrī and Vajrabhairava, had evolved to a point where his experience of the vision of Mañjuśrī felt almost like being in the presence of a real person.

There was one area of personal practice, though, where Tsongkhapa remained unsatisfied even at the end of his retreat period in the Wölkha Valley. This was his understanding and experience concerning the ultimate truth of emptiness. So, as he emerged from this long retreat period, he knew he still had more meditation practice to do. Although he would return to this beautiful valley for retreat right up to the founding of his own monastery, Ganden, in 1409, for now the time for intensive retreat was over.

CHAPTER 7

The Lhodrak Mystic

THE FIRST THING Tsongkhapa did after his long retreat in the Wölkha Valley was to pay a visit to Namkha Gyaltsen. Also known as Lhodrak Drupchen (literally, "the great adept of Lhodrak"), he was a mystic known to have a special connection with the meditation deity Vajrapāṇi. Tsongkhapa had received a letter from Lhodrak Drupchen toward the end of his stay in the Wölkha Valley. Drupchen—who had the rare distinction of being a Kadampa (stemming from Atiśa and Dromtönpa) with leanings toward Nyingma Dzokchen—had heard a ḍākinī say in a prophetic dream:

> There is an individual blessed by Maitreya (who is indivisible from Mañjuśrī) who is also being granted knowledge by the goddess Sarasvatī. You have a connection with him going back some fifteen lives, and in this life too, it will be auspicious to establish the bond of teacher and pupil. Thus, braving all hardships, you should invite him and confer all the teachings upon him. You should receive teachings from him as well.[234]

In his letter to Tsongkhapa, Drupchen extended his invitation, conveying his strong desire to inquire about certain points concerning the Dharma and to offer assistance with regard to ensuring Tsongkhapa's long life.[235] Thus, sometime in 1395, the Wood Pig year, in which he and his eight companions concluded their retreat in the Wölkha Valley, Tsongkhapa went to visit Drupchen at Drawo Monastery in Lhodrak, southern Tibet.

Meeting with Khenchen Chökyap Sangpo

On his way to Lhodrak, Tsongkhapa stopped in Nyal and spent some time with Khenchen Chökyap Sangpo. As a disciple and successor to the great Kadam masters Tsonawa and Möndrawa, he was a major lineage holder of the Kadam teachings. At that time, Khenchen was at the Drakor retreat center known as Rinchen Ling.[236] It had been forty years since Khenchen had vowed not to leave the place until he had attained the "signs of irreversibility." The night before Tsongkhapa's arrival, Khenchen dreamed of a monk wearing a red hat who said he was Atiśa. The monk said, "Tomorrow a monk will arrive capable of conferring all my instructions, so do request these instructions from him."

The next day, Tsongkhapa arrived with three of his attendants. Khenchen's attendant asked them to wait in the main prayer hall of the retreat. Khenchen asked, "Who is here?" to which the attendant replied, "Lobsang Drakpa has come to see you." Khenchen came out to meet Tsongkhapa and his students and invited them into his room upstairs. Tsongkhapa began a conversation with Khenchen, asking him important questions related to Sūtra and Tantra, to which Khenchen offered his responses. Similarly, Khenchen asked Tsongkhapa questions on various topics of Dharma.

Right there and then, it occurred to Khenchen that Tsongkhapa was indeed master Atiśa himself, as he had dreamed the night before. Moved by this thought, Khenchen asked Tsongkhapa if he would give him formal teachings. Tsongkhapa was taken aback by this request and responded, "It would be most inappropriate for a mere firefly to give a teaching to a sun-like mentor like you. If this is indeed your wish, since you as a yogi have mastery over the laws of dependent origination, please let me first receive teachings from you." Khenchen gave such transmissions as the reading of Atiśa's autocommentary on the *Lamp for the Path to Enlightenment* as well as the lamrim instructions stemming from master Tsonawa. In return, Tsongkhapa gave Khenchen transmissions of the entire cycle of instructions of master Atiśa, the five stages of the completion stage of the Guhyasamāja tantra, and the essential points of Nāgārjuna's teachings on both Sūtra and Tantra. Then, Khenchen gave Tsongkhapa the transmission of Drolungpa's *Great Exposition of the Stages of the Doctrine*, Sharawa's *Stages of the Path*, Potowa's instructions as recorded in Geshé Dölpa's *Blue Udder* and its commentary by Lhadri Gangpa, Śāntideva's *Bodhicaryāvatāra*, and Chekawa's *Seven-Point Mind Training*, as well as Tsonawa's extensive commentary on the *Root Lines on Vinaya*, Guṇaprabha's root lines on discipline.[237]

During his extended stay at Khenchen's retreat, Tsongkhapa also inquired about Lhodrak Drupchen, who he knew was Khenchen's student. Khenchen told Tsongkhapa that Drupchen was first a student of Thokmé Sangpo (a well-known master of Tibetan *lojong*, or mind-training instructions, as well as Śāntideva's *Bodhicaryāvatāra*) and later studied at the feet of Möndrawa, and that he was known to have visions of Vajrapāṇi. Khenchen told Tsongkhapa that his own teacher, Möndrawa (who had also taught Drupchen), had said that Drupchen was an emanation of the great second-century Indian master Āryadeva, the famed student of Nāgārjuna. Tsongkhapa then left for Lhodrak to visit Drupchen.

His time with Tsongkhapa had a powerful impact on Khenchen. Previously, Khenchen's reading of Nāgārjuna's philosophy of emptiness appeared to have been along the lines interpreted by Zhang Thangsakpa, a student of Patsap Nyima Drak—the translator of many of Candrakīrti's works into Tibetan. This made it hard for

Khenchen initially to follow Tsongkhapa's explanations on emptiness, but he strove mightily and had a breakthrough, attaining the signs of irreversibility.[238]

Meeting with the Mystic of Lhodrak

Tsongkhapa's visit to Drawo Monastery to see Lhodrak Drupchen happened to coincide with the sixth month of the Tibetan calendar. Understood to be the month when the Buddha gave his first public sermon at Deer Park in Sarnath, India, the sixth month is of special significance for the Tibetan tradition. As word came that Tsongkhapa was arriving, Drupchen went out to receive him and his small group.

It was a beautiful summer day in 1395, the fourth day of the sixth month on the Tibetan calendar, when Tsongkhapa and Drupchen first met. The mystic was already seventy years old. According to the sources, when Drupchen met Tsongkhapa he saw him in the form of Mañjuśrī, while Tsongkhapa saw Drupchen as Vajrapāṇi, wearing a spotted blue snake around his neck like a loose scarf.[239] That evening Tsongkhapa first received an empowerment of Vajrapāṇi from Drupchen. Around dawn, Drupchen dreamed of Maitreya, who instructed him to receive from Tsongkhapa a teaching on Śāntideva's *Compendium of Training* (*Śikṣāsamuccāya*). The next day, therefore, Tsongkhapa taught the text to Drupchen and his small community of monks. During this teaching, Drupchen had a series of profound experiences indicating that he was in the presence of a special being, someone blessed by many meditation deities—Maitreya, Mañjuśrī, Sarasvatī—and attended by powerful dharma protectors like Mahākāla. Tsongkhapa received from Drupchen the reading transmission of his collected writings, transmissions of the three lineages of lamrim stemming from Atiśa, and initiations for the various forms of Vajrapāṇi, including an empowerment of the meditation deity Hayagrīva.[240]

During one of their numerous conversations, Tsongkhapa shared with Drupchen that he still had lingering doubts about some aspects of his understanding of the view of emptiness and that he was planning to go to India. His hope was to go to the eastern part of India where the great yogi Mitrajogi was still alive on a forested mountain.[241] Tsongkhapa asked Drupchen if there were unforeseen obstacles to such a journey. In response Drupchen said:

> As for your questions on the view, I could ask my meditation deity [Vajrapāṇi]. Now, if you were to go to India, you would indeed meet with Mitrajogi, and you would become the abbot of Vajrāsana (Bodhgayā), thus being able to perform wondrous deeds beneficial to others. However, some of your companions would have obstacles to their life, and given that most of your companions are already on the paths of accumulation and preparation, it would be tragic if they were to fall victim to obstacles. And as for you, you would remain in India and never return. Thus, it would be better if you instead strive to serve the Dharma here in Tibet, so please do so.[242]

Heeding Drupchen's advice, Tsongkhapa decided against traveling to India.

Lhodrak Drupchen Consults Vajrapāṇi on Tsongkhapa's Behalf

As promised, Drupchen consulted Vajrapāṇi, presenting him with Tsongkhapa's questions about the view. The meditation deity gave a brief instruction entitled *Garland of Supreme Medicinal Nectar* (*Dutsi Menchok*) and said that this would dispel Matibhadra's lingering doubts. Later, Drupchen would write down this special instruction from Vajrapāṇi and send it to Tsongkhapa. "Who is Matibhadra?" asked Drupchen, to which Vajrapāṇi replied: "Lobsang Drakpa has already served the welfare of sentient beings for seven lives. In his previous life, he was born as Paṇḍita Matibhadra and was the abbot [at a monastery] in Kashmir." Vajrapāṇi then went on to say that even he, Vajrapāṇi, could not fathom the qualities of Tsongkhapa. "To be sure, he is blessed by the meditation deities; as for when he will attain enlightenment, I shall not speak about this, for Mañjuśrī and Avalokiteśvara will make this prediction."[243]

Then, at Vajrapāṇi's urging, Tsongkhapa composed his long hymn to Maitreya, "Brahmā's Diadem," and sent it to be chanted in the presence of Dzingchi Maitreya. It was both a hymn to the deity and a lamentation, expressing sadness for the long neglect both the temple and Maitreya's icon had suffered. Tsongkhapa also sent as offerings to the statue a set of robes, a monk's staff, an alms bowl, a square cloth to be used to spread over a cushion, and a water strainer—all of them items essential for a monk.[244] In the hymn to Maitreya, composed at Drupchen's retreat and sent to be chanted in Maitreya's temple, Tsongkhapa wrote:

> With constant gaze and full of compassion,
> You always look after all beings.
> Inspired every day by thinking of your qualities,
> I long to come and see you
> And be seated at your feet.
> But despite my desire, due to distance and my wish
> To continue to savor the taste of solitude,
> My body cannot undertake this long journey.[245]

Lhodrak Drupchen's Prophecies

During their visit, Drupchen told Tsongkhapa that he foresaw obstacles Tsongkhapa might encounter at around age forty-five in connection with his health. To help counter these potential obstacles, Drupchen gave Tsongkhapa the empowerment of Vajrapāṇi Great Wheel. He also advised Tsongkhapa that, from his hermitage, he should go to Tsari (one of the three sacred mountains in Tibet associated with Cakrasaṃvara) and Nyal, for this would be a source of great benefit to the Dharma and sentient beings. He further predicted that it would be in connection with the text of an Indian master that Tsongkhapa would attain a breakthrough in his understanding of the profound truth of emptiness.[246] "In the meantime," Drupchen asked, "could you teach the monks of my monastery?" Tsongkhapa complied. Drupchen was so inspired by his encounter with Tsongkhapa, over three decades his junior, that he composed the following verse of supplication:

> Tsongkhapa, you are Maitreya, the future guide of all beings,
> Who, out of concern for the beings of the degenerate age,
> Has appeared as the glory of the Land of Snows;
> I supplicate at your feet, O glorious guru.[247]

By the end of their stay, Tsongkhapa and his small group had spent seven full months at Drupchen's monastery retreat. Tsongkhapa would compose a prayer of supplication to Drupchen (using his alternate name, Namkha Gyaltsen) and would embrace him as the key source for the lineage of Atiśa's lamrim instructions and the cycle of practices associated with Vajrapāṇi. Later, when Tsongkhapa wrote his great synthesis on the path to enlightenment, based on Atiśa's lamrim instructions, and composed a prayer to the lineage masters of the bodhisattva ideal, he would include the following stanza to honor Lhodrak Drupchen:

> Through bodhicitta you see all beings as your children.
> You have been sustained and blessed by the meditation deity.
> You are the best spiritual mentor leading beings to freedom.
> I supplicate at your feet, O Namkha Gyaltsen.[248]

Vajrapāṇi's *Medicinal Nectar* Instruction

As mentioned earlier, Drupchen wrote down the instructions he received from Vajrapāṇi in response to Tsongkhapa's queries on the view of emptiness. That Tsongkhapa later received a copy of this text from Drupchen is evident from a reply he wrote to the mystic. The letter opens with seven verses of salutation and prayer for the master's long life and then acknowledges receipt of the text. Tsongkhapa writes:

> I received in particular the secret words of Vajrapāṇi, the *Garland of Supreme Medicinal Nectar*, bringing together the essential points of the intention of the buddhas and the bodhisattvas—namely, the instruction the Lord of Secrets [Vajrapāṇi] had conferred upon me and you put into words without any of the three faults: addition, omission, or error. When I received this instruction text, I felt the following:
>
> > The nectar of Vajrapāṇi's speech
> > Satiated my heart's yearning;
> > I have gained victory over the afflictions
> > And have just reached Aṭkāvatī heaven.[249]

Tsongkhapa's response letter to Drupchen ends by stating that, since he cannot find anyone else to whom he can address certain questions that he has, and since asking Drupchen is like asking an actual buddha (possibly referring to Drupchen's access to the deity Vajrapāṇi), he has tasked the bearer of his letter to ask additional questions.

One curious fact, rarely commented on by Tsongkhapa's biographers and commentators in the Geluk school, is how parts of the instructions on the view in the *Garland of Supreme Medicinal Nectar* strikingly echo the language of Dzokchen, a key perspective of the Nyingma tradition. In this letter, however, Tsongkhapa does not engage with the actual content of the text at all. Nor do we have any textual evidence of Tsongkhapa having engaged substantively with Dzokchen, apart from the simple fact that he was aware of this lineage. Nonetheless, this text, *Garland of Supreme Medicinal Nectar*, appears in both the collected works of Drupchen as well as those of Tsongkhapa. After the preamble, the actual instruction begins with the following:

> "O Karmavajra, get these words to Matibhadra's ears. With respect to the attainment of the great medicine—which represents the essence of the great mother Samantabhadrī's heart advice, the secret of myself, the Vajra Holder, and the apex of the vehicles—he should search for the clear light." I, Karmavajra (Drupchen), then asked, "What is the characteristic of this clear light?" The deity replied, "It consists of essence (*ngowo*), nature (*rangshin*), and compassionate energy (*thukjé*)." I then asked, "Are there any pitfalls related to the practice of clear light?" "Your question is excellent," the deity said and continued, "Should a person fail to understand it, there are pitfalls. This is fourfold: how one suffers the pitfalls, the signs of having fallen, the actual faults themselves, and the effects of such pitfalls."[250]

Those familiar with Tibetan Buddhism will immediately notice the strikingly Dzokchen-sounding phraseology in this brief opening exchange. "Mother Samantabhadrī" is a term unique to the Nyingma tradition, where she is conceived as the female counterpart of Samantabhadra, the primordial buddha. Possibly inspired by and modeled on the Mahāyāna figure of Mother Prajñāpāramitā—the perfection of wisdom portrayed in a feminine buddha form—Samantabhadrī is recognized as the primordial female buddha and the feminine aspect of the ultimate reality. Also, the language of the three attributes—essence, nature, and compassionate energy—is unmistakably Dzokchen, although these three are generally spoken of in Nyingma as characteristics of the ground (*zhi*) or primordial awareness (*rikpa*) rather than clear light (*ösel*), as presented in Vajrapāṇi's instruction here. Clear light, on the other hand, is a concept primarily emerging from the "new," non-Nyingma schools of Tibetan Buddhism, drawn from the authoritative Indian texts on Highest Yoga tantra, especially Guhyasamāja and Cakrasaṃvara. As we shall see later, "clear light" refers to the most subtle state of consciousness, which is experienced by an ordinary person at the moment of death, when all the processes of body and mind have come to an end. However, there are occasions in everyday life when even an untrained ordinary person may experience glimpses of clear light, such as when sneezing, fainting, sleeping deeply, and experiencing orgasm.

Toward the end of the long series of questions and answers between Drupchen and Vajrapāṇi recorded in the *Garland of Supreme Medicinal Nectar*, we find the following intriguing exchange:

> Karmavajra asked, "Is this Dzokchen an authentic view?" The deity replied, "Although Dzokchen is an advanced view, the view [of emptiness] that Nāgārjuna and Candrakīrti have

> expounded is flawless. Thus, without relying on their expositions it is impossible to attain genuine insight (*vipaśyanā*)."[251]

It is not clear to what extent Drupchen himself had any substantive exposure to Nyingma and Dzokchen teachings. In light of the available biographical material, his education and instructional upbringing appear to have been mostly Kadampa, with the great vinaya and lamrim masters Tsonawa and Möndrawa as his two principal teachers. Outside of his visionary experiences, the only reference we find is to a Dzokchen empowerment he is said to have received when he was five years old, suggesting a family connection with the Nyingma tradition. The available sources suggest that Drupchen's more esoteric instructions were received almost exclusively from his meditation deity Vajrapāṇi, in what the Tibetan tradition calls the state of pure vision (*daknang*). As we shall see later, for Tsongkhapa's immediate students, Drupchen's writings, containing revelations from Vajrapāṇi about Tsongkhapa's past lives and prophecies about his future lives, would play a crucial role in the sanctification of their master, especially after his entry into final nirvāṇa in 1419.

Still, we are left with something of a mystery—one that would be interpreted in very different ways centuries after Tsongkhapa's death when animosities developed between the Geluk and Nyingma schools. We have, on the one hand, explicit references to Dzokchen as well as uniquely Dzokchen terminology in Drupchen's record of Vajrapāṇi's instructions to Tsongkhapa. On the other, we have Tsongkhapa's silence concerning Dzokchen, even when transmitted by Drupchen as part of an oral instruction of Vajrapāṇi himself. Did Tsongkhapa study Dzokchen? And what was his attitude toward it?

On the whole, the mainstream Geluk commentators either choose to ignore the fact that Tsongkhapa received instruction with explicit Dzokchen content, or they suggest that the sections of Vajrapāṇi's instructions containing Dzokchen terminology might be later additions. In contrast, non-Geluk interpreters cite the presence of this unique instructional text as proof that Tsongkhapa's own final view was in accord with the Dzokchen view.[252] Given the dearth of Dzokchen references in the extensive records of teachings he received, it seems clear that Tsongkhapa had little contact with Nyingma teachings, including Dzokchen, although he was undeniably aware of them. No major seminaries or monasteries of the Nyingma school appear to have been active in central Tibet during Tsongkhapa's time, despite the fact that Longchenpa (1308–64), the great master responsible for systematizing the view and teachings of Dzokchen, had already authored his seminal works. Nonetheless, all available textual evidence suggests that Tsongkhapa was not aware of Longchenpa's writings. (In fact, it appears from the available textual evidence that most Tibetan scholars active in Ü-Tsang Province during the fourteenth and fifteenth centuries were not aware of Longchenpa's writings, which would later come to be recognized as the definitive exposition of Dzokchen according to the Nyingma school.)[253]

For his part, especially after his years at Tsal Gungthang, Tsongkhapa's own search seems to have focused entirely on reading, contemplating, and understanding the great Indian Buddhist sources, especially those of Nāgārjuna, Āryadeva, Buddhapālita, and Candrakīrti, as he sought to integrate the correct view of emptiness with the profound meditative techniques of Highest Yoga tantra.

Subsequent Correspondence between Tsongkhapa and Lhodrak Drupchen

Although Tsongkhapa and Lhodrak Drupchen kept in touch through letters, they would not see each other again.[254] Sometime after Tsongkhapa's departure, Drupchen recorded the details of his time with Tsongkhapa at the request of two of Tsongkhapa's direct disciples, Künga Sangpo and Gyaltsen Sangpo. Entitled *How I Met with Jé Tsongkhapa*, the text opens with the following:

> Once when I was conducting a teaching, many spiritual mentors who were students of Kashipa Lobsang Drakpa [Tsongkhapa]—Geshe Künga Sangpo and the Amdo student Vajrabhadra [Dorje Sangpo], the latter an individual who had been prophesied—came to see me. They said, "Whenever our teacher, the great Tsongkhapa, would mention your name, he would do so with much reverence, using phrases like 'the unrivaled Namkha Gyaltsen' and 'the most revered Vajrapāṇi yogi of Lhodrak would say this; he had been so kind.' Can you kindly tell us of any visions you had as well as what auspicious signs you observed?"[255]

In the preamble to another work by Lhodrak Drupchen, *A Secret Biography Dispelling Misconceptions*, Drupchen reports that several disciples of Tsongkhapa, including especially Jamyang Khaché (a senior teacher at Densa Thil and Tsethang Monastery)[256] and one Drakpa Lodrö, brought a letter from Tsongkhapa accompanied by some gifts. They then asked him (1) about how Tsongkhapa first generated the altruistic intention, (2) about how he engaged in deeds in the service of helping other beings, (3) whether he could share with them some prophecies, (4) what the best means would be to help Tsongkhapa to serve the Dharma and sentient beings effectively, and (5) what the best site would be for Tsongkhapa to found his own monastery.[257] As we shall see later, Vajrapāṇi's prophecies that Drupchen shared with Tsongkhapa's disciples would prove profoundly significant.

A Pilgrimage to the Holy Tsari Mountain

After spending over seven months at Drupchen's retreat in Lhodrak, Tsongkhapa and his small group of meditators left for the Nyal region. There, at Loro Tongtak, they stayed for five months, devoting themselves to intensive meditation practice. One day during their stay in Loro, someone brought a copy of Drolungpa's *Great Exposition of the Stages of the Doctrine*, which Tsongkhapa insisted on welcoming with a formal reception, with everyone standing in a receiving line. After making offerings to the text, Tsongkhapa read the entire work carefully. When he had finished reading, his appreciation of Atiśa's *Lamp for the Path to Enlightenment* (*Bodhipādaparidīpa*), the root text of lamrim instruction, was further deepened. He developed a renewed conviction that this instruction contains a powerful framework that structures the entire path to enlightenment in a comprehensive manner, one that is also in perfect accord with the stages of the practitioner's spiritual development.

In reading Drolungpa's extensive work, Tsongkhapa compared it to the shorter *Stages of the Doctrine* by Drolungpa's own teacher, the great translator Ngok Loden Sherap. He found that the presentations in these two Tibetan works were in perfect accord with his own personal understanding of the stages of the path to full enlightenment.[258]

Next, the group left Loro for Yarden Monastery in the lower region of Nyal, where they spent the rainy-season retreat (*yarné*). This is a period in summer, typically from July to the end of September, when monastic members undertake strict retreat by staying in one location and observing specific precepts. Dating back to the Buddha's time, the rainy-season retreat is practiced to this day in monasteries across all Buddhist traditions. It was during this summer of 1396 that Tsongkhapa composed his well-known hymn to Uṣṇīṣavijayā, an important goddess of longevity. Invoking the goddess, Tsongkhapa writes in the opening section of the poem:

> O goddess, you are a savior of sentient beings.
> When approached you grant supreme wisdom
> And turn Yama's [the lord of death's] club into a mere
> drawing;
> Uṣṇīṣavijayā, I offer these simple praises to you.[259]

Around this time, in the summer of 1396, during a session in which Tsongkhapa prayed fervently to Mañjuśrī, he had a vision in which the deity prophesied that through the help of an Indian text Tsongkhapa would soon gain final insight into emptiness. This was exactly what Lhodrak Drupchen had said earlier through his consultation with Vajrapāṇi, and the convergence of these two statements, coming from two independent sources, gave Tsongkhapa renewed energy to persevere in his long and earnest quest for the view of emptiness.

In the fall of 1396, Tsongkhapa was finally able to take Drupchen's advice to go on pilgrimage to sacred Tsari Mountain (Grass Mountain).[260] By then Tsongkhapa's group of wandering monastics had grown to some thirty in number.

Located on the border of southern Tibet and what is today the northern Indian state of Arunachal Pradesh, Tsari is one of the three most sacred mountains of Tibet, the other two being Mount Kailash and Lapchi. All three are associated with the meditation deity Cakrasaṃvara and his consort Vārāhī. Today, the town of Tsari, at the base of the mountain, is located in Luntse County of Lhoka Prefecture in the Tibet Autonomous Region. The original Tsari, to which devout pilgrims came from across Tibet, comprises the famed Dakpo Shelri—the Pure Crystal Mountain, which lies at nearly twenty thousand feet above sea level—and its surrounding region. The pilgrimage essentially consisted of circumambulation of the Crystal Mountain in a circuit. Two rivers, the Tsari and the Subhanshri, flow into their valleys from this region.

Tsongkhapa and his group stayed on the summit of Tsari Mountain for a few days, meditating, praying, and making offerings of tea and gifts to the long-term meditators living there as hermits. Tsongkhapa and his community of pilgrims performed the sādhana and self-initiation rites of Cakrasaṃvara, with Tsongkhapa experiencing a vision in which he received empowerment into Cakrasaṃvara's body maṇḍala—a visualization of the yogi's own body as the celestial mansion of the deity. However, Tsongkhapa did not perform the *tsok* ceremony, the ritual feast celebration of Cakrasaṃvara, on top of the mountain. As he was descending from the summit, suddenly he felt sharp pains in one of his feet, as if he had stepped on a poisonous thorn. His foot turned blue. He stopped right at that spot and made arrangements to have the tsok rite performed there. As if by a miracle, the pain in his foot went away.[261]

Later, a legend grew around this incident of Tsongkhapa's foot injury, a story heard and shared by successive generations of pilgrims. According to the legend, when Tsongkhapa failed to perform the ritual feast, ḍākinīs appeared and reminded him of the need to do so, since Tsari is a site of the Cakrasaṃvara maṇḍala. It is said that Tsongkhapa chanted the following lines, which later became a popular prayer chanted by pilgrims at Tsari:

> The glorious Tsari is the pure ḍākinī land of Kecara;
> Here I supplicate the sacred lineage masters and meditation deities,
> And the ḍākinīs and the guardians of the Dharma;
> Bless me so that my bad karma, nonvirtues, and defilements are cleansed.

Please help bring an end to all adversities and obstacles
And grant us attainments both common and supreme.[262]

After suffering sharp pains and subsequently performing the tsok rite, Tsongkhapa rested in a cave, which later came to be known as the Tsongkhapa cave (*Tsongkha phuk*); later, a mural of the master came to be drawn on the cave's wall. Once Tsongkhapa felt better, he and his companions resumed their descent to the valley and headed toward Nyal. Along the way, they stopped for the night at the base of a pass known as Mola. That evening, while the group was resting after a long day's trek, Tsongkhapa had a powerful vision of Maitreya.[263] It was a towering image, like a mountain rising high in the sky, pronouncing with the confidence of a lion's roar, "O son of the Buddha family, know that you shall resemble the Buddha reappearing on this earth." Hearing this, Tsongkhapa felt a surge of bliss shoot through his entire body, while his mind was utterly absorbed in a state of bliss and wonderment. Years later, Tsongkhapa's biographer and disciple, Khedrup, would memorialize this event in this popular hymn to Tsongkhapa:

"For the lotus grove of the Buddha's teaching in this world,
You shall resemble the sun-like Buddha himself"—
So declared the Lord Maitreya as if in person.
I supplicate you who have been so praised.[264]

Although by this time Tsongkhapa was best known for having a special connection with Mañjuśrī, Lhodrak Drupchen had emphasized Tsongkhapa's connection with Maitreya and had suggested that he compose the lengthy hymn to Maitreya entitled "Brahmā's Diadem." Perhaps Drupchen encouraged Tsongkhapa to go on pilgrimage to sacred Tsari Mountain based on a premonition that something like this vision of Maitreya was likely to occur. From a historical point of view, the greatest significance of Tsongkhapa's Tsari pilgrimage perhaps lay in its being the occasion for cementing his connection with Cakrasaṃvara, as he would later play a critical role in ensuring the flourishing of the teachings and practices of this important tantra.

A Profound Conviction in the Validity of the Kālacakra Tantra

After the trek from Tsari, Tsongkhapa and his group stopped at Sengé Dzong (Lion Fortress) in Nyal, where they remained for some time. There, Tsongkhapa focused his meditative practice specifically on the six yogas of the completion stage of the Kālacakra tantra, a system of tantra he was beginning to appreciate as being distinctly different from the other major tantras of the Highest Yoga class. He was aware that his own teacher, Rendawa, was skeptical about this particular tantra. But his own experience of receiving its transmission, according to both Butön's lineage and that of the Jonang tradition, as well as the extended periods he had already spent in its study and practice, had convinced him of its great importance.

Now, during his retreat at Sengé Dzong, Tsongkhapa gained unshakable conviction about the validity of this tantra and its overall place in the Vajrayāna tradition. During this time, Tsongkhapa had a dream one night in which the meditation deity Kālacakra appeared and told him, "With respect to this tantra you will become someone like Sucandra."[265] Tsongkhapa would later speak of this dream and tell Khedrup, his biographer, that prior to this sojourn at Sengé Dzong, he certainly had benefited from the expositions on the tantra he had received, but the effect was small. Perhaps, he suggested, the dream was an indication that he would now gain perfect understanding of the tantra.[266]

While at Sengé Dzong, Tsongkhapa and his group made extensive offerings to the Serché Bumpa stūpa, and Tsongkhapa taught the monks extensively on vinaya. He told the congregation that he had never committed an infraction of any of the important monastic precepts. Even when he had inadvertently transgressed one of the minor precepts concerning everyday conduct, he told them, he would immediately acknowledge and rectify the infraction. Sharing this, Tsongkhapa encouraged everyone gathered at the teaching to strictly follow the minute rules that govern a monk's daily conduct.[267] His institution of strict observance of the finest aspects of the vinaya rules, combined with a detailed exposition of the vinaya texts, laid a strong foundation for monastic culture in the monasteries that would come to be associated with Tsongkhapa's lineage.

Around this time, too, Tsongkhapa had a vision of Sarasvatī, who prophesied that he would live for fifty-seven years, during which he would be able to accomplish a great deal with respect to the welfare of others and himself. Being forty at the time, Tsongkhapa was mildly alarmed and invoked and prayed to Uṣṇīṣavijayā, the goddess of longevity for whom he had a written a popular hymn only a year earlier. Finally, word came from Tsongkhapa's student Tokden Jampel Gyatso that Mañjuśrī had told him that, although Tsongkhapa would find it difficult, the signs indicative of a shorter life span might be averted with the help of various rituals aimed at dispelling obstacles.[268]

In the meantime, Tsongkhapa had a more urgent matter to attend to: his ongoing struggle with the view of emptiness. He had been grappling with his own understanding of emptiness, delving ever deeper into its meaning, its radical implications, its relation to Vajrayāna perspectives and meditative practices, and how this view could be embodied in everyday life. Despite all his years of study, critical reflection, and meditation, including prolonged periods of silent retreat in the Wölkha Valley, Tsongkhapa retained lingering doubts connected with the radical implications of the view of emptiness. In short, he had not yet arrived at a point where he could be totally at home with the view of emptiness, when he could honestly say, "I've got it now." It is to this final phase in the story of this long quest that we now will turn.

CHAPTER 8

The Breakthrough

BY ALL MEASURES, Tsongkhapa's rapid rise as a scholar, practitioner, and teacher in the Tibetan Buddhist world in the latter part of the fourteenth century was remarkable. Before turning thirty, he had demonstrated his mastery of the great Indian Buddhist classics, the study of which constituted the core curriculum of the great learning centers of Tibet. With *The Golden Rosary*, he had authored, at thirty-one, one of the classics of Tibetan literature, admired to this day for its erudition, rigor, and sophisticated hermeneutics. Traveling from one monastery to another and from one retreat to another, over many years and great distances, Tsongkhapa had made sure to receive transmissions of all the important tantric lineages then current in Tibet. He had received transmissions of many important Tibetan instruction lineages as well. His personal development, through his insight into the subject matter of the great Buddhist texts and his own meditative practice, had continued to deepen. And he had been blessed with the unique facility to communicate with Mañjuśrī, first through a medium, the mystic Umapa; later through his disciple, Tokden Jampel Gyatso; and then by directly experiencing visions of the deity himself.

As noted, however, there was one area where Tsongkhapa never felt content with his progress: his understanding of the view of emptiness, with its implications for Buddhist thought, practice, and the entire path to full enlightenment. The breakthrough would come, finally, when he was forty-one, more than five years after his visionary encounters with Mañjuśrī. It is to this story that we now turn.

More Consultations with Mañjuśrī on the View

In the spring of the Fire Ox year (1397), shortly after their return from the Tsari pilgrimage, Tsongkhapa and his companions were staying at Sengé Dzong in the Nyal area. This was where, as mentioned in chapter 7, Tsongkhapa had entered into an intensive practice of the six yogas of Kālacakra tantra. At Sengé Dzong he once more sought the counsel of Mañjuśrī, asking the deity further questions on Sūtra and Tantra, especially concerning essential points on the attainment of tranquility and insight into emptiness. After offering brief responses to each of Tsongkhapa's specific questions, the deity then gave the following instruction:

> Now there is no more need to ask me questions frequently. If you explore with refined analysis the treatises composed by the great charioteers that set forth the meaning of the three baskets (*tripiṭaka*), as well as the four classes of tantra, you will find they are generally in accord with what I have revealed to you. Should there ever be any discrepancy, it is the oral instructions that must be abandoned, not the great treatises. With regard to oral instructions, you should rely on the authentic ones to serve as keys to help analyze the sūtras, tantras, and their commentarial treatises. Here is how to determine if your analysis has reached its culmination: *When you have gained conviction on a given point through scripture and reasoning and come to a conclusion, if no qualms remain, even in the deepest recess of your mind, then your analysis is complete.*[269]

Mañjuśrī then advised Tsongkhapa, "From now on, ensure that

whatever activities you might engage in through the three doors of your body, speech, and mind, you do so for the welfare of the Buddha's teaching and sentient beings." Tsongkhapa would later tell his attendants that he had followed this advice ever since.[270]

While in lower Nyal, Tsongkhapa decided to give some teachings for the monastic community. As news spread of his presence and ongoing teachings, many laypeople also came to attend his public teachings. This was perhaps the first time Tsongkhapa chose to conduct a large public teaching. Many among the gathering took the lay precepts and went for refuge to the three jewels: the Buddha, Dharma, and Saṅgha (spiritual community). As a purification practice, Tsongkhapa led everyone in constructing over a hundred thousand *tsatsa*s, small clay imprints of the Buddha and other figures.

Darma Rinchen, Tsongkhapa's Future Successor, Becomes His Student

Tsongkhapa and his monks next moved from the lower to the upper regions of Nyal, to Radrong Monastery, where they spent the summer of 1397. During this stay, Tsongkhapa met a man who would play a key role in ensuring his legacy, through both his influential philosophical writings and his leadership within Tsongkhapa's growing community of monks.[271] This was Darma Rinchen, later known as Gyaltsap Jé, literally, "the supreme regent."

A Sakya scholar of some repute, Gyaltsap was then known as Kachupa Dharma Rinchen—*Kachupa* meaning the master of ten treatises. Thirty-three at the time, he had just completed his last formal debate at Tsethang Monastery. Gyaltsap had briefly known Tsongkhapa before, as a fellow student of Rendawa, and had witnessed Tsongkhapa's remarkable rise in fame and esteem among their monastic peers. When Gyaltsap arrived at Radrong Monastery, Tsongkhapa led the entire community of monks in formally receiving him by standing in two lines outside the entrance of the monastery. Having heard so much about Tsongkhapa's growing fame, Gyaltsap was curious to see what Tsongkhapa was like now in person.

Once settled, Gyaltsap initiated a conversation with Tsongkhapa by asking a series of questions concerning various aspects of Buddhist philosophy and practice. Their conversation touched on what are called the four reliances, an important hermeneutic principle in Buddhist thought: rely not on the person but on the teaching, rely not on the words but on the meaning, rely not on the provisional meaning but on the definite meaning, and rely not on intellectual understanding but on experiential understanding through wisdom. Gyaltsap was deeply impressed by the depth and clarity of Tsongkhapa's understanding.[272]

Later that day or the day after, Gyaltsap attended the ongoing lectures Tsongkhapa was giving at the monastery. Tsongkhapa happened to be discussing how to apply the principles of logic and epistemology on the path to enlightenment, based especially on the second chapter of Dharmakīrti's *Exposition of Valid Cognition*. Tsongkhapa shared his view that the second chapter is a powerful application of the principles of logic to Buddhist soteriology. He argued that the text's rational explanation of the path to enlightenment sheds light on how to bring key philosophical insights into one's practice. This made a powerful impression on Gyaltsap, who realized that here finally was the master he was meant to be with. He sensed that, somehow, his own destiny was intertwined with Tsongkhapa's.

By the end of Gyaltsap's short stay at Radrong Monastery, he was deeply taken by Tsongkhapa. So, before he left for Sakya, Gyaltsap went to bid farewell to Tsongkhapa. Touching Tsongkhapa's feet with his bowed head, Gyaltsap told him that, for now, he needed to return to Sakya to speak about his experience, and with Rendawa's permission, he would like to come back. "If you would accept," Gyaltsap said to Tsongkhapa, "I would like to be an attendant accompanying you everywhere, as long as the lotus under your feet remains firm, just as a shadow follows the body."[273]

There is a more colorful version of the story found in a later biography of Gyaltsap, however. In that version, because of Gyaltsap's reputation as a great debater who had defeated two noted Sakya scholars—Yaktön Sangyé Pal (1350–1414) and Rongtön Shākya Gyaltsen (1367–1449)—Gyaltsap was initially motivated to meet with Tsongkhapa to engage him in debate. When Gyaltsap arrived, Tsongkhapa was in the middle of a lecture. Showing his intention to challenge Tsongkhapa to a debate, Gyaltsap sat in the congregation but kept his hat on. Seeing him, Tsongkhapa continued to teach but got down from the throne and sat on the floor, and Gyaltsap sat on Tsongkhapa's throne. As he continued to listen to Tsongkhapa's teaching, however, his demeanor slowly changed: first taking off his hat, then getting down from the throne, and eventually sitting together with Tsongkhapa's other students to listen to the master's teaching.[274]

That Gyaltsap was famed for his erudition as a sharp debater seems to have been widely known. Rendawa, in the course of listing his seven principal students, declared him "Darma Rinchen, one who is foremost in debate."[275] As we shall see later, when Tsongkhapa passed away, Gyaltsap would be chosen as his first successor, effectively becoming the head of both Ganden Monastery and the growing community of devotees across the Tibetan plateau beginning to view themselves as followers of Tsongkhapa's tradition. Tsongkhapa's biographers would interpret the story of Tsongkhapa's initial deference to Gyaltsap, including his respectful reception of him at their first formal encounter, as an auspicious indication of Gyaltsap's destiny.

The First "Great Session of Reading Scriptures"

Encouraged by the receptivity of the monks of Radrong Monastery to his teachings, as well as by the overwhelming enthusiasm displayed by the laity during his stay in the Nyal area, Tsongkhapa thought that instituting an annual Dharma celebration might be beneficial to the people of the region. He discussed this idea with the abbot of Radrong Monastery, who enthusiastically offered to sponsor such a celebration.

When a formal announcement was made of the celebration, it attracted monks from all the monasteries of the region, with provisions offered to everyone who attended.[276] This Dharma celebration, including the teachings Tsongkhapa gave at the time, came to be known as the "great session of reading scriptures" (*nyalgyi lungra chenmo*) and was later recognized as the second of "the four great deeds of Tsongkhapa."

Prevailing Tibetan Views of Emptiness in Tsongkhapa's Time

By the summer of 1397, Tsongkhapa had for many years been deeply engaged with the great Indian classics on emptiness, including Nāgārjuna's *Treatise on the Middle Way*, Candrakīrti's *Entering the Middle Way*, and Āryadeva's *Four Hundred Stanzas*. For each of these three root texts—which the Tibetans refer to collectively as *tsa juk zhi sum* (the first syllables of their titles in Tibetan followed by the word *three*)—Tsongkhapa had also carefully studied their important commentaries, especially those of Candrakīrti. He had further received expositions on each of these philosophical texts from his principal teacher, Rendawa, at the time an undisputed Tibetan authority on Madhyamaka philosophy.

Prior to meeting and studying with Rendawa, Tsongkhapa had

been exposed to what might be characterized as the received position in Tibet on the view of emptiness according to Candrakīrti. Sometimes referred to as "Shang Thangsakpa's position" (Thangsakpa was a principal student of Patsap Nyima Drak, the main translator of Candrakīrti's major writings into Tibetan), this view espoused a kind of agnostic quietism on the question of reality, literally denying the four possibilities of existence, nonexistence, both existence and nonexistence, and neither existence nor nonexistence. On this view, the Mādhyamikas (the proponents of emptiness) are said to have no position of their own and are concerned only with refuting others' positions. Hence, all the norms of logic and epistemology—reasoning, criteria of knowledge, law of causality—are valid only for the opponent. The Mādhyamikas themselves, according to this view, have no positions of their own, nor should they make any specific propositions.

An epistemological corollary to this is that there is no such thing as knowledge, except for the Buddha's omniscience, and that all perspectives of unenlightened beings are false, with no valid criteria to distinguish between something like water and a mirage. It is maintained that, given that reality cannot be described in any manner, the meditating mind must not engage with reality in any manner whatsoever. Genuine meditation on emptiness, therefore, entails total disengagement, not abiding in any point of view, and should be nonconceptual and free of any discursive activity. Tsongkhapa himself appears to have actually held more or less this point of view when he was writing *The Golden Rosary*, which he completed in 1388. There he states:

> In brief, the meaning of the statement, "In meditative equipose, Ārya's gnosis cognizes reality, the nature that transcends conceptual elaboration, and the ultimate truth," is this. Because all forms of subjectivity have dissolved for that

> gnosis, no perception whatsover arises with respect to these things. In fact, there is nothing that is being perceived and nothing that is doing the perceiving.[277]

Tsongkhapa was never quite happy with this widely shared Tibetan understanding of Nāgārjuna's philosophy of emptiness, supposedly read through Candrakīrti's so-called Prāsaṅgika understanding. He could not reconcile the widespread claim that the Prāsaṅgika view of emptiness was the highest philosophical position with what seemed to him to be a methodological sophistry—a philosophy concerned only with refuting others' views. Another complicating factor for Tsongkhapa was the rejection of principles of logic and epistemology other than upholding a principled skepticism. We recall how deeply inspired Tsongkhapa was by his careful reading of the second chapter of Dharmakīrti's *Exposition of Valid Cognition*—it often moved him to tears. There Tsongkhapa saw a powerful example of the application of principles of logic, reason, and epistemology to the Buddhist path. In Tsongkhapa's Buddhism, regardless of how lofty a view is proclaimed to be by its adherents, if the standpoint entails total rejection of fundamental truths of reason, reality, and knowledge, then something isn't quite right. On his view, one hasn't gotten to the bottom of the question yet.

One prevailing alternative to the "Thangsakpa position" in Tibet at the time was the so-called extrinsic emptiness (*shentong*) theory of the Jonang school. Briefly, this Shentong view draws a distinction between two senses of emptiness: intrinsic emptiness and extrinsic emptiness. According to this position, it is only the world of dependent origination, namely, the conditioned world governed by cause and effect, that is empty of intrinsic existence. In contrast, emptiness itself exists with its own intrinsic nature as absolute reality. The only way in which one can speak of the absolute truth as being empty is in the sense of it being devoid or empty of conditioned existence, things that are ontologically other than it, hence the term *extrinsic emptiness*. This absolute reality, according to its proponents, is an eternal, unchanging gnosis (*yeshé takpa*), the indivisible union of awareness and reality. And this, they assert, is the buddha nature, or buddha essence (*tathāgatagarbha*), in fact an essential buddha that is inherent in all beings.

The proponents of this view assert that "extrinsic emptiness" theory is the highest standpoint within Buddhist philosophy and is established in the mature works of Maitreya and Asaṅga, as well as in Nāgārjuna's poetic hymns (but not in his philosophical treatises). The most influential advocate of the Shentong view before Tsongkhapa's time was Dolpopa Sherap Gyaltsen (1292–1361).[278] Tsongkhapa's own teacher, Rendawa, was a vocal critic of this view.

Tsongkhapa was never attracted to this more absolutist reading of emptiness, and the extrinsic-emptiness view would become a major focus of his critique in his mature writings on the philosophy of emptiness. In fact, in his *Golden Rosary*, written about a decade earlier, Tsongkhapa already explicitly criticized this Shentong view. He wrote, "Some assert that the intended position of Maitreya's mature works and Asaṅga and his brother [Vasubandhu]'s treatises is that the unconditioned nature empty of all conditioned phenomena constitutes the absolute reality. Such an assertion is nothing but a trick conjured in the dark by those of a coarse intellect."[279]

Regarding the correct view of emptiness, there was still a third possibility of which Tsongkhapa was aware. This was an alternative reading of Nāgārjuna's philosophy of emptiness proposed by the Tibetan logician Chapa Chökyi Sengé (1109–69), who preferred the so-called Svātantrika-Madhyamaka line of thinking.[280] But because Chapa explicitly refuted Candrakīrti's interpretation of Nāgārjuna, Chapa's suggested reading was unacceptable to Tsongkhapa.

Tsongkhapa's Breakthrough

Content with what he had been able to achieve in Nyal, Tsongkhapa and his group, by now over thirty in number, returned once again to the retreat in the Wölkha Valley known as Lhading ("gods floating in the air"). He would remain there for a full year, continuing with his intensive meditative practice and conducting teachings for his small band of wandering contemplative monks. Throughout all this, taking to heart what his meditation deity Mañjuśrī had advised during their last encounter—that he should critically reflect on the great treatises and compare them against Mañjuśrī's own oral instructions—Tsongkhapa redoubled his efforts in the ongoing quest for deeper insight into emptiness. One night, he had a prophetic dream, in which he saw Nāgārjuna surrounded by four of his principal interpreters—Āryadeva (second century), Buddhapālita (fifth century), Bhāviveka (sixth century), and Candrakīrti (seventh century)—engaged in deep conversation. Then, one of the figures, said to be Buddhapālita, came over to Tsongkhapa bearing a wrapped text and touched the top of his head with it.[281]

Following the symbolism of his dream, the next morning Tsongkhapa plunged into Buddhapālita's exposition of Nāgārjuna's *Treatise on the Middle Way*.[282] Tsongkhapa read and read, reflecting every now and then, and meditating on crucial points of Buddhapālita's presentation of the philosophy of emptiness. As Tsongkhapa was reading and meditating on the eighteenth chapter, "Analysis of Self and Phenomena," all of a sudden everything became crystal clear. All of Tsongkhapa's long-standing doubts—especially regarding how to find the extremely fine line demarcating what is negated in emptiness and what is left untouched—vanished without a trace. He felt that nothing whatsoever was left for possible objectification—no object, no basis, no ground. Yet there was no danger, not even the slightest hint, of collapsing into nihilism or some kind of ineffable absolutism. Paradoxically, instead of being demolished, the world of cause and effect, right and wrong, saṃsāra and nirvāṇa seemed even more clear and regulated. Tsongkhapa knew exactly what Nāgarjuna meant when he wrote, centuries earlier:

> To whom emptiness is possible,
> For him all is possible;
> To whom emptiness is impossible,
> For him nothing is possible.[283]

Later, speaking of the impact of this experience, Tsongkhapa would tell his attendants the following:

> These days, with greater familiarity [with insight into emptiness], even in the postmeditation periods, I would have the perception of this entire world of diversity as being empty yet, in an illusion-like manner, maintaining its specific forms. And the perception of things as not "sealed" or marked by awareness of their emptiness—as objective facts with intrinsic reality—rarely arises in me now.[284]

Years later, Khedrup would memorialize Tsongkhapa's eureka moment in a hymn to the master:

> I supplicate you who, when Nāgārjuna and Āryadeva,
> Buddhapālita, and Candrakīrti blessed you,
> In that instant discarded all possible stains of error
> With respect to the profound ultimate truth.[285]

At the heart of Tsongkhapa's breakthrough experience was a profound realization of the equation of emptiness and dependent origination. It is one thing to declare there is no contradiction between emptiness and dependent origination—that the two can converge in a single locus without logical conflict. It is something quite different, however, to understand this at a level where emptiness *is* dependent origination and dependent origination *is* emptiness. In Nāgārjuna's language, the meaning of emptiness is dependent origination, which is another way of expressing the well-known formula from the *Heart Sūtra*, "Form is emptiness, emptiness is form; emptiness is nothing other than form itself; form is nothing other than emptiness." Speaking of this equation, a few years later Tsongkhapa would write:

> The statement that dependent origination becomes the meaning of *emptiness* is relevant only for the Mādhyamika who has negated intrinsic existence by means of valid cognition; it is not for just anyone. This is because, when such a Mādhyamika person ascertains external and internal phenomena as dependent originations, through the force of that very cognition itself he or she will realize that things are devoid of intrinsic existence.[286]

In a short verse work composed as a letter to his first attendant, Tsakho Ngawang Drakpa, Tsongkhapa would articulate this crucial point about the equation between emptiness and dependent origination:

When, with respect to all phenomena of saṃsāra and nirvāṇa,
You see that cause and effect never transgress their laws,
And when you have dismantled the focus of objectification,
At that point, you have entered the path that pleases the
buddhas.
As long as the two understandings—
Of *appearance*, the regulated world of dependent origination,

And of *emptiness*, the absence of all standpoints—remain separate,
You have not realized the intent of the Sage.
However, at some point when, without alteration and at once,
The instant you see that dependent origination is undeceiving
If the entire object of grasping at certitude is dismantled,
At that point your analysis of the view is complete.
Furthermore, when appearance dispels the extreme of existence,
And when emptiness dispels the extreme of nonexistence,
And you understand how emptiness arises as cause and effect,
You will never be swayed by views grasping at extremes.[287]

Following the bolt of insight triggered by his deep engagement with Buddhapālita's text, Tsongkhapa spent the entire spring and summer at the Lhading Retreat in single-pointed meditation on emptiness. He needed to bring his insight to life so that the view of emptiness permeated every fabric of his being—the way he viewed his own identity, how he perceived the world around him, and how the view affected even his emotional life. As a philosopher, Tsongkhapa also needed to understand how the view of emptiness would inform his entire worldview, especially his understanding of all the other important elements of Buddhist thought and practice, from the fundamental questions of knowledge and truth to moral and soteriological issues. Working out these implications, especially through writing, would come later. In the short term, however, Tsongkhapa was filled with an abiding sense of bliss, as well as profound feelings of gratitude and devotion for the Buddha, especially for his teaching of emptiness and dependent origination. To express these deep feelings, Tsongkhapa composed a hymn to the Buddha, praising him as the teacher of the truth of dependent origination. Here are a few selected stanzas from this hymn, which convey Tsongkhapa's exuberant feelings of joy, wonder, gratitude, and deep reverence for the Buddha:

Whatever degenerations there are in the world,
The root of all these is ignorance.
You taught dependent origination,
The seeing of which will undo this ignorance.
So how can an intelligent person
Not comprehend that this path
Of dependent origination is
The essential point of your teaching?
This being so, who will find, O Savior,
A more wonderful way to praise you
Than [to praise you] for having taught
This origination through dependence?[288]
Wondrous teacher! Wondrous refuge!
Wondrous speaker! Wondrous savior!
I pay homage to you, the teacher
Who taught well dependent origination.[289]

Speaking more specifically of what the Buddha's teaching on dependent origination consists of, he writes:

"All of this is devoid of essence,"
And "From this arises that effect."
These two certainties complement
Each other with no conflict at all.
What is more amazing than this?
What is more marvelous than this?
If one praises you in this manner,
This is a real praise, otherwise it is not.[290]

Deeply grateful that he had met with this precious teaching before his death, he writes:

Alas! My mind was defeated by ignorance;
Though I have sought refuge for a long time
In such an embodiment of excellence,
I possess not a fraction of your qualities.
Nonetheless, that I have found some faith
In you before the stream of this life,
Flowing toward death, has come to cease—
Even this I think is fortunate.
Among teachers, the teacher of dependent origination,
Among wisdoms, the knowledge of dependent origination—
You, who are most excellent like the kings in the worlds,
Know this perfectly well, not others.[291]

Over time, Tsongkhapa's hymn to the Buddha as the teacher of dependent origination, popularly known as "In Praise of Dependent Origination" (*Tendrel Töpa*), became a classic. It would come to be recognized as a freestanding treatise on emptiness and would attract numerous commentators, the earliest being those from Gungru Gyaltsen Sangpo (1384–1450) and Baso Chökyi Gyaltsen (1402–73),[292] both students of Tsongkhapa and the latter being a younger brother and student of Khedrup as well.

Correspondence with Rendawa on the View

Though it is difficult to piece together the chronology clearly, it appears that Tsongkhapa kept his teacher Rendawa abreast of his growing understanding on the view of emptiness, and Rendawa replied in kind. The exchanges between Tsongkhapa, who was at various retreat sites, and Rendawa, who spent most of his time at several monasteries, especially Sakya, represented a continuation of the dialogue they had begun years before.

Although we should be grateful to the editors who preserved some part of Tsongkhapa's communication with Rendawa on the view, it is unfortunate that these editors did not keep the scrolls holding this correspondence as separate documents. Instead, the scrolls seem to have been merged so as to produce a single text, thus making it impossible to discern which parts were written first and which parts came later. This situation is exacerbated by the confusing fact that Tsongkhapa's collected works contain two very similar entries, one entitled "Essential Points of Mañjuśrī's Path Presented as a Scroll to Master Rendawa," and another text, included in *Miscellaneous Writings*, which is a long letter sent in response to a letter from Rendawa. Except for the preambles and concluding parts, the main texts of these two entries are almost identical.[293] The following analysis of their correspondence on the view of emptiness is based on a careful comparison of the available letters preserved in their respective collected works.

It appears that sometime after his long retreat in the Wölkha Valley, Tsongkhapa wrote to Rendawa about his exchanges with Mañjuśrī concerning the view of emptiness. Tsongkhapa writes:

> With regard to several earlier and subsequent communications I have had [with Mañjuśrī], there have been numerous signs indicating that they are credible. It will not be possible to write about all of these here. In brief, although I had assumed that I gained the Prāsaṅgika view [of emptiness] that is devoid of all positions, I made careful inquiry about my view. But I was told, together with the reasons, that I still had not yet gained the understanding. I then entered into a prolonged debate about the view [with Mañjuśrī], who told me that the Prāsaṅgika view should be such and such but what you have in your mind is merely this and that. I then checked what the deity had said by consulting the treatises

> of Nāgārjuna and his disciples and realized that indeed I had not gained the understanding. I asked the deity about the means to help me gain such an understanding and pursued them. Now I have had a major insight, due to having gained a new understanding of the meaning of dependent origination that I had not understood before.[294]

Tsongkhapa goes on to describe this "major insight" (*ngeshé chenpo*) gained from a newfound understanding of the meaning of dependent origination. He writes:

> In general, it is common to all philosophical schools, right down to the Cārvāka [Indian materialist school], that *emptiness* dispels the extreme of existence and *appearance* the extreme of nonexistence. A distinctive feature of Prāsaṅgika Madhyamaka, however, is that appearance dispels the extreme of existence and emptiness the extreme of nonexistence; one understands how emptiness becomes [both] the cause as well as the effect. One thus accepts within one's own standpoint that effects arise in dependence upon their causes and that effects invariably follow their causes.[295]

Having thus identified what he understands to be a unique Prāsaṅgika way of seeing the relationship between emptiness and form, Tsongkhapa goes on to explore the implications of this view, especially for understanding what Nāgārjuna means by his equation of emptiness and dependent origination. Tsongkhapa writes:

> In light of this [unique understanding], there seem to be many things to say about this view, including how this understanding leads to a view of emptiness that eliminates all possible extremes. This, however, is not the standpoint that

> asserts that it is only from the perspective of the other party [in a discussion] that an effect invariably follows its cause, but that within one's own system one does not make any statements about veracity and nonveracity. When one leaves them unexamined, one perceives that effects never deceive their causes; when causes and effects are subjected to critical analysis, however, one does not find anything one can point to and say, "This is it." This said, some indeed observe cause and effect in their subsequent perceptions [after contemplating emptiness] and, recognizing their convergence on a single basis, speak of the fusion of emptiness and dependent origination. This, however, is not the true understanding. What is needed is the following. One needs to arrive at a standpoint whereby the very cognition that sees how effects never deceive their causes, without dependence on any other cognition, give rise to the understanding of emptiness that dismantles all possible bases for objectification. Similarly, the very reasoning [of dependent origination]—that effects never deceive their causes—this alone, without need for any further reasoning, establishes the emptiness that is free from all possible extremes. In this way, a depth of conviction in the efficacy of causality is brought forth, and this very insight seems to give rise to freedom from clinging through destroying the locus for objectification.[296]

Then, remarkably—acknowledging that Mañjuśrī had in fact given him instructions on the view described above, which he himself had failed to properly comprehend—Tsongkhapa mentions asking the deity whether Rendawa had attained the view or not. Tsongkhapa writes:

> When I compared these instructions [from the deity] against

> what I had heard previously from him, it appears that he had actually conferred instructions along the same lines in similar terms. But it seems I had missed their point and had thus failed to fully comprehend their meaning. Thinking that if I had not understood, since there is no difference between you and me [on the view], you too may not have understood this, so I asked the deity, "Does this mean that my master, too, has not understood this?" "He has understood it, though to what extent I am not sure," the deity replied. Thus, on the final points concerning the view, such as these, as well as the subtleties pertaining to the essential points about the [bodhisattva] deeds, whether or not one's practices actually hit the mark, and the difficult points concerning Sūtra and Tantra, previously I had lingering doubts. With regard to those points I had not been able to critically analyze before, when I viewed them on the basis of how they may be subjected to the force of reasoning, conviction began to arise in me, dispelling the stains of any lingering doubts.[297]

Of these four citations, the second and the third appear almost verbatim in the two texts concerning the view of emptiness said to have been sent to Rendawa—one dubbed by Tsongkhapa's editors the "Essential Points of Mañjuśrī's Path Sent to Rendawa as a Scroll," the other a lengthy letter included in his *Miscellaneous Writings*. The first citation, from the brief preamble of the scroll, and the fourth citation, concerning the question about whether Rendawa too had gained the view, is found only in the scroll. However, almost the entire text of the letter is contained in the scroll, thus making the relationship between the two texts, chronologically and with respect to content, unnecessarily obscure.

In any case, both texts address many questions of critical importance: the three essential elements of the path and their systematic cultivation and sequence; the importance of cultivating both tranquility and insight; the role of discursive or analytic meditation, especially in the context of developing insight into emptiness; the importance of beginning with the examination of one's own personal identity or self; the place of nondiscursiveness and nonmentation in meditative practice; the paradox of developing insight into the ultimate truth, which is beyond the bounds of language and logic, through the use of reason, language, and concepts; the thorny issue of whether or not Madhyamaka has a position of its own; and the critical question of whether or not the view of emptiness is the same in Sūtra and Tantra. Despite their brevity, the range of topics and questions raised in these letters to Rendawa, and the depth in which they are explored, is nothing short of amazing.

Toward the end of the letter version, there is the following personal note:

> If you plan to go into intensive practice, please do so. If, for the time being, we do not have the chance to see each other, then first—once you have performed some rites for your long life—contemplate the exalted Mañjuśrī for a year. If you are able to do this, there is no doubt that Mañjuśrī himself will directly confer instructions to you. So please, please do strive in this. Please do not take offense [at my making this suggestion].[298]

How did Rendawa respond to these letters from his pupil? We are fortunate that perhaps the most important of Rendawa's letters to Tsongkhapa has been preserved for posterity. It is a lengthy letter, some nineteen pages, sent from Sakya, possibly in response to the first scroll he received from Tsongkhapa about Mañjuśrī's instruction. The letter opens with the following acknowledgment:

> What you wrote in your letter touched upon points that I have already thought about, but it helped me greatly by strengthening my conviction and clarifying many details. In particular, sharing with me how the essence of Dharma is encompassed in the three [elements], such as renunciation and so on, was important, for I too have had the thought that to practice these three is like tapping into the life-vein of the path.[299]

The letter then goes on in some detail about Rendawa's understanding of how to cultivate and realize the first two essential points, renunciation and bodhicitta. Interestingly, Rendawa makes the case that, in fact, without the third point—the right view of emptiness—genuine bodhicitta might even be impossible. He then makes the following request:

> In this instructional lineage [of Mañjuśrī], it seems there is a unique approach to guiding a person through the cultivation of renunciation and bodhicitta, as well as the means for enhancing the two. If you could write these down in detail and have the letter sealed and sent via central Tibet, this would make a great difference. When guiding someone through instruction [on the three], I feel that I must do so by relating it to the stage of the person's mental development, while observing a definite sequential order. In my own case, I have practiced these three elements without confusing their proper sequence.[300]

Articulating his understanding of the third element, the right view of emptiness, Rendawa then writes of how, in the final analysis, the standpoints of all philosophical schools, Buddhist and non-Buddhist, remain within the boundary of conceptualization, and it is only at the stage of a noble one's nonconceptual gnosis and the stage of buddhahood that one transcends all views. Rendawa then offers his own understanding of the key difference between the two schools of Madhyamaka, Prāsaṅgika and Svātantrika, which represent two powerful currents of interpretation of Nāgārjuna's philosophy in India. For Rendawa, the two schools are equal in asserting the ultimate truth to be ineffable; their distinctiveness lies in the fact that while the Svātantrika of Bhāviveka and his like accepts the notion of dependent origination as a mere illusion (*tendrel gyuma tsam*), the Prāsaṅgika of Candrakīrti maintains dependent origination as a nominal reality and as mere designation (*takyö mingkyang tsam*).[301]

Rendawa then offers an intriguing observation about what he sees as four understandings of the view of emptiness—a perspective, so far as I am aware, unique to him. Given both the striking similarity as well as the recognizable difference between the views of Rendawa and Tsongkhapa on emptiness, having some clarity on what Rendawa characterizes as four progressive positions on the view could help bring Tsongkhapa's own view into sharper relief.[302] Rendawa writes the following in the same letter to Tsongkhapa:

> I have experienced four stages in the understanding of the Madhyamaka view [of emptiness]. First is a nihilistic emptiness, the second is [the union of] appearance and emptiness, the third entails understanding dependent origination as illusions, and the fourth is understanding dependent origination as mere designations and groundless.
>
> The first refers to emptiness according to which, like the breaking of a clay pot with a hammer, conventional reality is dismantled. It is as if a magician dismantles his conjurations created through some substances and incantations. Even

this level [of understanding of emptiness] helps overcome grasping at things as possessing some kind of analyzable existence, and it helps engender admiration for emptiness.

The second refers to the understanding whereby, at the very instant one perceives illusion-like phenomena, one also understands their lack of intrinsic existence. Although this understanding helps overcome reification and denigration of the external world of objects, it does not counter grasping at the inner world of subjective experience. Thus, this view does not go beyond that of the False Aspectarian branch of the Cittamātra [Mind Only] school.

As for the third, it recognizes that, given that the world of external objects and the world of inner subjects are both dependent on causes and conditions, like illusions, they merely appear as conventional realities but lack intrinsic existence. Although this view is free of grasping at any extremes, there still persists the notion of dependently originated things as not contingent upon language and thought and existing as illusions. This view does not go beyond that of Yogācāra-Madhyamaka.

In the fourth view, when dependently originated things are examined with correct reasoning, not even the tiniest intrinsic reality is found to exist. Yet when they are left unexamined, they remain as objects of [language and] conventions. They are thus understood to be designated by concepts and as mere nominal realities created by conventions. Only a mind that cognizes dependent origination in such terms would, without dependence on some additional understanding, give rise to the understanding of the invariable relation between cause and effect as well as the fact that dependent origination is free of all extremes of conceptual elaborations, such as eternalism, annihilationism, and so

> on. I do not believe there is anything beyond this view to be found. Until it is realized, one's view remains not final.[303]

Having described these four progressive stages in the deepening of one's understanding of the view, and having made the emphatic point that there is no higher view beyond the fourth stage—the stage that Rendawa understands to be the Prāsaṅgika view—Rendawa then has the following to say about Tsongkhapa's report of his own understanding of the relation of emptiness and dependent origination:

> Your present view about how you understand dependent origination is indeed extremely good. However, since there still remains some cognizance of illusion like reality, even if you were to gain ascertainment of this [final view of emptiness], it too could be dismantled. Therefore, you should continue to supplicate [Mañjuśrī] and engage in your own critical inquiry as well. Then, before too long, you will gain ascertainment. Also, remember that meditation deities reveal what is suited to the mental stage of the person, so do not be content with gaining some realization just once. For when you have gained insight into this view, convictions pertaining to both causality and emptiness will arise simultaneously. Furthermore, since what is to be abandoned as well as its antidote have both been realized to be rootless and groundless, even the notion that they are adventitious and exist as illusion-like dependent originations will come to be abandoned. And when the conventional reality of dependent origination is realized as mere nominal reality, there is no need to depend on some further reasoning to realize the ultimate truth, which is ineffable and space-like. This is because the very mind itself [realizing the nominal reality of

> dependent origination] will eliminate all doubts concerning the ultimate truth.[304]

At the end of this long letter, after commending Tsongkhapa for choosing to pursue intensive meditative practice in solitude, Rendawa expresses his wish that, barring ill health, they will see each other in three years' time. This suggests that at least this particular letter from Rendawa was sent during the time when Tsongkhapa was in the Wölkha Valley for his three-year retreat, before Tsongkhapa's great breakthrough in his view. Rendawa writes:

> It is most excellent that you have decided to devote yourself to virtuous deeds [by going on retreat]. There is no better offering to please the buddhas and the bodhisattvas than to engage in intensive meditative practice and shun all mundane activities, which is the heart of Dharma practice. Compared to this, the teaching and study being conducted today are mere similitudes of bringing about others' welfare. As for engaging in pseudoservice for others, I do not see that much meaning in performing empowerment rites as a means for gathering material things and giving reading transmissions and commentarial guides. Therefore, thinking that the teaching and study [of the great Buddhist texts] would be beneficial for the continuance of the Dharma, I told you earlier to continue in your teaching for the time being. Now, do not gather students other than those who are willing to dedicate their life to practice. Do not stay at one place for long; also, do not make efforts to establish a future base, such as by founding a monastery; and make sure that you keep your vow to complete your life in the mountains. If my health is good, let's seek the auspicious conditions for the two—the teacher and his pupil—to see each other within

> three years. Before that, if you want to write to me at Sakya about where you are and what you are doing, please do so. As for my own situation here, the two geshes will make this clear to you. This letter was sent on the tenth of the fourth month from the great learning center of glorious Sakya. May goodness and excellence prevail.[305]

So, what are we to make of this extremely interesting but chronologically uncertain exchange of letters? My own conjecture is this: Rendawa's lengthy letter, extensively cited above, was sent when Tsongkhapa was in the Wölkha Valley for his long period of meditative solitude, and part of what we read today in Tsongkhapa's "scroll," as well as his "reply" (contained in his *Miscellaneous Writings*), represents responses to this lctter from Rendawa. However, there are other parts of the scroll, including the opening section about the three principal elements of the path, that could only make sense as belonging to an earlier letter sent from Tsongkhapa to Rendawa. After all, Rendawa's lengthy letter opens with the acknowledgment and confirmation of that very statement about the three elements of the path.

But regardless of the exact timing of the letters, the point here is to give a taste of the depth of communication between Tsongkhapa and his teacher Rendawa on their evolving views on emptiness. Clearly, Tsongkhapa's views on emptiness had been shaped by his extensive study with Rendawa; it also appears, however, that Rendawa's own views on the subject may have later come to be affected by his prolonged engagement with Tsongkhapa's increasingly independent views.

How does Tsongkhapa's insight into the equation of emptiness and dependent origination compare to Rendawa's four progressive stages in the development of the view of emptiness? In his later, more substantive works, Tsongkhapa wrote extensively on the subject of emptiness and, in the process, changed the nature of Madhyamaka discourse in Tibet. In these writings, Tsongkhapa never explicitly addresses Rendawa's model of four progressive stages of the view. Perhaps Tsongkhapa wasn't particularly compelled by his teacher's delineation of these four stages and their perceived correlation to the philosophical standpoints of specific Indian Buddhist schools.

In Tsongkhapa's *Miscellaneous Writings*, however, there is a lengthy letter written in response to a series of questions posed by a student, one Jangchup Lama. One of the questions relates to Rendawa's four stages of the view, in particular the distinction between the last two. Jangchup Lama makes the acute observation that "If Rendawa's thought is that those who speak of mere illusions still possess some grasping at illusions, then this should apply equally to those who speak of mere designation and nominal reality, for they also would still possess some cognizance of the designations."[306] In response, Tsongkhapa defends his teacher's view and explains that the difference between the last two stages, in terms of the presence or absence of lingering apprehensions, has to do with the former still harboring some notion of objective intrinsic existence, while the latter rejects all objective standpoints involving any notion of intrinsic existence. But on this fourth stage, Tsongkhapa says that one cannot speak of a hierarchical difference among the following three: (1) understanding that all phenomena lack intrinsic existence and that they are like illusions, (2) perceiving all appearances to be devoid of intrinsic existence, and (3) cognizing the world of dependent origination as mere designations.[307] In brief, for Tsongkhapa, the understandings of dependent originations as "illusion-like" and as "mere designations" amount to the same thing.[308]

For Tsongkhapa, at the heart of the challenge posed by the Madhyamaka view of emptiness is this question: how do we square the regularity we perceive in the world of everyday experience, especially the regularity of cause and effect, with the fact that nothing possesses, even at the minutest level, any objective intrinsic existence? Over the next several years, in his authorship of substantial new works of writing, he would flesh out the far-reaching philosophical, ethical, and soteriological implications of his breakthrough on the view of emptiness as it relates to this question.

As the letters we have read here suggest, and as we shall see in the next chapter, a substantive change was taking place in Tsongkhapa's relationship with his teacher, Rendawa. Over time, the character of Rendawa's relationship with his pupil would shift increasingly toward collegiality. In his later letters, written when he was in retreat in Kyirong in western Tibet, Rendawa would even address Tsongkhapa as "the precious teacher Lobsang Drakpa" (*Lama Rinpoché Lobsang Drakpa*).[300] Yet Tsongkhapa's development from being Rendawa's student to being more of a colleague does not seem to have threatened their relationship. Until Rendawa's death, the two would maintain an ongoing communication on various topics of Dharma, including especially questions concerning Guhyasamāja, a system of the Highest Yoga tantra on which, as we shall see later, Tsongkhapa would become perhaps the greatest authority of his time.

To return to the narrative of Tsongkhapa's life—as noted earlier, the immediate effect of the breakthrough he experienced in the Wölkha Valley in the fall of 1397 appears to have been a powerful surge of joy, peace, and gratitude. The joy arose from the realization that finally he had arrived at the view hailed by the Buddha himself. He experienced an abiding sense of peace and freedom derived from "being at home," as it were, with the nature of reality, with no urge at all to resist, reify, or grasp at what he perceived, nor any desire for something beyond it. And he felt profound gratitude to the Buddha for having revealed the truth of emptiness and dependent origination. From this point onward, for Tsongkhapa, there would be no turning back insofar as the view of emptiness was concerned. His breakthrough would mark the beginning of an entirely original understanding of the philosophy of emptiness, not just for Tsong-khapa personally but for the entire tradition of Buddhism in Tibet.

CHAPTER 9

The Two Great Syntheses

FOLLOWING HIS BREAKTHROUGH on the view, in the fall of 1397, Tsongkhapa returned to his favorite hermitage of Lhading in the Wölkha Valley. He then moved his base to Garphuk, a hermitage closely associated with Gampopa, where he spent the winter of 1397 and the spring of 1398. Though mostly in retreat, Tsongkhapa sometimes gave formal teachings to the monks of the Wölkha Valley monasteries. He also conferred the oral instructions he had received from Mañjuśrī to a small group consisting of those who had accompanied him during the intensive retreat in the same valley a few years before.[310]

In the summer of 1398, Tsongkhapa and his students moved to E-Teura Hermitage, spending the rainy-season retreat there. During his stay, he gave teachings and conducted refuge ceremonies for the many lay devotees who came to see him.[311] It was during this summer at the hermitage that Tsongkhapa composed his first two works on lamrim, both written in the form of long letters of advice. The first is a prose work entitled "A Brief Presentation on the Stages of the Path" and sent to a senior monastic, Könchok Tsultrim.[312] The second is the well-known verse work entitled "Three Principal Elements of the Path," which was composed for Tsongkhapa's earliest attendant, Tsakho Ngawang Drakpa, who had returned to his native Gyalrong in eastern Tibet.

Milarepa's Song on "Critical Junctures"

One day during this period, while reading passages from Milarepa's songs, Tsongkhapa came across instructions on the practices to be undertaken at critical intersections, such as the following:

> If you wish to be free from the prison of existence,
> Then at the intersection of saṃsāra and nirvāṇa,
> You should establish the view of reality,
> Through introduction to the mode of being, the great seal.
> To train in the skills of mind and awareness,
> At the intersection of birth and death, the apparent world,
> You should strive on the paths of generation and completion.
> To help recognize the innate mind of clear light,
> At critical intersections while on the path,
> Implement the practices of ear-whispered instructions.
> To transform habits into aspects of the path,
> At the intersection of dream and sleep,
> Train in illusory body and clear light.[313]

Reading these lines brought Tsongkhapa a profound understanding of key features of the Highest Yoga tantra, especially what is known as the "nine mixings," which is central to the instructions of Milarepa's teacher Marpa on Guhyasamāja.[314] Contemplating these lines and delving into the sources that Milarepa so succinctly articulates, Tsongkhapa spent that fall and early winter at the Drakdong retreat in Wölkha, overlooking the valley of Dzingchi, devoting himself to the generation and completion stages of Guhyasamāja.

To Nyangpo Region and Return to the Holy City of Lhasa

In the new year of the Earth Rabbit (1399), Tsongkhapa once again visited the Maitreya Temple at Dzingchi. There, for fifteen days, he led a series of prayer ceremonies celebrating the Buddha's performance of the twin miracles at Śrāvastī. These ceremonies, as we shall see later, would be a rehearsal for the institution of the Great Prayer Festival at Lhasa.

That spring, Tsongkhapa taught a group of over two hundred monks, most notably Gyaltsap Darma Rinchen. It was during this teaching semester that Tsongkhapa first met Lodrö Gyaltsen, at the time only seven years old, who would later become one of his "great bodhisattva disciples."[315] Then, at the invitation of many devotees from the Nyangpo region, Tsongkhapa and his disciples visited Nyangpo Dangdo Monastery and observed the rainy-season retreat there.[316] By this time, the community of students traveling with him had grown to around two hundred. This meant that moving from one place to another had become a major undertaking. Two of Tsongkhapa's senior disciples, Gyaltsap and Dulzin Drakpa Gyaltsen, suggested that they start thinking about establishing a formal base for the community.

While at Nyangpo, Tsongkhapa received a visit from the abbot of Sangphu Monastery bearing a formal invitation from the local ruler of the Lhasa region, Neu Namkha Sangpo, who had earlier supported Tsongkhapa and his small meditating group in the Wölkha Valley and would later become his foremost benefactor. In the fall of 1399, Tsongkhapa traveled to Lhasa. He stayed at the Potala and conducted a series of teachings to a large gathering of monks from numerous monasteries in the Lhasa region, including the abbots of Sangphu, Nyethang Dewachen, Tsal Gungtsang, Gadong, Kyormolung, and Zulphu. Also in attendance was the

Sakya scholar Rongtön Shākya Gyaltsen (1367–1449).[317] Shākya Gyaltsen's philosophical writings would later play a key role in asserting Sakya standpoints on various issues that contrasted with those of Tsongkhapa and his immediate students, especially Gyaltsap. To this gathering of several hundred monastics, Tsongkhapa taught Kamalaśīla's *Light of the Middle Way* (*Madhyamakāloka*), texts on vinaya discipline, the stages of the path, and other topics.

It was also during this time in Lhasa that Shākya Sönam, later known also as the Radreng Bodhisattva, or Radrengwa, became a student of Tsongkhapa. Radrengwa was affected so profoundly by Tsongkhapa's lamrim teachings that it is said that bodhicitta arose spontaneously in him, leading Tsongkhapa to comment, "It was the bodhisattva Radrengwa who robbed my altruistic awakening mind!"[318]

A Reunion with Rendawa

The following year—1400, the Iron Dragon year—Tsongkhapa visted Gadong Monastery, where he taught the chapter on ethics from Asaṅga's *Bodhisattva Levels* (*Bodhisattvabhūmi*), *Fifty Verses on the Guru* (attributed to the second-century Buddhist master Aśvagoṣa), and explanations of the tantric vows. Toward the conclusion of this teaching series, Rendawa returned from western Tibet where he had been in the Kyirong Valley. Spending the summer rainy-season retreat at Taktsang Monastery in Tsang, Rendawa came to join Tsongkhapa at Gadong Monastery.

As Rendawa approached Gadong Monastery, he saw hundreds of monks waiting for him, all lined up on the two sides of the path leading to the monastery's main temple. Tsongkhapa wanted to receive his teacher with all the formality he could muster as a wandering monk. When Tsongkhapa prostrated to Rendawa, the latter tried to stop him from doing so.[319] Something had changed in the nature of their relationship. They were no longer simply teacher and student, and Rendawa was relating to Tsongkhapa more as a colleague than a student. At Gadong, Rendawa taught Candrakīrti's *Entering the Middle Way*, attracting over five hundred monks. During one of the sessions, a Sangphu geshé by the name of Könchok Sengé stood up and made the following plea:

> These days people speak of "Rendawa, the most learned one in Tsang," and "Tsongkhapa, the most learned one in Ü." Thus, the two of you, master and disciple, have become the custodians of the Buddha's teaching in Ü-Tsang. So this time, when you sit down to engage in deep conversations about topics such as the three vehicles and the tenets of the four philosophical schools, please do so not in private but in a public setting. This way, it will help clear the doubts of many of us who have keen interest in these subjects. Please turn the wheel of Dharma on the basis of expounding reasoning and drawing on scriptural citations in an authoritative way, so that what is and what is not becomes clear to us all. Thus, I appeal to master Rendawa not to say "I have to return to Gangbu-le Hermitage," and to master Lobsang Drakpa not to say "I have to return to Mount Odé Gungyal." Please remain with the monastic community of Ü-Tsang and engage extensively in serving the Dharma.[320]

Despite this public appeal, after the teaching series was over, Rendawa and Tsongkhapa indeed felt their great fondness for solitary places and so departed for Radreng, a monastery founded by Dromtönpa in 1056 as the primary seat of the Kadam school. The two masters were accompanied by a large number of monastics. They spent the winter of 1400 at Radreng Monastery.

While in retreat at Radreng, Rendawa taught the monks Nāgārjuna's *Five Stages of Completion*, a seminal work on the completion stage of Guhyasamāja tantra. He further gave guidance on the view of emptiness and instructed them in mind training. After the retreat, he gave formal lectures on Āryadeva's *Four Hundred Stanzas on the Middle Way* and Nāgārjuna's *Sixty Stanzas of Reasoning*.

Tsongkhapa, for his part, gave a detailed instruction on how to cultivate tranquility, drawing on Maitreya's *Ornament of Mahāyāna Sūtras* and *Differentiation of the Middle and Extremes*, as well as Asaṅga's *Compendium of Abhidharma* and *Śrāvaka Levels*.[321] Over many days, through a sequence of guided instructions, Tsongkhapa had the entire congregation undertake śamatha meditations step by step, so that by the end of the course some of the monks had gained profound experiences of tranquility.

In their private time, Rendawa and Tsongkhapa engaged in a series of conversations, sharing with each other their understandings, practices, and experiences. By then, as a result of the exchanges he had had with Tsongkhapa over the last few years, Rendawa's understanding of the view of emptiness appeared to have undergone some transformation. Thus, during this quiet time at Radreng, Rendawa received from Tsongkhapa an extensive exposition of the root tantra of Guhyasamāja and a detailed explanation of Candrakīrti's Guhyasamāja tantra, entitled *The Clear Lamp* (*Pradīpodyotana*), as well as Tsongkhapa's interpretation of Nāgārjuna's *Treatise on the Middle Way*.[322]

Also while at Radreng, Tsongkhapa received an invitation from Drigung Chökyi Gyalpo (1335–1407), the patriarch of the Drigung Kagyü lineage, whom he had first met when he arrived in central Tibet as a teenager. Thus, in the spring of 1401 (the Iron Snake year), Tsongkhapa once again returned to Drigung Thil Monastery. At Drigung, the patriarch had arranged for Tsongkhapa's room to be next to his atop the main temple. Taking their tea and meals together,

Tsongkhapa and the Drigung master had extended opportunities to engage in conversations about each other's Dharma practice and their understandings and experiences.[323] While Tsongkhapa conducted numerous formal teachings for the monks of Drigung, he himself received from Drigung Chöjé instructions on the six yogas of Nāropa and Mahāmudrā. At the request of senior members of the monastery, Tsongkhapa composed a praise to the Drigung patriarch.[324] He also composed the much-loved aspirational prayer, known as a prayer for the flourishing of "Goodness at the Beginning, the Middle, and the End." It concludes with this series of aspirations:

> Whoever sees or hears
> Or contemplates these prayers,
> May they never be discouraged
> In seeking the bodhisattva's amazing aspirations.
> By praying with such expansive thought
> Created from the power of pure intention,
> May I achieve the perfection of prayers
> And fulfill the wishes of all sentient beings.[325]

Today, this prayer is memorized by every monk of the Geluk school; it is chanted on important occasions such as the Great Prayer Festival and following a person's death. It was during this visit to Drigung Thil that many of the senior members of the Drigung lineage, most notably Dhöndrup Gyalpo, Drakpa Gyaltsen, and Tashi Rinchen, became students and devotees of Tsongkhapa.

A Rare Gathering at Namtsé Deng Monastery

While at Radreng, Rendawa and Tsongkhapa had received a personal invitation from Lochen Kyapchok Palsang to partake in a rare gathering at Namtsé Deng Monastery. Lochen was at that time based at this ancient monastery, which had been founded by Ar Jangchup Yeshé (eleventh century), a pioneering authority on Perfection of Wisdom studies in Tibet. After his brief visit to Drigung Thil, Tsongkhapa met up with Rendawa so that they could make the journey together.

On the way, at the invitation of Taklung Rinpoché Tashi Peltsek (1359–1424), the two masters visited Taklung Monastery. This is the seat of the Taklung Kagyü lineage, which was founded by Taklung Thangpa Tashi Pal in the twelfth century. Many people, both monastics and lay, came to greet the two famous monks.[326] Rendawa and Tsongkhapa met with Taklung Rinpoché, the head of the monastery. Over a cup of tea, they discussed important points of Dharma and spoke about the life of their mutual acquaintance, the fifth Karmapa, Deshin Shekpa. The two visiting teachers also gave formal teachings to the monastic community. As they were leaving, Taklung Rinpoché turned to Tsongkhapa and told him, "The reach of your activities will be equal to the sky itself. So please serve the tradition of the generation-stage and completion-stage teachings of Lord Marpa's lineage."[327]

From Taklung the two masters headed toward Namtsé Deng Monastery to join Lochen Kyapchok Palsang and observe the rainy-season retreat (summer 1401). Over six hundred monks had gathered to be part of this retreat, and the local ruler, Yönten Gyatso, served as the benefactor during the entire period. In the morning sessions, Lochen taught monastic discipline, Śāntideva's *Bodhicaryāvatāra*, Maitreya's *Sublime Continuum*, Candrakīrti's *Entering the Middle Way*, mind training, and the Hevajra tantra. During the early afternoon sessions, Rendawa taught monastic discipline, Nāgārjuna's *Treatise on the Middle Way*, Candrakīrti's *Entering the Middle Way*, the Guhyasamāja tantra, and a guide to the view of emptiness. In the late afternoon sessions, Tsongkhapa gave an extensive exposition of Guṇaprabha's *Root Lines on Vinaya*, the notes of which were compiled by Gyaltsap and later published as *Namtsé Deng Precepts of the Fully Ordained Monk*.[328]

On several occasions, "the three Dharma masters" held conversations covering a wide range of topics pertaining to Buddhist thought and practice, and these discussions were open to all who had gathered for the retreat. During some of these dialogues, Karma Könshön, a well-known Karma Kagyü scholar and a disciple of Karmapa Rolpai Dorjé (1340–83), served as a lead discussant as well. Calling both Rendawa and Tsongkhapa as witnesses, Karma Könshön challenged Lochen to a debate on emptiness, making the following opening statement:

> Some of Lochen's students seem to be saying that "conventional existence does not constitute existence," which means they are defying the validity of the law of karma. In fact, I could offer the same debate challenge to Rendawa as well. This time, I am not going to debate with the Dharma master Lobsang Drakpa [Tsongkhapa]. Because he generated the excellent mind of bodhicitta a long time ago, he does not react with attachment or aversion even toward defective philosophical views. As for Rendawa, it is thanks to him that today in this Land of Snows the word *Madhyamaka* falls from people's mouths and into people's ears. Before [Rendawa], there was a Madhyamaka corpse at Thangsak Monastery. Apart from this, "Madhyamaka" was nowhere to be heard.... In brief, if all the great minds of Ü-Tsang were to gather in one place, then in addition to the three masters [gathered here], the translator of Drakpa Gyaltsen should be here as well. Now if all four were to be present, then we would have the perfect gathering, with no one missing and no one extra.[329]

There is no textual record to tell us whether Lochen in fact took up the debate challenge or, if he did, what the result was.[330]

In any case, with the three great Dharma masters of Ü-Tsang[331] leading the assembly in formal teachings, Dharma discussions, and strict observance of monastic discipline, this summer retreat helped establish an enduring culture in Tibet of appreciation for the minute details of the monastic vows as well as the various rites for their regular renewal and restoration.

It was during this summer at Namtsé Deng that Tsongkhapa composed a four-line praise of Rendawa and offered it to the master. Rendawa then changed a few words and gave it back to Tsongkhapa, stating that the praise was actually more fitting for Tsongkhapa himself. In this slightly revised version, the prayer reads:

> You are Avalokiteśvara, great treasury of objectless compassion;
> You are Mañjuśrī, embodiment of stainless wisdom;
> You are the crown jewel among the learned of the Land of Snows;
> I supplicate at your feet, O Lobsang Drakpa.[332]

Later, a third line, "You are Vajrapāṇi, destroyer of all dark forces," was added so that Tsongkhapa could be praised as the embodiment of all three aspects of the Buddha's omniscient mind: compassion, wisdom, and power. Today, this is the official supplication prayer to Tsongkhapa chanted by all members of the Geluk school. Known as *Miktsema*, a name derived from three key syllables of the first line, this five-line prayer became the basis for an entire genre of guru yoga practices connected with Tsongkhapa.

With Lochen at Lion Cliff Hermitage

In the fall of 1401, after the end of the rainy-season retreat at Namtsé Deng, Rendawa returned to Tsang, while Tsongkhapa and Lochen, followed by a large number of monks, returned to Radreng. There they established their retreat at Drak Sengé ("Lion Cliffs"), a ridge overlooking the main monastery, which contains the meditation caves used by Dromtönpa.[333]

While at Radreng, Tsongkhapa received the sad news of the passing of Lhodrak Drupchen, the mystic from whom he had received many of the transmissions of Atiśa's lamrim instructions. Drupchen was seventy-five when he passed away at his hermitage.

One day, in the course of a chat, Lochen brought up the subject of how Tsongkhapa and Rendawa had once spent a few months in retreat here at Radreng and had engaged in a series of deep discussions of Dharma.

"What special attributes does Rendawa have?" asked Lochen.

"Obviously," Tsongkhapa replied, "all the qualities of a teacher—being learned, diligent in practice, and kind, as well as never divorced from meditative practice—are present in the master."

Persisting, Lochen said, "This time, do tell me something about Rendawa that is personal."

"Let me give you a simple example," Tsongkhapa replied.

He then told Lochen that ever since he had met Rendawa, he had not experienced even a single moment of anger. *That* had been the impact of Rendawa on him, he said. Relating this, Tsongkhapa was moved to tears. Seeing this, Lochen too had tears in his eyes.[334]

During their long retreat at Radreng, Lochen taught Middle Way philosophy to the monks while Tsongkhapa gave extensive instructions on lamrim. In the course of conducting this teaching on Atiśa's instruction, Tsongkhapa spent several days in intensive prayer in front of the famed statue of Atiśa, believed to have been scuplted by Dromptönpa himself as his master's portrait. At some point during these prayer sessions, Tsongkhapa had visions of the entire lineage of teachers, going all the way back to the original source, the Buddha, and all the way up to his own teacher, the

Lhodrak mystic, Drupchen Namkha Gyaltsen. Eventually, the three Kadam brothers—Potowa, Sharawa, and Phuchungwa—dissolved into master Atiśa, who placed his right hand on Tsongkhapa's head and made the following statement: "Work extensively for the Dharma, and I will support you in your quest for enlightenment and service to sentient beings."[335]

Tsongkhapa took this vision as an important indication of his role in disseminating Atiśa's teaching and legacy, especially his lamrim instructions. While all of this was happening, because of the extensive teachings Tsongkhapa had given on Atiśa's instructions on the stages of the path, many people independently requested Tsongkhapa to compose a text that would present his teachings on the topic. Prominent among those who made the requests were Lochen; the abbot of Sangphu Monastery, Könchok Tsultrim; and the grand abbot of Zulphu Monastery, Könchok Palsang.

Composing *The Great Treatise on the Stages of the Path*

Thus, in the fall of 1401 (the Iron Snake year), when Tsongkhapa was forty-four years old, he began the composition of what would become his most influential work, *The Great Treatise on the Stages of the Path to Enlightenment* (known in Tibetan by its shorter title *Lamrim Chenmo*). At Tsongkhapa's request, the statue of Atiśa made by Dromtönpa was brought into his room. Every morning Tsongkhapa would pray in front of this image and then proceed with his writing. It was also in the presence of this precious statue that Tsongkhapa wrote the prayer to the lineage masters of the stages of the path, a metrical hymn of invocation chanted to this day at the start of every formal teaching on lamrim.

For a while the writing went smoothly, but after Tsongkhapa completed the section on tranquility and was thinking about writing the final part, the section on the cultivation of insight and the view of emptiness, he began to have qualms. Given the difficult nature of the topic, he wondered if a lengthy exposition of the view of emptiness in this treatise would be of any real benefit to his readers.[336] As he was struggling with this question, he experienced a vision of Mañjuśrī, who urged him to continue with his writing and assured him that the insight section would be of benefit to his readers. Tsongkhapa, therefore, made fervent supplications to his meditation deity and to the lineage masters.

One day, as he was writing about some of the more challenging aspects of the view of emptiness, he had a vision of the names of the twenty types of emptiness in the form of silver characters standing vertically in space in front of him, as if they were inscribed on a parchment.[337] Encouraged and inspired, Tsongkhapa finished the final section of the text, and thus in 1402, Tsongkhapa completed his *Great Treatise*—in just over a year.

Tsongkhapa's *Great Treatise* was composed as a systematic presentation of all the stages of the path to enlightenment, based specifically on instructions appropriate to "the trainees of the three capacities"—beginning, intermediate, and advanced—as thematized in Atiśa's *Lamp for the Path to Enlightenment*. An ambitious work, *The Great Treatise* guides the student from the beginner's stage through initial awakening of their enthusiasm for the Dharma and up to the attainment of insight and buddhahood. In its scope and ambition, it is perhaps best compared to Buddhaghoṣa's *Path of Purification* (*Visuddhimagga*), a fifth-century Theravāda Buddhist classic still recognized as the most comprehensive map of the path to enlightenment according to the Buddhist traditions of Sri Lanka and Southeast Asia.

Although *The Great Treatise* sits comfortably in the stages-of-the-path genre, it can also be read as "an independent *summa* and synthesis of Buddhist ethical, religious, and philosophical thought and practice."[338] The role of *The Great Treatise* as a grand synthesis becomes clear if we look at what Tsongkhapa calls the four benefits of his text, which helps us to (1) recognize all of the Buddha's teachings to be free of contradictions, (2) perceive all scriptures as personal instructions, (3) easily discover the enlightened intention of the buddhas, and (4) guard against committing the negative deed of disparaging the Dharma. Years later, in a versified work articulating the essential points of lamrim based on his own practice, Tsongkhapa would describe the lamrim instruction in this way:

> Since it fulfills all the wishes of beings without exception,
> It is the king of kings among all quintessential instructions;
> Since it gathers into it thousands of excellent rivers of treatises,
> It is as well the ocean of most glorious well-uttered
> insights.[339]

The Scope and Structure of *The Great Treatise*

The Great Treatise is broadly structured into two parts: preliminary matters and the actual instruction on how to progress through the stages of the path. The preliminaries include a short biographical sketch of Atiśa, the source of the instruction, the greatness of the lamrim teachings, and how to both teach and listen to the instructions. The actual instruction is divided into two parts: how to rely on a spiritual mentor and how to engage in training the mind on the path on that basis.

The actual instruction on the path is structured within beginning, intermediate, and advanced capacities. This main part of the treatise, however, opens with a lengthy contemplation of the rare opportunities for Dharma practice accorded to us as human beings. The aim here is to inspire us to appreciate our current status and to drive home the rarity of this opportunity so that our human existence is not squandered. The text then defines each of the three capacities, explaining how anyone can progress through the three stages.

Briefly, the trainees of the three scopes are differentiated both by their primary goals and by their capacities. A trainee of beginning capacity is mainly concerned with ensuring a fortunate rebirth; one of intermediate capacity is mainly concerned with attaining freedom from cyclic existence; and one of highest capacity seeks to attain buddhahood for the benefit of all beings. The main focus of practice differs accordingly for each type of trainee. For those of beginning capacity, the main practice is basic morality and observance of the law of karma. For those of intermediate capacity, the main practice is the threefold training in morality, meditation, and wisdom. For those of the highest capacity, the primary focus of practice is the six perfections: generosity, morality, forbearance, diligence, concentration, and wisdom. Of these three types of trainee, the presentation of the practices of the person of the highest capacity takes up more than two-thirds of the text, with the section on insight and emptiness effectively forming an entire volume in itself.

The section on the practices for those of the highest capacity opens with a masterful presentation of the cultivation of universal compassion and bodhicitta. Tsongkhapa outlines what he sees as two different approaches to cultivating compassion and bodhicitta—one emphasized in the writings of Asaṅga, Kamalaśīla, and Atiśa, the other emphasized especially in Śāntideva's *Bodhicaryāvatāra*—presenting the steps through which each of the two approaches culminates in the arising of an uncontrived, spontaneous bodhicitta. Over time, this section on developing the intention and attitude of the practitioner of highest capacity became a definitive reference on the meditative cultivation of compassion and bodhicitta and the understanding of their underlying psychology.

Following the presentation on compassion and bodhicitta, Tsongkhapa turns to the first four perfections—generosity, morality, forbearance, and diligence—drawing extensively on Āryaśūra's *Summary of the Perfections* (*Pāramitāsamāsa*), Śāntideva's *Bodhicaryāvatāra*, and Maitreya's *Ornament of Mahāyāna Sūtras*. The last two perfections, concentration and wisdom, then receive extensive treatment, with the two correlated to the practices for cultivating tranquility (*śamatha*) and insight (*vipaśyanā*).

Contemporary scholar David Ruegg writes that the section on concentration is "nothing less than a searching and penetrating treatise on the subject of tranquility involving both bodily and mental calm.... [It] examines śamatha in the greatest detail with the view of defining its relation to insight and to establishing just how these two factors alternate at certain stages of practice and then mutually reinforce each other."[340] This observation, that this section on concentration is nothing short of a definitive treatise on the subject of tranquility, appears to have been shared by important Tibetan figures of the time. Gyaltsap, for example, simply refers his readers to this section of *The Great Treatise* when it comes to instructions on the cultivation of śamatha.[341]

The topics covered in Tsongkhapa's analysis of the fifth perfection include the definition, cultivation, and application of such faculties as attention (*manasikāra*), mindfulness (*smṛti*), meta-awareness (*saṃprajanya*), equanimity (*upekṣa*), natural quietitude (*praśaṭhavāhita*), mental pliability (*praśrabdhi*), and nonconceptuality (*nirvikalpitā*).

The actual instruction for cultivating tranquility is structured within a framework that uses Asaṅga's five hindrances and their eight antidotes: laziness, antidoted by confidence, aspiration, effort, and pliancy; forgetting the object of meditation, antidoted by mindfulness; laxity and excitation, antidoted by meta-awareness;

nonapplication of the antidotes, to be countered by intention to apply the antidotes; and inappropriate application, to be countered by equanimity. Tsongkhapa also makes use of the nine stages of attentional development—direct attention, continuous attention, resurgent attention, close attention, tamed attention, pacified attention, fully pacified attention, single-pointed attention, and balanced attention—found especially in Asaṅga's *Śrāvaka Levels*.[342] Two other important sources cited extensively in this section are the *Saṃdhinirmocana Sūtra* and Ratnākaraśānti's *Instructions on the Perfection of Wisdom*.

With regard to tranquility, Tsongkhapa was known for his amazing powers of concentration: his close attendants observed that once in meditative state, the master became oblivious to whatever might be happening around him. When asked when he started being like this, Tsongkhapa replied that this kind of absorption began during the Wölkha Valley retreat. "However," he continued, "I had this ability to be totally absorbed when engaged in a discursive contemplation of the view of emptiness much earlier."[343]

The final perfection, wisdom, is explored in *The Great Treatise* in the context of the cultivation of insight into emptiness, the ultimate nature of reality. Referred to as "The Great Treatise on Insight" (*Lhakthong chenmo*), this section of the text is often treated as an independent work on the philosophy of emptiness. Ruegg notes that the text is "concerned with the object of vipaśyanā, namely the theory of emptiness in its twin aspects of absence of self-nature or self-existence—i.e., the 'aseitas' of any entity posited as hypostatically established—and origination in dependence as expounded by Nāgārjuna and his great successors in the Madhyamaka school."[344]

Tsongkhapa begins this section with a discussion of how to gather the conditions essential for the cultivation of insight, especially insight into emptiness. These include, most important, cultivating a deep understanding of the truth of emptiness as expounded by Nāgārjuna and his principal interpreters, especially Buddhapālita and Candrakīrti.

The actual presentation on emptiness is then made in terms of three main points: (1) identifying what is being negated within the logic of emptiness, (2) the means by which such an object is negated, and (3) how the view of emptiness arises on the basis of applying such a method. In the first part, Tsongkhapa explores in great detail the critical importance of clearly delineating what is to be negated, avoiding the extremes of overnegation or undernegation. Central to the avoidance of overnegation, he argues, is the differentiation between two categorically distinct forms of analysis and their respective domains of discourse, namely, that of the ultimate truth and that of the conventional or relative truth.[345]

In the second part, exploring the method by which emptiness is established, Tsongkhapa analyzes in great detail the differences between what came to be referred to by Tibetans as Prāsaṅgika Madhyamaka and Svātantrika Madhyamaka. This is a topic he would return to and develop further in a subsequent work focused more specifically on questions of hermeneutics.

The third and final part of the presentation on insight contains a fine-grained explanation of emptiness in terms of the two forms of selflessness—that of the person and that of phenomena—as well as how familiarity with these two forms of selflessness results in the eradication of afflictions rooted in fundamental ignorance.

Tsongkhapa concludes the insight section with a lucid discourse on how the union of tranquility and insight arises through combined cultivation of two qualitatively different types of meditation—discursive analytic meditation and absorptive placement meditation. Years later, reading the insight section of Tsongkhapa's *Great Treatise*, Gö Lotsawa Shönu Pal, the noted Kagyü teacher and author of the influential historical work *The Blue Annals*, would remark that therein "the entirety of the Madhyamaka body is found complete."[346]

The Great Treatise concludes with a brief summary of the entire path to enlightenment as outlined in the treatise and then connects this summary with the trainee's entry into the Vajrayāna path. In this way, Tsongkhapa follows the structure of Atiśa's *Lamp for the Path to Enlightenment*, which states that, after having trained in all the aspects of the common path, the advanced student should enter the swift path of Tantra. Tsongkhapa concludes the treatise with these verses of aspiration:

> Through the twin collections gathered with prolonged efforts,
> [Merit and wisdom] as vast as expansive space,
> May I become a buddha, a savior for all those beings
> Whose minds' eyes have been blinded by ignorance.
> Throughout all my lives until I reach such a point,
> May I be sustained by Mañjuśrī with compassion,
> And, finding the supreme path complete in all the stages,
> May I please the buddhas through my meditative practice.
> Whatever essential points of the path I have realized,
> May I, stirred by forceful compassion, skillfully
> Dispel the darkness that lies within beings' minds,
> And may I uphold the Buddha's teaching for a long time.
> In places where the supreme precious teaching has not spread
> Or where it has declined though once flourishing,
> With my mind powerfully moved by great compassion,
> May I illuminate this treasure of happiness and benefit.
> May this treatise on the stages of the path to enlightenment,
> Arisen from the wondrous deeds of the buddhas and
> bodhisattvas,

Bring glory to the minds of those who seek liberation,
And may they long uphold the enlightened deeds of the
buddhas.
May everyone, both human and nonhuman, who helps
support
The cultivation of the excellent path and helps clear away the
obstacles,
Never be separated through all their lives
From the perfect path praised by the buddhas.
For my part, when I strive to engage in the supreme vehicle
Through the tenfold activities of Dharma practice,
May I always be aided by those who are powerful,
And may the ocean of goodness pervade all the directions.[347]

Additional Writing and Teaching at Radreng

Tsongkhapa carried forward the momentum of his writing even after the completion of *The Great Treatise*. He composed key texts on ethics, including an exposition of the chapter on bodhisattva ethics from Asaṅga's *Bodhisattva Levels*,[348] an extensive presentation on the tantric precepts entitled *Sheaves of Attainment*, and a commentary on Aśvagoṣa's *Fifty Verses on the Guru*. Tsongkhapa had previously authored seminal works on monastic discipline and basic ethics. Now, with these texts focused specifically on bodhisattva ethics, tantric precepts, and norms concerning relationship with one's guru, Tsongkhapa had effectively created adequate resources on the important question of the relationship between what the Tibetan tradition refers to as the three vows or codes (*domsum*). At the heart of this matter is the question of how three sets of vows (monastic, bodhisattva, and tantric) reside without conflict within a single practitioner—for instance, a monk yogi. In the concluding verses of his exposition of bodhisattva ethics, for example, Tsongkhapa speaks of how there is no path to buddhahood without engagement in the bodhisattva practices, and it is only by securing a firm foundation in the six perfections of the Sūtra path and bringing in the added dimension of the Tantra path that one can legitimately hope to attain buddhahood. Such an approach alone represents the excellent path, and everything else, Tsongkhapa writes, is mere chatter "to please the childish."[349]

Over the months during which Tsongkhapa was composing *The Great Treatise*, he told some twenty-five of his closest disciples, including Dülzin Drakpa Gyaltsen, that, as he now wished to give them formal Vajrayāna teachings, they should receive empowerments of Highest Yoga tantra from Lochen. As advised, they received from Lochen the full empowerment of Guhyasamāja.[350]

Lochen appears to have been at Radreng throughout the writing of *The Great Treatise*. Deeply impressed by Tsongkhapa's treatise, and taking a copy with him, he returned to Tsang Province.[351] As acknowledged in Tsongkhapa's colophon, the scribe for *The Great Treatise* was a student by the name of Sönam Sangpo, who would serve as Tsongkhapa's scribe for other major works as well. (Since the tradition of woodblock printing had not taken root in Tibet at this time, Tsongkhapa's scribe must have been working pretty much full time to produced copies of *The Great Treatise* to be offered to others.) Tsongkhapa himself stayed at Radreng for another year, altogether spending over two years at the hermitage, writing, meditating, and teaching his newly completed treatise.

It was at Radreng during this period of teaching that Palden Dhöndrup (who later founded several important monasteries and become the first lama in the Takphu reincarnation lineage) received full ordination from Tsongkhapa.[352] It was also at Radreng, sometime in the Water Horse year (1402), that Gungru Gyaltsen Sangpo became Tsongkhapa's student. He was eighteen years old when he first attended Tsongkhapa's teachings at Radreng.[353] Seven years later, Gungru would join Tsongkhapa's community and would remain with the master until the latter's death in 1419. He took full ordination from Tsongkhapa at Ganden in 1412,[354] composed an influential commentary on Tsongkhapa's autobiographical poem, wrote philosophical texts including expositions of major Indian classics, and served as the third abbot of Sera Monastery.

During his long stay at Radreng, Tsongkhapa taught Śāntideva's *Compendium of Training* (*Śikṣasamuccāya*), and the notes from this teaching were later compiled by Jamyang Chöjé as a major aid to understanding that important text. Tsongkhapa also gave an extended exposition of Maitreya's *Ornament of Realizations*, relating the key sections of the *Ornament* to their corresponding passages in the Perfection of Wisdom scriptures. During this particular teaching, Tsongkhapa assigned Gyaltsap to take notes, and he later authorized Gyaltsap to use these notes to compose a new commentary on Maitreya's text. Creating an updated version of his understanding of the *Ornament* and the Perfection of Wisdom scriptures was especially important to Tsongkhapa because the parts dealing with the view of emptiness in his much-admired earlier commentary, *The Golden Rosary*, were at odds with his later, mature view.[355]

Years later, in accordance with the master's advice, Gyaltsap would compose *Heart Ornament: An Exposition of the Ornament of Realizations*, a treatise that would become the standard text on Perfection of Wisdom studies in all Geluk centers of learning. Though based on Tsongkhapa's extensive instructions, Gyaltsap's work is by any standard an independent text presenting in depth his own careful reading and understanding of Maitreya's root text as well as its extensive Indian commentarial literature. He would also author a more practical text on how to apply the stages of realizations presented in Maitreya's *Ornament* in one's personal practice, thus directly relating Maitreya's text to the key instructions of Tsongkhapa's *Great Treatise*.[356]

During the Tibetan new year of the Wood Monkey (1404), right at the end of this long stay at Radreng, Tsongkhapa organized another extensive prayer festival, lasting fifteen days, celebrating the Buddha's miracles at Śrāvastī.

In Wön Dechen

After the prayer festival, Tsongkhapa and his community moved to Lhaphu Gönsar Monastery, north of the site of their own future Ganden Monastery. There, Tsongkhapa gave an extensive teaching on Dharmakīrti's *Exposition of Valid Cognition*, with emphasis on how Dharmakīrti's insights, especially his formal system of inference, his philosophy of language, and his epistemology, are directly relevant to one's understanding of the central issues of Buddhist thought and practice. This special teaching on epistemology, it is said, was responsible for silencing the widespread view that epistemological texts, such as those of Dharmakīrti, were mere polemical works with no relevance or value for actual Dharma practice.[357] The notes taken by Gyaltsap from this series of lectures on Dharmakīrti's primer were later compiled and included in Tsongkhapa's collected works.

In response to repeated invitations from the Phagdru ruler, Miwang Drakpa Gyaltsen, Tsongkhapa visited Wön Dechen, where he and his students observed that year's rainy-season retreat. During that summer he gave teachings on his newly composed *Great Treatise* as well as lectures on Madhyamaka philosophy and on pramāṇa epistemology. It was at Wön that the famed meditator Götruk Repa (b. 1364), met Tsongkhapa and received teachings, especially on the stages of the path. Moved to see the tattered clothes the meditator was wearing, Tsongkhapa gave him one of his own *tögak*, the vest worn by Tibetan monks.[358]

After the rainy-season retreat, Tsongkhapa and his students returned to his favorite hermitage, Jampa Ling in the Wölkha Valley. There, at the request of his students, he taught the stages of the path, as well as the generation and completion stages of Highest Yoga tantra.

A Great Treatise on the Vajrayāna Path

During the winter of 1404, when Tsongkhapa and his close disciples were in strict retreat at Wölkha, he once again had a vision of Mañjuśrī. At his deity's urging, Tsongkhapa composed his influential commentary on Nāgabodhi's *Guhyasamājasādhana-vyavasthāli*, a major text on the practice of the Guhyasamāja tantra. In the opening section of his text, Tsongkhapa acknowledges his debt to Mañjuśrī, stating that it is thanks to the deity's kindness that his mind has been satiated by the taste of the great bliss that is engendered by deepened understanding of the essential points of tantra.[359] Composing this text marked a turning point in Tsongkhapa's writing career, which until then had been concerned primarily with non-Vajrayāna topics. He would later tell some of his close students:

> At that time, it had in fact been over ten years since I had gained clear and in-depth understanding of the five stages of completion in general and, more specifically, the essential points of the root and explanatory tantras of Guhyasamāja, such as, in particular, the cultivation of the third stage of illusory body, based especially on the unique explanations of Nāgārjuna and his disciples. Until that point, however,

> I did not have the courage to speak about these matters. But now I have begun speaking of them.[360]

Now that Tsongkhapa had formally started to teach Vajrayāna, especially Highest Yoga tantra, requests began pouring in to compose a major synthesis on tantra, one akin to his *Great Treatise on the Stages of the Path*. In particular, Lochen Kyapchok Palsang, who had been so impressed by Tsongkhapa's *Great Treatise*, sent repeated requests to the master to compose such a definitive synthesis on tantra. According to the colophon of *Great Treatise on the Stages of the Path of Tantra*, Tsongkhapa was urged also by the Phagdru religious patriarch Chenga Sönam Sangpo (1368–1415) to compose "an extensive exposition of the stages of the path of tantra."[361]

Tsongkhapa acceded to these requests, and in the Wood Bird year of 1405, when he was forty-eight, he completed his second great treatise. Like its counterpart on the stages of the path, the treatise on tantra is an ambitious work, both in scope and in length. Containing fourteen chapters and running over four hundred folios (approximately six hundred pages) in length, it begins with a lengthy section situating the teachings and the path of tantra within the larger framework of the Buddhist path to enlightenment. The body of the text is structured around the four classes of tantra, with the longest part, comprising more than three quarters of the total, covering the essential points of the Highest Yoga tantra. What is remarkable about Tsongkhapa's synthesis is how it brings together a vast array of tantric material, drawn from diverse approaches and distinct instructional lineages, into a coherent system that clearly outlines the broad structures of the tantric path.[362]

Seeing these two great treatises, Bodong Choklé Namgyal (1376–1451), a rising scholar who would later become the most prolific of all Tibetan authors (with collected works amounting to some 137 volumes), wrote a letter in verse to Tsongkhapa containing the following lines:

> Your liberating activities both great and most great
> I hear about even as I live far from you.
> I have seen your two treatises, on Perfection and Tantra.
> This too brought joy to my mind.
> As for me, if I am not called in the near future
> By time's messenger to life's other shore,
> I wish to see you, the Buddha's emanation,
> And meet with the learned adepts residing with you.
> My mind is focused single-pointedly
> On traveling to you and listening to your words,
> Just as Sadāprarudita sought the perfection of wisdom.[363]

Despite Bodong's express wish to see Tsongkhapa, the two would know of each other only by reputation and would never meet.

Later biographers saw the composition of *The Great Treatise on Tantra* as the fulfillment of a prophecy made more than a decade earlier by the mahāsiddhas in a vision Tsongkhapa experienced at Gya Sokphu, to the effect that if he were to author a treatise based on Abhyākaragupta's writings, it would bring great benefit to the Dharma.[364] *The Great Treatise on Tantra* would later become a major source text and a model for subsequent Tibetan masters writing on tantra, not just among the Geluk. Tsongkhapa himself would send copies of the two, especially *The Great Treatise on the Stages of the Path*, to his far-flung students, such as Tsakho Ngawang Drakpa, who had returned to his native eastern Tibet.

In all, Tsongkhapa stayed for two years in the Wön Dechen area during this visit. In addition to teaching his new *Great Treatise on Tantra*, he gave teachings on the entire corpus of Cakrasaṃvara, a major class of Highest Yoga tantra, which had been translated into

Tibetan. From then on, that region came to be known as Sangak Nang, "Home of the Tantras." During these extensive teachings, it is said, some signs of obstacles appeared, including portents of the untimely death of two members of Tsongkhapa's wandering monastic community. To counter these obstacles, Tsongkhapa and a few of his closest students observed a strict retreat and performed various rites. During this retreat, Tsongkhapa also composed his major sādhana of Vajrabhairava, along with its fire-offering rite.[365] That winter of 1405, Tsongkhapa stayed at the Jangchup Ling Hermitage in Wölkha and taught the monks there his recently completed *Great Treatise on Tantra*.

Now, with these two grand syntheses in place—one on the general Mahāyāna path, the so-called Sūtra system, and the other on Tantra, or Vajrayāna—Tsongkhapa's students had two standard treatises to use to organize their understanding and practice. As we shall see, evidence suggests that both syntheses were commissioned to woodblock printers, so that they spread quite fast and widely, much more so than mere manuscripts could.[366]

CHAPTER 10

Hermeneutics and Philosophical Analysis

IN THE SPRING of the Fire Pig year of 1406, Tsongkhapa went to Kyishö, the lower region of the Kyichu River near Lhasa. While there, he and his community of students were supported by the Neu ruler of the region, Namkha Sangpo, and his family, who provided for their everyday needs. To observe the rainy-season retreat that summer, Tsongkhapa moved to Sera Chöding, a small hermitage on the ridge of a hill. One day the great monastic university of Sera would be founded by Jamchen Chöjé, an important student of Tsongkhapa, on the slopes of that same hill.

During this stay at Sera Chöding, Tsongkhapa met someone who would later play a critical role in consolidating his legacy. Khedrup Gelek Palsang (1385–1438) would help to define Tsongkhapa's followers as a distinct school of Tibetan Buddhism called Geluk—literally, "the tradition of Geden (spelled also as Ganden) Monastery." A brilliant young scholar from Sakya who, according to some early sources, defeated the great Bodong Choklé Namgyal in a debate in 1400, Khedrup in 1406 was twenty-eight and in the midst of his formal debate rounds, traveling from one monastery to another in central Tibet to obtain his qualification as a kachupa.[367] Bearing a formal letter of introduction from Rendawa, Khedrup had come to see Tsongkhapa, who was then forty-nine years old.

The night before he met Tsongkhapa, Khedrup had an unusual dream in which it was as if a thick blanket of darkness had descended on the earth and left him walking in the dark. He felt disoriented and frightened that he was lost. After a while, he saw a brilliant light in the east coming from a circle of blazing swords, their handles touching in the middle. On this sword platform sat Mañjuśrī. Appearing in his orange-colored form, he wielded a sword of wisdom in his right hand, and in the left he held the stem of a lotus on which lay a scripture. Mañjuśrī then rose up, moving toward Khedrup, and merged into his body. As this happened in his dream, Khedrup felt as if, suddenly, the sun had appeared, dispelling the darkness without a trace.

The next morning, when Khedrup finally met Tsongkhapa, the young monk had a powerful experience, a sense of déjà vu that somehow he had known the master long before.[368] Khedrup then asked Tsongkhapa a series of questions, sharing his uncertainties about many Tibetan interpretations of the Indian classics. He also asked questions pertaining to the practice of both Sūtra and Tantra. Tsongkhapa was deeply impressed and responded to each question with care, commending Khedrup for his acumen.[369]

Khedrup then described to Tsongkhapa the dream he had had the night before. Tsongkhapa commented, "It is wonderful that you have seen the indivisible union of the guru and meditation deity. It appears you are an excellent receptacle for the teachings of Tantra, a jewel-like student." Tsongkhapa then asked Khedrup whom he took to be his main meditation deity. Khedrup replied that he took his main deities to be Vādhisiṁha Mañjuśrī and Red Yamāntaka. Tsongkhapa responded:

> In general, Mañjuśrī will sustain one regardless of which of the three aspects of Yamāntaka—Red, Black, or Vajrabhairava—is taken as one's meditation deity. However, do know that

> the lineage I have is blessed especially by Mañjuśrī. In this lineage, Vajrabhairava is given particular emphasis because in the sādhana practice of Vajrabhairava, Mañjuśrī is present both at the causal Vajradhara stage [when generating the deity] as well as at the resultant Vajradhara stage [i.e., oneself arising as the deity in his complete form]. Some people are simply not cognizant of this uniqueness. The significance of it is the presence of a practice that combines both the peaceful and wrathful aspects of the meditation deity, an instruction I heard directly from Mañjuśrī himself.[370]

Sharing these thoughts, Tsongkhapa then made preparations to formally confer on Khedrup the empowerment of Vajrabhairava, and he conducted the ceremony right then and there. From that day on, Khedrup embraced Vajrabhairava as his principal meditation deity and undertook the sādhana practice on a daily basis.

Over time, Khedrup would come to be known not only as one of the "principal disciples of Great Tsongkhapa" but also as the sole inner disciple (*nang thugkyi séchik*). His statue would be placed on Tsongkhapa's left in iconographic depictions of "the foremost father and his two sons" (*jé yabsé sum*), the other being Gyaltsap.

As we shall see, Khedrup would also become an important custodian of many of Tsongkhapa's Vajrayāna transmissions. Khedrup later composed *Ocean of Attainments*, an authoritative presentation on the generation stage, as a companion to Tsongkhapa's *Lamp to Illuminate the Five Stages* on the completion stage of the Guhyasamāja tantra. Khedrup also wrote *General Principles of Tantra* as a supplement to Tsongkhapa's *Great Treatise on Tantra*. He compiled notes from Tsongkhapa's lectures on the Kālacakra tantra to produce a general exposition of this unique system of tantra, and he also wrote his own extensive exposition of the Kālacakra tantra, the *Illumination of the Principles*. Last, Khedrup would become the conduit for the dissemination of some of the one-to-one pith instructions from Tsongkhapa on guru yoga practice and instructions on the Madhyamaka view of emptiness.

A Brief Disappearing Act

During the summer of 1406 at Sera Chöding, Tsongkhapa remained in strict retreat. At the request of some of his close disciples, however, he taught a small group of around twenty-five students the five stages of the Guhyasamāja tantra. (Gyaltsap's notes from the teaching would later be formalized and included in Tsongkhapa's collected works.) He also taught them the completion stage of the mother tantras, especially Cakrasaṃvara.[371]

One day, Tsongkhapa told some of his senior students, including Gungru Gyaltsen Sangpo (1384–1450), that he saw potential obstacles for himself and his students and that he needed to go away for a few months. When asked where, Tsongkhapa replied that this time it was important that he not reveal his location. Thus, accompanied only by his two senior students—Dülzin and Gyaltsap—one night Tsongkhapa left undetected. He and his two disciples went to Raga Drak Hermitage and entered strict retreat.[372]

It was during this retreat, sometime in 1407, that Tsongkhapa had another vision of Mañjuśrī. The deity raised essential philosophical points of the two Mahāyāna schools, Cittamātra (Mind Only) and Madhyamaka (Middle Way), and then urged Tsongkhapa to write a treatise on these essential points of the tenets of these schools. This inspired the writing of his *Essence of True Eloquence* (*Lekshé Nyingpo*),[373] a work that presents a particular approach for ranking the views of the Buddhist philosophical schools on the topic of the ultimate truth. As indicated by the subtitle, "Distinguishing between the Provisional and the Definitive," the methodology of the text is best described in contemporary terms as hermeneutical—a systematic approach to applying the theory of textual interpretation. This medium-length text, running to just over a hundred folios, was so influential that it established a new field of scholarship in Tibet devoted to hermeneutics. This field is known as *drang ngé*, literally, "the provisional and the definitive."

"Is This Definitive or Provisional?"

The Essence of True Eloquence begins with an acknowledgment of the critical importance of textual hermeneutics within Buddhist thought—especially in the Mahāyāna tradition, which accepts a vast array of disparate scriptures as the infallible word of the Buddha. The teachings of these diverse scriptures can be reconciled only if there are criteria for determining whether what a given scripture states is definitive, and thus to be accepted literally, or whether its meaning must be treated as provisional, requiring further interpretation. This kind of adjudication, Tsongkhapa argues, cannot be based on the authority of a scripture, for to take such an approach simply begs the question, "What verifies the definitive status of *that* scripture?" Relying on a scripture as the final authority, therefore, would involve infinite regress. It is only on the basis of sound reasoning that the statements found in a given scripture can be established as either definitive or provisional. And, writes Tsongkhapa, "to uphold a philosophical position that is contrary to reason negates the credibility of the speaker."[374]

With these preliminary points established, Tsongkhapa structures the remainder of the text in reference to two authoritative systems of hermeneutics, those of Asaṅga (part I) and of Nāgārjuna (part II). Tsongkhapa understands these two systems to be based on specific Mahāyāna sūtras: *Unraveling the Intention of the Buddha* (*Saṃdhinirmocana Sūtra*) for Asaṅga's system and *Questions of Akṣayamati* (*Akṣayamatinirdeśa Sūtra*) for Nāgārjuna's approach.

Tsongkhapa viewed the systems of both Nāgārjuna and Asaṅga as representing authentic philosophical traditions of Mahāyāna Buddhism, and he wanted to offer a clear account of the textual hermeneutics and philosophical reasoning that underpin these two important but different systems of thought.

At the heart of these two hermeneutical systems lies their interpretations of the Perfection of Wisdom sūtras, the archetypal example being the *Perfection of Wisdom in Eight Thousand Lines*. Asaṅga's system, relying on the *Saṃdhinirmocana Sūtra*, interprets the statement in the Perfection of Wisdom scriptures—that everything is empty and devoid of essence—in terms of the theory of the three natures. On this understanding, emptiness, or the ultimate nature of reality, referred to as the *perfected nature*, is defined in terms of the negation of *imputed nature* (the reified concepts we impose on actual reality) that is projected onto the *dependent nature*. Of these three, it is only the imputed nature that can be said to be truly empty and devoid of intrinsic existence. In contrast, dependent phenomena, such as causes and effects, as well as their ultimate truth, which is characterized by the negation of imputed nature on dependent phenomena, possess intrinsic existence. The result of this approach is that what is being negated is defined contextually and relative to the class of phenomena in question.

Part I of Tsongkhapa's *Essence of True Eloquence*, on Asaṅga's system, addresses two broad topics: the presentation of the three natures in the *Saṃdhinirmocana Sūtra* and how Asaṅga interprets the intent of that sūtra. This second topic is further explored in terms of how Asaṅga relies primarily on this sūtra and how, on that basis, he presents his view of the ultimate nature of reality. The main presentation on Asaṅga's understanding of the ultimate truth is developed in some detail, with Tsongkhapa's analysis organized around the following three subjects: (1) how Asaṅga abandons the two extremes of reification (absolutism) and denigration (nihilism) in general; (2) how he eliminates the extreme of reification in particular; and (3) how, based on these, he distinguishes between the provisional and definitive scriptures. Drawing on Asaṅga's key works, especially *Bodhisattva Levels* (*Bodhisattvabhūmi*) and *Summary of the Bases* (*Vastusaṁgraha*), as well as Maitreya's *Ornament of Mahāyāna Sūtras* (*Sutrālaṃkāra*) and *Differentiation of the Middle and Extremes* (*Madhyāntavibhāga*), Tsongkhapa develops a comprehensive presentation of Asaṅga's Mind Only understanding of the ultimate nature of reality.

Part II of *The Essence of True Eloquence* follows a similar format, framing its presentation with two broad topics: a presentation of the hermeneutic system found in *Akṣayamatinirdeśa Sūtra* and a discussion of how the intent of this sūtra's hermeneutic approach is interpreted. Of these two topics, the second is further divided into two: how Nāgārjuna himself interprets the intent of the sūtra and how Nāgārjuna's followers interpret the intent of the sūtra. Tsongkhapa presents Nāgārjuna's own interpretation through two main points: how Nāgārjuna interprets the meaning of dependent origination in terms of emptiness and how he then hails this equation of emptiness and dependent origination as the heart of the Buddha's teaching. In the second part of the presentation of Nāgārjuna's hermeneutical system, Tsongkhapa makes a cogent analysis of the key differences between the two main strands of interpretation of Nāgārjuna, which Tibetans came to refer to as the two subschools of Madhyamaka: the Svātantrika and the Prāsaṅgika.[375]

Central to Tsongkhapa's differentiation of the two Madhyamaka subschools is the assertion that Svātantrika Madhyamaka holds on to a residual notion of objective intrinsic existence. Tsongkhapa's claim is based on a careful reading of key parts of Bhāviveka's writings and of an important section of Candrakīrti's *Entering the Middle Way* wherein Candrakīrti demonstrates three unwanted consequences for those who subscribe to a notion of intrinsic existence.

Tsongkhapa takes the target of this critique to be Svātantrika thinkers, especially Bhāviveka. The second objection, the crucial one, involves the charge that if things were to possess intrinsic existence, this would entail that conventional reality, such as the everyday world characterized by causes and effects, would be able to withstand the scrutiny of ultimate analysis. The point is a subtle one, and to understand it requires some background on the important Buddhist philosophical concept of the two truths: the conventional or relative truth and the ultimate truth.[376]

The *conventional truth* pertains to statements about our everyday world within the provisional framework of shared convention and language. This is the realm in which all the norms that govern everyday reality—cause and effect, temporality, laws of nature, and logical principles—hold sway and help explain the world. The *ultimate truth*, on the other hand, pertains to statements about the way in which things can be said to exist in an ultimate sense. For Nāgārjuna and his Madhyamaka followers, there is only one ultimate truth, namely, emptiness, which is nothing but the absence of intrinsic existence.

These two truths do not describe two separate and independent realms of existence; instead, they are two epistemically defined aspects of one and the same world. They are the truths produced by reality when viewed from two different perspectives. Given the distinct scope and domain of each of these two truths, Tsongkhapa, following Candrakīrti's lead, maintains that to subject conventional truths to ultimate analysis—an analysis that seeks the ultimate mode of being of things—is to commit, to borrow the British philosopher Gilbert Ryle's phrase, "a category mistake."

For example, if one were to reject the reality of, say, a table, on the grounds that when one seeks to find out exactly what it is and where it is (the legs, the top, the shape, the collection of its parts, and so on), one cannot find anything that could be pointed at, this is to subject a conventional reality to an ultimate analysis. This is because terms like *real* and *existence* are defined within the framework that is relational and contingent, not independent and absolute. In fact, Tsongkhapa sees the conflation of these two domains of analysis—conventional and ultimate—at the root of many of the earlier (and in his view, mistaken) Tibetan interpretations of emptiness that entail the rejection of reality, true knowledge, and the principles of logic.[377]

In part II of *The Essence of True Eloquence*, Tsongkhapa elaborates further on many of the philosophical points he had explored in the insight, or emptiness, section of his *Great Treatise on the Stages of the Path to Enlightenment*. These include:

1. Making the critical conceptual distinction between *existence* and *intrinsic existence*, the latter being rejected even on the conventional level;
2. Differentiating the domains and scope of *conventional analysis* and *ultimate analysis*;
3. Identifying *what is to be negated* in the context of emptiness;
4. Arriving at a clear understanding of the notion of *ultimacy* in the context of the statement that things do not exist on the ultimate level;
5. Defining *emptiness* in terms of the categorical negation of intrinsic existence (i.e., emptiness must be defined, in technical Buddhist language, in terms of *nonimplicative negation*);[378]
6. Respecting the *apparent world of conventional truth* and not denigrating it through taking it to be mere illusion with no causal efficacy;
7. Interpreting *emptiness* in terms of the truth of *dependent origination* (i.e., emptiness = dependent origination);
8. Differentiating between the standpoints of Svātantrika

and Prāsaṅgika on the basis of acceptance or rejection of the notion of intrinsic existence, especially on the conventional level; and

9. Developing a *unique Prāsaṅgika standpoint* on key questions of ontology, epistemology, and soteriology, in the wake of rejecting intrinsic existence even at the conventional level.

In describing his sense of indebtedness to Candrakīrti, especially for his reading of the insights of Nāgārjuna, Tsongkhapa writes toward the end of *The Essence of True Eloquence*:

> I revere from the depths of my heart the excellent
> explanations
> Of these great learned ones who are ornaments of the world.
> Yet, when one's eyes of intellect, the night-lily garden,
> Have been opened by the moonlight of Candra's insights—
> Where all bases for objectification are dismantled
> Through the reasoning of dependent origination, of saṃsāra
> and nirvāṇa—
> And when one thus sees the path revealed by Buddhapālita,
> Who would there be who would not uphold supreme
> Nāgārjuna's most excellent system?[379]

The Essence of True Eloquence is a carefully organized and tightly woven work, employing literary embellishments only in the opening and concluding poetic verses. Composed in the manner of an authoritative root text, it is written in a concise style that naturally lends itself to easy memorization and group chanting.[380] Reading the text gives a sense of a masterly voice distilling the philosophical essence of the Mahāyāna Buddhist tradition. In Tsongkhapa's concluding verses, the reader can intuit the deep sense of joy and fulfillment he must have felt as he neared the end of his writing:

> One moment, you swell with joy of faith in the buddhas;
> The next, you remember the kindness of the charioteers;
> At others, reverence for the wise spiritual teacher,
> And heartfelt compassion for the suffering beings,
> And the wish for the precious teaching to long endure—
> These feelings rise up as if competing with each other.
> At this time, you realize that such is the magic of the path
> Of reason, so hard to find yet longed for for so long;
> Shouting "Oh, yes!" and "How wonderful!,"
> Even when you are alone, joyful exclamations come forth!
> Moonlike speech will honor such a person
> Repeatedly with garlands of praise like the following:
> "Meditator of the highest wisdom";
> "Leader of those pure in ethical discipline";
> "Buddha heir who has discovered the definitive meaning."
> The intelligent who wish to win such honors from the Buddha
> Should immerse themselves in this clear exposition
> And purify the eyes of their intellect
> Through the path of philosophical reasoning.
> By whatever merit I may have gained through this effort
> In differentiating the two systems of the charioteers,
> May I uphold all the sublime teachings of the Buddha,
> Just as Nāgārjuna and Asaṅga did.[381]

According to one source, Tsongkhapa sent a copy of *The Essence of True Eloquence* to the great Sakya scholar Yaktön Sangyé Pal, partly in response to a series of questions the Sakya master had asked him on hermeneutics.[382] Khedrup would later compose a supplement to Tsongkhapa's *Essence*, entitled *The Great Summary: Opening the Eyes of the Fortunate*,[383] using the same format but offering much more context and supporting material from authoritative Indian sources. A key reason Khedrup would give for authoring his text would be to help reveal to the reader in a few words the meaning of the "adamantine words" of Tsongkhapa's *Essence*.[384] Over time a large body of exegetical literature would evolve that took Tsongkhapa's *Essence* as the root text.[385]

An Official Invitation from China's Yongle Emperor

While Tsongkhapa and his small group of close students were in retreat at Raga Drak, his main community at Sera Chöding Hermitage had an unexpected disturbance. A large convoy of people headed by four emissaries of the Ming dynasty Chinese emperor Yongle arrived unannounced at Sera Chöding, wanting to see Tsongkhapa. Fearing that he would refuse to meet with the delegation, the emissaries made a night journey from the Phenpo region timed to arrive at Sera Chöding in the early morning, and they pretended they were there simply bearing gifts for the master.[386] Their unexpected arrival so early in the day caused a commotion, forcing many monks to break their retreat sessions. Not only was Tsongkhapa not in residence, in fact, no one seemed to know where the master might be. This was highly embarrassing. The Neu governor Namkha Sangpo had to act as a guarantor that the delegation would indeed meet with the master.

It was later learned that the principal task of the Chinese emissaries was to escort Karmapa Deshin Shekpa to Beijing, where he had been invited by the Yongle emperor. Having heard of Tsongkhapa's great fame, the emperor had also sent gifts as well as a formal letter of invitation to Tsongkhapa to visit China. After some time, the emissaries learned that Tsongkhapa was in retreat at Raga Drak, but the master turned down their initial request for a meeting. However, through the efforts of the Phagdru ruler Miwang as well as Neu Namkha Sangpo, the Chinese emissaries were able to meet Tsongkhapa and present him with the Yongle emperor's letter of invitation. Tsongkhapa politely declined the emperor's invitation and explained why he could not accept it, asking the emissaries to offer his sincere apologies.[387]

Tsongkhapa, Gyaltsap, and Dülzin then returned to Sera Chöding, possibly at the beginning of the summer of 1408. There, Tsongkhapa wrote a formal response to the emperor apologizing for his inability to fulfill the emperor's wish and handed it to the chief emissary, together with some gifts. Below is the text of Tsongkhapa's letter:

> OṂ May goodness prevail! In the presence of the great emperor who, through the power of great waves of merit, reigns lawfully over the vast earth reaching as far as the oceans, I, the Buddhist monk Lobsang Drakpai Pal, who lives in the central part of the Land of Snows, would like to state the following. Great righteous emperor, your merits stand high like the towering Mount Meru; your subjects live with happiness comparable to that of the celestial realms; your command is received by the crowns [of the rulers of] numerous smaller kingdoms. In order to enhance the power of the three jewels, you deputized emissaries bearing your command to this part of the world. They brought with them your royal letter, with gifts such as a roll of red silk with floral and cloud patterns, a blue roll, three rolls of green silk, seven rolls of silk of multiple colors, a yellow robe made of silk brocade, a cloak, a silk shirt, a sleeveless vest, a gown, a moonstone rosary, a bell and vajra, two cymbals, two fine china dishes, two brocade tablecloths, three towels, three wall hangings

adorned with a maṇḍala pattern, a sash, two sets of hand bells, a pair of boots, fifty *gyamas* of tea, and a lump of sandalwood. Please know that I received these gifts you have sent.

Your majesty has expressed your wish that I come once to your part [of the world], and I have understood well what your emissaries as well as Miwang emphatically told me with respect to your majesty's command. It is not that I have failed to comprehend that your majesty's command comes from your thoughts for the Buddha's doctrine, nor is it that I am disrespecting your command or belittling it. It is that whenever I happen to be [for long] in a large crowd of people, I fall victim to severe illness. Because of this I am not able to comply with your command. Thus, I would like to request that you, with your mind as deep and expansive as the sky itself, not be displeased. The great Dharma kings who appeared in the past shouldered the responsibility of spreading just laws governing the norms of this world as well as the norms of the Dharma relevant to fate in the afterlife. In the same manner, in our time as well, you, the great emperor, also uphold pure intentions and engage in deeds of great wonder. I have repeatedly heard this wonderful news, a story that is a source of delight for the entire world, including the gods. Please know that in this part of the world too, we senior members of the monastic community constantly pray with pure intention for your majesty's long life, as well as the longevity of your reign. As for how you, your majesty, should engage in deeds appropriate to an emperor, this is something you yourself know. I, for one, do not dare to say anything specific about it.

This is a letter from me offered with humility. To assist in presenting this letter before your eyes, I send the following gifts: a statue of Avalokiteśvara brought from Khotan, a

> golden statue of the Buddha, a golden statue of Mañjuśrī, a three-chambered casket containing relic pills of the Buddha, another piece of the Buddha's relic, and a relic from the great master and unique lord Atiśa, who was a great Indian adept who made great contributions to the flourishing of the Buddha's teaching in both India and Tibet.
>
> This letter was sent from central Tibet on the nineteenth day of the sixth month of the Rat Year (1408).[388]

Tsongkhapa was aware of the patron-priest relationships that important Tibetan lamas had enjoyed with some of the rulers of China ever since a special relationship was formed between Sakya patriarch Phakpa Lama and Kublai Khan, the founder of the Mongol Yuan dynasty in thirteenth-century China. Later, two of Tsongkhapa's own students would become priests at the Ming court. Personally, however, Tsongkhapa does not appear to have been interested at all in establishing any formal relationship with the Chinese imperial family. Even his relationship with Tibet's Phagdru dynasty Tsongkhapa seems to have kept mostly informal and personal, rather than assuming any formal role vis-à-vis the Phagdru court. Although the explicit excuse Tsongkhapa offered was his tendency to fall ill when spending much time in a large crowd, which was partly true, one suspects the main reason for his declining the Yongle emperor's invitation may have had more to do with his having little time or patience for things overtly mundane and connected with status and power.

Six years later, Tsongkhapa would receive another letter from the Yongle emperor, once again inviting him to China. The emperor's letter read:

> From his heavenly mandate the Ming emperor states the following to Lama Lobsang Drakpa. Your knowledge of

> the path is most profound, highly advanced, perfect, and vast. Through loving-kindness and compassion, you bring great benefit to sentient beings, and you place others on the Mahāyāna path. Because of this, I long ago came to recognize you as a perfect master. Today, I have sent emissaries, led by Tai Gyin Hou Han, with instructions to invite you in accordance with the dual norms [of religion and society]. If you care for the flourishing of the Buddha's teaching, do come to the Central Land (Middle Kingdom) and fulfill my wish.[389]

The emperor's letter then continues with a long list of gifts, including a vajra and bell, a rosary made of ivory, a lump of sandalwood, a large variety of silk brocades, and numerous other exotic articles. The emperor's letter—written on yellow Chinese paper three and half *thos* (the measure of a closed fist with the thumb extended) in width and an arm's length in length and decorated with a five-finger dragon claw—contained the Tibetan text first, followed by Chinese characters.[390] This time, still unwilling to go himself, Tsongkhapa would, however, send one of his senior disciples, Jamchen Chöjé Shākya Yeshé (1354–1435), in his stead. Traveling along the southern route via the Lokha region and Litang in Kham, Jamchen Chöjé reached the imperial capital of Beijing in 1415.

Unlocking Nāgārjuna's Logic of Emptiness

Having returned to Sera Chöding, Tsongkhapa began composing another important work: *Ocean of Reasoning*, an extensive commentary on Nāgārjuna's *Treatise on the Middle Way*. This work of Nāgārjuna, his most well known, ushered in a revolution in Indian Buddhism as well as in the larger Indian philosophical and religious world of his time. Beginning with a salutation to the Buddha for teaching the truth of dependent origination, the text is ostensibly dedicated entirely to elucidating this teaching. It is written in verse and consists of twenty-seven chapters of varying length, each addressing an important metaphysical concept—causation, motion, self, nature, time, and so on—and subjecting it to a thoroughgoing deconstruction to demonstrate the untenability of any notion of independent objective reality. For some time Tsongkhapa had been approached by numerous students, including the Phagdru ruler, Miwang Drakpa Gyaltsen, requesting him to write an authoritative exposition of Nāgārjuna's primer. When Tsongkhapa was writing his *Essence of True Eloquence* a year earlier, he had already made the decision to comply with his students' request and pen a commentary on Nāgārjuna's text.[391] Tsongkhapa set to the task and completed the work by the end of 1408.

In the opening verses, he writes of the reason he felt it necessary to compose this commentary on Nāgārjuna's *Treatise on the Middle Way*:

> As I have been urged by many spiritual friends
> Who aspire to ascertain the definitive meaning,
> And by the illustrious ruler of the kingdom,
> It brings joy to my mind to explain this profound Middle Way.
> Those who are content with the mere phrase *definitive meaning*
> Or are satisfied by just a glimpse of partial meaning,
> And those in whom the desire for practice arises from the heart
> But who shun the excellent treatises, may not need this.
> However, those who wish to dispel through perfect reasoning
> The darkness caused by not knowing, misknowing, and doubts
> Pertaining to the perfection of wisdom, the essence of the
>   definitive scriptures,
> Which is the path traversed by millions of accomplished
>   yogis,

And who aspire to contemplate Nāgārjuna's intent just as it is,
Through the view decisively establishing the truth of reality—
For those intelligent ones I shall expound well
This root text on the Middle Way, so respectfully do listen.[392]

Ocean of Reasoning is a careful and refined exposition of Nāgārjuna's root verses. Tsongkhapa weaves together the interpretations of Buddhapālita and Candrakīrti, the two Indian commentators on Nāgārjuna whom, as we saw in his *Essence of True Eloquence*, Tsongkhapa considered to be most authoritative. Tsongkhapa writes of how, because of the difficult nature of the subjects, the study of two key commentaries on Nāgārjuna's treatise—Buddhapālita's bearing his own name *Buddhapālita* and Candrakīrti's *Clear Words* (*Prasannapadā*)—has declined in Tibet. Seeing this, Tsongkhapa states, he composed his own *Ocean of Reasoning* in accordance with the views of these two great Indian masters, based on his extensive study of the Middle Way thought and "relying uninterruptedly on Mañjuśrī, the treasure of wisdom." Tsongkhapa's teacher Rendawa had also spoken of this "decline" of Madhyamaka in Tibet—such as how, when he was a student at Sakya, people spoke of there being "only one Madhyamaka text at the monastery" and did not view its study to be worthwhile. "Today, however," Rendawa adds, "people value Madhyamaka texts, and this is a contribution I have made to the doctrine."[393]

In addition to interpreting Buddhapālita and Candrakīrti, Tsongkhapa sought to make his own contributions to the understanding of the *Treatise on the Middle Way*. In contrast to the Indian commentators, one of Tsongkhapa's key objectives was to draw out the profound implications of Nāgārjuna's rejection of any notion of objectivity or intrinsic existence (*svabhāva*) with respect to all categories of ontology, epistemology, and soteriology. Tsongkhapa is not content with only a clear explanation of what exactly is being negated by Nāgārjuna's philosophy of emptiness; he is equally, if not more, interested its exploring what this negation means with respect to the entire spectrum of Buddhist thought and practice. How, he wants to know, does Nāgārjuna's standpoint not collapse into nihilism or paralyzing skepticism? What is the fine line between denial of any form of objective reality characterized by some kind of independent essence, on the one hand, and maintaining a robust notion of reality within which the norms of logic, language, epistemology, and causation do not fail to operate? How, if everything is empty and nothing exists in terms of intrinsic reality, do Buddhists motivate themselves to endeavor on the path to enlightenment?[394]

In the introductory section of *Ocean of Reasoning* (just over thirty pages in the English translation), Tsongkhapa explores the central question with particular intensity. How does one espouse a standpoint that negates every possible basis for objectification or reification, while at the same time according robust reality to our everyday world of lived experience? This introduction, which can be treated as a stand-alone essay, should be read by anyone who is perplexed by the way Buddhists fuss about the meaning of emptiness: Tsongkhapa's comments make it very clear why it matters. *Ocean of Reasoning* ends with the following words of humility:

> This profound truth is most difficult to fathom indeed.
> My intellect is limited and my perseverance weak.
> Therefore, if there are any shortcomings in this work,
> I offer apologies for them from the depths of my heart.
> By whatever virtue I may have created through this effort—
> Pure as the whiteness of moonstone and night-lily—
> May all beings, tightly chained by extreme views,
> Easily attain the view that is free from extremes.
> May the Buddha's teaching be upheld by countless masters
> Who realize the truth of dependent origination,

Which comes from Nāgārjuna, chief among all philosophers,
Who is the single eye through which one can view
The truth of reality as taught by the Buddha.
May I too, being sustained through all my lives by Mañjuśrī,
The great wisdom treasure [of all the buddhas],
Uphold sublime Dharma even at the cost of my life, and
Especially never abandon the teaching on dependent
origination.[395]

Having finished writing this major work on Nāgārjuna's philosophy, Tsongkhapa now had authored three substantive works that present in detail his unique understanding of emptiness: the "insight" section of his *Great Treatise on the Stages of the Path*, *The Essence of True Eloquence*, and the newly completed *Ocean of Reasoning*. He next began a series of formal teachings at Sera Chöding Hermitage to a gathering of over six hundred monks, including the abbots of surrounding monasteries, such as Gadong, Kyormolung, and Zulphu, as well as the former abbot of Thangsak Monastery. Tsongkhapa began the lecture series with his new *Ocean of Reasoning*, followed by his *Great Treatise on the Stages of the Path to Enlightenment*, his *Essence of True Eloquence*, an exposition of Āryadeva's *Four Hundred Verses*, his own *Great Treatise on Tantra*, a presentation of the tantric vows, and Aśvagoṣa's *Fifty Verses on the Guru*.

It was during this teaching series at Sera Chöding that the hermit Sangyé Pal (better known as Kuchor Tokden), an important figure in the dissemination of the nyungné fasting practice in Tibet, became a disciple of Tsongkhapa, who gifted him with a monastic robe and an alms bowl. Soon afterward, Tokden had a son, and he saw Tsongkhapa's gifts as a sign that his son had a destiny to be a monk. Later known as Phakpa Lha (1439–87),[396] the boy indeed became a monk as well as a key figure in the spread of Tsongkhapa's tradition in the Kongpo and Nyang Valley regions and also in eastern Tibet. With all of their provisions provided by the Neu governor and his family, Tsongkhapa and his students stayed for around two years at Sera Chöding Hermitage, departing at the end of the summer rainy season of 1408.

CHAPTER 11

The Lhasa Prayer Festival and the Founding of Ganden Monastery

IT WAS DURING his two-year stay at Sera Chöding, between 1406 and the summer of 1408, that Tsongkhapa first had the idea of hosting a grand prayer festival at the holy Jokhang Temple in Lhasa. So, from 1407 on, Tsongkhapa set aside for this project most of the offerings he received from his devotees. He also approached his main benefactor, Neu Namkha Sangpo, for material support for this ambitious plan. As noted, Tsongkhapa had already staged two smaller prayer festivals celebrating the Buddha's miracles at Śrāvastī—the first one in the presence of the Maitreya statue he helped restore inside the ancient Dzingchi Temple, and the second at Radreng Monastery. These would become "rehearsals" for the real thing, to be held in the holy city of Lhasa in the Jokhang Temple itself.

The Jokhang, Tibet's Holiest of Holies

The Jokhang is undisputedly the holiest temple in the devoutly Buddhist land of Tibet. If Lhasa were Vatican City, the Jokhang would be St. Peter's Basilica; if Lhasa were the Byzantine capital Constantine, the Jokhang would be the Church of the Holy

Apostles. Located about three thousand feet to the east of Mount Marpori ("Red Hill"), where today the majestic Potala Palace sits, the Jokhang Temple complex covers an area of over six acres. All early historical sources, including those from Tibet's imperial period, attribute the founding of the Jokhang to Tibet's powerful seventh-century emperor Songtsen Gampo (b. 612). Later, post-imperial Tibetan sources present a mythical account of the events surrounding the construction of the temple, including the exorcism of demons that were obstructing the construction work. Part of this exorcism ritual involved imagining the Tibetan plateau in the shape of a supine demoness and pinning her down through vital points on her body.[397]

According to the early sources, in 639, when the emperor was twenty-three years old, the foundation for the temple was finally laid, a major undertaking that also involved filling a small lake. Songtsen's Nepalese queen, Princess Bhṛkuṭī, was said to have taken charge of the temple construction, employing the skills of Newari artisans accompanying the Nepalese crown prince Narendradeva, then living in exile in central Tibet.[398] The main entrance to the Jokhang faces west, toward Nepal, an orientation that the sources state was chosen out of respect for Bhṛkuṭī's father, the Newari king at the time. Modeled on that of Indian *vihāras* (Buddhist monasteries), the basic plan of the temple, a square, remained unchanged through the ages, with "each successive building having been added to the ancient core."[399] The Jokhang first came to be known as "the Magical Temple of Rasa" (*rasa trulnang gi tsuklak khang*), Rasa being the name of Lhasa in ancient times. It might have meant "Walled City," a name possibly deriving from it being "part town, part fortress."[400] Some traditional Tibetan sources explain the meaning of *Rasa* as "land made through earth brought by goats," alluding to the mythical story that the earth used for reclaiming the temple land was brought on the backs of goats. Over time, the word *Rasa* changed to *Lhasa*, "the land of gods."[401] The construction of the temple is said to have been completed within a single year.

The Jokhang Temple consists of three stories, and modern scholars have found architectural and textual evidence to indicate that the second floor may have been part of the original structure.[402] Legend has it that the emperor had a vision of various Buddhist deities discussing the Dharma among themselves in the various inner chapels of the temple, so he decided to install statues of those deities in each of the chapels. Early Tibetan sources speak of the emperor originally bringing nine statues, including the Self-Originated Great Compassionate One, Avalokiteśvara, to be installed inside the newly built temple.[403] According to the legend, these nine statues miraculously appeared inside the Jokhang, with the Great Compassionate One flanked by eight other images: on his right were Lokeśvara, Bhṛkuṭī, and Sarvanivāraṇa, while on his left were Avalokiteśvara Khasarpaṇi, the goddess Sarasvatī, Tārā, and Hayagrīva.[404] Other sources mention that the following images were originally installed on the ground floor of the Jokhang: as one enters the main, western entrance, to the left in the northern chapel was the Great Compassionate Avalokiteśvara; on the eastern side were three chapels, with the center chapel housing the Buddha Akṣobhya that was brought to Tibet by Princess Bhṛkuṭī, and the two side chapels occupied from left to right, respectively, by Amitābha and Akṣobhya.[405]

According to traditional sources, Emperor Songtsen is said to have hidden a large cauldron filled with treasures under the temple so that "repairs could be made to the Jokhang Temple if and when it suffers damage and decay, and also to ensure the honoring of this temple for a long time."[406] He also is reputed to have buried objects and written prophecies under or inside some of the pillars. Some four centuries later, one of these buried treasures, the so-called *Pillar*

Testament (*Kachem kakhol ma*), would be retrieved by the Indian Bengali master Atiśa, who had come to revive Buddhism in Tibet. As we shall see later, specific passages from this "retrieved" text, supposedly recording the testaments of the seventh-century emperor, would play an important role in the sanctification of Tsongkhapa's name after his death. This apocryphal work contains certain passages that came to be widely cited and interpreted as prophecies of historical events and personalities, including those who would play key roles in the long history of the Jokhang Temple itself. For example, the text mentions Atiśa by name and contains allusions to several Kadam masters, as well as the great translators Rinchen Sangpo and Ngok Loden Sherap. There is a passage that speaks of how a bodhisattva will "honor the Buddha's icon for up to two hundred years,"[407] which is traditionally understood to prophesy Dakpo Gompa Tsultrim Nyingpo (1116–69), a student of Gampopa who undertook a major renovation of the Jokhang in the twelfth century. Around a century earlier, another important renovation was overseen by one Zangkar Lotsawa, who lamented how "the great skill of Newari artists had been transformed into a beggars' home."[408]

Preparing for the Great Prayer Festival

As part of the preparations for the great festival he envisioned, Tsongkhapa wanted first to have some much-needed renovation work done, both outside and inside the temple. He had prayed in the Jokhang on numerous occasions and had once even observed the nyungné fasting retreat inside the temple. Like every educated Tibetan, he was familiar with the history of the temple as well as the legend surrounding its two most important icons: the statue of Śākyamuni brought to Tibet by the Chinese princess Wencheng as part of her dowry and the Five-Faceted Self-Originated Great Compassionate One.[409] Originally, it was another statue of Akṣobhya (Jowo Mikyö Dorje), said to have been brought to Tibet by the Nepalese princess Bhṛkuṭī, which was housed in the newly constructed Jokhang Temple. Later, during the reign of Tridé Tsukden (704–c. 754), Akṣobhya was moved to another temple, Ramoché, and the Buddha image brought to Tibet by Wencheng was installed inside the Jokhang as its principal icon.[410]

Though the Jokhang was constantly visited by pilgrims from all parts of Tibet, Tsongkhapa found it to be in dire need of care and renovation. Many of the statues and murals were covered in thick dust, soot, and dirt, which obscured their original colors.[411] Some of the chapels were in a dilapidated condition and were even being used as dwellings by beggars, who lit fires for cooking and left dirty rags, personal belongings, and leftover food on the statues. Thus, the first step in the renovation was to relocate the beggars who called some of the chapels home. They were given food and alternative shelter and were asked to respect the sanctity of the Jokhang. The chapels were then locked at night while the renovation work took place.[412]

The central skylighted structure topped with a gilded roof and supported by twelve pillars was renovated. To prepare for the large gathering of monks for the prayer festival, a major extension was undertaken. This included a new assembly hall, the *dukhang*, whose central area, known as *khyamra*, is open to the sky. Leading to this multipillared new prayer hall was a hallway opening onto a large portico with "six large fluted wooden pillars, four fronting the street and two behind them."[413] This portico, in essence, became the main entrance of the temple. In front of the Jokhang, a large square was created by laying stone slabs in such a way that the temple would stand out in the Lhasa landscape, and the thousands of pilgrims and devotees who would gather for the festival could move around with greater ease.[414]

Tsongkhapa's main benefactor, Neu Namkha Sangpo, oversaw the procurement of all the necessary provisions to support the crowd of monastics expected to gather in Lhasa for the sixteen-day festival, the largest such gathering ever at that time. With the help of his benefactor and students, Tsongkhapa sought out the best artisans and craftsmen and procured the gold sheets, cleaning materials, and paints to restore the sculptures and murals. He also obtained many bolts of fine silk for the robes.[415] While the architectural renovation was going on, the artisans, assisted by devout volunteers, cleaned the statues and the murals, restoring them to their former glory. All the statues received a fresh layer of gold leaf on their faces and had their eyes and other facial features retouched. The craftsmen created crowns of gold and silver, and tailors made silk robes to be offered to the images during the prayer festival.

For his part, Tsongkhapa created a compilation of liturgical texts, mainly prose and verse passages selected from sūtras and other important Indian works, to be chanted during the festival. He also composed two dedication prayers, one for the benefit of deceased benefactors and the other for the living ones, to be used at the prayer festival when acknowledging the day's generous benefactors and dedicating their merit.[416]

After the end of the 1408 rainy-season retreat at Sera Chöding, Tsongkhapa, followed by some five hundred monks, traveled to Drumbu Ling Monastery at the invitation of Miwang Drakpa Gyaltsen. This gave Tsongkhapa an excellent opportunity to seek Miwang's support for the Great Prayer Festival, and support it he did, using all the authority and power of his office as the de facto king of Tibet at the time. Many monks from other monasteries in various parts of central Tibet came together to Drumbu Ling to attend Tsongkhapa's teachings, bringing the total number of monastics gathered there to around a thousand. They spent the winter together, during which time Tsongkhapa taught lamrim, the sādhana practice of Cakrasaṃvara according to the tradition of the mahāsiddhi Lūipa, and the completion stage meditations of mother tantra, especially Cakrasaṃvara.[417]

The Jokhang Temple in Colors and Splendor

Toward the end of the twelfth month of the Tibetan year (January 1409), Tsongkhapa returned to Lhasa to inaugurate the much-anticipated Mönlam Chenmo, the Great Prayer Festival. On the eve of the Tibetan New Year, January 16, 1409, he convened a preliminary prayer session with a formal public announcement. According to the *Catalog of the Great Prayer Festival* compiled during the festival, Tibet's ruler, Miwang Drakpa Gyaltsen, had issued a decree about the festival and had instructed his various ministers to get out the word and help with procuring necessary provisions. Over eight thousand monastics had come to participate, not just from central Tibet but from other regions as well, including remote places like Kham and Amdo.[418]

Tsongkhapa joined the congregation in the performance of the fortnightly confession ceremony to review and restore their monastic vows. To prepare them for the multiday festival, all the statues were dressed in appropriate attire, with monastic robes for the Buddha images and colored silk robes for the others. For the central image of Śākyamuni, Tsongkhapa had commissioned a crown of solid gold, studded with precious jewels, and for Akṣobhya and Avalokiteśvara there were crowns made of pure silver. A large silver bowl, representing a monk's alms bowl, had been made for the occasion and was placed in front of Buddha Śākyamuni.[419]

The rooftops of the entire temple complex were decorated with a network of colorful prayer flags, interspersed with silk banners with jingling bells. Outside the temple, on the circumambulation route known as the Barkhor, a column was erected of fifteen tall wooden poles with fluttering banners printed with the mantras and prayers of the fifteen directional guardians. Between these tall columns were other shorter poles with fluttering flags of different colors. All of these flagpoles were connected with strings of colorful prayer flags interspersed with small bells.

In front of the temple's main entrance, where the ninth-century treaty pillar (*do ring*) stood,[420] there was a massive square cauldron filled with butter, with a powerful flame burning from a huge wick. On either side of this enormous butter lamp stood, on a square platform, a gigantic *torma* offering made of *tsampa* (roasted barley) and decorated with colored butter scriptures. These offerings were renewed every few days, with the old ones given away to the multitude of beggars who had also gathered for the festival. All around the Jokhang circuit were lamps burning from large clay pots filled with butter and bearing wicks the size of a man's arm. The brilliance of the light from all these butter lamps made them difficult to look at. From a distance one felt as if the brightly lit night sky studded with sparkling stars had descended to the earth. During the prayer festival, a large number of butter lamps were also lit at Ramoché Temple, the Potala, and Tsal Gungthang Monastery, such that, it is said, one could see the shadows of the willow trees just as clearly at night as in daytime. Inside the Jokhang were laid out thousands of water bowls filled with water sprinkled with saffron, filling the entire surrounding area with their sweet perfume. Plumes of smoke from incense burners both inside and outside the temple filled the air with the aromas of juniper, sandalwood, and other sweet scents.

The Great Prayer Festival

What was Tsongkhapa's Great Prayer Festival celebrating? It was held to honor the Buddha's performance of miracles at Śrāvastī in central India, which, according to the Tibetan calendar, occurred in the first month of the year. In fact, the Tibetans refer to their first month as *Chötrul Dawa*, the "Month of Miracles."

The early Buddhist texts speak of the Buddha's twin miracles (*yamakaprātihārya*) performed in response to a public challenge by a group of six ascetics. The miracles involved the production of two contradictory phenomena at the same time: flames flared from the upper part of the Buddha's body while water streamed forth from the lower part. The Buddha also created doubles of himself that filled the sky. In later Mahāyāna retellings, the Buddha's miracles are described as lasting for multiple days. It is this latter account that inspired Tsongkhapa's Great Prayer Festival, which served both to celebrate the Buddha's miracles and to dedicate the month of their occurrence to a special time of prayer.

When dawn broke on the first day of the Tibetan New Year of the Earth Ox (1409), Tsongkhapa oversaw the first formal session of his long-awaited Great Prayer Festival. With the chanting of prayers in full swing, he offered the gold and silver crowns to the central images and had the large silver bowl placed in front of the Buddha. Next he offered to the temple a camel-headed chalice said to be a drinking cup of Songtsen Gampo, which the emperor had buried along with six other similar silver cups. Tsongkhapa is believed to have rediscovered this silver cup in the Tölung Valley.[421] Today, this silver drinking cup is housed in the Songtsen chapel on the second floor of the Jokhang.

Each day of the festival was divided into four sessions: an early morning prayer, a teaching session, a noon prayer, and an afternoon prayer. Throughout the fifteen days of the festival, the teaching session was dedicated to reading from Āryaśura's *Garland of Birth Stories* (*Jātakamāla*), a fourth-century poetic retelling of thirty-four of the most famous of the Buddha's former lives, or Jātakas. This tradition of reading from the Jātaka tales survives to this day as an important part of the Great Prayer Festival. On the fifteenth and final day of the festival, which was a full-moon day, Tsongkhapa performed a large public ceremony of the generation of bodhicitta, the Mahāyāna aspiration to attain buddhahood for the benefit of all beings.[422]

On the first day of the festival, Tsongkhapa himself and his close students were the benefactors for the tea, food, and monetary offerings to the thousands of monks in attendance. On this same day, the religious patriarch of Phagdru Kagyü, Chenga Sönam Sangpo, made extensive offerings to the sacred icons as well as to Tsongkhapa. On the second day, Tibet's ruler, Miwang Drakpa Gyaltsen, sponsored offerings to both the sacred images in the temple and the large congregation of monastics present there. The names of the benefactors for the individual days of the festival constitute a virtual "who's who" of central Tibet at the time: political leaders, powerful religious hierarchs, monasteries, and wealthy merchants. The honor of sponsoring the eighth day, a day of special religious observance according to the Tibetan calendar, went to Tsongkhapa's principal benefactors, the Neu governor Namkha Sangpo and his wife Rinchen-Drön. (The Neu family appears to have been both devout and generous. Tsongkhapa's writings contain dedication prayers celebrating the family's commissioning of a special selection of key Mahāyāna scriptures—the *Perfection of Wisdom in One Hundred Thousand Lines*, the *King of Meditations Sūtra*, the *Lotus Sūtra*, the *Lalitavistara*, the "Five Supreme *Dhāraṇīs*," and the *Sūtra of the Fortunate Aeon*—all inscribed in gold on thick dark-blue paper.)[423]

As the festival progressed, more and more laypeople came to pay homage and take part in the celebration, circumambulating the temple, topping off the numerous butter lamps, chanting prayers, and making prostrations to the Jokhang. One evening, one of the large butter lamps was not refilled on time, so the thick oil-soaked wick burst into flame, causing the gathered devotees to panic. Seeing this, Tsongkhapa entered into meditation and, thankfully with very little wind blowing, the fire did not get out of control.[424]

Sources speak of crowds of over ten thousand laypeople in addition to around eight thousand monastics taking part in the prayers.[425] Never before had the holy city of Lhasa witnessed such a congregation of so many people at the same time. At Tsongkhapa's urging, hundreds of laypeople volunteered during the festival to help build a stone wall on the banks of Lhasa River to protect against possible future flooding of the Jokhang.[426]

The festival formally came to a close on the sixteenth day, with a session of thanksgiving. The grand finale took the form of a procession of a statue of Maitreya, the future Buddha, around the Jokhang on the Barkhor circuit. The Maitreya image was carried in a palanquin decorated with colorful silks and accompanied by musicians playing various instruments, such as clarinets, cymbals, and drums. At each cardinal direction, an ablution rite was performed for Maitreya, followed by the chanting of hymns and prayers, offerings to the local spirits, and recitations of auspicious verses. All the participating monks were offered sums of money that had been left over from the offerings received for the festival. Similarly, all leftover provisions, butter, tsampa, and so on were distributed among the various monasteries and temples or given to beggars and the poor.

By all accounts, Tsongkhapa's Great Prayer Festival in Lhasa was a resounding success. For him, it was the realization of a deep aspiration. He had wanted to do something about the decaying state of the holy Jokhang Temple. He had also wished to see the Jokhang images of Buddha Śākyamuni and the Self-Originated Avalokiteśvara honored as never before, so that their status as the paramount icons of Tibet (together with Akṣobhya at Ramoché Temple) was once again proclaimed loudly and widely. He wanted to restore the Jokhang's original role, not just as a temple but as a place for monastics to gather and pray. By the end of the Great Prayer Festival, Tsongkhapa had achieved all of these aspirations. And by skillfully selecting the texts and passages to be chanted, he created a shared liturgy for the monks of all Tibetan Buddhist traditions, so that everyone participating in the prayer festival could feel included. No wonder that some biographers list his hosting of the Great Prayer Festival as the third of the "four great deeds of Tsongkhapa," the first two being the restoration of the Dzingchi Maitreya and the institution of the Great Scriptural Festival of Nyal.[427]

The festival also helped consolidate and institutionalize, at the national level, an approach Tsongkhapa had been advocating in Tibet for some time: making the historical Buddha a robust presence in the vision and lives of his fellow Tibetan Buddhists, who often seemed excessively focused on the gurus and deities of their own lineages. After his breakthrough to a profound realization of emptiness at the age of forty-two, Tsongkhapa strove to focus the minds of his students and fellow Tibetans on the Buddha himself. In a deeply inspired state, he had penned a short ode to the Buddha, "In Praise of Dependent Origination," and had later composed another hymn to the Buddha, a short twenty-verse piece entitled "Swift Entry of the Buddha's Blessings." Better known as *Kapsumpa*, it would later become a key part of the liturgy of the annual Great Prayer Festival.

It appears that, for the next few years, it was the monasteries in the vicinity of Lhasa, such as Kyormolung and Gadong, that continued the tradition of annual Great Prayer Festivals at the Jokhang. In 1417, a year after the founding of Drepung Monastery, one of Tsongkhapa's senior students, Jamyang Chöjé Tashi Palden (1379–1449), took charge of staging the annual Mönlam Chenmo. The tradition, however, was interrupted between 1498 and 1517 when the Rinpungpas, the then rulers of central Tibet who were closely allied to the

Karma Kagyü lineage, banned the attendance of all Geluk monks from the Great Prayer Festival. Except for this interval, Drepung Monastery retained control of the annual prayer festival until the political tragedy that befell Tibet in the mid-twentieth century. (Following the exodus of many Tibetans to India in and immediately after 1959, the annual prayer festival has been continued in the major Tibetan Geluk monasteries in exile.)

Over time, a tradition emerged whereby the candidates for the Geshé Lharam degree (the highest academic qualification in Tibetan Buddhism, equivalent to a doctorate in divinity) from the major Geluk monasteries of central Tibet, especially the Three Great Seats of Learning (*densa chenpo sum*), namely, Ganden, Drepung, and Sera, would sit for their formal oral examinations during the intervals between the formal sessions of the Great Prayer Festival.[428]

The Founding of Ganden Monastery

The year 1409 also saw another legacy-shaping contribution by Tsongkhapa: the founding of the "mother monastery" (*magön*) for what would later become Tsongkhapa's Geluk school. For several years, some of Tsongkhapa's closest disciples, moving from one monastery or hermitage to another, had complained about the peripatetic lifestyle necessitated by being part of his community. As Tsongkhapa was aging, and experiencing recurring backaches, he too must have begun to feel the hardships of a life that entailed extensive walking. Whatever the reason, in 1409, Tsongkhapa was ready to listen to his senior students' pleas for a more permanent base for the community.

In any case, it appears that as he was planning the Great Prayer Festival, Tsongkhapa was also thinking about finally establishing a home for his growing community of monks. Given his popularity and his close connections with the ruling families of different regions in central Tibet, Tsongkhapa received various suggestions about where to locate such a base. Some benefactors offered him older, existing monasteries, while others proposed to build a new monastery for his community within their area.[429] According to some sources, one intriguing site was connected with a prophecy Lhodrak Drupchen had communicated to Tsongkhapa nearly a decade earlier. The prophecy read:

> On the slopes of Wangkur Mountain,
> On the side where the queen soared high,
> Countless monks will be brought together.
> On this mountain Mañjuśrī will teach.
> It will be a sublime object of worship for those
> From central Tibet, Dokham, and China, drawing forth goodness.
> It will be the refuge for the entire northern realm up to Ngari;
> From it, monasteries will spread to all ten directions.[430]

During the Great Prayer Festival, Tsongkhapa conducted a series of observations, which included examining his dreams and making fervent prayers in the presence of the image of Buddha Śākyamuni in the Jokhang. By the end of the festival, he had made his decision: as prophesied by Lhodrak Drupchen, Tsongkhapa's monastery would be built on Wangkur Mountain. He would name it Ganden ("Land of Joy"), another name for Maitreya's heavenly realm, Tuṣita.

So, immediately after the completion of the Great Prayer Festival, accompanied by Gyaltsap, Dülzin, and other senior disciples, Tsongkhapa visited the site of his future monastery.[431] Wangkuri, or Wangkur Mountain, is located around twenty-five miles northeast of Lhasa at an altitude of over fourteen thousand feet. Its name, Wangkuri, derives from its fame as having supposedly been the summit where Emperor Songtsen Gampo was enthroned at the age of thirteen.[432] *Wangkur* means "coronation," while the syllable *ri* means a mountain or a hill. As a longtime enthusiast for mountain retreats and hermitages, Tsongkhapa immediately fell in love with the site. The vista from the summit, with its dramatic view of the valleys beneath the mountain, was spectacular. And Tsongkhapa appreciated the site's proximity to Lhasa and other central Tibetan sites he had come to cherish—his favorite hermitages in the Wölkha Valley; Nedong, the base of his principal benefactors; and other such locations must have also factored into the choice. Standing at the summit of the mountain, Tsongkhapa could envision how his monastery complex could nestle on the upper part of the slopes like a great tapestry hanging down and covering an entire face of the mountain.

Tsongkhapa performed the traditional rites required for the construction of a new monastery: examining the site for its appropriateness and auspiciousness, formally requesting permission from the earth and the local spirits to build there, and expelling forces that might hinder the construction and long-term sustainability of the monastery on that site.

Later biographies report that during the digging for the laying of the foundation, two notable objects were discovered. The first was a large conch. The second was a mask, which Tsongkhapa and his senior disciples took to be the mask of the Dharma protector deity Kālarūpa, belonging to the Yamāntaka class of deities (those who put an end to the Lord of Death). The discovery of the two objects, especially the large conch, would evolve into a legend that purported to trace them to the time of none other than the Buddha himself. One version cites a passage said to exist in a Chinese translation of the *Laṅkāvatāra Sūtra*, which relates the following story. Once the Buddha and his monks were sitting on the shore of Lake Manasarovar, observing their rainy-season retreat. At that time, the nāga king Anavatapa offered a large conch to the Buddha, who, in turn, gave it to Maudgalyāyana and instructed him to bury it in Tibet, the "land of the red-faced people." He then prophesied that in the future a monk "bearing the demeanor of a lotus" would spread his teachings there and use the conch to summon his congregation. "So," the Buddha concluded, "bury this and let it be guarded by a stone shaped like a monkey."[433] According to a later source, Tsongkhapa gave this conch to Jamyang Chöjé, who, after the founding of Drepung Monastery, placed it there, where it would be a prized object of veneration.[434]

Once the ground-breaking ceremonies and the foundation laying for the first building were complete, Tsongkhapa delegated supervision of the actual construction to two of his most trusted senior students, Gyaltsap and Dülzin. Most of Tsongkhapa's students remained with the two senior monks to assist in the large-scale construction work. Some of Tsongkhapa's disciples who had been major benefactors of the Great Prayer Festival contributed generously toward the construction project, as did many ordinary devotees. The work proceeded so well that a substantial part of the monastery complex was completed before the end of the Earth Ox year (1409). This included the main temple, Tsongkhapa's personal chambers, and some seventy cells for the monks, with the foundations laid for over one hundred more monks' cells.[435]

Back in the Wölkha Valley

Tsongkhapa himself, accompanied by a small group of monks, returned to Sera Chöding in the early spring of 1409 to conduct a series of teachings for an assembly of over six hundred monks. He taught Nāgārjuna's *Treatise on the Middle Way*, the chapter on ethics from Asaṅga's *Bodhisattva Levels*, and the stages of the path, as well as teaching the sādhana text entitled *Samantabhadra* and giving some other tantric teachings.

Next, at the invitation of Chenga Sönam Sangpo (1380–1417), the religious patriarch of Densa Thil and Tsal Gungthang Monastery who was closely associated with the Phagdru dynasty, Tsongkhapa visited Chin Hermitage on Mount Sangri. Sönam Sangpo, who also happened to be Miwang Drakpa Gyaltsen's brother, was already an admirer of Tsongkhapa's and counted among those who requested the master to compose his grand synthesis of tantra, completed in 1405. Tsongkhapa and some two hundred students visited Chin Hermitage on Mount Sangri. There, Tsongkhapa taught a large gathering of monastics, including those from Densa Thil, on lamrim and various other instructions.[436] By this time, Chenga Sönam Gyaltsen (1386–1434), another younger brother of Miwang, had already been a student of Tsongkhapa for a few years.[437] He would later request Tsongkhapa to compose his authoritative work on the six yogas of Nāropa, entitled *A Guide Endowed with Three Convictions*.[438]

For the rainy-season retreat of 1409, Tsongkhapa returned to his beloved Wölkha Valley region, making Samten Ling Hermitage his base. There he gave extensive teachings to monks from both the Wölkha and Dakpo regions.[439] A well-known local teacher from Nyal, Rapdrong Geshé, had recently passed away, but not before asking his wealthy relatives to make a substantial offering of gold to his teacher, Tsongkhapa.[440] Accepting this gift, Tsongkhapa made offerings in turn to his fellow monks but set aside a substantial portion for the construction of Ganden Monastery. Tsongkhapa stayed at Wölkha Samten Ling Hermitage for the entire summer and fall of 1409. During the fall, he went into a strict silent retreat, focusing principally on his Vajrayāna practice, especially that of the Guhyasamāja tantra. He was joined by just five of his closest and most senior students in this retreat, during which he carefully guided them through the successive phases of the generation and completion stage meditations of Guhyasamāja.[441] Speaking of this unique meditation retreat, Tokden Jampel Gyatso, one of the earliest disciples, would state, "When the master taught the generation and completion stages of Guhyasamāja at Wölkha, I joined in the meditation practice. All six of us, master and disciples, experienced clear indications of transformation in our minds. . . . I attained realizations connected with the [Guhyasamāja] tantra after cultivating them for twenty-six days."[442]

Having studied, reflected on, and meditated on the essential points of the Guhyasamāja tantra, as well as having composed a sādhana—a meditation manual to generate oneself as the deity through stages of visualization—Tsongkhapa began to think of authoring a comprehensive exposition of the advanced completion stages of this "king of tantras." During this retreat, therefore, Tsongkhapa supplicated the meditation deity and the great lineage masters of the Guhyasamāja tradition, and he began jotting down the first set of notes during the intervals in the retreat.[443] One night, he had an unusual dream, pregnant with symbolism. He wrote about this dream a few days later, on the seventh day of the twelfth month of the Earth Ox year (January 12, 1410), in a cryptic eighteen-line poem preceded by a salutation to his guru and meditation deity, Mañjuśrī.[444] Below is a paraphrase of a prose summary offered by Khedrup on the meaning of Tsongkhapa's lines:

> On the *third* day of the twelfth month of the Earth-Ox year, I saw the entire maṇḍala assembly of the nineteen-deity Mañjuśrīvajra, with the principal deity adorned by fine jewels and holding a vase filled with precious nectar. This nectar was said to be the same nectar that was produced through the power of dialogue between Mañjuśrī and Maitreya in the presence of master Atiśa when he was on the banks of the Kyichu River in Nyethang. "It has been three hundred ten years since the time of the great Atiśa, and I have not found anyone to whom to pass this on," said Mañjuśrīvajra.

> When this was spoken, both of the dialogue partners (Mañjuśrī and Maitreya) were present. On the night of the *fourth*, I dreamed of the great Butön, who gave me a wrapped text and said, "You should now be the custodian of this." So saying, he recited mantras and performed hand gestures, circled it over my head three times, and placed it on my head. On the *fifth*, I was able to attain mastery over the instruction on "mixing and transference," which lies at the heart of Marpa's teachings. On the *sixth* day, I was able to recognize that this instruction of Marpa constitutes an excellent teaching that represents the enlightened intention of Ārya Nāgārjuna and his immediate disciples. On the *seventh* day, as I read Āryadeva's *Lamp on the Compendium of Practices* (*Caryāmelāpakapradīpa*), I gained the deep conviction that this text had laid the basis for the special instructions connected with the mixings during the sleep and dreaming states. In this way, I gained most firm conviction. It was on this day that I understood the phrase "timely food at the point of death" (*shi zan*), which I had dreamed of writing underneath a thangka of Cakrasaṃvara decorated with a line of offerings. Thus, on the seventh day I understood this phrase to mean that my role will also involve restoring the teaching and practice of Cakrasaṃvara—as if reviving someone when they are about to die of starvation.[445]

With these dreams and the series of important insights and convictions that ensued from them, Tsongkhapa would come to recognize that the time had finally arrived for him to take the next major step in contributing to the Buddhadharma in Tibet: composing major works on the advanced stages of Highest Yoga tantra and their associated instructions and practices.

The Tibetan tradition, drawing on its Indian sources, speaks of four important qualifications for authoring a major work on tantra: (1) receiving the specific instructions through an unbroken lineage of transmission; (2) gaining good knowledge of the instructions and the practices; (3) attaining some personal realizations through meditative practice; and (4) obtaining some special signs from the meditation deities indicating their permission to write. Tsongkhapa had received the transmissions of the specific teachings long ago; his knowledge of the tantras, both the root texts and their commentaries, was by then perhaps unrivaled in Tibet; and, thanks to his constant retreats in multiple hermitages, he had gained profound personal realizations through his meditative practices. He had been unsure, however, whether he met the fourth qualification, receiving special signs from the meditation deities. Now, however, at the age of fifty-four, Tsongkhapa felt he had received those signs and therefore met the crucial fourth criterion as well.[446]

CHAPTER 12

Yogi of Glorious Guhyasamāja

On the fifth day of the second month of the Iron Tiger year (March 11, 1410), around a year after laying the foundation for Ganden, Tsongkhapa returned to his new monastery. The master's return had been eagerly awaited by the large community of monks there, especially by Gyaltsap and Dülzin, who had overseen the construction. As Tsongkhapa and his entourage, approaching from the south, reached the base of Wangkur Mountain, they must have been impressed to see the upper part of the mountain covered with a complex of buildings, with lime-finished walls topped with a maroon band and studded with narrow Tibetan-style windows. By then, many of the edifices, including the main prayer hall, Tsongkhapa's private residence, and over a hundred monks' cells, had been completed.

Tsongkhapa presided over the formal consecration ceremony and made offerings to the sacred images installed in the prayer hall as well as to the assembled monks. Many of Tsongkhapa's benefactors attended the consecration and offered gifts of money to the monks. As part of the consecration, Tsongkhapa conducted a series of teachings in the new prayer hall. Topics and texts included his own *Great Treatise on the Stages of the Path to Enlightenment*; Candrakīrti's extensive exposition of the root tantra of Guhyasamāja, *The Clear Lamp*; and Nāgārjuna's *Five Stages of Completion*. In addition, he taught Asaṅga's *Compendium of Abhidharma* and the essential points of his

Śrāvaka Levels and *Bodhisattva Levels* as well as lecturing on difficult points in Buddhist logic and epistemology.

It was during these teachings at the newly opened Ganden Monastery that Shönu Gyalchok, who would later author a much-admired work on mind training entitled *A Compendium of Well-Uttered Insights*, became Tsongkhapa's student. Shönu Gyalchok had been sent to Ganden by a senior student of Tsongkhapa, Sempa Chenpo Künsang (1366–1444), who had been impressed by the young monk's intellect and told him that he would benefit greatly from studying with Tsongkhapa.[447] For his part, Sempa Chenpo would remain deeply devoted to Tsongkhapa throughout his life, sharing with his own students, including Gö Lotsawa Shönu Pal, his feeling of indebtedness to the great teacher. When speaking of Tsongkhapa, Sempa Chenpo would later say to Gö Lotsawa, with tears in his eyes, "Had I not met the precious Jé Tsongkhapa, I could have died of thirst for Dharma."[448]

Now that Tsongkhapa and his community of monks finally had a base at their new monastery, he wanted to ensure that the daily life of the monks residing there would be guided by codes of conduct in accord with the discipline established by the Buddha himself. While the lives of individual Buddhist monks were bound by a set of precepts that each had taken at the time of their full ordination—a tradition going back to the time of the Buddha—they were also required to adhere to a set of rules governing their conduct as members of a community. The Tibetan tradition refers to these two sets of rules as, respectively, the internal rules of vinaya discipline and the stipulated rules for members of a monastery.[449] In the first set, every monk, regardless of their level of education, is expected at the very least to know the basic list of the precepts—36 for novices and 253 for the fully ordained—and seek to live according to the guidelines established by their vows. In contrast, the second set of rules falls into two broad categories: (1) regulation of communal activities that pertain to restoration and reaffirmation of the monastic vows, such as participation in the fortnightly confessional ceremonies; and (2) rules aimed at fostering harmony and healthy community life, including how to address disputes when they arise.

Tsongkhapa had already composed two monastic rule books, a longer one and an abridged version, for the monastic hermitage of Dzingchi Jampa Ling located in his favorite Wölkha Valley.[450] Thus, it was relatively easy for him to establish guidelines for the members of his new Ganden community. The two earlier rule books cover such matters as how monks should gather with dignity when a gong calls them to prayer or to a meal; how laypeople who are brought into a prayer ceremony must be led in by the disciplinarian; how resident monks should not wear clothes with sleeves; how the sick should be treated with special care, with no expense spared for their medication; how the environment of the monastery must be kept clean; how there should be no shouting in the monastery; and how the everyday life of a monk should be dedicated to study, contemplation, and meditation. This emphasis on the strict observance of "individual" vinaya precepts and adherence to explicit rules for everyday conduct by community members set the pattern for all the subsequent monasteries established in Tsongkhapa's Ganden tradition. Speaking of the wider influence of this tradition in Tibet on the flourishing of vinaya practice, *The Blue Annals* notes, "Thanks to the example they [Tsongkhapa's followers] set, the vinaya tradition has become [pervasive] in this land of Tibet like the light of a shining sun."[451]

The Buddha himself is reported to have declared that after his death, when a follower of his teaching pays homage to the three scriptural collections of sūtra, vinaya, and abhidharma, the second is worthy of receiving an additional homage, the first homage being to the vinaya in its own right and the second as the substitute for him, the teacher. Similarly, scriptures state that where the rites of the three vinaya activities of ordination, fortnightly confessional ceremony, and rainy-season retreat remain active, the Buddha's teaching will flourish. Other scriptures declare that any land where the four categories of the Buddha's disciples are present (monks, nuns, laymen, and laywomen)[452] should be considered a center of Dharma. Earlier, we saw how Tsongkhapa taught vinaya on numerous occasions and how he composed two influential works on the precepts of fully ordained monks and those of novices, both referring in their titles to the site, Namtsé Deng, where he wrote them. Furthermore, by the time Ganden was founded, Tsongkhapa's extensive notes on Guṇaprabha's Indian classic, the *Root Lines on Vinaya*, had become an important resource on the topic.[453]

As the monks at Ganden, many of whom had come from different monasteries to join the new community, gradually settled in, Tsongkhapa began to think systematically about how to utilize his new base to further the mission of developing a lineage that would combine what the Tibetan tradition calls the three spheres (*khorlo sum*): study and critical reflection, meditative cultivation, and active engagement in the welfare of others.[454] For Tsongkhapa, the focus of study and meditative cultivation had to be on the union of Sūtra and Tantra. This can be roughly characterized as the union of the foundational aspects of the Buddhist path (essentially the three principal elements of the path: renunciation, bodhicitta, and the view of emptiness) and advanced Vajrayāna practices.

Thus far, Tsongkhapa had written and taught at length on the Sūtra-based traditions, especially through his extensive dissemination of lamrim instructions. He also had taught substantially on the great Indian Buddhist classics, such as Nāgārjuna's *Treatise on the Middle Way*, Asaṅga's *Compendium of Abhidharma* and *Bodhisattva Levels*, Candrakīrti's *Entering the Middle Way*, and Dharmakīrti's primer on logic and epistemology. With respect to tantra, however, apart from his *Great Treatise on the Stages of the Path of Tantra* and a few expository works, he had chosen not to write on the topics related to the completion stage of Highest Yoga tantra. From 1410 onward, however, Tsongkhapa would shift his priorities significantly, making the advanced levels of Highest Yoga tantra the main focus of his writing and teaching.

A New and Final Phase of Writing

Tsongkhapa began what might be called his final literary phase with the composition of detailed explanations of the *Questions of Four Goddesses* (*Caturdevīparipṛcchā*) and *Compendium on Wisdom Vajra* (*Vajrajñānasamuccaya*), two of the most important explanatory tantras of the Guhyasamāja cycle. As part of his efforts to expound these two tantric texts, Tsongkhapa produced a reliable critical edition of the tantras themselves based on a careful comparison of the texts, a process he would later repeat for the Guhyasamāja root tantra itself.[455]

In the spring of the following year, 1411, Tsongkhapa took a vow not to leave Ganden for several years and to remain in retreat meditating, teaching advanced tantric practices to a select group of students, and writing. In a letter Tsongkhapa wrote to Karmapa Deshin Shekpa, who had recently returned to central Tibet from China, he apologized for not being able to come see him:

> Although I should come to see the victorious banner that is your physical presence, I made a pledge early in the spring of the Rabbit year (1411) not to descend from this mountain for several years, thinking this would be a most wonderful thing to do. I am therefore bound by this oath and am unable to see you for the time being. However, "Though my body remains afar, / In my heart our friendship remains undimmed; / Just

as the sun and a lotus grove remain connected / Though separated by a distance of countless leagues."[456]

This letter was accompanied by several gifts, most notably a statue of Maitreya that once belonged to Atiśa.

It was during this retreat period that began in 1411 that Tsongkhapa wrote two of his most influential works on tantra: his *Lamp to Illuminate the Five Stages*[457] and *A Practical Guide to the Five Stages in One Sitting*. In writing these texts, he drew on his experience acquired over years of meditative practice and, more immediately, the notes he had taken during his retreat in Wölkha in 1409.

The first work, *Lamp*, is an authoritative and detailed exposition of the five stages of the completion stage of Guhyasamāja tantra, based on Nāgārjuna's *Five Stages of Completion*. With the body isolation (the clear visualization of oneself as a buddha deity) being part of the generation stage, the five stages of completion are (1) speech isolation, primarily involving the yoga of winds (*prāṇayāma*); (2) mind isolation, principally entailing meditations on the nature of mind and entering into progressively subtler levels of consciousness; (3) illusory body, assuming a subtle form that is composed of subtle winds; (4) clear light, evoking the subtlest state of awareness (akin to consciousness at the moment of death); and (5) the union, namely, the coalescence of the last two stages into an indivisible union of a buddha's perfected, enlightened body and mind.

The second work, *A Practical Guide to the Five Stages in One Sitting*, takes Nāropa's *Lucid Summary of the Five Stages* (*Pañcakrama-saṃgraha-prakāśa*) as its main framework and offers a practical and experiential instruction on the specific completion stages and their key elements. Of Tibetan authorities, Tsongkhapa relies primarily on two important figures in the transmission of Guhyasamāja in Tibet: the celebrated translator Marpa (1012–95), who was the teacher of Milarepa, and the translator Gö Khukpa Lhatsé (eleventh century). Though he draws on others, Tsongkhapa uses Gö Khukpa Lhatsé as his major Tibetan source when it comes to conceptual and theoretical explanations of the tantra, and Marpa when it comes to the more experiential aspects.[458]

As noted earlier, one critically important qualification for any Tibetan master aspiring to write about tantra is the receipt of signs indicating they have permission to write on esoteric matters, what the Tibetans call "receiving a reliable sign from the meditation deity." Tsongkhapa explicitly refers to having received such a sign at the end of each of these two tantric works, which is quite remarkable given his usual reticence in speaking about his own spiritual attainments. In the colophon of his *Practical Guide to the Five Stages in One Sitting*, he writes:

> Those who fail to differentiate correct and incorrect paths
> Will not understand this teaching, no matter how long they
> strive;
> Seeing this, I prayed for a long time and, as a result,
> When I received a reliable sign from my meditation deity,
> I composed this work for my own benefit and that of others.[459]

We find similar statements about receiving such signs in the colophon of Tsongkhapa's *Lamp to Illuminate the Five Stages*. Indeed, we see in that colophon a detailed explanation of the efforts Tsongkhapa felt he needed to make to reach the milestones before embarking on the task of writing such a significant work on tantra. As he puts it:

> The glorious Guhyasamāja, king of tantras, as renowned as the sun and moon, is the ultimate of all the Buddha's teachings and the sole jewel of the three worlds explained by the prophesized master Nāgārjuna, teacher of the ultimate

definitive meaning of the Buddha's words, and by his disciples, who had realized the meanings of the tantra and commented accordingly on its glorious five stages: This work has been a clear and complete explanation of all their points.

I realized that if you do not understand just what the superior paths are superior to, and if you do not properly understand the lower tenets, you will not understand the subtle and exclusive features of those superior paths and of the higher tenets. Especially, if you do not truly discover the ultimate definitive meaning that is the profound emptiness and the definitive teachings of the Buddha by using analytical intelligence trained well in the subtle paths of reasoning presented by the master Nāgārjuna, then you will not discover the general points of the paths to liberation and omniscience. In particular, you will not properly recognize the innate exalted wisdom that arises from a practice that has bliss and emptiness united, which is the essential subject matter of the two kinds of nondual tantra (father and mother tantra). Though you may have great liking for it, it will never go beyond mere faith. Realizing this, I trained myself well in ours and others' traditions of the Great and Lower vehicles of our own tradition, the Mantra and Perfection vehicles, and the four tantra classes of Vajrāyana.

Also, I familiarized myself for a long time with enthusiastic application to the ways that disciples are guided by the stages of the complete corpus of each of these paths, ornamented by relevant core teachings; to the ascertainment of emptiness and, having ascertained it, to the way to meditate upon it; to the ways that each Guhyasamāja tradition has been explained; and to all the genuine Indian works of the Ārya tradition that have been translated into Tibetan, together with their core teachings. With this, I compared

> the root tantra and the explanatory tantras, and with much prayer and request I received special signs of permission to compose this work. Then, with a pure motivation for the severely weakened Guhyasamāja Ārya tradition to be restored and remain strong for a long time, I composed this work.[460]

In this passage, we hear the voice of someone who speaks from a place of authority rooted in both mastery of the topic and deep personal experience. In fact, we notice that from 1410 onward, from the beginning of what I see as the final phase in Tsongkhapa's writing, he refers to himself in the colophon of his works on tantra as "Tsongkhapa Lobsang Drakpa of the eastern regions, a monk of much learning and a yogi of glorious Guhyasamāja."[461]

Tsongkhapa's *Lamp to Illuminate the Five Stages* is broadly structured into two main parts: an introduction and the main presentation of the five stages. The lengthy introductory section addresses general topics important to the Guhyasamāja tantra. The main part of the text opens with a second introductory section, this one dealing with specific issues related to how to engage in the Guhyasamāja path. A special focus here is the interrelation between the two stages of the Highest Yoga tantra path. Tsongkhapa also details the Vajrayāna union of method and wisdom in terms of the union of bliss and emptiness as symbolized by the word EVAṂ, a fusion of the two Sanskrit syllables *e* and *vaṃ*. (EVAṂ literally means "thus" and features as the first word in a Buddhist sūtra as part of the phrase "Thus have I heard once. . . .") The two stages within the Highest Yoga tantra are the generation stage, framed within the sādhana practice of imaginatively generating oneself into the meditation deity, and the completion stage, which involves effecting progressive stages of transformation of body and mind through yogic methods centered on channels (*nāḍi*), winds (*vayu* or *prāṇa*), and drops (*bindu*). Having addressed these preliminary issues, Tsongkhapa then offers one of the most comprehensive explanations of each of the five (six, if we include the body isolation) stages according to Nāgārjuna in his *Lucid Summary of the Five Stages*, and subsequently elaborated by an entire lineage of great Indian masters.

Nāropa's Unique Instruction on the "Ninefold Mixing"

Tsongkhapa's second work on tantra, *A Practical Guide to the Five Stages in One Sitting*, is quite different from his *Lamp* in both structure and style. It is much shorter, about one-third the length of the *Lamp*, and closely follows Nāropa's *Lucid Summary of the Five Stages*.

As its title suggests, the work is primarily an instruction manual explaining how to undertake the practice of all five stages in a meditation session. It opens with a brief instruction on such preliminary practices as (1) training one's mind in the foundational aspects of the Buddhist path, (2) becoming initiated into the tantra through an empowerment ceremony, (3) observing the vows and commitments taken at the time of initiation, (4) engaging in the purification practice of Vajrasattva meditation and recitation, and (5) invoking the blessings of one's gurus through guru yoga meditation. The actual instruction on the practice of the five stages is organized in terms of the trio of ground, path, and result (*zhi lam dré sum*), an approach that became hugely popular in Tibet. The Tibetan tradition defines the three more specifically as (1) understanding the ground, the nature of reality; (2) how to traverse the stages of the path; and (3) how the result comes to be actualized. Nāropa's root text puts this succinctly:

> There is the nature of reality, the path,
> And stages in the arising of the result.[462]

Nāropa's text is one of the earliest, if not the first, to explicitly present this powerful framework of ground, path, and result. Though the structure was initially developed in the context of an advanced Vajrayāna instruction, Tibetan masters often adopted this framework more broadly, using it to present the Buddhist perspective in many contexts. Thus, we find such phrases as the presentation of "the ground, the understanding of the two truths; the path, the union of method and wisdom; and the result, the union of the two buddha bodies."[463] The framework captures a fundamental insight utilized by the Buddha in teaching on the four noble truths—suffering, its origin, cessation of suffering, and the path to such a cessation—namely, that it is through knowledge of reality and transforming one's mind through bringing that knowledge onto the path that one gains freedom from bondage. Tsongkhapa was so impressed by the succinctness and lucidity of this short text of Nāropa's that, in addition to using this as the framework for his *Practical Guide to the Five Stages in One Sitting*—which opens with a summary of Nāropa's verses—he later composed a word-by-word commentary on the root text itself.[464]

Tsongkhapa speaks of Marpa having received from Nāropa's lineage, among others, the following four important transmissions associated with four specific tantras: (1) based on the Hevajra tantra, the tummo (or "inner fire" practice), which is known as "grabbing emptiness with your bare hands"; (2) based on Mahāmāyā tantra, the practice of prāṇayāma (breath yoga), known as "the method of practicing the white and red drops"; (3) based on the Caturpītha tantra, the practice of *phowa* (or transference of consciousness into another); and (4) based on the Guhyasamāja tantra, instruction on completing the five stages in one sitting.[465] Of these, Tsongkhapa states, the fourth instruction is based on Nāropa's short text entitled *Lucid Summary of the Five Stages*. In speaking of the importance of the practical understanding gained by the great Tibetan translators in interpreting the great Indian tantric works, Tsongkhapa expresses his deep appreciation of Marpa's contribution:

> These great works [of the Indian masters] are extremely profound in their meaning. Thus, without the help of very clear instructions from excellent teachers, later trainees will not gain complete understanding of the essential points of the instructions. Therefore, the instructions of the great Tibetan translators who studied at the feet of numerous Indian masters and received the transmission perfectly are most critical. Among these, the two traditions—of master Marpa and of master Gö—are the best. Now, to gain decisive understanding of the instructional aspects of this Guhyasamāja tantra rooted in the treatises of the Ārya tradition, it is necessary to rely on the instructions stemming from master Gö. However, to gain decisive understanding not just of the explicit but also the implicit points in the treatises on the basis of elucidating the details of numerous unique meditative practices relevant for today's practitioners, it is necessary to rely on the instructions of master Marpa.[466]

One of the most important instructions—not explicit in many of the treatises of the Ārya tradition but made explicit by Marpa's instruction stemming from Nāropa—is that on "the ninefold mixing." This is a unique meditation practice that utilizes the three states of waking, dreaming, and deep sleep, as well as death, the intermediate state, and rebirth, and correlates them with the resultant states of buddhahood: the *dharmakāya*, *saṃbhogakāya*, and *nirmāṇakāya*. In his *Lamp to Illuminate the Five Stages*, Tsongkhapa would develop a comprehensive presentation of the practice of the ninefold mixing. Later, on another ocassion, when Tsongkhapa assigned Jamchen Chöjé to go to China in his stead, he would write a short work at the disciple's request on the instructions on the ninefold mixing and transference of consciousness.[467]

The purpose of this instruction on "the ninefold mixing" is to prepare the yogi so that at the critical moment of death they will be able to ensure the "meeting of the mother and child clear lights." Here, the "mother clear light" refers to the clear light that arises naturally at the point of death, when all activities, both physical and mental, cease and only the empty expanse of pure consciousness remains. In contrast, the "child clear light" refers to the clear-light state evoked through meditative practice and attained through progressive dissolution of consciousness and arrival at a realization of the total emptiness of mere luminosity. Experienced yogis, who have familiarized themselves with the critical signs of dissolution and can deliberately evoke the state of clear light through meditative practice, will then be able to maintain their awareness at the point of death, when only pure consciousness remains. Even though this pure consciousness of mere luminosity arises at the moment of death for all of us—free, devoid of subject-object duality, ego-consciousness, or any form of conceptuality—an untrained ordinary person is simply swept away by the power of the state. The yogi, on the other hand, has the chance to seize the moment and merge their awareness with that pure state.

The Union of Bliss and Emptiness

Like the great Tibetan masters before him, Tsongkhapa never questioned the basic assumption that the path of Tantra, or Vajrayāna, was superior to the general Mahāyāna, or the Sūtra path. Yet he did develop his own unique perspective on how the profundity of Tantra lies principally in two areas: the richness of its meditative techniques and the nature of the mind that actualizes the ultimate truth, emptiness. For Tsongkhapa, however, Tantra's profundity did not lie in the revelation of some new "truth" or ultimate reality not discovered through the Sūtra path. Indeed, Tsongkhapa specifically insisted that there is no special or different emptiness to be discovered through Tantra that is somehow more advanced than the one taught in the Perfection of Wisdom sūtras and so clearly expounded by Nāgārjuna and his Indian commentators. In other words, for Tsongkhapa, there was no difference between Sūtra and Tantra when it comes to the view of emptiness. In Tsongkhapa's words, "For the definitive understanding of emptiness, there is nothing beyond what is found in the Madhyamaka."[468] In this respect, Tsongkhapa agreed with Sakya Paṇḍita, who had earlier stated that if there is something beyond emptiness, this would mean that emptiness is not beyond conceptual elaboration.[469]

The heart of the tantric approach for Tsongkhapa was the indivisible union of bliss and emptiness—the realization of emptiness by a unique subject permeated by the experience of great bliss. In what sense are bliss and emptiness fused so as to constitute an indivisible union? According to Tsongkhapa, given that bliss, like anything else, is inseparable from its own emptiness, it too is empty. So, in an objective sense, there is no need for bringing the two into union; they already are indivisibly one. Nor is it a matter of generating two streams of consciousness, one a blissful state and the other the wisdom of emptiness, and somehow linking the two. What then is the meaning of their union? Tsongkhapa writes:

> How then is this union developed? The subject consciousness, arising in the nature of innate bliss, is fused with its object, emptiness, in the manner such that it perceives emptiness without any distortion. This uniting of subject and object is the inseparable joining of bliss and emptiness. At the time of the arising of actual innate bliss, object and sub-

> ject become of one taste, like milk poured into water, and even the subtlest dualistic appearance has ceased. Before the actual innate bliss has arisen, given that the ultimate reality has not yet been perceived directly, one has to engage with the ultimate reality through simulation. Thus, there is only the imagination of these two being of one taste. This is the way of uniting nondually with the object, emptiness. Therefore the way that the mind cognizing emptiness and the bliss are inseparably united entails the generation of two mental states into a single entity not separate in nature.[470]

In brief, this union of bliss and emptiness is defined in terms of the inseparable and nondual fusion of a subject with its object, a blissful state of mind perceiving emptiness in a nondual way. This, then, is the unique notion of the subject that realizes emptiness in the tantra: a state of mind that is blissful, nondual, and free of conceptuality. Until the yogi has reached the stage where the innate great bliss has arisen, such a union, including the realization of emptiness, will remain only at the level of simulation and imagination.

For Tsongkhapa, the wisdom of emptiness remains at the heart of the journey to enlightenment on the tantric path, just as it is on the general Mahāyāna path. What is different is that in tantra this insight into emptiness must occur at the subtlest level of consciousness, which can be brought about only through generating the experience of great bliss arising from the entry of winds into the central channel. This, in essence, is the wisdom of the union of bliss and emptiness.

The Nature of Great Bliss in Tantra

If, as Tsongkhapa states, there is no difference between Sūtra and Tantra when it comes to emptiness, then everything hinges on the other member of the pair in this union: the bliss. What, then, is this bliss? Tsongkhapa advises us to be discerning in our understanding of the meaning of *bliss* in the context of the union of bliss and emptiness and not to confuse it with other types of bliss. In particular, he identifies two categories of bliss in the Buddhist sources. The first is the deep feeling of bliss that comes with the arising of physical and mental pliancy when one has successfully quieted the mind and attained tranquility. The second is a pervasive experience of bliss that arises through breath-based techniques, as presented in nontantric sources as well as the Action and Performance classes of tantra.

In his *Lamp*, Tsongkhapa describes this second type of bliss as arising through "preventing the breath from leaving the body and holding it inside, which is taught as *prāṇāyāma* deity-yoga meditation."[471] In both of these cases, meditators can attain a state that is characterized by bliss, clarity, and nonconceptuality. The problem with both of these types of bliss, however, is that neither of them has arisen from the "melting of drops caused by the ignition of tummo [inner heat] through the entry of the winds into the central channel triggered by penetrating the vital points of the channel centers in the body."[472] What then is the right kind of bliss? Tsongkhapa writes:

> Therefore, *innate joy* is the bliss spoken of with respect to "uniting bliss and emptiness," and it initially arises from bringing the winds of the left and right channels into the central channel to ignite the *caṇḍālī* (tummo) fire, which then causes the bodhicitta to melt. . . . This bliss is also called the *object-less compassion*.[473]

Here we see a highly complex and intriguing notion of bliss that is essentially sexual in nature and presupposes a unique tantric physiology. According to this view of the subtle human body, winds or subtle energies course through the body in a network of channels, with winds serving as media for consciousness. These multiple channels stem from three principal channels: a central channel flanked by two side channels, with the three channels forming "knots" at crucial junctures of the body. These junctures where the two side channels intersect with the central channel—the crown, throat, heart, navel, and sexual organ (sometimes the midbrow and base of the spine are added, making seven altogether)—are known as *cakras* or channel centers and are an important focus of attention in tantric yoga. On this view, all activities of our mind, including sensory perceptions, emotions, thoughts, concepts, and so on, are functions of the movement of winds within the channels. Except at the point of death, when all thought processes cease and the clear-light mind, the subtlest level of consciousness, arises, very little activity occurs within the central channel. There are, however, occasions in everyday life when even for an ordinary person this clear light is thought to manifest briefly, as when fainting, yawning, and—crucially—during orgasm.[474]

Steeped in this Indo-Tibetan tradition of psychophysiology, Tsongkhapa envisions a two-pronged approach to tantric meditation. One is to deepen one's understanding and realization of emptiness, while the other is to focus on generating bliss through the ignition of tummo by applying yogic techniques that cause the winds to enter the central channel. Two distinct types of technique for the second purpose are identified, one involving the explicit evocation of sexual energy, through union with either a live partner ("action seal") or with a visualized consort ("wisdom seal"), and the other involving the yoga of channels, winds, and drops. As a celibate monk, Tsongkhapa understandably cautions against the use of a live partner, "since this requires for both partners the presence of all the specific qualifications stipulated in the tantras, which is most rare."[475] Tsongkhapa further maintains that most features of the experience from sexual union with a living partner can be effected on the basis of a visualized consort as well. Thus, by relying on sexual union with a visualized consort, one can cause the winds to enter the central channel.

As for the second type of method, Tsongkhapa identifies various techniques presented in the different tantras. Indeed, he understands the difference between the major tantras of the Highest Yoga class (Guhyasamāja, Cakrasaṃvara, Hevajra, and Kālacakra) largely to be a function of their different methods toward the same end: igniting the tummo fire. Briefly, they are the method of vajra repetition (*dordé*) wind yoga and vase-breath (*bumchen*) yoga as presented in Guhyasamāja tantra; the various yogas focusing on the subtle drops (*trathik*) as presented in the works of Cakrasaṃvara mystic Ghaṇṭapā; and tummo meditations as presented in the works of Ḍombi Heruka and Kṛṣṇācārya. These techniques differ also in which specific point on the body is taken to be the principal focus and how it is used. For example, Tsongkhapa explains, in the approach of Ḍombi Heruka and Kṛṣṇācārya, the navel cakra is the focus of the tummo practice. Kālacakra tradition also focuses on the navel cakra but uses it as a locus for its vase-breath technique. In the Ārya tradition of Guhyasamāja, by contrast, the sexual-organ cakra is chosen first, and the yogi then shifts the focus to the heart cakra.[476]

In sum, Tsongkhapa understands tantra to be offering sophisticated techniques to bring the subtle levels of mind to the fore. Progressive dissolutions of the grosser levels of activity of both body and mind lead eventually to a subtle state of mind free of duality or conceptuality and permeated by bliss. Paradoxically, this is not an acquired or generated bliss but innate to our consciousness. It is as if consciousness, freed from its habitual bondage to objects, concepts, and sensations, has returned home, to a pure luminosity whose basic tone is bliss. The goal in tantra is to utilize this most subtle level of mind to perceive emptiness, and when this can be done, the effect is said to be simply immeasurable. Tsongkhapa compares the realization of emptiness by an ordinary intellect and by such innate great bliss mind to the difference between the space covered by an open palm and that of the entire sky.[477]

Nonconceptuality in Tantra

Just as Tsongkhapa admonishes us to be discerning in our understanding of what is meant by *bliss*, he draws our attention also to the multiple meanings of the problematic term *nonconceptuality*. He writes:

> Generally, merely resting the mind in a stable and nonconceptual or nondiscursive (*mitokpa*) manner is common to Buddhists and non-Buddhist [paths], as well as to both Mahāyāna and the Lesser Vehicle. In particular, an uncontaminated meditative state dwelling nonconceptually on emptiness is also shared with the Perfection Vehicle. So, to develop these states, there is clearly no need to meditate by applying the techniques of penetrating the vital points of the body through wind yoga. Also, it makes no sense to say that such a meditative state will bring about great bliss through the force of the winds dissolving into the central channel. Therefore, the "stable mind" one is instructed to develop in the context of stability of the mind attained through stopping the movement of the action winds is the mind of *innate bliss*. . . . Developing this depends upon the winds dissolving into the central channel and the blazing of the tummo fire. Thus the [varying types of] nonconceptual mind and bliss referred to earlier may have similar names but, in actual fact, they are completely different from one another.[478]

Perhaps the most controversial aspect of Tsongkhapa's exposition of tantra for some of his Tibetan peers was his insistence on the importance of discursive or analytic meditation even in advanced Vajrayāna practice. If, as Tsongkhapa maintains, there is only one and the same emptiness for general Mahāyāna and for Tantra, there is then no substitute for going through the progressive stages of deconstruction of our concepts, characteristic of meditation on emptiness. This clearly requires discursive analysis using all the resources offered by Madhyamaka reasoning. In other words, Tantra does not offer any easy shortcut. The only difference, as noted earlier, is the need to generate bliss through progressive dissolution of our ordinary consciousness. However, Tsongkhapa admits that there are certain occasions when discursiveness should not be employed, including especially when, through yogic techniques, the innate joy and clear-light mind have arisen and bliss and emptiness are truly united. Only when the yogi rises from such a state should he or she once again employ discursive meditation.[479]

It seems that, soon after the appearance of Tsongkhapa's *Lamp* and *Practical Guide*, a tradition developed among his followers to teach, study, and ground one's practice of the completion stage of the Guhyasamāja tantra by combining these two works. Indeed we find in Tsongkhapa's collected works an instruction on the completion stage based on the two texts together. Similarly, Khedrup explicitly combines the instructions in Tsongkhapa's two texts in a guide on the completion stage.[480] In fact, Khedrup would compile "twenty-one short pieces on Guhyasamāja," based on notes taken from Tsongkhapa over ten months, which he utilized as the main resource for his meditative practice for six years before compiling the notes as a special collection of oral instructions (*shalshé*).[481] Tsongkhapa's own collected works contain a special set of oral instructions covering various facets of the completion stage of the Guhyasamāja tantra.

A Long Retreat at Ganden Monastery

To return to our narrative, by the time Tsongkhapa had consecrated Ganden Monastery and written his two important works on tantra, it was 1411, and the great master was now fifty-five years old. He was cognizant of the prophecy he had received six years earlier, at the hermitage of the Lhodrak mystic Drupchen Namkha Gyaltsen, foretelling threats to his health when he turned fifty-seven. So, accompanied by a group of some thirty close students, Tsongkhapa entered a long retreat at Ganden. During the retreat, they performed various rites for averting obstacles.[482]

Around this time, having seen Tsongkhapa's two major works on tantra, Rendawa, who had been in retreat in western Tibet, sent an intriguing request to his former pupil. Rendawa asked if Tsongkhapa would request the meditation deity Mañjuśrī to provide a short experiential instruction on how to engage in practice in the most efficient manner. The result is a remarkable short instruction, running to eight folios, summarizing the entire map of the Vajrayāna path to buddhahood. Tsongkhapa sent this with another work—an instruction on the sādhana practice of the peaceful and wrathful aspects of Mañjuśrī—on the fourth day of the sixth month in the Tibetan calendar (June 25, 1411), recognized in the tradition as the auspicious day when the Buddha gave his first sermon in the Deer Park at Sarnath. In the colophon of this text, Tsongkhapa writes, "Please do not share this with others. As for the detailed explanations I received on each of the main points, I would like to offer these when we meet in person."[483]

Alas, Tsongkhapa would never have the chance to see his beloved teacher again. A year later, in the winter of 1412 (the Water Dragon year), Rendawa passed away at the age of sixty-four at the hermitage of Lötsé Pal. At the time, Rendawa was teaching Candrakīrti's *Entering the Middle Way* to a group of over one hundred monks at the retreat. In accordance with his wishes, Rendawa's attendant sent Tsongkhapa the small gold statue of Mañjuśrī seated on a silver base, which the master always kept next to him. It was accompanied by a letter and a portion of Rendawa's ashes. Tsongkhapa had a similar gold statue, so he had the two statues housed together in the altar of the main prayer hall at Ganden Monastery.[484] Perhaps Tsongkhapa wanted his and Rendawa's inseparability to be symbolized in some tangible form, even when the law of impermanence had forced the physical separation of the two on this earth.

Throughout 1411 Tsongkhapa and a small group of close disciples remained in strict retreat. About a year into the retreat, sometime in the spring of 1412, he told his students that he had so far not seen any indication that the obstacles had been cleared. One night, however, he had a powerful dream in which a stream of light stemming from the tip of his nostrils, the upper end of the central channel, flowed downward into his body through the central channel. The following day, when he engaged in his meditative practice, he experienced a powerful surge of bliss permeating his entire being, an innate bliss fused with spontaneous awareness of emptiness, the ultimate nature of reality. He had attained the true union of bliss and emptiness, direct realization of emptiness by the most subtle mind of clear light.[485] Earlier, thanks to his realization of emptiness, Tsongkhapa had been able to spontaneously perceive everything as illusion-like, without solidity or substantial reality. Now, with this arising of innate bliss, he would perceive everything as the manifestation or play of the union of bliss and emptiness. It appears that as Tsongkhapa's meditative experiences were progressing by leaps and bounds, crossing ever more thresholds, signs of his imminent ill health were also becoming starker by the day.

The Master Falls Ill at Ganden Monastery

In the autumn of 1412, as the new year of the Water Snake was approaching, Tsongkhapa called together his closest disciples and said, "I do not know if I will be able to teach again and again as before. As a basis for establishing your aspiration, I would like to give explanations on each of the four classes of tantra." However, the disciples begged Tsongkhapa in unison to continue to focus on countering the obstacles to his health by remaining in retreat. Thus, on the seventh day of the eighth month of the Tibetan Water Dragon year (September 22, 1412), Tsongkhapa and his closest disciples began another period of intensive retreat. Despite all their efforts, in the eleventh month, Tsongkhapa began to experience the beginning signs of ill health. When the new year of the Water Snake (1413) began, Tsongkhapa fell ill, just as the prophecy had warned. The chronic back pain he had suffered in his early twenties resurfaced, this time affecting much of the lower part of his body. At one point, the pain prevented him from getting a good night's sleep for almost three weeks.[486] For his part, however, Tsongkhapa continued his daily meditation practice, often equipoised in the experience of the union of bliss and emptiness. As the master appeared increasingly frail, his students became alarmed and undertook a series of healing rites. Many of Tsongkhapa's benefactors came to Ganden to see him and to sponsor ritual ceremonies for his well-being. During this period, seven devoted students helped nurse the master: Gyaltsap, Khedrup, Hortön Namkha Pal, Sharpa Rinchen Gyaltsen, Jamchen Chöjé, Lekpa Sangpo, and Shönu Gyalchok. Shönu Gyalchok, the youngest in the group, served as the ritual assistant during many of the healing rites.[487]

Tsongkhapa began to feel a little better, and he decided to undertake an intensive retreat on Vajrabhairava, the wrathful form of Mañjuśrī, with special focus on visualization of the protection circle and invocation of the wrathful guardians. In the evenings, Tsongkhapa would return to his equipoise on the union of bliss and emptiness. Gradually, his health continued to improve. One day, during a session on Vajrabhairava meditation, Tsongkhapa experienced a powerful vision of a massive image of the Buddha resplendent within a large halo of light floating up above in space. The Buddha was performing the gesture of conquering the *māras*, the forces of darkness. While maintaining his meditative focus, Tsongkhapa willed the image of the Buddha to enter his body and dissolve into him. This then led to a cascade of other visions—powerful protectors led by Mahākāla, with Kālarūpa dragging the obstructive forces, which were chased by Kṣetrapāla from behind. These obstructive forces were then brought before Tsongkhapa, where the protectors sliced them into pieces and buried them inside a deep pit. With this vision, Tsongkhapa's health began to improve noticeably by the day.[488]

It was toward the end of 1413, too, that Tsongkhapa received the second formal letter of invitation from the Chinese Yongle emperor. As noted before, this time, Tsongkhapa sent Jamchen Chöjé, one of his senior students, to Beijing in his stead, bearing a letter and gifts for the emperor.[489]

One day in the first month of the Wood Horse year (1414), Tsongkhapa had a vision of Mañjuśrī, who told him, "From now on, you should concentrate your practice on the generation and completion stages of tantra. If you do this, you will attain the realizations of the Highest Yoga tantra. Among your students, too, such extraordinary realizations will arise in the mind streams of seven who are specially fortunate."[490] Emerging from this long period of ill health, Tsongkhapa told his close students that perhaps he should not take this particular vision of Mañjuśrī seriously, as it could be the aftereffects of his illness. Later, he would ask Tokden Jampel Gyatso, the longtime disciple who constantly had visions of Mañjuśrī, to see if he could consult the deity. Tokden said, "There is no need; the deity has told the same thing to me, too, about how the union of bliss and wisdom has arisen in you and that, just as clouds gather into a larger cluster, all the conditions to increase the union will come to you."[491]

By the summer of 1414, Tsongkhapa had completely regained his health and had resumed writing.[492] There was one important lacuna that needed to be filled to complete his writings on the Guhyasamāja tantra, namely, the exposition of the root tantra itself. Thus, in 1414, while still in strict retreat, he embarked on his final work on Guhyasamāja. As a methodical author, he first produced a critical edition of the root tantra and of Candrakīrti's extensive commentary *The Clear Lamp* (*Pradīpodyotana*). He then produced a comprehensive outline of the entire tantra and commentary, as well as an analytic exposition of the critical points of the tantra. Finally, he produced a detailed annotation of Candrakīrti's commentary, creating the basis for what came to be known as the four interwoven explanations of the tantra.[493] These are (1) Tsongkhapa's summary outline, (2) Candrakīrti's commentary, (3) Tsongkhapa's annotations, and (4) his analytic exposition. With these works complete, Tsongkhapa had produced a comprehensive and authoritative resource on the study and practice of this important Buddhist tantra.[494] Years later, the influential historical work *The Blue Annals* would remark:

> With respect to the successive lineages stemming from Gö Lotsawa [Khukpa Lhatsé], I perceive Butön to be the most learned. He taught the Guhyasamāja cycle to Khyungpo Lhepa, from whom the great master Tsongkhapa received it. The latter made, in general, great contributions to the

Buddha's doctrine, and in particular, it was great Tsongkhapa who made Guhyasamāja spread across the entire face of the earth.[495]

A Teaching Festival at Tashi Dhokha

In the summer of 1415, the Wood Sheep year, Tsongkhapa descended Ganden Mountain at the invitation of Miwang Drakpa Gyaltsen to spend the summer rainy-season retreat at Tashi Dhokha Hermitage, near Densa Thil Monastery, in the Wön region.[496] He had not left Ganden since arriving in the spring of 1410 to formally consecrate the new monastery. At Tashi Dhokha, Tsongkhapa gave various teachings to around seven hundred monastics, as well as numerous layfolk, on lamrim; the Madhyamaka philosophy of emptiness; pramāṇa epistemology; Śāntideva's *Bodhicaryāvatāra*; his own hermeneutic monograph, *The Essence of True Eloquence*; his commentaries on the *Fifty Verses on the Guru* and on *Root Vows of Tantra*; and so on. Among those attending this lengthy teaching series at the hermitage were some of the most powerful members of the Phagdru dynasty.[497]

At this Tashi Dhokha retreat, Tsongkhapa forged connections with a number of important people who would have an impact on his legacy. It was there that he first met Gendün Drup (1391–1474), who would play a crucial role in the diffusion of Tsongkhapa's lineage in Tsang Province and later would be recognized as the first Dalai Lama.

Gendün Drup was twenty-four and had come to the hermitage from Narthang Monastery as an attendant to Sempa Chenpo Künsang, the latter already a disciple of Tsongkhapa. Two of Gendün Drup's teachers, Sempa Chenpo Künsang and Sherap Sengé, both students of Tsongkhapa, spoke to Tsongkhapa about the young scholar's clear intellect.[498] Gendün Drup felt an immediate connection with Tsongkhapa and seized the opportunity to ask questions on the important points of Buddhist epistemology. Tsongkhapa, too, was impressed by the young scholar and gave him one of his spare robes as a memento. Gendün Drup would later compose a work compiled from his notes on the lectures Tsongkhapa gave at Tashi Dhokha on Dharmakīrti's *Pramāṇaviniścaya*.[499] For the next three years, Gendün Drup would spend extended periods of time at Ganden Monastery to deepen his command of Madhyamaka and epistemology studies, studying at the feet of Tsongkhapa, Gyaltsap, and Dülzin.[500]

Other notable figures in attendance were the meditator Götruk Repa and Ngorchen Künga Sangpo (1382–1456), an important member of the Sakya Ngor lineage.[501] It was also at this hermitage that Gö Lotsawa Shönu Pal (1392–1481), the author of *The Blue Annals*, first became Tsongkhapa's student. He was twenty-three years old and would later compile the notes from Tsongkhapa's teaching on the six yogas of Nāropa to produce an instruction manual on the practice. Later, Gö Lotsawa would say, "When it comes to not confining one's understanding merely to what one has learned but to critically examining the texts through one's own intelligence, and when it comes to everyday conduct, it is for Tsongkhapa alone that I have the deepest admiration."[502]

Another young monk who would meet Tsongkhapa at Tashi Dhokha was Jampa Lingpa Sönam Namgyal (1400–75), a student at Tsethang Monastery who was at the time barely fourteen years old. (Jampa Lingpa would later emerge as a major author on two important tantras, Kālacakra and Cakrasaṃvara.) Impressed by the young monk's composure and sharp intellect, Tsongkhapa complimented him and gave him some gifts.[503]

During this two-month summer retreat, two important figures took full ordination from Tsongkhapa. One was Chenga Sönam Sangpo, the younger brother of Miwang; the other was Jamyang

Chöjé, the eventual founder of Drepung Monastery. The latter, who was then thirty-six years old, offered a pledge to Tsongkhapa that he would teach 108 volumes. It was also at this hermitage that Tsongkhapa instructed Jamyang Chöjé to establish Drepung, with financial support from Tsongkhapa's loyal longtime benefactor, Neu governor Namkha Sangpo. After receiving this instruction, Jamyang Chöjé had a prophetic dream in which a local spirit showed him the site of the new monastery and pledged to attract five thousand monks there. In the dream, Jamyang Chöjé saw himself walking across a large valley up a hill, where he came across a spring. Tsongkhapa was sitting next to the spring and urged Chöjé to drink from it, describing it as "the spring of study and critical reflection."[504]

On the devotional side, it was at Tashi Dhokha Hermitage that a set of seven revered statues of Tsongkhapa were constructed—remarkably, according to some sources, by the fourteen-year-old Jampa Lingpa Sönam Namgyal. Each of these seven statues contained hair from one of Tsongkhapa's seven head-shavings while at the hermitage. These statues, about the size of a closed fist (five inches or so) and reputed to be consecrated by the master himself, came to be known as the Tashi Dhokha Tsongkhapa icons.[505] After a stay of over two months, sometime in the fall of 1415, Tsongkhapa returned to Ganden.

CHAPTER 13

Yogi of the Cakrasaṃvara Tantra

IN THE FALL of 1415, following the rainy-season retreat and his extended stay at Tashi Dhokha Hermitage, Tsongkhapa returned to Ganden Monastery.[506] He had always been a focused person, but after his return from Tashi Dhokha, those around him noticed an additional intensity of focus in his activities. With the benefit of hindsight, we can see that during his final four years, Tsongkhapa was essentially filling what he perceived to be important gaps in his life's work.

One important lacuna was his dearth of writings on the Cakrasaṃvara tantra, another supremely important system of Buddhist tantra. Perhaps Tsongkhapa had a premonition that his end was approaching; after all, it had been just over a year since he had come out of his two-year spell of ill health, and an old prophecy had given him a life span of only fifty-seven years. Whatever the cause, one couldn't help noticing a certain sense of urgency in Tsongkhapa. A few years earlier, in 1412, his own teacher Rendawa—with whom he had remained close ever since they met in 1376, and who over time had also become a colleague—had passed away. Another important figure in his life, Lochen Kyapchok Palsang, the senior personage who made the formal request to Tsongkhapa to author his two grand syntheses, too, was no more. More recently, Karmapa Deshin Shekpa, another important Tibetan religious figure to whom Tsongkhapa was close, had passed away at the age of thirty-two. It was as if the truth of impermanence was closing in on him.

The first thing Tsongkhapa appears to have done after his return to Ganden, however, was to compose a shorter, more practice-oriented version of his magnum opus, *The Great Treatise on the Stages of the Path to Enlightenment*.[507] This was perhaps the easiest piece of writing he had undertaken, as it involved simply trimming down a longer work, while adding only a few new materials to the original. The original version, composed in 1402, ran to some 519 long folios, and after thirteen years, Tsongkhapa had taught that text numerous times. Over time, he had come to appreciate the need for a more manageable version that would contain the essence of his earlier text while omitting the elaborate citations from the various Indian sources he used to substantiate the points he was making. The result was yet another authoritative presentation of the stages of the path based on Atiśa's instruction in terms of practitioners of the three progressive levels of spiritual capacity, this version about one-third shorter than the original *Great Treatise*.

One topic found in this shorter text but not in the lengthier version is the explicit presentation of the two truths. Another important addition is a more explicit discussion of the status of "nonmentation" meditation. This is a kind of deliberate nondiscursive meditative practice involving, as Asaṅga puts it in his *Śrāvaka Levels*, "the absence of engagement of thought (*drenpa mepa*) and of conscious attention (*yila jepa mepa*)," such that one's mind abides free of the perception of signs, devoid of conceptuality, and tranquil.[508] In his *Great Treatise on the Stages of the Path*, Tsongkhapa did speak of a way of cultivating tranquility that involves not taking on any external object but rather simply abiding within a nonconceptual or nondiscursive state. Here, however, Tsongkhapa explores what such a "nonconceptual state" might entail and discusses whether it can be recognized as genuine nonconceptual realization of emptiness, the ultimate nature of things. For example:

> As you rest your mind devoid of thought and attention, unable to link with subsequent [mind] moments any more than bubbles arising one after another in water, your thoughts will naturally come to cease on their own. As you continue to maintain this meditation, even the awareness of subjective experience, as well as the sense of bliss [that arises], will be unable to stand on their own, without your having to stop them, just like an old skin being shed [naturally by a snake]. At that time, when you remain in meditative equipoise, you will have no perception whatsoever of your body, and as for the mind, you will experience a sense of its being indistinguishably fused with empty space. When you rise from the meditative state, you will feel as if you have suddenly acquired a body.[509]

For Tsongkhapa, on its own, such a state of nondiscursiveness and nonconceptuality represents the attainment of tranquility focused on one's mind but does not constitute nonconceptual realization of emptiness as understood by Nāgārjuna. If, however, such a nondiscursive and nonmentational state is accompanied by a genuine understanding of the truth of no-self, it then becomes part of a genuine path to enlightenment. "So," Tsongkhapa writes,

> with respect to the meditative state devoid of thought and attention, a state characterized by bliss, clarity, and nonconceptuality [often] referred to by phrases such as "uncontrived by the intellect" (*lö machöpa*) and "devoid of subjectivity" (*dzinmé*), there are two kinds: one that is genuine emptiness meditation equipoised on ultimate reality and another type that is not. It is therefore important to clearly differentiate between these two. This is because even when someone has

> not yet gained realization of emptiness, they still are in great danger of mistakenly thinking that they have done so.[510]

Over time, this shorter version of the stages of the path would be recognized as the middle-length version, with Tsongkhapa's verse "Songs of Experience on the Stages of the Path" identified as the short version of his lamrim text.

Filling in the Gaps in the Cakrasaṃvara Literature

With this shorter version of his *Great Treatise* complete, Tsongkhapa turned his attention to composing major works on the Cakrasaṃvara tantra. Cakrasaṃvara belongs to what is known as the mother tantras within the Highest Yoga tantra class. Tsongkhapa began this phase by first composing a detailed exposition of Lūipa's sādhana of the meditation deity. Lūipa (possibly tenth century and known also as Lūipada, whose name may be translated either as "Scribe" or "Fish-Gut Eater") was a Buddhist mystic said to have been born into royalty. Repulsed by wealth and power early on, he chose to lead the life of a wandering yogi. A well-known verse of praise to Lūipa reads:

> The fortunate one born into the scribe caste:
> Living on fish entrails, he attained *siddhis*;
> I prostrate to that guru,
> Who is known as Lūipa.[511]

Lūipa was a disciple of the great mystic Śavaripa, from whom he received his initiation into the Cakrasaṃvara tantra. Wandering through various places in India, Lūipa eventually ended up on the banks of the River Ganges in Bengal, where he lived on fish entrails. As a result of his intensive meditative practice, he attained advanced tantric realizations, which included experiencing a vision of the great mother-tantra deity Cakrasaṃvara. The lineage of Cakrasaṃvara practice stemming from this mystic's vision came to be known as the Cakrasaṃvara Lūipa tradition, which together with two other lineages stemming from Lūipa's lineage—those of Ghaṇṭapa and Kṛṣṇācārya—became widespread within Tibetan Buddhism.

The introductory section of Tsongkhapa's commentary on Lūipa's sādhana, entitled *Milking the Wish-Granting Cow*, presents a remarkable survey of Cakrasaṃvara literature as well as an account of the transmission of the tantra in Tibet.[512] The main part of the text is a detailed explanation of the generation stage of Cakrasaṃvara, based on Lūipa's lineage, including a word-by-word exposition of the mystic's own sādhana.

Tsongkhapa followed up on the writing of this important work by composing two sādhanas of his own, one a lengthy meditation manual on imaginatively generating oneself into the deity and the second a practical step-by-step manual, written in a chantable liturgical style, on how to engage in the sādhana meditation practice of the tantra.[513] The second, shorter text is still used in Geluk monasteries as the main sādhana for the practice of Lūipa's tradition of Cakrasaṃvara.

To accompany his lengthy exposition of Lūipa's Cakrasaṃvara sādhana and his own two shorter generation-stage sādhanas, Tsongkhapa then composed a presentation of the completion stage of Cakrasaṃvara. Entitled *Sheaves of Attainments*, the work grounds the practice of the completion stage of this tantra on an interwoven interpretation of crucial passages from Lūipa's sādhana pertaining to the completion stage and their sources in the tantras. A special focus of the Cakrasaṃvara tantra, especially what is called "the great yoga of the completion stage," is the evocation of "innate great bliss," especially through the use of sexual yoga. Implied in this is the intriguing idea that if properly understood and tapped into, something as mundane as the sex act could hold the key to the most profound wisdom immanent within a human being. Speaking of this, Tsongkhapa quotes the following famous lines from Saraha's *Dohākoṣagīti*: "Although they talk about it at homes here and there, / no one understands the nature of great bliss."[514] Even so, he also points out that alternative methods exist for invoking this innate bliss without engaging in actual sexual activity. These involve various yogic techniques focused on specific cakras in the yogin's body, all aimed at facilitating the entry of the winds into the central channel. In a rare sharing of what it feels like to have such an experience, Tsongkhapa writes the following:

> Then, due to the force of having applied [the appropriate techniques to] the vital points of the body as well as the mental absorptions, as you observe the tip of your nostrils you will notice that air would flow from the two nostrils in a balanced manner. If this happens once or twice, you cannot take it seriously. If, however, there are no countervailing conditions and the air flows from the two nostrils in exactly equal manner, with no difference at all in force and pace, then, through this process you will have the ability to experience the entry of wind into the central channel. This said, such an entry occurring once does not preclude the wind flowing through the either of two side channels. In any case, this marks the entry of the wind into the central channel. . . . A point will arrive when, as you observe, you will notice that even the slight movement of breath has come to cease. Now, if you find this difficult to discern, try out the following: Sit with your back straight and avoid any movement of the body. And then observe if there is movement of your belly or not. If there is even a slight movement of the

> belly, this is a sign that [the movement of wind in the side channels] still has not ceased....[515]

In the opening part of his text, Tsongkhapa explains his main reasons for writing this text on the completion stage:

> As for the great yoga of the completion stage according to Lūipa's tradition, even today, the visualization practices based simply on the passages cited in the sādhana do exist. However, no tradition of explanation seems to exist today that is based on a clear understanding of how and where all the elements of the practice are presented in the root and branch tantras of Cakrasaṃvara. It is most appropriate for those who are intelligent and interested, and have a keen aspiration to see what the tradition of the great adept (*mahāsiddha*) might be [like], to inquire into what such an explanation would look like and search for it. This tradition of Lūipa is known to be at the root of Cakrasaṃvara tantra [practice] in India, and this adept appears to have been followed by many other mahāsiddhas as well. Thus, this is an extremely important tradition [of tantric instruction].[516]

Thus, having composed an extensive exposition of the completion stage of Cakrasaṃvara, just as in the case of the generation stage, Tsongkhapa wrote a short step-by-step practical instruction on how to engage in the completion stage practice of the deity, entitled *A Succinct Guide to the Stages of Completion of the Great Yoga of Cakrasaṃvara According to the Lūipa Tradition*.[517] The main section of the guide is structured into discussions of (1) how to cause the entry of the winds into the central channel, (2) how to engage in the stages of completion following the entry of the winds into the central channel, and (3) how to correlate the stages of the Cakrasaṃvara path with the six yogas of Kālacakra and the fives stages of Guhyasamāja. This comprehensive guide to the most advanced practices of the Cakrasaṃvara system is written in a lucid instructional style and peppered with nuggets of insight rooted in personal experience; indeed, the *Succinct Guide* is a remarkable handbook for any yogi dedicated to making Cakrasaṃvara the principal focus of their meditative practice.

The next set of writings Tsongkhapa undertook focused on the cycle of Cakrasaṃvara practices according to Ghaṇṭapa, another Indian yogi instrumental in the propagation of this particular tantra. Ghaṇṭapa was born a prince but later gave up his royal life to become a monastic at Nālandā Monastery. He eventually became a disciple of the mystic Dārikapa, who was himself a disciple of Lūipa.[518] A specialty of Ghaṇṭapa's particular lineage is a sophisticated "body maṇḍala" meditation that involves visualizing the meditator's "grosser" body as the external maṇḍala and the subtler dimension of the body—the channels and the elements that flow within them—as deities of the maṇḍala.

Tsongkhapa first composed a sādhana of Ghaṇṭapa's Cakrasaṃvara body maṇḍala, then followed it up with an instruction on how to perform the rite of entering the maṇḍala and receiving the empowerment.[519] The colophon of the second text states that it was written at the request of Gelek Pal, most probably Tsongkhapa's student and future biographer, Khedrup. Tsongkhapa says that he wrote the text after "having familiarized myself with the Cakrasaṃvara root tantra itself and numerous Indian works, including especially all the treatises of the great siddhas connected with this cycle of tantra."[520] Tsongkhapa speaks of taking the tradition of the Sakya masters as his main basis and complementing it with insights from the writings of other Tibetan masters.

Tsongkhapa then took on the task of producing an authoritative work on the completion stage of Cakrasaṃvara according to the

Ghaṇṭapa tradition. He produced a word-by-word explanation of Ghaṇṭapa's short text *The Five Stages of Cakrasaṃvara* (*Śrīcakrasaṁvarapañcakrama*), entitled *Opening the Eyes to View the Hidden Meaning*, indicating how the central aim of Ghaṇṭapa's short text is to help open the eyes of the meditator so as to see the profound practices of Cakrasaṃvara's completion stage. Just as in his later writings on Guhyasamāja, where Tsongkhapa would refer to himself in the colophons as "a yogi of glorious Guhyasamāja," here too, in his later works on Cakrasaṃvara, he calls himself "a widely read monk and a yogi of Cakrasaṃvara by the name of Easterner Tsongkhapa Lobsang Drakpa."[521]

A Guide to the Six Yogas of Nāropa

One other work of note composed by Tsongkhapa around this time is his acclaimed instruction for engaging in the practice of the six yogas of Nāropa. Entitled *A Guide to the Six Yogas of Nāropa Endowed with Three Convictions*,[522] the text was written at the explicit request of Miwang Drakpa Gyaltsen and Miwang's brother, the Kagyü teacher Chenga Sönam Gyaltsen. Sönam Gyaltsen had been a disciple of Tsongkhapa since he was eighteen years old. He had also recently received an oral teaching on the topic from Tsongkhapa when the master taught the six yogas of Nāropa as part of the series of discourses at Tashi Dhokha Hermitage in 1415. At that time, Chenga made a formal request to Tsongkhapa to compose a guide to the six yogas.[523] In speaking of his relationship with Tsongkhapa, Chenga would later write:

> Having observed the insights of the All-Knowing Glorious Lobsang Drakpa on a number of essential points related to tantra, in particular his instructions on Guhyasamāja, I have gained much understanding of tantra in general and

> of the unique instructions of master Nāropa and his spiritual sons in particular. I have, therefore, developed the strong conviction that [Tsongkhapa] is identical with Vajradhara himself.[524]

Given the special history of the six yogas of Nāropa within Kagyü tradition, in presenting his own guide to this important practice Tsongkhapa draws extensively on the teachings of Marpa and Milarepa, and, when it comes to specific practical instructions, on Phagmo Drupa (1110–70), the founder of the Phagdru Kagyü tradition. Tsongkhapa describes his guide as being endowed with three convictions: (1) the instructions on the specific practices are clear and well organized, (2) each of the six yogas has been presented in such a way as to lead to in-depth understanding, and (3) the practices themselves are grounded in authoritative Indian sources. The following lines capture well Tsongkhapa's profound admiration for the tradition of the six yogas:

> The excellent instruction of great siddhas Tilopa and Nāropa,
> Hailed as "the six yogas of glorious Nāropa"—
> It is this instruction that offers the supreme Vajrayāna feast
> To countless fortunate ones in this Land of Snows.[525]

Chenga Sönam Gyaltsen, who was the principal person requesting Tsongkhapa to compose an instruction on the six yogas of Nāropa, would later list Tsongkhapa as the source of his own transmission of the six yogas;[526] he considered Tsongkhapa to be one of his three most important gurus, crediting the master with granting him the intellect to penetrate the profound meaning of the sūtras, treatises, and tantras without exception.[527]

Constructing the Yangpachen Tantric Temple

During this period of intensive writing on Cakrasaṃvara, Tsongkhapa had also been giving teachings to the larger community of monks at Ganden and also to a select group of around a hundred of his senior students, giving the latter group advanced tantric instructions. Because the main prayer hall was open to all, and seeing the need for a separate, dedicated space for the teaching and group practice of the more advanced tantric meditations, Tsongkhapa began planning the construction of a separate complex called Yangpachen (Vaiśālī). Vaiśālī is a sacred Buddhist site in north-central India, the location of the Buddha's favorite residence, the Jetavana Grove, a place later Buddhist traditions also came to associate with the teachings of Vajrayāna scriptures. The foundation stone for Yangpachen was laid by Tsongkhapa at Ganden in the summer of 1416 (the Fire Monkey year), with construction work on the complex beginning immediately after.[528]

Earlier in the year, Tsongkhapa had received word from Jamchen Chöjé Shākya Yeshé, the senior student he had sent in his stead to the Ming court of the Yongle emperor, that he would be returning to Tibet soon. He reached Ganden in the late fall of 1416, bearing gifts for his master, the most important of which was an entire set of the earliest Northern Ming block prints of the Kangyur.[529] This print version of the Kangyur brought by Jamchen Chöjé deeply impressed Tsongkhapa, who would soon commission the woodblock-print publications of many of his own major works.[530] Jamchen Chöjé's return to Ganden occurred while Tsongkhapa was in the middle of conducting an extended series of teachings, so the former was able to join the congregation in time to receive Tsongkhapa's teaching on Nāgārjuna's *Treatise on the Middle Way*, a transmission of Tsongkhapa's own *Great Treatise on the Stages of the Path* and *Great Treatise on Tantra*, and an exposition of the five stages of Guhyasamāja.

Another important event that occurred in 1416 was the founding of Drepung Monastery by Jamyang Chöjé Tashi Palden, who had taken his full ordination vows from Tsongkhapa only the year before. Over time, Drepung would become reputedly the largest monastery in the entire world, with a population at one point of nearly ten thousand monks. Drepung's success in becoming the largest monastery in Tibet was likely due to its excellent location (neither too far from nor too near to Lhasa), the ingenuity of its founder Jamyang Chöjé, and the attractive monastic curriculum it offered from its inception.

While the construction work on the new Yangpachen Temple was under way, Tsongkhapa began to receive a large number of offerings from various parts of the country, which were intended to help with the construction of the temple and especially the installation of sacred icons inside it. With the funds at hand, in the third month of the Fire Bird year (1417), a select group of Tibet's best craftsmen and sculptors gathered at Ganden and began their work.[531] Before the end of that year, both the construction of the temple and the sculpting of the images were complete. The Yangpachen Temple was two stories high, with a main hall of seventy-two pillars on the ground floor and several smaller halls on the upper floor. Inside the main hall was a large statue of the Buddha, slightly taller than the one inside Lhasa's Jokhang Temple. The upper floors contained three-dimensional maṇḍalas of three key tantric deities: the thirty-two-deity maṇḍala of Guhyasamāja, the sixty-two-deity maṇḍala of Cakrasaṃvara, and the Vajradhātu maṇḍala. Tsongkhapa himself supervised the measurements of these three-dimensional maṇḍalas as well as of the miniature statues of the deities placed inside them; the notes on these measurements prepared by Tsongkhapa were later transcribed as an instructional guide by one of the attendants.[532] The statues of the principal deities were made of pure silver, those of the retinue deities of bronze. These images, as well as the celestial mansions, were studded with turquoise, coral, and other precious gems.

Aside from these three-dimensional maṇḍalas and their deities, major statues of other important deities were made, including golden statues of Mañjuśrī, Amitāyus, Maitreya, and Vajrabhairava, each about "an arrow's length" in height (approximately 29 inches). Two larger golden statues were also made, one of the goddess Uṣṇīṣavijayā (the Victorious One) and one of Sitātapatrā (the White Umbrella). In addition, a special clay icon of the meditation deity Vajrabhairava, about twelve feet in height, was constructed.[533] When the smaller images of the maṇḍala deities were being cast, the sculptors were said to have been surprised to see that most of the statues came out so clean that they required no further refinement, with no rough parts to be filed off, as is normally the case. One image in particular, of Khaṇḍakapāla from Cakrasaṃvara maṇḍala, came out of the cast so brilliant that it radiated the colors of the rainbow.[534] Seeing this, Tsongkhapa instructed the sculptors not to do any further work on the statue but simply to clothe it in a silk robe. Deeply inspired by the sight, Tsongkhapa wrote the following spontaneous hymn to Cakrasaṃvara:

From Heruka's celestial mansion,
As an excellent source of merit for beings,
Cakrasaṃvara, lord and consort, have appeared,
Adorned with skulls and in sexual union;
With colorful hues and wondrous signs they've come.
Their arrival here is most excellent indeed![535]

Tokden says that when the Cakrasaṃvara maṇḍala was being consecrated, Tsongkhapa had a vision of all the deities of the maṇḍala and heard hymns and songs being sung by ḍākinīs in the space above.[536] Moved by this experience, Tsongkhapa wrote the following poetic lines:

> Beautiful forms with exquisite eyebrows drawn by the brush
> of meditation,
> Their bodies are slim and slender, resembling young trees;
> Their glowing faces rob even the moon of its splendor;
> Sporting eyes of blue lotus, their full lips red,
> They bear in their hands excellent garlands of flowers.
> Emanating many such forms associated with sexual bliss,
> To bring joy to the deities of the maṇḍala,
> I honor you with the bliss of goddesses bearing sense objects.[537]

It was at this time, too, Tsongkhapa composed his famed "Song of the Spring Queen," a series of verses invoking innate bliss through describing the celebrations of yogis and yoginis assembling to partake in a feast of songs, dances, and evocations of sexual bliss. Ever since its composition, "Song of the Spring Queen" has been sung or chanted by Tsongkhapa's followers every time a ritual feast is performed on the tenth and twenty-fifth of every Tibetan month—two dates of special significance in the Cakrasaṃvara cycle of tantra.

Once the construction of all the images was complete, Tsongkhapa led the official consecration ceremony for the Yangpachen Temple and its newly installed sacred icons. The entire Ganden community joined in the ceremony, along with monks from neighboring monasteries and thousands of lay devotees. When the consecration of the large Vajrabhairava was performed, Tsongkhapa's senior disciple Tokden Jampel Gyatso writes:

> A great clap of thunder arose from a clear blue sky and was heard by everyone inside the hall. Some of the yogis prac-

> ticing the five stages of Guhyasamāja and Cakrasaṃvara experienced visions of likenesses of Vajrabhairava appearing from all four directions and dissolving into the clay image.[538]

Tsongkhapa then led a series of rites of cultivation and propitiation for the meditation deities in their respective halls. According to Khedrup, "since that day crops have thrived in central Tibet, with rains falling on time, and the activities of teaching and practice of Dharma also have flourished as never before."[539] All in all, Tsongkhapa instituted the great *drupchö* festivals—the sādhana practice, rites of propitiation, and self-initiation—of the following main meditation deities at Ganden: Guhyasamāja according to the Ārya tradition, Lūipa's Cakrasaṃvara, thirteen-deity Vajrabhairava, Kālacakra, Vajrapāṇi Mahācakra, Vajradhātu, Sarvavid, Vairocana Abhisambodhi, nine-deity Amitāyus according to Jitari's transmission, and Akṣobhya. The institution of the annual rites and practice of these tantric deities at Ganden came to be recognized as the fourth of "the four great deeds of Tsongkhapa," the other three being the restoration of the Maitreya temple at Dzingchi, the Great Scriptural Festival of Nyal, and the establishment of the Great Prayer Festival of Lhasa. These drupchö related to the major tantric deities were maintained uninterruptedly until the political tragedy that swept central Tibet in 1959. Today, these traditions have been revived at the reestablished Ganden Monastery in southern India.

Around this same year (1417), the young Chenga Lodrö Gyaltsen (1402–72) of Gyama Rinchen Gang Monastery[540] came to Ganden to receive teachings from Tsongkhapa. Earlier, two of his predecessors, *chengas* (abbots) from Gyama, Chenga Kunga Lodrö and Chenga Shönu Wö, had attended Tsongkhapa's teachings. His elder brother, Namkha Tenpai Gyaltsen, already was a student of the master.[541] Lodrö Gyaltsen was then only fifteen years old. He would later play an important role in the dissemination of Tsongkhapa's instructions on lojong—practical instructions on how to cultivate universal compassion and bodhicitta and live in accordance with these ideals on a daily basis—as well as the master's teachings on lamrim and instructions on cultivating the view of emptiness. Lodrö Gyaltsen also would write the official biography of Tsongkhapa's student Tokden Jampel Gyatso, who early on had served as a medium between Tsongkhapa and Tokden's meditation deity, Mañjuśrī.

Another figure who would play a crucial role in disseminating Tsongkhapa's teachings on lojong was Hortön Namkha Pal (1373–1447). By 1417, Hortön had been a student of Tsongkhapa for nearly a decade. He would later compile the notes he took at Tsongkhapa's teaching on Chekawa's *Seven-Point Mind Training* combined with critical passages from Śāntideva's *Bodhicaryāvatāra*. The result is the well-known text entitled *Rays of Sun: A Mind-Training Guide*, which effectively set forth Tsongkhapa's tradition on the Kadam lojong instructions. Following the salutation verses, the text opens with the following:

> I pay homage to the great Mañjuśrī Tsongkhapa,
> The second Buddha of our era of degeneration;
> His supreme instruction containing excellent insights
> On how we should train our mind in bodhicitta,
> This excellent teaching, I shall present exactly as it is.[542]

One more disciple of Tsongkhapa critical for the transmission of the master's instructions on bodhicitta and lojong was the Sangphu teacher Shākya Yeshé, popularly known as Jangsem Radrengwa, "the bodhisattva from Radreng Monastery." Radrengwa would later compile yet another set of notes from Tsongkhapa's teachings on bodhicitta and lojong, known as "The Great Ear-Whispered Teachings on Mind Training."[543]

Lecture Series on the Kālacakra Tantra

In 1418 (the Earth Dog year), Tsongkhapa conducted a series of teachings at Ganden almost uninterruptedly. He first gave the transmission of his recently composed interlinear annotated commentary on Candrakīrti's extensive exposition of the Guhyasamāja root tantra. He also taught the following: his own commentaries on the various "explanatory tantras" of Guhyasamāja; Nāropa's great commentary on the Guhyasamāja tantra; his own two works on the Guhyasamāja completion stage, *Lamp to Illuminate the Five Stages* and *A Practical Guide to the Five Stages in One Sitting*; the six yogas of Kālacakra; Cakrasaṃvara; the Cakrasaṃvara body maṇḍala; Kṛṣṇācārya's *Spring Drop* (an instruction on the completion stage of Cakrasaṃvara); the six yogas of Niguma; the generation and completion stages of Vajrabhairava; and such non-Vajrayāna texts and topics as the Madhyamaka philosophy of emptiness, pramāṇa epistemology, lamrim, and Maitreya's *Sublime Continuum*.

In particular, Tsongkhapa gave an extended teaching on the Kālacakra tantra based on the most authoritative Indian exposition of the tantra, Puṇḍarīka's *Stainless Light*.[544] Thanks to Khedrup's brilliant note-taking, we have an extensive record of this important discourse on Kālacakra, running to over a hundred long folios.[545] In his *Great Treatise on Tantra*, written nearly a decade earlier, Tsongkhapa had already shared his observations about the uniqueness of the Kālacakra. Earlier, Rendawa had penned an open letter in the form of a series of critical questions about the authenticity of Kālacakra as a Buddhist tantra. Rendawa began with the observation that there is no discussion in the Kālacakra root tantra of the crucial Highest Yoga tantra notion of EVAṂ, while the condensed tantra is replete with internal contradictions.[546] Roughly stated, Rendawa raised the following thirteen objections against the Kālacakra:

1. On the philosophical level, the tantra presents a notion of emptiness as a material form, which is utterly at odds with any Buddhist doctrinal perspective;
2. It describes sentient beings as fully awakened buddhas;
3. It asserts that the worlds of both "the container" and "the contained" (the physical world and its inhabitants), including especially the four castes of India, emerge from the mouth of the Kālacakra deity;
4. It describes the bliss of sexual emission as the principal cause of cyclic existence;
5. It presents a cosmology that is at odds with the Abhidharma account;
6. Its presentation of the inner channels and winds is in contradiction with those of the other, more established tantras.
7. On the level of the path, its presentation of tantric empowerments and commitments is at odds with those of the other tantras;
8. Its generation stage cannot be a cause for achieving the supreme attainment;
9. It asserts the empty form of the completion stage to be the dharmakāya;
10. It suggests that one cannot attain buddhahood in the intermediate state of existence;
11. It presents the body and mind of the resultant state of buddhahood to be of the same single entity;
12. It denies the existence of any materially composed phenomena on the resultant level of buddhahood; and
13. It describes the saṃbhogakāya as being of the nature of speech.[547]

Perhaps as a mark of his deep respect for his teacher, Tsongkhapa never names Rendawa in his Kālacakra lecture when responding to an objection, but he takes up almost every single critical point his teacher raised about the tantra. For example, Tsongkhapa takes great pains to underscore the point that the empty form of Kālacakra is different from the emptiness of intrinsic existence articulated by Nāgārjuna. The empty form of Kālacakra is induced through the experience of immutable great bliss, whereas Nāgārjuna's emptiness is achieved by destroying conceptual elaborations that grasp at signs.[548]

One of the unique features of the Kālacakra tantra, according to Tsongkhapa, is its presentation of the fourth, or word, empowerment. Unlike Guhyasamāja and Cakrasaṃvara, where the fourth empowerment is conferred in a hidden manner with the oblique line "The fourth, too, is similar to this," in the Kālacakra tradition the fourth empowerment is conferred in an explicit way and in its own terms.[549] For reasons such as this, Tsongkhapa would characterize Kālacakra as an "explicit tantra," in that what remains hidden and oblique in many other tantras is laid out plainly in the Kālacakra. According to this tantra, the definitive fourth empowerment is identified as nondual gnosis, which is in turn defined in terms of the nonduality of empty form and immutable great bliss. Thus, emptiness in the context of the union of bliss and emptiness is referred to as "object endowed," for it is perceived in terms of color and shape, while the immutable bliss is awareness that cognizes the suchness of things, and therefore often is described as "objectless."[550]

Tsongkhapa also takes on the challenge of understanding how the dematerializing of the corporeal body envisioned in Kālacakra practice does not undermine our ability to experience great bliss and how this concept differs from the idealism of the Mind Only school.[551] He also addresses a key objection raised by Rendawa regarding the incoherence of the notion of the Buddha's body and mind being of a single entity. For Tsongkhapa, perhaps the most compelling reason for accepting Kālacakra's authenticity as a Buddhist tantra is its acceptance by highly authoritative figures like Abhyākaragupta and Nāropa (ca. tenth to eleventh century), the latter being a master whom, as we know, Tsongkhapa deeply revered. Tsongkhapa's instructions on the six yogas of the completion stage of Kālacakra would be compiled by his student Gyaltengpa and later included in the master's collected works.

In *The Blue Annals*, we read the following comment on Tsongkhapa's lectures on Kālacakra:

> The great master Tsongkhapa too had received the Kālacakra cycle of teachings from Gongsum Dechenpa. In the Earth Dog year (1418), he taught the complete exposition of the great commentary on the tantra [entitled *Stainless Light*]. As my teacher states, given that he was the lord of the Buddha's doctrine, when the All-Knowing Lord Tsongkhapa taught this system even once, it was, compared to others teaching the tantra a hundred times, like hoisting a victory banner that will never be lowered.[552]

Sometime during this period of extensive teaching, Tsongkhapa also composed a sādhana of the thirteen-deity Vajrabhairava (or Yamāntaka), entitled *Jewel Casket.* The sādhana was written at the request of one of Tsongkhapa's oldest disciples, Tsakho Ngawang Drakpa, who had returned to his native Gyalrong many years earlier.[553] A wrathful form of Mañjuśrī, this meditation deity had been an important part of Tsongkhapa's tantric practice since his childhood. He had been initiated into the practice by his early teacher, Chöjé Döndrup Rinchen, and had undertaken several retreats on it, which included reciting the Vajrabhairava's mantra hundreds of thousands of times.

Earlier, while in retreat at his favorite hermitage on the slopes of Mount Odé Gungyal in the Wölkha Valley region, Tsongkhapa had composed a sādhana of Solitary Vajrabhairava (the meditation deity without a consort). Later, when staying at the Chin retreat on Sangri Mountain, Tsongkhapa had authored a sādhana of Kṛṣṇa Yamari, another form of Yamāntaka. To accompany this sādhana, Tsongkhapa also wrote a lengthy text on the rites of empowerment of the same meditation deity, entitled *Precious Garland: A Rite of Initiation into the Maṇḍala of Thirteen-Deity Yamāntaka*. The text opens with a discussion of the authentic Indian roots of the practice of Yamāntaka and its transmission to Tibet.[554] Key figures in the origin of this tantra were the Indian mystics Lalitavajra and Śrīdhara, and the Tibetan translators Nyö Yönten Drak and Ra Lotsawa (b. 1076). The sādhana of Solitary Yamāntaka would become an important part of daily practice for the monastic followers of Tsongkhapa's tradition.[555]

It was during this summer and fall that, based on Tsongkhapa's own careful instruction, the murals inside the Yangpachen Temple were completed. Tsongkhapa also initiated the project of having some of his major compositions committed to woodblock prints, including especially his interlinear annotations on the Guhyasamāja root tantra and Candrakīrti's commentary on it, *The Clear Lamp* (*Pradīpodyotana*).[556] Other texts commissioned for printing probably included *The Great Treatise on the Stages of the Path*, *The Great Treatise on Tantra*, *The Essence of True Eloquence*, and *The Lamp to Illuminate the Five Stages*.

Sometime in the winter of 1418, Tsongkhapa began speaking openly of his long-standing, mysterious relationship with the Dharma protector Kālarūpa, recognized as Mañjuśrī in the form of a fierce Yama spirit.[557] With an ash-blue body and a buffalo head projecting two long, sharp horns, and clasped on his left hip by the goddess Cāmuṇḍī, Kālarūpa strikes a ferocious pose, riding on a water buffalo and holding a club in his right hand and a noose in his left. He had been a constant companion of Tsongkhapa at some mysterious level for a long time. At the request of Tokden Jampel Gyatso, his longtime student and retreat companion, Tsongkhapa composed, in a poetic style evocative of grandeur and majesty, a hymn to the protector that is chanted to this day in all Geluk monasteries. Though originally entitled "Hymn to Yama King Kālarūpa in His Inner Aspect: Crushing the Forces of Demons," the hymn would come to be known, on the basis of the first syllables of its opening verse, as *Kyang Kum Ma* ("legs extended and bent"):

> The slightest stomping of your legs, one extended and the other bent,
> Could shake Mount Meru itself along with its base of four elements;
> The thundering noises bellowing forth from your buffalo mouth,
> Fierce and wide open, could fill the entire realm of the triple world;
> Blessed Yamāntaka, you're the fierce form assumed by Mañjuśrī,
> The father of all the buddhas, to help tame the forces of darkness.
> As I pay homage to you and sing your praises, O king of Yama,
> The time has come now to pacify all obstructive forces.[558]

The poem consists of six four-line stanzas (with each line running to twenty-one syllables), written in a chantable style that demonstrates an impressive mastery of the natural rhythms of the Tibetan language. Hearing it chanted by a group employing the deep, resonant throat singing so typical in Tibetan monasteries, one can't help feeling the power and majesty of the hymn, with its evocation of the image of the fierce protector as he was experienced by Tsongkhapa.

Two Last Major Writings

One important task Tsongkhapa took on throughout 1418 was to write an extensive exposition of Candrakīrti's *Entering the Middle Way*, including its autocommentary. Candrakīrti's work is an independent treatise written as a comprehensive supplement to Nāgārjuna's *Treatise on the Middle Way*, authoritatively establishing the meaning of emptiness and drawing out its larger philosophical and soteriological implications. These two Indian works would effectively become for the Tibetan tradition the foundational classical Indian texts concerning the philosophy of emptiness.

As a young monk, Tsongkhapa had memorized *Entering the Middle Way*, taken classes on it from Rendawa, debated and meditated on its meaning, and eventually taught the text himself numerous times. Not long before, two of his senior Tibetan colleagues, Lochen Kyapchok Palsang, a senior Kadam-Sakya master who had requested Tsongkhapa to write his two great syntheses, and Tsongkhapa's own teacher, Rendawa, had written commentaries on this influential work.[559] Tsongkhapa himself had already written a great deal on the topic of emptiness, with his extensive commentary on Nāgārjuna's *Treatise on the Middle Way*, his hermeneutically oriented *Essence of True Eloquence*, and the sections on emptiness in his earlier and later surveys of the stages of the path. However, given the renewed enthusiasm for Candrakīrti's interpretation of Nāgārjuna in Tibet—thanks especially to the propagation of his Madhyamaka writings by both Rendawa and Tsongkhapa himself—many students had requested the master to compose an authoritative commentary on Candrakīrti's primer. In explaining his reasons for composing this major work, Tsongkhapa writes:

> It was written at the strong urging of the spiritual mentor Lhula Lekpa Pal, one versed in the ten treatises, who offered a maṇḍala of forty silver coins, and in response to requests from many spiritual mentors who deeply admire this teaching and themselves possess no small aptitude for comprehending its meaning. They have emphatically urged me to write an extensive work that contains a comprehensive explanation of the difficult points in Candrakīrti's autocommentary that is lucid in its explanation of the words [of the root text] and thorough in its analysis of the broader points.[560]

The result is perhaps the single most influential Tibetan exposition of Candrakīrt's *Entering the Middle Way*. It presents not only explanations of the root text but also a detailed analysis of Candrakīrti's autocommentary. Tsongkhapa employs his typically careful approach, comparing the two different Tibetan translations of the Sanskrit original, one by Patsap (b. 1055) and the other by Naktso Lotsawa (1011–64). Though ostensibly belonging to the genre of commentary as a formal exposition of an existing text, Tsongkhapa's work would come to be treated as a freestanding text and referred to as *Madhyamaka Elucidation of the Intent* (*Uma Gongpa Rapsel*). Over time, it effectively became the primer on Madhyamaka philosophy among Tsongkhapa's followers, giving rise to a great deal of secondary pedagogical literature.[561]

The Tibetan new year of the Earth Pig fell on February 4, 1419; it would turn out to be the last year of Tsongkhapa's life. Tsongkhapa began the year with a final major writing project, his monumental and detailed explanation of the root tantra of Cakrasaṃvara, entitled *Illuminating All the Hidden Meanings*. As in the case of previous tantras, here too Tsongkhapa first prepared what he considered to be an accurate Tibetan edition of the root tantra itself, based on a comparative reading of the various translations in light of authoritative Indian commentaries. By midsummer Tsongkhapa had completed his work, so that he was able to give an oral explanation of the Cakrasaṃvara tantra, based on his own text, to a large number of monastics at Ganden Monastery.[562] During the teaching sessions, with Jamyang Chöjé serving as the chant master, the senior disciples would read aloud sections of Tsongkhapa's newly authored text as the master moved through it chapter by chapter.[563] Commenting on Tsongkhapa's legacy with respect to the Cakrasaṃvara tradition in Tibet, Gö Lotsawa Shönu Pal observes in his *Blue Annals*:

> In later times, following the lineage of Butön Rinpoché, the revered great Tsongkhapa also composed a commentary on the root tantra, excellently bringing its explanatory tantras together with the great Indian commentaries. He also wrote sādhanas and maṇḍala rites connected to the Ghaṇṭapa tradition, and exposition of the five stages according to the Ghaṇṭapa tradition, instructions on how to engage in the meditative practice of the Great Yoga completion stage of the Lūipa tradition, as well as an exposition of Lūipa's sādhana entitled *Milking the Wish-Granting Cow*. Thus he brought back to life the tradition of Cakrasaṃvara that had declined [in Tibet].[564]

Tsongkhapa also conducted additional specialized teachings for select groups of senior disciples. For example, he gave a small group of disciples, including Khedrup and his brilliant young protegé Shangshung Chöwang Drakpa, an important teaching on how to understand the ultimate perspective of Maitreya's *Ornament of Realizations*—an Indian classic typically interpreted according to the so-called Yogācāra-Madhyamaka tradition of Vimuktisena and Haribhadra—as that of Candrakīrti's Prāsaṅgika Madhyamaka school. Khedrup would later write a short text distilling the essential points of this teaching.[565]

The master also gave advanced Cakrasaṃvara completion-stage instructions according to the Ghaṇṭapa tradition to a select group of senior disciples, the notes of which were compiled by the Cakrasaṃvara yogi Chetön Kunga Sangpo, known also as "the great bodhisattva Kunsang." Tsongkhapa's oral instructions on the six yogas of the completion stage of Kālacakra, also taught around this time, were compiled by his student Gyaltengpa; and his special teaching on the sādhana chapter of the Kālacakra tantra was compiled by Khedrup. Other compilations from this period include a lengthy but unfinished exposition of the Hevajra tantra, the most important system of tantra for the Sakya tradition, by Tsongkhapa himself, and a brief but lucid exposition of Śāntarakṣita's *Ornament of the Middle Way* written by Tsongkhapa's senior student Gyaltsap. All of these notes are preserved in the master's collected works.

One other highly important set of notes to emerge from this period of Tsongkhapa's teaching is the text entitled *Door-Frame Essential Instructions.* Containing nine distinct notes on key aspects of the advanced Vajrayāna path, this compilation consists of highly practical instructions to meditator yogis, most notably on what to do when encountering difficulties in specific areas of their practice.[566] In another set of notes, entitled *The Cycle of Short Instructional Pieces on Guhyasamāja*, which may be an alternative compilation of the same set of oral instructions, we find a reference to the "Vajra Lines on the View [of Emptiness]" composed by Tsongkhapa himself. In this instruction on the view, Tsongkhapa differentiates four distinct forms of understanding and experiencing emptiness.

First, at the beginner's stage, when we are cultivating our experience of the view of emptiness, Tsongkhapa advises us to avoid any form of affirmation after negating intrinsic existence.

Second, while we are cultivating tranquility and insight focused on emptiness, he instructs us to maintain a fine balance between the single-pointed absorption characteristic of tranquility practice and ascertainment of the nature of reality born of analytic meditation. Here, to overemphasize absorption and neglect discursive analysis would be a flaw.

Third, when we are meditating on emptiness based on having attained tranquility, it is analytic meditation that will give rise to mental and physical pliancy, resulting in a perfect union, or equilibrium, in which analysis itself gives rise to absorption and the absorbed mind can engage in fine analysis. Tsongkhapa advises the meditator to be acutely aware of these two dimensions of the meditative state.

Fourth, at the stage where we directly realize emptiness, the subject (the meditating mind) and the object (emptiness) have fused into a single taste. In that state, apart from this total fusion of mind and emptiness, not even the concept or mental image of emptiness remains.

With respect to meditation on emptiness in the context of Highest Yoga tantric practice, however, Tsongkhapa instructs that once we have gained a basic conceptual understanding of emptiness, during the actual meditation on emptiness there is no need to cultivate tranquility first and follow it with cultivation of insight. This is because here, unlike in non-Vajrayāna practice, the subject or the mind employed in emptiness meditation is the subtle mind conjoined with innate bliss. Given the subtlety of the mind employed, there is no need for any discursive analysis; rather, the mind's absorption into emptiness itself gives rise to the attainment of the union of tranquility and insight.[567]

Sometime in this Earth Pig year (1419), perhaps with a premonition of his own end, Tsongkhapa composed an instructional text on transference of consciousness (phowa), one of the six yogas of

Nāropa. In this text, *Guide to Transference of Consciousness Opening the Golden Door*, Tsongkhapa offers an instruction based on a detailed exposition of the practice in a section of the *Saṁpuṭa Tantra*, as well as on instructions found in other sources, in particular the explanation of the Indian master Abhyākaragupta. This text would become the primary manual on transference of consciousness for members of Tsongkhapa's tradition.[568]

One important work that Tsongkhapa would leave unfinished is an extensive analytical commentary on Śāntarakṣita's *Ornament of the Middle Way*, which is a brief work of ninety-seven four-line stanzas accompanied by an autocommentary.[569] Śāntarakṣita's text, which is considered a foundational work of the Yogācāra-Madhyamaka school, contains one of the most cogent and comprehensive presentations of the style of Madhyamaka reasoning known as "the absence of one and many" argument. On the philosophical level, Śāntarakṣita's text investigates a series of concepts (what contemporary philosophers call "primitives") given ontological status by proponents of real existence—self, space, eternal indivisible atoms, eternal consciousness, and so on—and demonstrates the incoherence of each of them. In his own opening verses, Tsongkhapa speaks of how ensuring the continuity of the study and teaching of Śāntarakṣita's works is an unrivaled act of paying homage to the master, expressing the Tibetan people's gratitude toward his memory.[570]

CHAPTER 14

Nirvāṇa

IN THE FALL OF 1419, Tsongkhapa began to experience pains in his legs, possibly due to the resurgence of his chronic back pain. Some of his close students urged him to visit the hot springs in the Tölung region, so Tsongkhapa left Ganden on a trip for the first time since his return from the now legendary teachings at Tashi Dhokha Hermitage in the fall of 1415. He stopped for few days in Lhasa, where he visited the Jokhang Temple and paid homage to the sacred Buddha images, made offerings, and prayed and meditated in their presence.[571] It had been ten years since he had last visited the Jokhang, at the time of the first Great Prayer Festival. To be back inside Tibet's holiest temple, with both the exterior and inside looking well cared for, must have been for Tsongkhapa a source of both joy and deep inspiration.

To Tölung Hot Springs, Lhasa, and Drepung Monastery

From Lhasa he left for the Tölung hot springs (today known as Yangpachen hot springs), which lies about fifty-four miles northwest of Lhasa. Once at the site, apart from dipping his feet into the springs, Tsongkhapa showed little interest in seeking any serious or prolonged therapy. Instead, he attended to the requests of the many devotees, both monastics and lay, who had come to see him and receive teachings: Tsongkhapa gave numerous public discourses, conducted blessing ceremonies, and accepted the various offerings people made to him.[572]

From the hot springs, he went to Drepung, the monastery his student Jamyang Chöjé had founded 1416 at the foot of Mount Gephel, around five miles west of Lhasa. *Drepung* (literally, "heap of rice") is the Tibetan translation of the Sanskrit *Dhanyakaṭaka*, a sacred site in southern India (identified with modern-day Amaravati in Andra Pradesh) that is associated with the origin myth of the Kālacakra tantra. Probably because of his leg pains, Tsongkhapa was carried to the monastery on a palanquin, and he was formally received by hundreds of monks lining the two sides of the road leading to the monastery's main prayer hall.[573] Jamyang Chöjé was eager to receive his master and profoundly grateful to have his new monastery blessed by Tsongkhapa's visit. As Tsongkhapa's convoy approached Drepung, a brilliant rainbow appeared right over the master's palanquin, which everyone saw as a sign of great auspiciousness.[574]

Over two thousand monks had gathered at Drepung for the occasion of Tsongkhapa's visit.[575] During this period, all the necessary provisions were offered by Tsongkhapa's longtime benefactor, the Neu family. Tsongkhapa officiated at the consecration ceremony for the monastery and the sacred images installed in the main prayer hall. As part of the consecration rites, Tsongkhapa requested the protectors, six-armed Mahākāla and Kālarūpa, to inhabit their newly sculpted representations. In this way, the master assigned these protectors the task of guarding the newly established monastery. Impressed by what Jamyang Chöjé had accomplished so far, Tsongkhapa told his student, "Even though it has been [only] around four years, a lot has been achieved. You should continue to be the main custodian of the monastery in the future, too."[576] Prostrating at the master's feet, Jamyang Chöjé offered his pledge that he would fulfill Tsongkhapa's wish to the best of his ability.

While at Drepung, Tsongkhapa gave a series of teachings on, among other topics, Candrakīrti's *Entering the Middle Way* and a number of works of his own: his lamrim, his guide to the six yogas of Nāropa, and *The Clear Lamp*, his annotated commentary on Candrakīrti's Guhyasamāja commentary.[577] This time, Tsongkhapa allowed many laypeople, including even some beggars, to attend his teachings on the stages of the path and on the Madhyamaka philosophy of emptiness. He taught the nontantric texts and topics in the morning and the Guhyasamāja tantra in the afternoon.

One day, Tsongkhapa asked Jamyang Chöjé to have a large silver statue of Vairocana made and to pursue the work discreetly. Tsongkhapa then gazed for a while in the direction of Ganden Monastery as if longing to be there. One day, after about a month and half's stay at Drepung, Tsongkhapa abruptly announced that he needed to return to Ganden soon. As he was in the midst of the ninth chapter of the Guhyasamāja tantra, his students and the benefactors sponsoring the teachings requested the master to stay at least two more weeks, so he could complete the series. "At least," they pleaded, "do not leave the teaching of the Guhyasamāja tantra unfinished." Tsongkhapa replied that at this point it was best for him to leave for Ganden. He said that he had already decided the day before to leave the lamrim and Guhyasamāja tantra teachings unfinished.[578] His followers would later interpret this as an auspicious sign for the continual flourishing of these teachings. Thus, Tsongkhapa left Drepung for Lhasa, heading toward his home monastery, Ganden. It would be the master's only visit to Drepung.

Final Visit to Sera Chöding Hermitage

On his way home to Ganden, Tsongkhapa stopped in Lhasa. Once more, he visited the Jokhang Temple to honor the sacred Buddha image with prostrations, offerings, and meditation. He made a fervent prayer in the Buddha's presence that the teachings of the Buddha remain on this earth for a long time. Then, at the request of his student Jamchen Chöjé, Tsongkhapa paid a short visit to Sera Chöding Hermitage. There, he reiterated his aspiration for the emergence of a monastery dedicated to the propagation of the study, teaching, and practice of the great tantras. The master then shared this wish with some of his other senior disciples and spoke of the need to establish a community whose members would live strictly according to the vinaya discipline but would be dedicated to the study, teaching, and practice of the Guhyasamāja and Cakrasaṃvara tantras.[579]

One day, at a gathering of many of his closest disciples, Tsongkhapa hoisted in his right hand a copy of the volume of his annotated commentary on the Guhyasamāja root tantra and asked, "Who will volunteer to be the custodian of this lineage of exposition of the stainless tantric teaching, which is the authentic scripture of Vajradhara?"[580] Hearing no response, he repeated the question a second time, but still no one came forward. When the master asked the question a third time, Sherap Sengé stood up. Prostrating three times at Tsongkhapa's feet, he pledged, "O my guru, you who are identical with Lord Vajradhara himself, I shall keep your sacred command in my heart and pursue your wish to the best of my ability." Although some of his fellow disciples felt that Sherap Sengé was being a bit presumptuous, Tsongkhapa was deeply pleased and blessed him. He gave him a skull cup (a ritual object used in advanced tantric practice) filled with black tea, a golden statue of the Guhyasamāja deity, a copy of the four interwoven commentaries on the Guhyasamāja root tantra, other texts on the generation and completion stages, and a mask of the protector Kālarūpa and some of the deity's paraphernalia, including a club and noose. In this way, Tsongkhapa confirmed Sherap Sengé as custodian of his own approach to Highest Yoga tantra and sowed the seeds for the establishment of the first tantric college.[581]

Then, as a mark of auspiciousness and to bring blessings to this important initiative, Tsongkhapa and his community of monks performed the fortnightly confession rite. He also led two teaching sessions, one on Guhyasamāja and the other on Cakrasaṃvara, each involving a short reading from the opening section of their respective root tantras.[582] At one point during a teaching session, Sherap Sengé stood up and requested Tsongkhapa pray for him, as he felt he did not have the capacity to propagate the Vajrayāna teachings by himself. Tsongkhapa replied:

> You don't need to be afraid. I have assigned the oath-bound protector Kālarūpa to assist you. There is a mountainous place in the shape of a bell a few leagues from here. On this mountain lives a yogi who has been sustained by Yamāntaka for numerous lives. He will become your disciple and will help propagate the teaching.... Furthermore, there is a female *yakṣa* (fierce spirit) residing on a mountain that resembles an ogress lying on her back. She too will assist you in the task. The rest you will find out yourself.[583]

Thus, Tsongkhapa prophesied the founding of the tantric monastery he desired.

Jamchen Chöjé, who was the host of Tsongkhapa's visit to Sera Chöding, conveyed to the master his wish to establish Sera Monastery. Deeply pleased to hear this, Tsongkhapa said, "This is most excellent! This monastery will make great contributions to the long-term survival of the exposition and practice of both Sūtra and Tantra, and thus it will be a source of benefit to countless sentient beings." Tsongkhapa then gave specific advice on the location and design of the buildings of the monastery complex.[584] Soon after Tsongkhapa left, Jamchen Chöjé began construction work, and by the end of 1419 he had established what would become Sera Thekchen Ling Monastery, which one day would become one of "the three great centers of learning" in central Tibet and one of the largest monasteries in the world.

During this brief stay at Sera Chöding, Tsongkhapa also gave a select group of about a hundred students an instruction on the completion stage of Cakrasaṃvara according to the Indian mystic Kṛṣṇācārya. This was an advanced teaching based on the Indian mystic's short text entitled *Spring Drop* (*Chithik*), which presents the completion stage under four headings: continuum (the nature of the body), mantra (tummo practice), wisdom (the arising of the four joys), and secret (how to engage in the actual practices). At least two different sets of notes from this special instruction, one by Gyaltsap and the other by Sempa Chenpo Künsang (using his tantric name Mikyö Dorjé), would later be compiled into instructional manuals and included in Tsongkhapa's collected works.[585]

On his way back to Ganden from Sera Chöding Hermitage, Tsongkhapa stopped in Lhasa yet again and visited the Jokhang Temple as before, praying, making offerings, and meditating in front of the sacred Buddha image. The young Gendün Drup, who had accompanied Tsongkhapa from Sera to Lhasa, bade farewell to the master, informing him that he planned to spend some time studying vinaya and Abhidharma. Tsongkhapa gave Gendün Drup personal advice and some gifts to help pay for provisions during his studies.[586]

After leaving Lhasa, Tsongkhapa stopped at Dechen Tsé, where the master instructed the *dzongpön* (lord) of Drakar Dzong and his wife to establish a monastery there dedicated to the study, teaching, and practice of Guhyasamāja. He also made a significant contribution toward the establishment of such a monastery from the various offerings he had received during this trip. For his part, the dzongpön pledged to help sponsor the establishment of such a monastery as Tsongkhapa instructed. Saying he might never have the chance to perform such a rite again, Tsongkhapa supervised an elaborate consecration ritual at the site. He also gave the future monastery a name: Sangak Khar ("Tantra Fort").[587] The master then left for Drakar, stopping en route at Drushi Monastery, which is located in the Taktsé Dzong region. On the evening of Tsongkhapa's arrival at Drushi, many of the monks heard the sound of the gong being struck and wondered what it meant. Upon investigation, it was found that no one had actually struck the gong, even though many heard the sound.[588] Later, Tsongkhapa's followers and his biographers would interpret this event as the announcement by celestial beings of the great Tsongkhapa's impending nirvāṇa.[589]

Returning Home to Ganden

From Drushi Monastery, Tsongkhapa finally headed back to Ganden. Upon arrival, he first visited the Yangpachen Temple, which he had built specifically for tantric teaching and practice. Saying that he might not come to the temple again, he asked his students to prepare an elaborate set of offerings before the sacred icons: the large Buddha in the main hall and the meditation deities on the upper floor. In addition to various supplication prayers, Tsongkhapa led the chanting of the aspirational prayers he himself had composed at the end of the sādhanas of the three major meditation deities: Guhyasamāja, Cakrasaṃvara, and Vajrabhairava. Then, at the request of the benefactor who was offering tea to the monks, Tsongkhapa attended the prayer session inside the main prayer hall. There, without being requested, the master led the chanting of his extensive prayer for rebirth in the Sukhāvatī pure land and various aspirational prayers and verses of auspiciousness. He made a fervent prayer that Ganden Monastery flourish as a seat of study, teaching, and practice of the Buddha's teaching to serve the well-being of the Dharma and sentient beings for a long time to come.[590]

When all the public events were over, Tsongkhapa finally returned to his own residence. As he entered, he told his attendants, "At last, I am home in our own monastery where I can be free. I can relax now."[591] Around midnight of the same day, the twenty-first day of the tenth month (November 8, 1419), Tsongkhapa began to feel unwell. The next day, the entire Ganden community performed specific rituals dedicated to their master's health. For two days, while the monks were performing the rituals, Tsongkhapa said that, apart from some pain in certain parts of his body, what he was going through was not unbearable. Mostly, he felt tired and lacking in appetite. On the second night of his illness, Tsongkhapa told Sharpa Rinchen Gyaltsen that he and Gyaltsap needed to ensure the well-being of Ganden Monastery.

The next day, Tsongkhapa's senior disciples came to see their master. It turned out that Tsongkhapa had already spoken with Gyaltsap at some length before his departure for the Tölung hot springs, sharing his thoughts and aspirations with Gyaltsap on how best to look after the well-being of the Ganden community and serve the Buddhadharma. Now, at this gathering of his closest disciples, Tsongkhapa grabbed his yellow paṇḍita hat by the tip and threw it into Gyaltsap's lap. He also gave his outer ceremonial gown to Gyaltsap and anointed him his successor. Then, turning to the rest of the group, including Rinchen Gyaltsen, he said, "Please understand the point I am making here. And everyone should always practice bodhicitta."[592] He continued,

> For those future students who might be saddened by not having met me in person, I would say this: Read the two

> syntheses I have written, one on Sūtra and the other on Tantra. If you do so, this will be no different from having met me in person. In these texts, I have condensed the essence of all eighty-four thousand teachings of the Buddha and explained them in an integrated way. So even if you had met me in person, I would have had nothing more to say beyond what is found in these works.[593]

Entering the Peace of Nirvāṇa

Throughout his final illness, Tsongkhapa maintained his daily routine of meditation practice: rising early in the morning, engaging in sādhana practices, performing self-empowerment rites, and most important, remaining absorbed in silent meditative states. On the evening of the twenty-fourth day of the tenth month (November 11, 1419), Tsongkhapa performed the self-empowerment rite of the thirteen-deity Vajrabhairava maṇḍala, followed by an elaborate offering rite of Cakrasaṃvara. He then asked for a skull cup filled with clarified butter and performed an extensive inner-offering ritual, concluding it with the gesture of tasting it sixteen times, twice.[594] He then remained seated cross-legged in deep meditation throughout the night.

Based on the changed pattern of the master's breathing, those in attendance opined that he was now in "vajra repetition" yoga, which gives rise to the entry, abiding, and absorption of the winds in the central channel.[595] As dawn broke on the twenty-fifth day of the tenth month (November 12, 1419), Tsongkhapa entered nirvāṇa, actualizing the dharmakāya, the buddha body of ultimate truth, the pure luminosity of the subtlest clear-light mind. He remained seated cross-legged, with his eyes cast downward; his left palm was upturned on his lap in the gesture of meditation, while his right hand rested on his right knee with the palm facing out, in the gesture of granting wishes. As the morning sunlight illuminated the day, the senior disciples attending to Tsongkhapa instantly noticed that there had been a remarkable change in the master's physical appearance. Previously, his ill health had made him appear feeble, with a pallid complexion and the skin on his face sagging. Now the master's face looked fresh and young, bearing no evidence of his age or illness. His face, in fact, was glowing. Some disciples spoke of seeing orange light rays emanating from his body; others described the light as pale yellow; still others spoke of the light radiating from the master's body as golden in color.[596]

Speaking of this phenomenon, Khedrup writes in his official biography of Tsongkhapa:

> When he entered nirvāṇa, the skin tone of master's body assumed the appearance of a youthful body. In brief, it was as if his human body had transformed into that of a celestial being. One might ask, "Has anyone heard of something like this happening in the past? Can anyone offer explanations for the reason behind this?" I have heard that when the Indian paṇḍita and siddha Gayadhara passed away at Kharek, his body shrank in size and became like the body of a young child. However, I have not heard anything like that with respect to a Tibetan lama.[597]

Once the rest of the Ganden community heard of the master's passing, everyone was gripped by a feeling of profound loss. While emissaries were sent to make offerings before the sacred Buddha image in the Jokhang Temple in Lhasa, as well as to the monks of nearby monasteries, some of Tsongkhapa's close students who were not at Ganden at the time—Khedrup, who was in Tsang at his Changra Monastery; Sherap Sengé, who was at Narthang; and Jamyang Khaché, a senior teacher at Tsal Gungthang Monastery—

rushed back to Ganden to join in the ceremonies honoring their great master.

On the fifteenth day of the eleventh Tibetan month, in the third week following Tsongkhapa's nirvāṇa, as Jamyang Khaché was participating in the fortnightly confession ceremony at Ganden, he felt a powerful surge of the pain of his own loss.[598] He missed Tsongkhapa's calm and reassuring presence, his warm and soothing voice, and his love and kindness toward his students. Missing his master so deeply, that afternoon Jamyang Khaché composed what became a celebrated eulogy to Tsongkhapa, later known as "Eighty Tsongkhapas," because it contained repeated mentions of the name Tsongkhapa. The poem is divided into three parts. The first part is a long eulogy reviewing Tsongkhapa's entire life, the second is an alphabetical poem, and the third is a seven-limb worship. Here is the alphabetical poem:

ka: Just like Mañjukīrti in [the Shambhala kingdom of] Kalāpa,
kha: Here in the land of snows, to uphold the Buddha's doctrine,
ga: You are unrivaled when viewed from any angle;
nga: O Tsongkhapa, you are my crown jewel.
ca: Shunning idle speech, you sing out the music of insight;
cha: You wear the appealing attire of the three robes;
ja: With no craving for tea and the like, you lived with simple
needs;
nya: O Tsongkhapa, you are like Lūipa.
ta: You're the bodhisattva prophesied by the Tathāgata;
tha: To tame the desperate beings of this Land of Snows,
da: You're known today as Lobsang Drakpa;
na: O Tsongkhapa, you are a manifestation of Nāgārjuna.
pa: Just as the moon is amid [other] celestial bodies, like Venus,
pha: You're unrivaled among the multitude of scholars;
ba: Like a cowherd, you resided in the wilderness

ma: And strove in meditation, O Tsongkhapa.
tsa: In sacred places such as Tsari Mountain,
tsha: Braving all obstacles, such as heat and cold,
dza: To tame this wild mind of ours,
wa: You remained single-pointed, O Tsongkhapa.
zha: You honored your teachers like a crown on your head;
za: You lived on food both excellent and ordinary;
'a: For those of us wandering in the ocean of saṃsāra,
ya: You showed the wondrous liberation path, O Tsongkhapa.
ra: Like Ra Lotsawa, you've perfected the generation stage;
la: Like Lvavapa, you've realized the completion stage;
sha: Like Śaripūtra, you've directly perceived the truth;
sa: O Tsongkhapa, you're unrivaled on this earth.
ha: As I pray to you with fervent admiration,
a: O Tsongkhapa, you who have realized the unborn truth, the meaning of *a*[599]—
Your body hoists the victorious banner of monastic robes;
Your speech proclaims the eighty-four thousand heaps of Dharma;
Your mind never sways from the expanse of ultimate reality;
I praise you, O Dharma king, Buddha Tsongkhapa.
To you my glorious guru, the Buddha's regent,
I prostrate once again at your feet
And make offerings both actual and imagined;
I declare each instance of my past negative karma,
And I rejoice in all the good deeds I have performed;
I request you to turn the Dharma wheel for the countless beings;
Wherever you reside, pray do not enter nirvāṇa;
I dedicate the merit of this effort toward great awakening.
On the fifteenth day of the month in the third week
After the supreme savior Dharma lord's departure to other realms,
As the monks were in the fortnightly confession rite,

I repeatedly missed my guru, who had sustained me
So much through the wealth of his sublime teachings;
Because of this and at the urging of others—
Upholders of the three baskets wishing to join in the prayers—
This eulogy was composed at the victorious Ganden,
A site filled with many who strive in study and practice,
By a monk from the borderlands,
A clear-minded hermit called Jamyang Khaché Dubha Punyaśrī.
Alas, the beings of this degenerate era
Embrace their own faults as if they were virtues,
And they shun others' virtues as if they were faults,
So it might not be appropriate to say what I've said here.
Nonetheless, if fortunate [people] who seek liberation
Supplicate constantly with faith and devotion
Their guru who is the embodiment of all buddhas,
All wished-for attainments will be realized, no doubt.
Why? As it has been stated in numerous sūtras and tantras:
"Compared to honoring all the buddhas of the ten directions,
Honoring a sublime and qualified guru accrues
A far greater store of merit."
Should there be any flaws in this writing of mine,
I ask the gurus, meditation deities, and protectors,
As well as all unbiased, learned scholars,
For their forgiveness and corrective help.
Through the merit created by my effort here,
May I be sustained through [all my] lives by Guru Vajradhara,
And by pursuing all my guru's instructions,
May I quickly attain the state of complete buddhahood.[600]

In the days after Tsongkhapa's passing, monks from nearby monasteries, as well as many lay devotees, including ruling members of the Phagdru dynasty who had been Tsongkhapa's principal benefactors, began converging at Ganden Monastery to pay their respects to the great teacher. In honor of their master, the monks at Ganden engaged in a series of rituals and prayers, and chanted various texts, including, most notably, Tsongkhapa's own hermeneutic text *The Essence of True Eloquence*. The curtains on all the three-dimensional maṇḍalas of the great meditation deities—Guhyasamāja, Cakrasaṃvara, Vajrabhairava, Vajradhātu, and Vairocana Abhisambodhi—were opened as monks performed their self-empowerment rites. The main prayer hall, the various halls at Yangpachen Temple, and, of course, Tsongkhapa's own residence were all lit with butter lamps. At night, thousands of butter lamps burning on the window sills of the various temples and of individual monks' cells turned all of Ganden Mountain into what seemed like a mirror reflecting the stars that filled the night sky.[601]

Tsongkhapa appears to have remained in *thukdam* (the clear-light meditative state) for thirteen days.[602] Throughout this period, it is said, the azure sky above Ganden remained absolutely spotless, without even a speck of cloud. A sense of stillness pervaded the atmosphere, with only an occasional gentle breeze brushing across the mountain slopes. It was as if even the air were holding its breath out of deference. On several days, rainbows could be seen in different parts of Ganden Monastery and in the valleys below. Speaking of this, Tsongkhapa's longtime attendant Lekpa Sangpo writes:

> For thirteen days, the whole sky remained devoid of any cloud or other obstruction. All forms of blustery winds ceased and the sunlight had a very special character. The significance of this is that the master, through his mastery of the unique meditative state of bliss and emptiness, was sending a signal or offering a proof. From this, I understand that the monastery will grow and flourish [through] up to thirteen successive abbots.[603]

Once the main rituals in honor of Tsongkhapa connected with the meditation deities were completed, the senior members of Ganden Monastery, led by Dülzin Drakpa Gyaltsen, formally requested Gyaltsap to ascend to Tsongkhapa's Ganden throne in accordance with the wish of their late master. Gyaltsap was thus enthroned as the "regent of the second Buddha" and as "the lord of the great kingdom of Buddhadharma."[604] At this ceremony, Khedrup, who had been a student of Gyaltsap as well, chanted aloud a tribute to the new abbot that he had composed for the occasion, which begins with the following:

> You who are empowered to ascend the fearless lion throne
> By [Tsongkhapa], the progenitor of glorious enlightened
> qualities,
> O Dharma master, regent of the second Buddha,
> May you, the second Maitreya, remain victorious![605]

In his new role as the head of Ganden Monastery, Gyaltsap began taking charge by first completing the important projects Tsongkhapa had begun. This included, in particular, the sculpting of a Vairocana statue, which the master had instructed to be made when he was at Drepung. Also, when Tsongkhapa finally came out of the clear-light state, Gyaltsap led the discussion on whether to cremate the master's body or embalm it. The disciples chose the second option. They then began construction of a stūpa to contain the master's embalmed body. The stūpa was made of pure silver and studded with various precious stones, as well as turquoise and coral. The body was placed inside the bulbous vase of the stūpa, facing to the east.[606]

Thanks to large donations from the ruling Neu family and offerings sent from various parts of the country, Gyaltsap was able to supervise the construction of a new hall to house the master's stūpa. He also commissioned the sculpting of a large golden Buddha, around two feet taller than the sacred Buddha image inside the Jokhang Temple. By the end of the Iron Bird year (1420), all the work was completed, and the stūpa containing the master's embalmed body was installed inside the new temple.

On the day of the official consecration of the temple and the installation of the stūpa, a brilliant rainbow appeared in the sky above Ganden Monastery.[607] As the first anniversary of the master's nirvāṇa approached, the monks at Ganden engaged in multiday rituals, performing the sādhanas and self-empowerment ceremonies of Guhyasamāja, Cakrasaṃvara, Vajrabhairava, Hevajra, Kālacakra, Vajrapāṇi Mahācakra, Amitāyus, and Vairocana. This series of prayers and rituals culminated on the twenty-fifth day of the tenth month, the first anniversary of Tsongkhapa's nirvāṇa. Elsewhere, Tsongkhapa's principal benefactor Neu Namkha Sangpo and his family invited Jamchen Chöjé to lead a large-scale commemoration of Tsongkhapa's nirvāṇa at Raga Drak Hermitage, where the master had meditated and taught.[608] Since that first anniversary, this commemoration day of Tsongkhapa's nirvāṇa has come to be known as Ganden Ngamchö Chenmo, "the Great Ganden Celebration of the Twenty-Fifth,"celebrated across Tibet and, later, elsewhere in the Tibetan Buddhist cultural sphere, such as Ladakh, Buriyatia, and Mongolia. A characteristic of this festival, which typically occurs in late November or December, is the lighting of butter lamps on rooftops and window sills, making it, in effect, Tibet's annual festival of light.

CHAPTER 15

Canonization and the Master's Legacy

BY THE TIME Tsongkhapa passed away, he had acquired a preeminence unmatched across the entire Tibetan plateau. Through his extensive teachings and his authoritative writings over some thirty years, he had attracted a huge following, with many of Tibet's greatest minds as well as members of powerful ruling families becoming his students. Pawo Tsuklak Trengwa's influential sixteenth-century Kagyü-oriented Tibetan historical work *Feast for the Learned* speaks of so many monks flocking to join Tsongkhapa that at one point many Kagyü monasteries were in danger of emptying out.[609] Similarly, Shākya Chokden, a prominent critic of Tsongkhapa belonging to Sakya tradition, writes of how in the fifteenth century most people in the Land of Snows were embracing Tsongkhapa's tradition.[610] It was thanks to the long-standing financial and political support of the Phagdru ruler Miwang Drakpa Gyaltsen, and most of the powerful political figures of central Tibet, that Tsongkhapa had been able to carry out his mission, including most notably the institution of the Great Prayer Festival at the Jokhang Temple in Lhasa and the founding of Ganden Monastery.

Tsongkhapa's prioritization of the authority of original Indian Buddhist sources over their Tibetan interpretations; his emphasis on insights gained through personal understanding rather than the authority of tradition; his insistence on developing an integrated understanding of the entire Indian Buddhist philosophical and spiritual heritage, both Sūtra and Tantra; his strong advocacy of vinaya ethics as the indispensable foundation of spiritual life; and his call for engaging in meditative practice, even of a specific instruction, with an overall understanding of the entire Buddhist path—all of these inevitably led to the emergence of an entirely new tradition in Tibet, whether or not Tsongkhapa himself intended to create one.

With the establishment of Ganden Monastery in 1409, followed by the founding of Drepung in 1416 and Sera in 1419, Tsongkhapa's followers had permanent monastic bases in central Tibet where they could put into practice their master's vision of a comprehensive and fully integrated Buddhist tradition.

Many of Tsongkhapa's influential works—including *The Great Treatise on the Stages of the Path to Enlightenment*, the hermeneutical text *The Essence of True Eloquence*, and his expositions of the Guhyasamāja tantra—had been published on woodblock prints for wider distribution, thanks once again to the Phagdru ruler, who had instructed his minister Gongkar Zhizompa to oversee the project.[611] In fact, before his death in 1405, the religious patriarch of Densa Thil, Chenga Sönam Sangpo, who had received his full ordination from Tsongkhapa, commissioned most of Tsongkhapa's collected works to be produced.[612] According to one source, it was the Phagdru ruler Miwang Drakpa Gyaltsen himself who first commissioned the entire collection of Tsongkhapa's writings for woodblock printing at Lhokha.[613] By the end of the fifteenth century, the entirety of Tsongkhapa's known writings would be compiled as his *Collected Works* (*sungbum* or *kabum*), covering some eighteen or nineteen large volumes. Tsongkhapa's collected works would later be joined by the collected works of two of his most important disciples and immediate successors, Gyaltsap and Khedrup, comprising eight and twelve large volumes, respectively. Together known as the "Father and Sons Collected Works" (*jé yapsé ungbum*), these volumes would become the major canonical collection for members of Tsongkhapa's Geluk school.

By the time of his death, Tsongkhapa's uniqueness on the Tibetan religious scene was beyond question. For his followers, he had become none other than the second Buddha. For those outside the Geluk, Tsongkhapa remained a force to be reckoned with, someone whose vision, ideas, and writings had to be understood in relation to their own cherished lineage and tradition. Indeed, the question that occupied the great Tibetan minds of the fifteenth, sixteenth, and following centuries was, "What does Tsongkhapa mean for the Tibetan Buddhist tradition as a whole and for the teachings of the specific lineages?" Buddhist thought in Tibet, especially systematic philosophical discourse, inevitably came to be shaped by the agenda set by Tsongkhapa's influential works. Many of the new developments in Tibetan philosophical thinking after Tsongkhapa took the form of either consolidating his thought further or opposing his views, particularly concerning the interpretation of Nāgārjuna's philosophy of emptiness, the relationship between ontology and epistemology, the philosophy of language, and the role of reason and thought in the soteriological process.

In the immediate aftermath of his passing, however, Tsongkhapa's disciples were keen to ensure the memory and legacy of their great master. By preserving his body in a special stūpa and installing it in a new temple, Tsongkhapa's followers had created a sacred monument that would comfort the devotees that the great master was still present at Ganden.

The "Conventional" and "Secret" Biographies

The next important task was to enshrine the memory of the teacher in writing. Tsongkhapa himself, sometime after 1410, had written an autobiographical poem entitled "Realizations Narrative" (*tokjö dunlekma*), which recounts how he first dedicated himself to extensive study, how all the great treatises then dawned upon him as personal instructions, and how he finally dedicated himself to single-pointed practice.[614] In a sense, this short poem sums up his entire life:

> First, I sought out a learning that is wide and extensive;
> In the middle, I perceived all teachings as personal
> instructions;
> Finally, I engaged in meditative practice day and night;
> All of this I have dedicated toward the flourishing of Buddha's
> teaching.[615]

Tsongkhapa's autobiographical text is quite brief, however. What was needed now was to create a work that would capture the recollections of the disciples who had been with Tsongkhapa the longest and served him most directly. Principal among them was Tokden Jampel Gyatso, who, like the master himself, also hailed from Amdo and was only a year older than Tsongkhapa. He had been with Tsongkhapa for over three decades, including accompanying him during the long, intensive retreat in the Wölkha Valley, and had, in the early years, served also as the medium for Tsongkhapa in his communication with the meditation deity Mañjuśrī. In addition, there were the notes of two of Tsongkhapa's attendants, Rinchen Pal and Lekpa Sangpo, who had nursed the master during his two-year illness in 1412–14. According to the colophon of Lekpa Sangpo's biography, the text was based on notes taken over a period of twenty-one sessions with Tsongkhapa and had been checked for accuracy by the master himself.[616]

The first biography of the master written by a student seems, intriguingly, to be Tokden Jampel Gyatso's brief "secret biography" of Tsongkhapa,[617] written at the request of Tsongkhapa's senior student Sharpa Rinchen Gyaltsen (founder of Shartsé College of Ganden Monastery), Sherap Sengé from Amdo, and Namkha Sangpo from Ngari, the latter two being Tokden's own students as well. This brief text deals with but a single theme: how, according to a prophecy stated by Mañjuśrī, Tsongkhapa would in the future display the deeds of the buddha Siṁhasvara ("Lion's Roar") in the buddha field called Adorned with Various Arrays of Amazing Wonders. The text goes into some detail about the physical appearance of this buddha, including his height, hand gestures and implements, color, and so on, and lays out the specific meritorious conditions devotees must gather in order to be reborn in Siṁhasvara's buddha field. In the colophon, Tokden Jampel Gyatso states that he had composed the text "in exact accordance with the instruction of the Venerable [Mañjuśrī], on the eighth day of the eighth month of the Rabbit Year."[618] There are two possibilities for this year: 1411 and 1423. Given that the tone of the biography suggests that Tsongkhapa was still alive when it was composed, my guess is that it was written in 1411, around the time when Tsongkhapa had made a pledge not to leave Ganden Mountain for few years so as to engage in continual retreats and focus on writing about the Guhyasamāja tantra.

The assignment to write the official, "great biography" of Tsongkhapa, however, fell to Khedrup, who was comparatively junior among the late master's disciples. Khedrup was, in fact, also a student of Gyaltsap, Tsongkhapa's formal successor to the Ganden throne. Khedrup probably was chosen because of his writing skill; by then he had established his authorial reputation with his remarkable text on the three vows, *Dusting the Buddha's Doctrine*. Khedrup had also compiled the authoritative notes from Tsongkhapa's lectures on Kālacakra as well as an important set of notes on the master's lectures on the perception chapter of Dharmakīrti's *Exposition of Valid Cognition*. Whatever the reason he was chosen, Khedrup would in fact write two biographies of the master: a conventional life story entitled *Entryway of Faith* and a secret biography entitled

Sheaf of Precious Jewels. As noted, a secret biography concerns the more esoteric dimension of a spiritual master's life, including especially their visionary experiences, and is meant to be read by the faithful so as to deepen their devotion to the master as a highly realized—indeed, enlightened—being. Intertextual evidence reveals that Khedrup wrote the conventional biography first and the secret biography later.

Khedrup's two biographies of the master were soon followed by three others of note: a conventional biography by Tokden Jampel Gyatso and two biographies by Tsongkhapa's attendant Lekpa Sangpo. The colophon of Tokden's text, entitled *A Compendium of All Excellent Utterances*, describes it as a "supplement" (*surdep*), suggesting he wrote it as a complement possibly to Khedrup's official biography.[619] Lekpa Sangpo characterizes his first biography of the master as conventional and the second as secret, following Khedrup's approach exactly.[620] Since Lekpa Sangpo's conventional biography of Tsongkhapa explicitly mentions Khedrup's secret biography of the master, it is clear that both of his texts were completed after Khedrup's two biographies. Similarly, if we take the explicit reference in Tokden's *Supplement* to Khedrup's *Secret Biography of Great Tsongkhapa* to be his own, given that Tokden passed away in 1428, nine years after Tsongkhapa, we can conclude that both of Khedrup's biographies of Tsongkhapa were written sometime between 1419 and 1427, less than a decade after the master's nirvāṇa.[621]

From a contemporary reader's perspective, these biographies may be regarded as engaging in a form of mythmaking, creating an official narrative of a deeply revered founding figure so that generations of future followers will be able to make a special emotional connection with him. I am using the term *myth* in the sense of a story that "accomplishes something significant for adherents,"[622] while leaving open the question of its objective truth. What these biographies aimed to do was, to borrow the language of the Catholic Church, canonize Tsongkhapa—to transform a flesh-and-blood historical personage into a transpersonal and mythic figure who thereby becomes an object of worship and emulation for the spiritual aspirant. In the case of Tsongkhapa, however, sanctification alone would not be adequate; what was required was the transformation of their master into none other than a fully enlightened buddha. In this process, two crucial factors proved indispensable. One was the role of secret biographies in recounting the deeply mystical dimension of his life, especially his numerous visionary experiences, to make the powerful point that the master had attained capacities far beyond the ordinary. The second was the role of prophecies indicating that the coming of the master had been predicted long before by various enlightened beings. Ostensibly intimating events yet to occur, some prophecies also have a retrospective dimension, revealing notable former lives of the subject, echoing the age-old tradition of the Jātaka tales, the stories of the Buddha's former lives. Tibet's own tradition had already produced an early equivalent of the Jātakas in the form of the narration of Dromtönpa's former life stories in *The Book of Kadam*.[623]

While the details of Tsongkhapa's secret biography would remain almost unchanged, the volume of prophecies predicting the master's coming would increase substantially as generations of Tsongkhapa's followers came to "discover" further such accounts. Over time, a more extensive list of Tsongkhapa's former births, known as *trungrap* ("successive births"), would be established. During Tsongkhapa's own life and immediately after, however, almost all the material for both his secret biography and the prophecies predicting his coming came from two sources: (1) visions of Mañjuśrī experienced by Lama Umapa or Tokden Jampel Gyatso and (2) visionary experiences of the Lhodrak mystic Drupchen Namkha Gyaltsen.

Briefly stated, the key elements of the past and future deeds of Tsongkhapa described in these two sources are the following:

- Throughout numerous past lives, Tsongkhapa was a student of Mañjuśrī, the buddha of wisdom.
- As a bodhisattva in a former life, Tsongkhapa made the aspiration in the presence of the buddha Indraketu to spread the teachings of Vajrayāna, as rooted in the understanding of the perfect view of emptiness, in the worlds inhabited by imperfect beings.
- Impressed by the young bodhisattva's courage and noble intention, the gathered buddhas prophesied in unison at that time that he would display the deeds of a fully awakened buddha as the tathāgata Siṁhasvara (Lion's Roar).
- During Śākyamuni's time, Tsongkhapa was born as a Brahmin who as a boy offered the Buddha a crystal rosary and thereafter generated bodhicitta. The Buddha then prophesied to Ānanda that the young Brahmin would one day revive the Buddha's doctrine and would found a monastery called Ganden.
- According to a variation of the same prophecy, the Buddha stated that Tsongkhapa would be reborn as the bodhisattva Mañjugarbha in the Tuṣita heavenly realm of the future Buddha Maitreya.

That Tsongkhapa had been the recipient of numerous visions of Mañjuśrī was widely known during his lifetime, since he himself and his principal teacher Rendawa both reported such events on several occasions. Furthermore, Drupchen's visions were well documented by the mystic himself in his collected writings. Jamyang Khaché's eulogy "Eighty Tsongkhapas," written in the third week after Tsongkhapa's death, confirms all the major elements of the master's life, including the visions recorded in the secret biographies and his offering of a crystal rosary to the Buddha in a former life.

All of this is evidence that these events were well known even while the master was alive.[624]

What Khedrup, as the official biographer, added was the crucial piece about the master's attainment of buddhahood. Using the Vajrayāna interpretation of buddhahood as the realization of the "three buddha bodies" (dharmakāya, saṃbhogakāya, and nirmāṇakāya), Khedrup declared that Tsongkhapa had attained the full awakening of buddhahood immediately following his death:

> Therefore, our great master... actualized at that point the ultimate truth of clear light and, by transforming death into dharmakāya, he arose as an illusory body during the intermediate state. Thus, there is no doubt that our master attained supreme saṃbhogakāya during the intermediate state.[625]

Khedrup reconciles his statement about Tsongkhapa attaining buddhahood in the intermediate state with a well-known prophecy that speaks of the master departing to the heavenly realm of Tuṣita after his passing[626] by comparing it to two seemingly contradictory statements concerning Nāgārjuna: one, that he died while on the first bodhisattva level and was reborn in Sukhāvatī; the other that he attained the Vajradhara state of full buddhahood as envisioned in tantra. Khedrup explains that the first version is presented from the perspective of Nāgārjuna's display of the deeds of an unenlightened being still on the path, while the second represents the definitive standpoint.[627] By the same token, Khedrup reads the claim that Tsongkhapa was reborn in Tuṣita after his death as provisional, and the assertion that he attained buddhahood in the intermediate state as definitive.

Khedrup would later compose a thirty-six-verse biographical hymn to Tsongkhapa, which would come to be memorized by all young monks in Geluk monasteries and chanted as the standard prayer honoring the great Tsongkhapa. This hymn would later be complemented by another verse hymn composed by Jamyang Chöjé (founder of Drepung Monastery), "The Secret Biography of the Great Tsongkhapa,"[628] which focuses specifically on the esoteric and visionary dimension of the master's life.

"The Master Was Prophesied in the Scriptures"

To return to our discussion of mythmaking, it appears that two significant new biographies of Tsongkhapa appeared before the end of the fifteenth century: Khedrup Norsang Gyatso's (1423–1513) *Short Account of the Great Tsongkhapa and His Disciples* (written in 1491) and Nenying Kunga Delek's (1446–96) *Doorway to Faith*, composed the next year. In addition to these, the Nyingma teacher Neringpa Chimé Rapgyé (fifteenth century), whose grandfather had been a devoted follower of Tsongkhapa, wrote four short biographical pieces related to the master: two on his immediate disciples; one on his qualities of learning, discipline, and compassion; and the last, an unfinished work, on his threefold activity of teaching, debate, and composition.[629]

One remarkable feature of Norsang Gyatso's biography is his use of various epithets for Tsongkhapa, which shows that by the end of the fifteenth century, Tsongkhapa's followers had developed many ways of referring to their great teacher. Norsang Gyatso describes the subject of his biography as:

> The protector and refuge of all sentient beings, including the gods; the light of Buddha's doctrine; the regent of Buddha Śākyamuni; the embodiment of the wisdom and compassion of all the buddhas; the crown jewel of humans of the last five-hundred[-year] period [of the Buddha's teaching]; the

> one the dust from whose noble feet graces the crown of all the great scholars; the one whose enlightened activities pervade the entire ocean-colored sky; the one unrivaled by anyone in hoisting the victory banner of the Tathāgata's doctrine right up to the peak of existence; the emanation of Mañjuśrī hailed as the Dharma king Tsongkhapa, whose fame thunders aloud like a banner flapping across all three worlds.[630]

The second major late-fifteenth-century biography, *Doorway to Faith* by Nenying, was written in 1492. As the title indicates, it is intended in part as a guide to Khedrup's *Entryway of Faith*. More than a mere gloss, however, it also is the first biography of Tsongkhapa to attempt to produce a seamless portrayal of the master's remarkable life by combining material from both the conventional and secret lives available to the author. Another innovation of this new biography is its identification of a passage in *The Pillar Testament*—a seminal work attributed to the seventh-century emperor Songtsen Gampo, said to have been extracted by Atiśa from underneath a pillar in the Jokhang Temple—as an important prophecy concerning Tsongkhapa.[631]

In his lengthy *History of Kadam Tradition*, which appeared two years after Nenying's biography, Lechen Kunga Gyaltsen (1432–1506) identifies this same passage from *The Pillar Testament,* along with a passage from *The Book of Kadam*, as prophecies of Tsongkhapa, and portrays Atiśa as a former life of Tsongkhapa.[632] Lechen's citation from *The Book of Kadam* reflects the influence of his teacher Gendün Drup (the First Dalai Lama), who was instrumental in the transmission of this esoteric *Book of Kadam* teaching within Tsongkhapa's new Geluk school.

Gendün Drup's successor, Gendün Gyatso (1476–1542)—later recognized as the Second Dalai Lama—introduced still another element by identifying Tsongkhapa as part of a series of previous births that includes not just Atiśa but the Indian tantric teacher Padmasambhava as well. In a famous hymn, he writes:

> Padmasambhava, lord among knowledge-bearing siddhas:
> You are glorious Dīpaṃkāra, the crown jewel of humans of this last five-hundredth;
> You are glorious Lobsang Drakpa, Lord Vajradhara himself—
> To you who perform the play of various forms I pray.[633]

Panchen Sönam Drakpa (1478–1554), who was a disciple of Gendün Gyatso and later became tutor to the Third Dalai Lama, Sönam Gyatso, explicitly speaks of Tsongkhapa's identification with Padmasambhava in his 1529 *History of Old and New Kadam Traditions*, which is effectively the first official history of the Geluk school. Panchen finds the following prophecy concerning Tsongkhapa in a major Nyingmapa *terma* (a treasure text) revealed by Ratna Lingpa (1403–79), *The Testament of Padmasambhava* (*Pemai Kachem*):

> At the sacred site of the monastery known as Ganden,
> A person by the name of *lo* (intellect) and *sang* (excellent) will appear:
> As a supreme scholar, he will be learned in all the sūtras and tantras;
> An emanation of Vajradhara, he will open the doors of tantric scriptures;
> Such a guide of beings, expert in showing the way, shall appear,
> And one bearing the tantric name Karmavajra shall grant him bliss.[634]

This search for prophecies concerning Tsongkhapa, beyond the traditional sources—the well-known visions of Mañjuśrī and

Lhodrak Drupchen's visions—was probably motivated in part by the wish to ground the canonization of Tsongkhapa in authorities more widely revered within the Tibetan tradition.

The first known Geluk work to compile a comprehensive list of prophecies about Tsongkhapa in Indian scriptures as well as Tibetan terma texts appears to be Ngawang Chödrak Gyatso's *Poetic Narrative on the Life of Jé Tsongkhapa: A Cluster of Flowers Adorning the Buddha's Doctrine*, written in 1560.[635] This is a poetic rendering of Tsongkhapa's life written almost entirely in verse, with the exception of the chapter dedicated to various prophecies about Tsongkhapa. In that chapter, the author, who was a student of Panchen Sönam Drakpa, was essentially completing what his teacher initiated in the *History of Old and New Kadam Traditions*. This poetic work was followed in the seventeenth century by Kharnak Lotsawa's *History of Ganden Tradition*. Written in 1629, when the Fifth Dalai Lama was a thirteen-year-old boy, the opening biographical section on Tsongkhapa begins with an impressive list of citations from sūtras and tantras, complemented by citations from authoritative Tibetan sources, including the revealed terma texts. Kharnak Lotsawa cites from two sūtras, one the chapter on cleansing the doctrine from *Imparting the Instructions Sūtra* and the other from the so-called Chinese version of the *Descent to Lanka Sūtra* (*Laṅkāvatāra*). The first citation reads:

> Ānanda, this young boy who has offered me a crystal rosary
> will revive my doctrine.
> In the future, during the age of degeneration,
> He will found a monastery called Virtuous (*Ge*)[636]
> At the meeting points of Dri and Den.
> He will be called by the name Lobsang
> And will attract a large circle of students,
> And will establish the tenfold Dharma practice.

Inside the temple, its pillars adorned with leaf motifs,
He will offer crown ornaments
To my two embodied images.
Like a teacher chanting sūtras,
He will sing supplications in melodious tunes,
And through his offering supplication to me,
The doctrine will last up to a thousand years.
He then will depart to the east,
To the Excellently Arrayed realm,
Where he will become [Buddha] Siṁhasvara.
Those who have faith in him will be born there;
This buddha realm is most excellent indeed.[637]

The second sūtra citation, from the Chinese version of the *Laṅkāvatāra*, essentially centers on the story of how the Buddha asked Maudgalyāyana to bury a large conch offered by the nāga king Anavatapta under Mount Gogpari, and prophesied that it would eventually be extracted by Tsongkhapa.[638] Kharnak then identifies two passages from the root tantra of Mañjuśrī, the second of which contains what appear to be explicit references to Tsongkhapa. This citation reads:

When I enter nirvāṇa
And when the earth becomes barren,
You'll assume the form of a youth
And will perform the deeds of a buddha;
At that time there will be a great monastery,
Most joyful (*ga*), in the Land of Snows.[639]

Kharnak cites a passage from yet another sūtra, the *Questions of the Goddess Vimalā*:

In the northern land of snow mountain ranges,
In a place endowed with virtue (*geden*),
The sublime Dharma will come to flourish.[640]

The practice of reading passages in authoritative scriptures as prophecies of one's master was not new, nor was it even a Tibetan innovation. The seventh-century Indian philosopher Candrakīrti, for example, speaks of Nāgārjuna as prophesied by the Buddha in the sūtras.[641]

In any case, in addition to finding these canonical sources, Kharnak goes on to cite various Tibetan sources, such as the "Prophecy" chapter of *The Book of Kadam* and these lines from *The Pillar Testament*:

Next, there will a monk bodhisattva born in the east
Who will honor [the temple] in a most extensive way,
A great yogi who will teach the tantras;
Such a great being with heart shall come to appear;
Changing the face [of the Buddha], he will honor the
temple.[642]

The other sources Kharnak brings to our attention include a statement from the famed woman mystic Machik Lapdrön (1055–1149) and treasure texts discovered and revealed by Ratna Lingpa (cited earlier), Dorjé Lingpa (1346–1405), and one Chöjé Gönpo Rinchen.[643] Later Geluk biographers would discover other prophecies in the terma literature, including from the well-known *Testament of Padmasambhava* (*Pemai Kachem*):

There will appear Lobsang Drakpa, an upholder of Sūtra and
Tantra doctrine,

A Mañjuśrī emanation and a master of doctrine for the students.
Departing from this realm, he will go to the presence of
Maitreya.[644]

Almost exactly the same prophecy is found in a treasure text revealed by Dorjé Lingpa:

There will appear Lobsang Drakpa, an upholder of Sūtra and
Tantra doctrine;
For seven generations he will reveal the scriptures (*piṭakas*)
and the tantras;
Departing from this realm, he'll go to the presence of
Maitreya.[645]

Ratna Lingpa's treasure text on the life of Padmasambhava is said to contain the following remarkable statement, addressed to the Tibetan emperor and his ministers by the Indian tantric master:

There will appear a Mañjuśrī emanation,
An ordained monk who is a vajra holder [*tāntrika*];
He will serve the Jowo [the Jokhang Buddha image]
excellently;
He will make Nāgārjuna's tradition flourish;
He will live for sixty-four years
Then will depart toward the northeast.[646]

These lines explicitly identify key characteristics of Tsongkhapa: he was known to be an emanation of Mañjuśrī; he was a fully ordained monastic but also a master of Vajrayāna; he honored the sacred Buddha image in the Jokhang Temple in Lhasa; he ensured the flourishing of Nāgārjuna's philosophy in Tibet; and he lived to the age of around sixty-four (according to Tibetan counting).

The "discovery" of all of these prophecies concerning Tsongkhapa, both in canonical sources and in terma texts, including an intriguingly negative prophecy warning that Tsongkhapa would appear as a kind of Antichrist,[647] would animate the subsequent biographical literature on Tsongkhapa during the seventeenth and eighteenth centuries. The lineage coming from Gendün Gyatso, the Second Dalai Lama, who received and transmitted several terma-based instructions associated with Padmasambhava[648] (whom Tsongkhapa himself revered), descended through authors like Kharnak Lotsawa, the Great Fifth Dalai Lama, and his regent Desi Sangyé Gyatso, who also would celebrate the prophecies found in the Nyingma treasure texts. In fact, the Desi would question the authenticity of the citations from the "Chinese version" of the *Laṅkāvatāra Sūtra*, the *Sūtra Imparting Instructions*, and the *Questions of the Goddess Vimalā*, on the grounds that the cited passages are not to be found in the Tibetan canonical collection, the Kangyur, and would instead emphasize prophecies found in the Tibetan treasure texts.[649] Not all of Tsongkhapa's followers would share such enthusiasm for Nyingma terma texts, however. The Geluk historian Sumpa Khenpo Yeshé Paljor (1704–88), for whom the authenticity of many of the treasure texts remained at best an open question, felt that acceptance of these passages as prophecies of Tsongkhapa was unnecessarily problematic.[650]

From a critical historical perspective, one significance of these Nyingma terma prophecies about Tsongkhapa—all of which were "extracted" and revealed either toward the end of Tsongkhapa's life or soon after his passing—is to understand them as a means of accommodating the phenomenon of Tsongkhapa vis-à-vis the Nyingma tradition. As we have already observed, these terma texts are believed to have been hidden by the great Padmasambhava, to be revealed at an appropriate time in the future, so the statements prophesying Tsongkhapa confer legitimacy on the master by invoking the authority of none other than Padmasambhava himself. As noted earlier, of the major Tibetan Buddhist schools during Tsongkhapa's time—Nyingma, Kadam, Sakya, and Kagyü—he appears to have had the least interaction with the teachings and institutions of the Nyingma tradition, and even the simple question of what Tsongkhapa thought of Dzokchen would remain a mystery.[651] In contrast, as we have observed in the preceding chapters, Tsongkhapa had extensive interactions with both the teachings and the institutions of the other major Tibetan schools.

In the late eighteenth and early nineteenth centuries, perhaps in response to a felt need among many of Tsongkhapa's Geluk followers, three voluminous and comprehensive biographies of the master would emerge. The first was *Source of All Joys and Goodness*, an extensive biography in nine chapters written by the ethnic Mongol author Chahar Lobsang Tsultrim (1740–1810).[652] In addition to bringing together material from all preceding biographies, this work is unique in presenting much of Tsongkhapa's recorded correspondence with various contemporaries, in what the biographer deemed appropriate chronological order. Chahar's biography was soon followed by *Entryway to the Ocean of Pure Faith*, written by yet another Mongol monk, Yeshé Döndrup (1792–1855). Finally, in 1845, Gyalwang Chöjé Lobsang Trinlé composed what would eventually become the *Namthar Chenmo*, the standard "great" biography of Tsongkhapa. Collating all the various sources—Mañjuśrī's visions as narrated by Umapa and Tokden, Vajrapāṇi's prophecies as narrated by Lhodrak Drupchen, the prophecies found in the sūtras and tantras as well as in such Tibetan scriptures as *The Pillar Testament* and various Nyingma treasure texts, and statements by great masters like Khenchen Chökyap Sangpo—Lobsang Trinlé provides the following "definitive" list of Tsongkhapa's twenty-seven former lives, not enumerated in strict chronological order:

1. Tathāgatha Nāgagotrottama
2. Tathāgatha Möpa Raptu Gawai Nyingpo
3. Mañjuśrī
4. Bodhisattva Mahāsattva
5. Bodhisattva Maṇibhadra
6. The Brahmin boy who offered a crystal rosary to the Buddha
7. Bhikṣu Kamalaśīla
8. Arhat Upāli
9. Arhat Upagupta
10. Padmasambhava
11. Nāgārjuna
12. Ḍombi Heruka
13. Lvavapa
14. Lūipa
15. Kawa Drimé Wö
16. Bodhisattva Raśmamālī
17. Atiśa
18. Marpa Chökyi Lodrö
19. Nyantön Chöbar
20. Gampopa
21. Denbak Mawai Sengé
22. Bodhisattva in the guise of a caretaker of Swayambhu stūpa in Nepal
23. Dharma Sengé
24. Kadam master Tsonawa
25. An Indian Nāgarāja
26. The Brahmin girl Saten
27. In his immediately preceding life, a Kashmiri paṇḍita by the name of Matibhadra.[653]

The Role of Art and the Rise of Guru Yoga Devotional Practice

Another strand in this mythmaking took place in the domain of art, with the iconographic depiction of the great master and his life, especially the events from his secret biography. As we have seen, the tradition of creating statues and paintings of Tsongkhapa seems to have begun during his life. Then there was the official statue of the master sculpted immediately after his death to be housed in the stūpa temple. Sometime toward the mid-fifteenth century, a thangka portrayal of Tsongkhapa as a focus of the guru yoga meditation practice *Hundred Deities of Tuṣita* (*Ganden Lhagyama*), stemming from the Sé lineage of Dulnakpa Palden Sangpo (1402–73), emerged. This painting depicts Tsongkhapa seated on a throne with his two hands in the teaching gesture, with each holding the stem of a lotus, on which are placed a sword of wisdom on the right and a scripture on the left. Tsongkhapa and the two principal disciples (Gyaltsap and Khedrup) flanking him are all on a mass of white clouds emerging from the heart of Maitreya, the future Buddha residing in Tuṣita above.

Another portrayal derives from visions of the master experienced by Khedrup, as recorded in his biography by Chöden Rapjor (fifteenth century).[654] According to this biography, on several occasions when Khedrup missed Tsongkhapa, he burst into tears. During some of these moments, Khedrup had visions of Tsongkhapa in five different forms: two in his usual appearance as a monk seated cross-legged on a lotus on a throne, one riding on a white elephant, another seated on a white lion, and finally one riding a fierce tiger.[655] This particular thangka portrayal of the master would be known as *Je Sikpa Ngaden*, the "Master in Five Visions." Evidence also indicates that by the mid-sixteenth century there was a tradition of depicting the events of Tsongkhapa's life in a series of paintings. One Namkha Wöser, a student of the second Dalai Lama, was commissioned to write an explanatory text for "Tsongkhapa's Biography in Painting" (*namthar redrima*), which he completed in 1513.[656] Judging by this text, there appears to have been a set of sixty-one paintings, a large central thangka and sixty smaller paintings, the first thirty numbered alphabetically with the thirty consonants and the next thirty numbered with the consonants accompanied with the vowel *i*. By the time Jamyang Shepa (1648–1721) wrote his *Garland of Cintamani Gems*, a description of biographical paintings, the number of individual items in the paintings had grown to 205.[657] It is not clear from either Namkha Wöser or Jamyang Shepa whether each of these smaller paintings represents an individual thangka or whether they were somehow grouped together in sets, although my own sense is that it is the latter. There is, for example, the established tradition of creating a set of sixteen thangkas, known as "Eighty Tsongkhapas" (*Tsogkha Gyechu*), depicting the life of the master.[658]

The Emergence of the Ganden (Geluk) School

Tibetan historians understandably consider the founding of Ganden Monastery in 1409 to be the starting point of Tsongkhapa's Ganden or Geluk school.[659] However, the actual story of how and when the Geluk school emerged as a distinct, self-consciously identified tradition within Tibetan Buddhism is more complicated. Some modern scholars contend that Tsongkhapa himself never intended to create a new Tibetan Buddhist school and that the credit for the emergence of the new school must go to, if to anyone at all, Khedrup Gelek Palsang. In some ways, this is a moot point. In the preceding chapters we discovered enough evidence to indicate that, over time, Tsongkhapa did come to recognize that his was a unique tradition in Tibet, grounded primarily in his personal understanding and realizations based on careful study of the Indian Buddhist sources and the instructions he received from Mañjuśrī on various occasions. Tsongkhapa never identified himself as a member of any specific Tibetan school of his time, including the Sakya tradition of his main teacher, Rendawa. Even during his student years in central Tibet, when he spent time in monasteries belonging to most of the major lineages of the time—Kadam (Sangphu, Narthang, and Dewachen at Nyethang), Sakya, Shalu (Butön's monastery) and Kagyü (Drigung, Densa Thil, Tsethang, and Tsal Gungthang)—Tsongkhapa does not seem to have committed himself to any specific tradition.

Tsongkhapa was a maverick: a hermit at heart, a seeker moving from one monastery to another and one teacher to another, receiving what he felt to be the best instruction on whatever subject, text, or practice most interested him at a given time. Although he studied the Indian philosophical classics with a number of Sakyapa teachers, most notably Rendawa, it is unclear whether Tsongkhapa ever received the full transmission of the lamdré (path and fruits) cycle of teachings, a key instruction of the Sakya school. He received teachings at Kagyü monasteries on the two signature instructions of Kagyü tradition, Mahāmudrā and the six yogas of Nāropa, and he cherished Marpa and Milarepa's unique insights into the "mixings" practice connected with the Guhyasamāja tantra and also their instructions on the tummo practice connected with the mother tantras, even composing his own guide to the six yogas of Nāropa. Yet he never considered himself a member of the Kagyü lineage.

He admired Butön's teachings on Kālacakra and the Jonang tradition's unique instructions on the six-yoga completion-stage meditations of that late Indian tantra, but he did not see himself as a member of either Butön's Shalu tradition or the Jonang tradition. The one Tibetan school with which Tsongkhapa probably felt the greatest affinity was the Kadam tradition of Atiśa and Dromtönpa. In fact, Tibetan historians of Buddhism would sometimes characterize the Geluk school as neo-Kadam (*kadam sarma*). Even here, though, his focus was largely confined to Atiśa's lamrim teaching and the lojong instructions centered on bodhicitta practice that evolved from Atiśa's oral teachings; he showed considerably less interest in the more esoteric teachings connected with *The Book of Kadam*, which are a Tibetan innovation.

In his mature period, following the completion of his studies, Tsongkhapa moved around constantly, choosing initially to remain for the most part in various hermitages, engaging in intensive meditative practice. From the time his teaching career took off in the late 1390s until the founding of Ganden Monastery in 1409, Tsongkhapa did not base himself at any one monastery. Rather, he maintained his peripatetic lifestyle, somewhat like that chosen by the Buddha some two millennia earlier. Although he traveled throughout much of central Tibet, Tsongkhapa appears to have avoided teaching in Tsang Province, where Sakya Monastery is based—perhaps out of deference to his teacher Rendawa, who was a self-identified Sakyapa. Because he did not venture into Tsang in his mature teaching period, Tsongkhapa never met one of the important intellectual and literary figures of his era, Bodong Choklé Namgyal, who was active primarily in Tsang. Ironically, Tsongkhapa's two immediate successors on the throne at Ganden, Gyaltsap and Khedrup, were both originally Sakyapas and hailed from Tsang; indeed, the next five monks to ascend to the Ganden throne would all be from Tsang.[660]

Tsongkhapa's mode of study also showed his independence. In his quest to gain insight into the ultimate truth of emptiness as expounded by Nāgārjuna, Tsongkhapa had pursued an approach that carefully combined the following: (1) a close reading of Nāgārjuna himself, guided especially by the interpretations of two Indian masters, Buddhapālita and Candrakīrti; (2) prolonged contemplation grounded in critical engagement with these texts; (3) occasional personal instructions from his meditation deity, Mañjuśrī;

and (4) deep meditative practice over a long period. In his advanced Vajrayāna practice, all the evidence indicates that he concentrated solely on instructional lineages that he believed to be reliably rooted in Indian traditions. Whether his focus was meditative practices pertaining to the Guhyasamāja, Cakrasaṃvara, Kālacakra, or Yamāntaka cycles of tantra; tummo practice; the yoga of channels, winds, and drops; the union of innate bliss and emptiness; or the illusory body, Tsongkhapa did seek out the extant Tibetan transmissions of these teachings. But he appears to have relied for his own understanding and practice primarily on a careful comparative study of the Indian texts themselves. Thus, when, at a gathering of a few of his closest disciples a few weeks before his nirvāṇa, Tsongkhapa asked, "Who will volunteer to be the custodian of my explanatory tradition on Guhyasamāja?"[661] he clearly seemed to be speaking about a unique transmission lineage of the tantra in Tibet.

In any case, with the founding of the three great monasteries of Ganden (1409), Drepung (1416), and Sera (1419), by the time Tsongkhapa passed away, the conditions were in place for the emergence of a unique lineage or school within Tibetan Buddhism. There was a shared conviction among Tsongkhapa's closest disciples that in their master's teachings they had found the true revelation of the Buddha's enlightened intention. Not all of Tsongkhapa's disciples would identify with the new Ganden school. While revering Tsongkhapa as a key teacher and embracing many of his teachings, a number of important figures chose to remain within their own original lineages, including Chenga Sönam Gyaltsen (a Kagyü master at Densa Thil Monastery), Jamyang Khaché (another important master of Densa Thil and Tsethang), Khenchen Sengé Gyaltsen and Sempa Chenpo Namkha Wöser (senior disciples of Lochen Kyapchok Palsang and founding abbots of Chökhor Gang Monastery),[662] Gö Lotsawa Shönu Pal (a Kagyü master and author of *The Blue Annals*), Götruk Repa (a Drukpa Kagyü contemplative), Shönu

Gyalchok (a Kadam and Sakya teacher), and Könchok Palsang (the abbot of Zulphu Monastery).[663]

Many others, however, would identify themselves primarily as members of the new Ganden tradition. It is these disciples, many with a missionary zeal, who would spread Tsongkhapa's teachings across the Tibetan plateau as they founded new monasteries and converted existing ones. Never before had Tibet witnessed such a rapid rise of a new tradition or focused to such a great extent on the legacy of a single master. By the end of the fifteenth century, just over eighty years after Tsongkhapa's death, his new Ganden tradition had spread through the entire Tibetan cultural area, with monasteries upholding the tradition located in western Tibet, in Tsang, in central and southern Tibet, and in Kham and Amdo in the east.[664] Observing this fact, Gö Lotsawa Shönu Pal would remark, "By that time, the entire face of this great earth was covered by the one white canopy of Tsongkhapa."[665]

Interestingly, until around the end of the fifteenth century, the teaching of some of Tsongkhapa's key texts appears to have continued to be transmitted by masters outside the new Ganden tradition. Taktsang Lotsawa's biography, for example, records his receiving transmissions of various works of Tsongkhapa, especially on Guhyasamāja, from his teacher Drakpa Sangpo.[666] Similarly, Shamar Chödrak Yeshé's (1454–1526) biography of the third Shamarpa, Chöphel Yeshé (1406–52), reveals him receiving transmissions of Tsongkhapa's writings on Guhyasamāja tantra.[667] As for the fourth Shamarpa himself, he in fact speaks of receiving transmissions from Gö Lotsawa Shönu Pal on several texts composed by Tsongkhapa, including *The Middle-Length Treatise on the Stages of the Path*, *The Essence of True Eloquence*, *The Great Treatise on Tantra*, and the extensive commentary on the Cakrasaṃvara tantra.[668] Sönam Gyaltsen, a key teacher at Densa Thil Monastery, who had requested Tsongkhapa to compose a guide to the six yogas of

Nāropa, would continue to revere the memory of the master, never missing an annual commemoration of his passing,[669] and in his own instruction on the six yogas of Nāropa he listed Tsongkhapa as the source of his transmission.[670] Furthermore, in his replies to a series of questions on the teachings of Kagyü tradition, Sönam Gyaltsen would emphatically make the point that master Tsongkhapa's view of emptiness is in perfect accord with the view inherent in the Kagyü Mahāmudrā teaching.[671]

There is no doubt that Khedrup did play a critical role in consolidating the identity of Tsongkhapa's new Ganden school in the immediate aftermath of the master's passing. On the one hand, for members of the new school, especially those who upheld important teaching traditions, Khedrup emphasized the need for what could be described as "doctrinal purity," a strict loyalty to the writings of the master himself. Notoriously, Khedrup is believed to have chided Gungru Gyaltsen Sangpo, a noted student of Tsongkhapa, for being unfaithful to the master's writings, prompting Gungru to write the following lament:

> All the people run after the powerful;
> All the narratives run after the famous;
> While Lobsang Drakpa resides in Tuṣita heaven;
> I, Gyaltsen Sangpo, am left here alone.[672]

To be fair, Khedrup did not exclude himself from this requirement for loyalty to the master's writings. In a lengthy letter to one Tharpa Gyaltsen, Khedrup writes:

> Whatever writings may have been produced by the master's disciples, myself included, you should not simply follow their letter but examine with an objective mind whether or not they include anything that contradicts the master's

> scriptures, either directly or indirectly. If, as a result of such examination, [we see that] there are such contradictions, [we] should cast these away as if spitting something out.[673]

In another short work, entitled *Lamp Dispelling the Darkness of Erroneous Paths*, Khedrup speaks of the critical importance of not diluting the purity of Tsongkhapa's teachings on emptiness by introducing terminology and concepts borrowed from indigenous Tibetan traditions. In suggesting this, Khedrup does not appear to be sectarian; rather, he seems to be advocating an approach involving strict fidelity to Tsongkhapa's view, while respecting the integrity and uniqueness of the approaches presented in other instructional lineages. What he is condemning is a kind of naïve syncretism that combines the terminology and concepts of distinct and specific approaches. It is in this text that we encounter the descriptor "those who aspire to uphold the lineage of the All-Knowing Great Tsongkhapa."[674]

The second task Khedrup seems to have chosen, as the guardian of Tsongkhapa's tradition, was to write rebuttals of any critiques of the master's writings. Khedrup speaks of how the responsibility of being the custodian of the great master weighs heavily on his heart but he does not feel wearied by the challenge. Also, he says it is he who holds the sword to guard the Buddha's doctrine, so he cannot afford any distractions, such as traveling in response to invitations.[675] Two figures whom Khedrup singled out for criticism were Ngorchen Kunga Sangpo, the great master of the Sakya Ngor tradition,[676] and the influential Sakya scholar Rongtön Sheja Kunrik, both of whom Khedrup saw as having raised doubts about Tsongkhapa's works. However, as we shall see later, the main critiques of Tsongkhapa would appear years after Khedrup's death, at the hands of a trio of Sakya scholars: Taktsang Lotsawa, Gorampa, and Shākya Chokden. Although Ngorchen Kunga Sangpo appears to have initiated the process,[677] it was Gorampa in particular who played a key role in hardening the sectarian divide between Sakya and Tsongkhapa's new Ganden school.

The recognition that Tsongkhapa had initiated a unique lineage within Tibetan Buddhism appears to have been shared by prominent members of other Tibetan schools, including Tsongkhapa's most fervent critics. For example, Shākya Chokden speaks of Tsongkhapa as having "set forth all sorts of positions with respect to Madhyamaka and Cittamātra [philosophies], as well as the sūtras and tantras."[678] Gorampa even raises the possibility that the visions of Mañjuśrī that form the basis for Tsongkhapa's new tradition could have been a delusion.[679] On a more positive note, Shamar Chödrak Yeshé (1453–1524), who was a student of Gö Lotsawa, speaks of how, having gained the view himself, Tsongkhapa established a new interpretation of Madhyamaka in Tibet that emphasized the role of critical reasoning, and developed both a view and meditative practice that are superior to those of earlier traditions in Tibet. He also acknowledges that Tsongkhapa established a tantric tradition endowed with unique features respecting the understanding and practice of the five stages of completion and the six yogas of Nāropa. Seeing this, he notes, many people in Tibet have flocked to follow this new tradition.[680]

Critiques of Tsongkhapa's Works in the Fifteenth Century

Although Tsongkhapa's junior contemporaries Rongtön Shākya Gyaltsen (1367–1449) and Ngorchen Künga Sangpo (1382–1456),[681] both important figures in the Sakya school, were known to be critical of some aspects of Tsongkhapa's writings, there is no record of Tsongkhapa responding to their critiques. Tsongkhapa's writings do, however, include a response to one Sasang Lotsawa Ngawang, who Tsongkhapa says "had raised objections to the Vajrabhairava sādhana I had written."[682]

As for Rongtön, Shākya Chokden's biography states that his written critiques generally focused on three main areas: (1) some early Tibetan views on the differentiation of the four classical Indian Buddhist schools, (2) the very unusual views presented in Dolpopa Sherap Gyaltsen's works, and (3) the tenets established by the precious master Lobsang Drakpa.[683] The biographer, however, does not provide any specific critiques Rongtön leveled against Tsongkhapa's views. It is well known that Rongtön's writings on Maitreya's *Ornament* became the "rival" exposition of the Indian text against Tsongkhapa and Gyaltsap's reading of this influential Indian text. Rongtön's own writings on Madhyamaka, especially in his *Presentation of the Difficult Points of [Nāgārjuna's] Madhyamaka Analytic Corpus,* indicate that his view on emptiness in fact appears to be quite close to Tsongkhapa's, with a few differences in specific areas.[684] As for Norchen's criticism of aspects of Tsongkhapa's tantric writings, Khedrup would pen a scathing rebuttal.

These few instances aside, it was only after the death of both Tsongkhapa and Khedrup that more systematic critiques of his writings began to emerge. The first among these came from Taktsang Lotsawa. Born in 1405, fourteen years before Tsongkhapa's death, Taktsang became a student of Jamyang Chöjé at Drepung Monastery.

Taktsang criticized aspects of Tsongkhapa's Madhyamaka thought that he deemed to be at odds with the views of Lochen Kyapchok Palsang and Rendawa.[685] His critiques focused on Tsongkhapa's insistence on the need to maintain a robust notion of conventional truth grounded in some verifiable criteria of validity, even within the Madhyamaka system that espouses all phenomena to be empty of intrinsic existence. Taktsang's own preferred standpoint can be characterized as a form of epistemological skepticism. For

Tsongkhapa, however, Nāgārjuna's equation of emptiness with dependent origination means that one needs to take the world of conventional truth seriously. Espousing emptiness does not mean "anything goes" or that nothing can be said to exist. Even a Mādhyamika, in Tsongkhapa's view, must accept the difference between the veridicality of the perception of water as water and a mirage as water. For Taktsang, this kind of insistence on the part of Tsongkhapa reflects a dangerous mixing of Nāgārjuna's philosophy of emptiness with Dharmakīrtian epistemology, which remains untenable. Taktsang famously leveled "eighteen heavy loads of contradiction" against Tsongkhapa, most of which centers on what he saw as serious problems resulting from Tsongkhapa's integration of Madhyamaka ontology and Dharmakīrtian epistemology.[686]

Despite questioning aspects of Tsongkhapa's views, Taktsang Lotsawa held Tsongkhapa in enduring esteem, deeply admiring his extensive achievements. In fact, disturbed by the overtly sectarian tone of some criticisms of Tsongkhapa, Taktsang wrote the following lament:

> The act of ruining the teaching through the demon of
> sectarianism
> By those who target you primarily with bigoted attitudes—
> may this too
> Be dispelled swiftly by you who embody unbiased admiration
> for all,
> And may all upholders of Dharma live in perfect harmony.[687]

The most vehement critiques of Tsongkhapa's writings in the fifteenth century came from two Sakya scholars who were born after Tsongkhapa's death and had studied as young monks at the feet of Rongtön: Gorampa Sönam Sengé (1429–89) and Shākya

Chokden (1428–1507). Gorampa sees Tsongkhapa's insistence on defining emptiness in terms of the absolute negation of intrinsic existence—pure and simple absence—as a form of nihilism. He also takes issues with other important aspects of Tsongkhapa's work, such as his characterization of conventional truth and his differentiation of the two subschools of Madhyamaka.[688]

Shākya Chokden, on the other hand, took issue with Tsongkhapa for having propounded so many new tenets. To be accused of innovation in the traditional world of Tibetan scholarship is to be accused of committing a serious fallacy, of conjuring things up with no authoritative sources. The irony is that Shākya Chokden himself would later come to be accused of exactly the same fallacy, that of innovation!

At the heart of Shākya Chokden's objections is the rejection of Tsongkhapa's claim that, insofar as the view of emptiness is concerned, there is no difference between Sūtra and Tantra. Shākya Chokden himself advocated what could be called a "contextual view" of emptiness, not that dissimilar to Dolpopa's so-called extrinsic emptiness (*shentong*), whereby the view of emptiness presented by Nāgārjuna in his *Treatise on the Middle Way* represents the "philosophical" and "rational" view, while the view found in Nāgārjuna's collection of poetic hymns represents the "meditator or yogi's view." According to him, this latter view is found also in the Yogācāra writings of Asaṅga and Vasubandhu.[689] More broadly, Shākya Chokden sees Tsongkhapa as disrespectful of the views of earlier Tibetan masters, not only on philosophy but also on meditative practice and Vajrayāna instructions. Even so, he does acknowledge the importance of Tsongkhapa's contribution to Buddhism in Tibet, writing, "When the sun of the Buddha's doctrine was in decline in Tibet, the full-moon light of the great intellect from the Tsongkha region in the east appeared."[690]

The Geluk response to these critiques took two forms. The

first was direct rebuttal, as in Lekpa Chöjor's (a.k.a. Jamyang Galo, 1429–1503) reply to Gorampa and Jetsün Chökyi Gyaltsen's response to both Gorampa and Shākya Chokden. A second form of response, paralleling these scholarly rebuttals, was, as suggested above, the discovery and revelation of important prophecies concerning Tsongkhapa in authoritative scriptures.

How Tsongkhapa Came to Be Viewed after the Fifteenth Century

As the fifteenth century drew to a close, and as Tsongkhapa's new Ganden or Geluk community flourished across the Tibetan plateau, admiration for Tsongkhapa continued to be expressed by major religious and intellectual figures in other Tibetan traditions. For example, in a remarkable praise to Tsongkhapa written on a visit to the sacred Tsari Mountain, a site associated with Cakramsaṃvara and visited by Tsongkhapa, Mikyö Dorjé (1507–54), the eighth Karmapa, lists various unique features of Tsongkhapa's Ganden tradition, calling the master "the reformer of Buddha's doctrine," "the great charioteer of Madhyamaka philosophy in Tibet," "supreme among those who propound emptiness," and "one who had helped spread robe-wearing monastics across Tibet and from China to Kashmir." Speaking of Tsongkhapa's establishment of a new tradition in Tibet, the eighth Karmapa writes:

> When the Buddha's doctrine approached its demise
> Through the decline of Sakya, Dakpo, and Saṅgphu, the
>   upholder of Kadam vinaya,
> You spread your new doctrine across the land;
> I praise you, the man from Geden mountain.[691]

Similarly, while responding to what he considered to be an unfair critique of Kagyü Mahāmudrā in one of Tsongkhapa's early works, *Queries from a Sincere Heart*, Drukpa Pema Karpo (1527–92) wrote a short poem paying homage to Tsongkhapa. The tone of Pema Karpo's work is captured in the following lines:

> When the enlightened qualities of all the buddhas are weighed
> On a scale against yours, no differences exist at all;
> You're worthy to be the crown jewel of humans of the last
> five-hundredth;
> I pay homage to you, All-Knowing One.[692]

For Tsongkhapa's own Geluk followers, the way they felt about their master and understood his uniqueness may have been captured best by the Fifth Dalai Lama, who was known for his ecumenism in general and his affinity for Nyingma traditions in particular. In the course of describing Tsongkhapa's many stellar qualities, he writes:

> One might say that these alone do not prove that he indeed rose high above all [other] learned ones. There were, for example, the three Kadam brothers, as well as Langri Thangpa and Sharawa, all of whom were bodhisattvas who held others dearer than themselves. There were also siddhas like Chegom Dzongpa, Drokmi Lotsawa, Marpa Lotsawa, and Milarepa, who had attained the state of union in their lifetime or in the intermediate state. There had also appeared countless scholars, such as Sakya Paṇḍita, Ngok Loden Sherap, and Butön Rinchen Drup, who were versed in the five fields of knowledge.
>
> This reasoning does not apply in the present context. Yes, if one were to put all these great beings together, their

qualities could match the qualities of this sublime master [Tsongkhapa], but not when they are taken individually. Here is the reason. Although it is true that this sublime teacher does not possess bodhicitta superior to that attained by the paṇḍitas, translators, emperors, and bodhisattvas of the first diffusion of Buddhism in Tibet and the great Kadam masters of the later diffusion of the doctrine, they did not possess the mastery of philosophy and the whole of Tantra that this teacher attained. Similarly, though it is true that with respect to the attainments of the generation stage and completion stage of tantra, the twenty-five realized beings of the first diffusion period and Lochen, Drokmi, the "three white patriarchs" [of Sakya: Sachen Kunga Nyingpo, Sönam Tsemo, and Drakpa Gyaltsen], Marpa, and Milarepa are all equal [to Tsongkhapa], there does exist a difference when it comes to vinaya discipline and mastery of the standpoints of the four classical Buddhist philosophical schools, as well as the conventional fields of knowledge like linguistics and pramāṇa epistemology. Also, there may be no difference between this teacher and Sakya Paṇḍita, Ngok Loden Sherap, Shongtön Lotsawa, Pangtön Lotsawa, Butön, and others when it comes to having engaged in critical scholarship in all five fields of knowledge, but it has been established by observable evidence that, thanks to the kindness of the guru and guardian Mañjuśrī, this sublime teacher decisively established the view of emptiness—the explicit subject matter [of the Perfection of Wisdom sūtras] and the intent of the glorious master Nāgārjuna—as well as the profound themes of the glorious Guhyasamāja tantra, including especially the topic of the illusory body, which had remained beyond the comprehension of past scholars and realized meditators.[693]

In brief, the Fifth Dalai Lama is saying that Tsongkhapa is unique in his achievements. He may be comparable to other great Tibetan figures in specific areas, but only the combination of many of his predecessors could match the totality of his qualities as an embodiment of Mahāyāna Buddhism's ideal of great compassion, his advanced meditative realizations, and his accomplishments as one of Tibet's intellectual giants.

If we were to search for a more measured assessment of Tsongkhapa's legacy by a non-Geluk author whose perspective is not colored by exultant veneration of the master typical of his own devout follower, what Taklung Ngawang Namgyal (1571–1626), the author of a history of Taklung Kagyü tradition, wrote might be a good candidate:

> Among all the great beings who have appeared in Tibet, this Land of Snows, it is glorious Tsongkhapa Lobsang Drakpa from eastern Tibet who is unmatched with respect to his perfect enlightened activities, such as the threefold pursuit of the learned: teaching, debate, and composition. In particular, he established the custom of meticulous observance of all the precepts of omission and commission of the sublime vinaya discipline; with the keys of exposition, he unlocked the Guhyasamāja tantra, which had been sealed with "six boundaries" and "four modes," and ushered in the emergence of monastic communities engaged in the study and teaching of this tantra even in this era of degeneration. These communities serve as exemplars for the transmission of the exposition of tantras. In brief, for the Buddha's doctrine as a whole, he performed the task of being the second Buddha.[694]

Epilogue

TRADITIONAL BIOGRAPHIES of Tsongkhapa conclude with a list of the master's principal disciples. These lists generally include over a hundred recognizable names, such as his three principal disciples, Gyaltsap Darma Rinchen, Dülzin Drakpa Gyaltsen, and Khedrup Gelek Palsang;[695] the mystic Tokden Jampel Gyatso; Jamyang Chöjé and Jamchen Chöjé, the founders of Drepung and Sera monasteries, respectively; and the First Dalai Lama, Gendün Drup. In later biographies, written during and after the sixteenth century, the list of Tsongkhapa's principal disciples came to be organized according to specific attributes shared by several individuals, such as "the eight disciples who accompanied Tsongkhapa during his long retreat in Wölkha." One such group is "the seven great banners who upheld the tradition in distant lands," which includes (1) Shangshung Chöwang Drakpa, (2) Gugé Ngawang Drakpa, (3) Gyaltsen Sengé, (4) Denma Yönten Gyatso, (5) Sönam Sherap, (6) Rongpo Jaknakpa, and (7) Wöser from Amdo. In addition, there were "the two Sherap Sengpos," one from western Tibet and the other from eastern Tibet, who were instrumental in spreading Tsongkhapa's tradition in their respective native regions. Thus, it was primarily due to the missionizing activities of these disciples of Tsongkhapa and their students that, by the end of the fifteenth century, Tsongkhapa's Geluk tradition had become widespread on the Tibetan plateau.

In 1426, seven years after the master's passing, Segyü, the first monastery to uphold and perpetuate Tsongkhapa's tantric teachings, was founded in Tsang Province. This was followed in 1433 by the founding of another tantric college, this one near Lhasa, by Sherap Sengé, who had famously pledged to serve as the custodian of Tsongkhapa's Vajrayāna traditions. A nearby offshoot of this college was founded by Kunga Döndrup in 1475. Based on their geographical locations, these two colleges later came to be known as Gyümé (the lower tantric college) and Gyütö (the upper tantric college), respectively.

In 1447, Gendün Drup, who would later be recognized as the First Dalai Lama, founded Tashi Lhünpo in Tsang Province. Located near the historic town of Shigatsé, Tashi Lhünpo became the fourth (with Ganden, Drepung, and Sera) major Geluk monastic university in central and western Tibet as well as, from the seventeenth century on, the official base of Tibet's Panchen Lamas. The presence of these major monastic centers, along with the three founded before Tsongkhapa's death, would cement Tsongkhapa's legacy in both central and west-central Tibet. In fact, as noted earlier, both of Tsongkhapa's principal disciples and immediate successors, Gyaltsap and Khedrup, hailed from Tsang, thus establishing a special bond between Tsongkhapa's legacy and the province.

The first to bring Tsongkhapa's tradition to western Tibet were two of his three well-known western Tibetan students, Gugé Ngawang Drakpa and Sherap Sangpo. (The other was Shangshung Chöwang Drakpa.) Gugé Ngawang Drakpa's fame reached the then Gugé rulers of western Tibet, who invited the monk to their domain and appointed him abbot of the best-known monastery in western Tibet, Thöling, which was founded in 997. From then on, Thöling became part of Tsongkhapa's tradition. Sherap Sangpo, on the other hand, actively missionized in the Mangyul region of western Tibet, as well as certain areas of modern-day Ladakh and Zangskar.

In the south, several of Tsongkhapa's students, including the great bodhisattva Kunga Sangpo, established their own monasteries in the Lhodrak and Nyal regions. In the southeast of Tibet, including the areas of Wölkha and Dakpo, where Tsongkhapa had spent considerable time in various retreats, especially the hermitages of Wölkha Chölung and Samten Ling, existing monasteries like Dzingchi converted to Geluk, and new monasteries, such as Chusang, Nyima Ling, and Riwo Serling, were established by Tsongkhapa's immediate disciples.[696] In Kham, in eastern Tibet, the first major monastery of Tsongkhapa's new Geluk tradition was Jampa Ling, founded in 1437 by Tsongkhapa's disciple Sherap Sangpo. Other key figures in the spread of Tsongkhapa's tradition in eastern Tibet include Tsakho Ngawang Drakpa, a close student of the master and his earliest attendant, who founded several monasteries in the Gyalrong area; Shangshung Chöwang Drakpa, the brilliant student of Khedrup known for his famed poem *The Tale of Rāma*, who founded monasteries in the Nakshö region; Tsongkhapa's disciple Denma Yönten Pal, who brought the master's tradition to the Denma region; Lhula Kachupa, a student who brought the tradition to the Tsulkhang region; and Sangyé Pal, who introduced it to the Pombor region by founding Gitigang Monastery. Later, Phakpa Lha, a student of Lodrö Chökyong (1389–1463), founded several monasteries, including Tashi Chölung, Demo Latsa, and Chötri Thang, while Kunga Gyaltsen, a student of Khedrup, founded Samdrup Gön Monastery in the Dzachu River valley.

Although Tsongkhapa himself speaks of his student Jang Lama as having established five major monasteries[697] in the northeastern region, Amdo, the first known Geluk monastery to appear probably was Taktsang Lhamo Kirti, usually known simply as Kirti Monastery. It was founded in 1472 by a student of Tsongkhapa's named Rongpa Jaknakpa. The next known major Geluk monastery to appear in Amdo was Kumbum, which, in fact, grew from a smaller monastery that had been founded to honor the site of Tsongkhapa's birth. In 1583, the earlier monastery at the site, Gönpa Lung, was expanded and renamed Kumbum ("One Hundred Thousand Sacred Images") based on the instruction of the third Dalai Lama, who had come to pay homage to the site of Tsongkhapa's birth.[698] The third major Geluk monastery in Amdo, Gönlung Jampa Ling, was founded in 1604 by Dönyö Chökyi Gyalpo; it eventually became the seat for high-ranking lamas of the Geluk school, especially those in the incarnation lineages of Changkya and Thuken. Finally, the most famous Geluk monastery in Amdo, Tashi Khyil, better known as Labrang, was founded in 1709 by the first Jamyang Shepa, Ngawang Tsöndrü (1648–1722). By the middle of the eighteenth century, Tsongkhapa's Geluk tradition had become the dominant lineage throughout Amdo Province.[699]

Beyond the borders of Tibet, thanks to Jamchen Chöjé's two visits to China in 1414–16 and 1425–35 as well as the activity of Jang Darma, another disciple of Tsongkhapa, Tsongkhapa's tradition began to draw attention in China, especially at the imperial court. The patron-priest relationship between Tsongkhapa's tradition and China's imperial family would be further strengthened in the seventeenth century, following the Fifth Dalai Lama's visit to Beijing in 1652. During the Manchu Qing dynasty, thanks to the close personal relationship between the Qianlong Emperor (1711–99) and the Geluk master Changkya Rolpai Dorjé (1717–86), the entire Qing court would become followers of Tsongkhapa's Geluk tradition.

With respect to Mongol regions, in 1578, the Third Dalai Lama, Sönam Gyatso, met with the powerful Mongol chieftain Altan Khan, who bestowed upon the Tibetan teacher the title "Dalai Lama." Literally meaning "the Ocean Lama," the title possibly refers to the second part of the lama's name, Gyatso, which is the Tibetan word for "ocean." This relationship between the Third Dalai Lama and Altan Khan would pave the way for the spread of Tsongkhapa's tradition across the vast Mongolian cultural area. Ever since, a special bond has existed between the Dalai Lamas and Mongol Buddhists. An important legacy of this relationship has been the tradition of young Mongols studying at the great Geluk centers of learning in Amdo and central Tibet, a custom that, though disturbed when Mongolia became Communist in 1924, lasted until the political upheavals that shook the Tibetan plateau in the mid-twentieth century. Some of these monks—for instance, Dzaya Pandita Lobsang Trinlé (b. 1642), Khalkha Ngawang Palden (b. 1797), Tendar Lharam (1759–1831), and Lobsang Tamdrin (1867–1937)—went on to become recognizable names within the Geluk tradition, with their works valued as major contributions to the elucidation of Tsongkhapa's philosophical thought.

On the Tibetan plateau itself, in 1642, with the help of the Mongol chieftain Tenzin Chögyal, also known as Gushri Khan, the Fifth Dalai Lama assumed political leadership of all of Tibet. Thus began the rule on the plateau by the Dalai Lamas, which would last until the mid-twentieth century. The Fifth Dalai Lama's rule would bring Tibet into a semblance of political unity for the first time since the collapse of the Tibetan empire some seven hundred years earlier, in the later half of the ninth century. The Great Fifth, as he often is called, established a formal theocratic system of government, with both monastic and lay officials occupying important leadership positions. He built the majestic Potala Palace, overlooking the Lhasa valley; revived the status of Lhasa as the preeminent sacred site of the Tibetan Buddhist world; and spurred a major renaissance in art and book printing. Although the Fifth Dalai Lama was personally an ecumenist who revered Tibet's other major Buddhist traditions, especially the Nyingma, his rule led to Tsongkhapa's Geluk tradition becoming effectively the "state church." With this, the incarnation lineages of the Dalai Lama (originally based at Drepung Monastery) and Panchen Lama (based at Tashi

Lhünpo Monastery from the time the widely revered Panchen Lobsang Chökyi Gyaltsen made it his residence) effectively became Tibet's national institutions. The fate of the Tibetan state and that of Tsongkhapa's Geluk school thus remained intertwined from the founding of the Dalai Lama's rule in the mid-seventeenth century.

Tibet and its culture were rudely awoken to modernity in the form of Communist China's invasion in 1950, with many of Tibet's cultural and religious monuments and institutions suffering serious injury, especially during the Cultural Revolution. As noted in the preface, Tsongkhapa's embalmed body, so devoutly worshipped for centuries at his Ganden Monastery, was tragically burned to ashes. Following the Dalai Lama's escape to India in March 1959, joined by some eighty thousand Tibetans, most of Tibet's historically important monasteries, including those belonging to Tsongkhapa's tradition, were reestablished in India. Today, as Tibet's Buddhist culture engages ever more deeply with the forces of modernity—pluralism, rejection of tradition, the scientific worldview, secular values, and so on—Tsongkhapa's philosophical legacy, with its emphasis on the role of reason even in the domain of religious faith and practice, may offer an important resource for the Tibetan tradition as it struggles to assure that its soul is not lost in translation. Thanks to the Fourteenth Dalai Lama's farsightedness, the great monastic institutions of Tsongkhapa's tradition—Ganden, Drepung, Sera, and Tashi Lhünpo—have embraced contemporary science as part of their regular curriculum.

With respect to the outside world, numerous Dharma centers teaching Tsongkhapa's tradition have emerged across North America and Europe, as well as in East and Southeast Asia. Even an endowed chair named after Tsongkhapa, the "Je Tsongkhapa Professorship in Tibetan Buddhist Studies," has been established at Columbia University in New York. As I write, the entirety of Tsongkhapa's collected works, as well as those of his two principal students, Gyaltsap and Khedrup, are being edited to produce a comparative modern edition, with all the citations in the texts sourced and annotated. This forty-two-volume set is scheduled to be released to mark the six-hundredth anniversary of Tsongkhapa's nirvāṇa, in December 2019.

In short, as Tibetan tradition engages with contemporary society and culture worldwide, there may still be new chapters to write in the ongoing legacy of the great Buddhist master from the northeast reaches of Tibet.

APPENDIX

The Four Disciplines of Classical Buddhist Scholarship in Tsongkhapa's Student Years

TSONGKHAPA'S formal education in central Tibet, like that of his monastic peers, revolved primarily around a set of key Indian Buddhist texts that pertain to four major scholarly disciplines. Each of these four disciplines has one or two root texts (*tsawa*) that constitute its principal book, whose study is supplemented by authoritative Indian commentaries.

1. Perfection of Wisdom Studies (*prajñāpāramita*; Tib. *pharchin*)

ROOT TEXT: Maitreya's *Ornament of Realizations* (*Abhisamayālaṃkāra*).

MAIN INDIAN COMMENTARIES: Haribhadra's (ca. 770–810) *Clear Meaning* (*Sphuṭārthā*), supplemented by his *Explanation of the Eight Thousand Lines on the Perfection of Wisdom* and Vimuktisena's (sixth century) *Light on Perfection of Wisdom in Twenty-Five Thousand Lines*.

Attributed to Maitreya (ca. fourth century) and written entirely in verse as an instruction on the Perfection of Wisdom, the *Ornament* is a dense work aimed at summarizing the entire contents of the three-volume *Perfection of Wisdom in Twenty-Five Thousand Lines*, a key Mahāyāna scripture. The text is divided into eight chapters and structured around three key themes: (1) the path of the threefold knowledge (chapters 1–3); (2) the four practices (chapters 4–7), the means by which these paths are cultivated; and (3) the resultant state of buddhahood (chapter 8). While the explicit subject matter of the Perfection of Wisdom scriptures (the doctrine of emptiness) is expounded in Nāgārjuna's works, the implicit subject matter of these scriptures (the stages of the path and their cultivation) is understood to be Maitreya's principal topic. The work is an encyclopedia of the important topics of Mahāyāna Buddhism, including the following: preparing the mind to enter the path, cultivation of compassion and bodhicitta, the four noble truths and the twelve links of dependent origination, the two truths, cultivation of tranquility and insight, attainment of meditative absorptions, the thirty-seven aspects of the path to enlightenment according to Mahāyāna, the six perfections, the five levels of the path, the ten bodhisattva grounds, and the resultant state of buddhahood defined in terms of the three buddha bodies (kāyas). In contemporary terms, the subject matter of *Ornament* can be characterized as "religious studies" according to classical Indian Mahāyāna Buddhism. In brief, Maitreya's *Ornament* serves as an exhaustive table of contents for the voluminous Perfection of Wisdom scriptures. Traditionally, a monastic student memorizes the *Ornament* at a young age, as Tsongkhapa did at the feet of his first teacher, Chöjé.

2. Logic and Epistemology (*pramāṇa*; Tib. *tsema*)

ROOT TEXTS: Dignāga's *Compendium on Valid Cognition* (*Pramāṇasammucāya*) and Dharmakīrti's *Exposition of Valid Cognition* (*Pramāṇavārttika*) and *Determinations on Valid Cognition* (*Pramāṇaviniscaya*).

MAIN INDIAN COMMENTARIES: Devandrabuddhi's *Pramāṇavārttikapañjikā*, Śākyabuddhi's *Pramāṇavārttikaṭīkā*, Prajñakāragupta's *Pramāṇavārttikālbhāṣyam*.

Although historically Dignāga's *Pramāṇasammucāya* (fifth century) is most important as it established pramāṇa (logic and epistemology) as a formal discipline within Buddhism in India, in Tibet the study of this topic focused principally on the influential writings of Dharmakīrti (seventh century). Dharmakīrti's primary work, *Pramāṇavārttika*, is written entirely in verse (some 1,450 stanzas). Typically, the works belonging to this discipline cover topics of inquiry and interest for logic (criteria of a sound proof, theory of inference, the role of example in inference, fallacies of argument, norms of debate, and so on) as well as questions of epistemology, cognitive science, and philosophy of language (theory of knowledge, perception, memory, concept formation, concept of universals, meaning and reference of words, and so on). Dharmakīrti's *Pramāṇavārttika*, which by Tsongkhapa's time was the standard text on logic and epistemology, is divided into four lengthy chapters. The first, "Inference for Oneself," broadly addresses three main topics: nature and types of inference, reference of words, and the critique of the assertion that sacred Vedas are authorless and represent valid utterances. In chapter 2, "Established Validity," Dharmakīrti applies the principles of inference presented in the preceding chapter to establish the validity of the Buddha as a reliable teacher and the veracity of his path concerning the knowledge of the four noble truths. The third chapter, "Perception," the longest in the text, presents in great detail the theory of perception—its nature, types, validation, and effects, as well as numerous arguments to establish cognitions as necessarily involving self-cognition. A topic in this chapter is the distinction between perception and conceptual cognition, two modalities of knowing that Dignāga and Dharmakīrti both see as categorically different from each other. The fourth and final chapter, "Inference for the Other," examines what constitutes a legitimate thesis in the context of a logical syllogism, the types of formal argument, and what defines an invalid argument. Dharmakīrti himself wrote a lengthy commentary on the first chapter, with his student Devandrabuddhi composing commentaries on the remaining three chapters.

3. Abhidharma (*ngönpa*, literally "higher dharma")

ROOT TEXTS: Asaṅga's *Compendium of Abhidharma* (*Abhidharmasamuccāya*) and Vasubandhu's *Treasury of Abhidharma* (*Abhidharmakośa*) as well as his autocommentary on the text.

MAIN INDIAN COMMENTARIES: Yaśomitra's *Abhidharmasamuccāyavyākhyā* and his *Abhidharmasamuccayabhāṣya* and *Abhidharmakośaṭīkā*; Pūrṇavardhana's *Abhidharmakośaṭīkālakṣaṇānusāriṇī*.

Of the numerous Indian Buddhist works on Abhidharma, two texts became central to the study of the discipline of Abhidharma in the Tibetan tradition: Asaṅga's *Compendium of Abhidharma* and Vasubandhu's *Treasury of Abhidharma*, referred to respectively as upper Abhidharma and lower Abhidharma, possibly alluding to the Tibetan view that, within the four classical Indian Buddhist philosophical schools, Asaṅga's Yogācāra should be recognized as being more advanced or "higher" compared to Vaibhaśika, the standpoint represented in Vasubandhu's *Treasury*. Despite this view, it is in fact Vasubandhu's work that is adopted as the textbook for Abhidharma study, with Asaṅga's *Compendium of Abhidharma* used mainly as a point of contrast on important topics, such as mental factors, afflictions, and the specific Yogācāra theory of mind. Unlike Asaṅga's text, which is in prose, Vasubandhu's is composed in verse (around 600 stanzas) and divided into eight chapters. The author himself wrote the first commentary on his verses, adding a ninth chapter examing the topic of Buddhist rejection of the concept of self. Written as a distillation of the multivolume *Great Treatise on Differentiation* (*Mahāvibhāṣā*), the definitive text of the Sarvāstivāda Abhidharma, Vasubandhu's text is fairly straightforward in structure. Defining *abhidharma* as "immaculate wisdom together with its attendant factors," the *Abhidharmakośa* is amazingly comprehensive in its scope, covering all important topics of interest for Indian Buddhist schools in the first few centuries of the first millennium.

Chapter 1, "Elements," explores the Buddhist analysis of the factors of existence within the framework of the five aggregates: matter, feelings, perception, mental formations, and consciousness. Chapter 2, "Faculties," examines the faculties implicated in sentient beings' entrapment in unenlightened existence as well as those faculties that could help lead toward freedom from such bondage. A key topic in this chapter concerns the taxonomy of mental factors, in terms of their natures, functions, and interrelationships. Chapter 3, "Cosmology," presents cosmology as well as the theory of the emergence of humans on earth. Chapters 4 and 5 present, respectively, the topics of karma and afflictions, the two factors that together constitute the cause of birth in the cycle of existence. These two chapters represent one of the most systematic and comprehensive accounts of the Buddhist understanding of karma and what could be called the Buddhist psychology of emotions. Chapter 6, "Path and Beings," presents the object of the path, the four noble truths, the path itself in terms of the thirty-seven aspects of the path to enlightenment, and the types of persons on this path. Chapter 7, "Types of Knowledge," explores further the presentation of the path, examining the finer distinctions within the aspects of the path as well as contemplations of the qualities of the Buddha's enlightened mind. Finally, chapter 8, "Meditative Attainment," presents in detail the dhyānas, or states of concentration, that constitute the basis for the arising of various forms of knowledge, including those of the Buddha's fully awakened mind. In many ways, Vasubandhu's text is comparable to the influential fifth-century Theravāda classic *Path of Purification* (*Visuddhimagga*) by Buddhaghoṣa. Typically, a monastic student would memorize Vasubandhu's root text and undertake its study with the help of important commentaries, such as Vasubandhu's own autocommentary as well as the commentaries of Yaśomotra, Pūrṇavardhana, Sthiramati, and others.

4. Vinaya (*dulwa*, monastic discipline)

ROOT TEXT: Guṇaprabha's *Root Lines on Vinaya* (*Root Lines on Discipline*).

MAIN INDIAN COMMENTARY: Guṇaprabha's own *Vinayasūtravṛttyabhidhanasvavyākhya*.

Some one hundred long folios, Guṇaprabha's *Root Lines on Vinaya* is a manual on Buddhist monastic discipline according to the Mūlasarvāstivāda lineage of ordination. The author himself wrote a lengthy commentary on his own root lines, an exposition that fills two large volumes. The *Root Lines on Vinaya* presents everything that is important in the Buddha's teachings on basic ethics and monastic discipline, as understood by the Mūlasarvāstivāda school. The topics include the enumeration and definition of each of the multitude of precepts (253 for a fully ordained monk and 364 for a fully ordained nun); what constitutes their infraction; the means for restoring the secondary precepts; the various rites to be performed by the monastics, including the rite of ordination; matters concerning disciplinary actions; how to resolve disputes within the order; and so on. Once again, a monastic student would memorize Guṇaprabha's *Root Lines on Vinaya* and engage in its study with the help of his extensive commentary. By Tsongkhapa's time,

Tsonawa Sherap Sangpo's commentary had become a standard Tibetan exposition to be studied alongside Guṇaprabha on the discipline of vinaya.

5. Madhyamaka[700] (*Uma*, Middle Way philosophy)

ROOT TEXTS: Candrakīrti's *Entering the Middle Way* (*Madhyamakāvatāra*) together with the author's own commentary *Madhyamakāvatārabhāṣya*, complemented by Nāgārjuna's *Treatise on the Middle Way*.

MAIN INDIAN COMMENTARIES: The three main Indian commentaries on Nāgārjuna's *Treatise:* Buddhapālita's *Buddhapālita*, Bhāviveka's *Prajñādīpa* (*Lamp of Wisdom*), and Candrakīrti's *Prasannapadā* (*Clear Words*).

Although historically Nāgārjuna's *Treatise* remains the fundamental text of Madhyamaka philosophy, Candrakīrti's *Entering the Middle Way* became the root text of choice in Tibet for the formal study of the discipline. The work is structured on the framework of the ten bodhisattva levels on the path to full awakening and consists of ten chapters, followed by a lengthy section on the attributes of the ten levels as well as the presentation of the final level of buddhahood. The root text is composed entirely in verse, with the main chapter, the sixth, running to 226 stanzas.

The sixth chapter of *Entering the Middle Way* serves as a standalone work on Madhyamaka philosophy; it can be divided into three broad parts: (1) a presentation of the selflessness of phenomena, (2) a presentation of the selflessness of persons, and (3) the categories of emptiness established through reasoning. In the first section, the author presents in great detail Nāgārjuna's arguments against the concept of intrinsic existence through demonstrating the untenability of any objective notion of causation in terms of arising from self, from other, from both, and from no cause at all. As part of deconstructing assertions concerning causation from "other," Candrakīrti covers a range of important topics: the presentation of the two truths, a critique of Yogācāra's concept of consciousness, its theory of the three natures, and so on. In the second section, Candrakīrti presents his famed "sevenfold analysis of the person," and in doing so develops a detailed exposition of Nāgārjuna's critiques of the concept of self and its existence. In the final section, Candrakīrti takes up the varying classifications of emptiness into four, sixteen, twenty, and so on, found in the Perfection of Wisdom sūtras, which are the source sūtras for Nāgārjuna's Madhyamaka philosophy of emptiness. The chapter's concluding point is that the existence of things is analogous to illusions and thus can only be understood in terms of constructs and mere imputations.

An important topic discussed in the concluding part of *Entering the Middle Way*, the presentation of the attributes of the ten levels and the resultant level of buddhahood, is how Buddha's enlightened mind—utterly free of concepts and devoid of conscious intent—perceives reality as it is and also helps perform altruistic deeds to fulfill the welfare of other sentient beings. In Tsongkhapa's Geluk monasteries, Tsongkhapa's own *Elucidation of the Intent: An Extensive Exposition of "Entering the Middle Way"* became the standard textbook for the study of Madhyamaka philosophy.

Chronology

YEAR	EVENTS IN TSONGKHAPA'S LIFE	CULTURAL HISTORICAL EVENTS
1354		Phagdru dynasty rule begins in Tibet.
1357	Born in Amdo, northeastern Tibet.	
1360	Fourth Karmapa, Rolpai Dorjé, on his way back from China, blesses young Tsongkhapa and gives him the name Künga Nyingpo.	
1363	A local lama, Chöjé Dhöndrup Rinchen, takes custody of young Tsongkhapa; the boy moves to Jakhyung Monastery to live with the master.	Nyingma master Longchenpa dies; Tsalpa Künga Dorjé completes his historical work *The Red Annals*.
1364	Receives novitiate vows from Chöjé.	Phagdru ruler Jangchup Gyaltsen and Butön Rinchen Drup die; Tsongkhapa's future successor at Ganden Monastery, Gyaltsap, is born.
1368		Yuan dynasty falls and Ming rule begins in China.

YEAR	EVENTS IN TSONGKHAPA'S LIFE	CULTURAL HISTORICAL EVENTS
1372	After nine years of study with Chöjé, Tsongkhapa departs for central Tibet to further his monastic education.	
1373	Arrives in central Tibet, first landing at Drigung Thil Monastery.	Second Phagdru ruler, Shākya Gyaltsen, dies.
1374	Senior Sakya master Lama Dhampa Sönam Gyaltsen gives his ceremonial hat to young Tsongkhapa, predicting that the latter will become a chief custodian of Butön's lineages.	Drakpa Jangchup becomes third Phagdru ruler; fifth Phagdru ruler Miwang Drakpa Gyaltsen, who will become Tsongkhapa's most important patron, is born.
1375	Sits for his first formal drakor debates, on Perfection of Wisdom studies, at several important monasteries.	Lama Dhampa dies.
1376	Meets Rendawa, who will become his most important teacher.	
1378	Receiving a request from his mother to return home before she dies, Tsongkhapa decides against the trip and instead sends her a self-portrait; he authors his first two works, a lengthy essay on the topic of "twenty persons" and a treatise on the Yogācāra theory of mind.	Rendawa completes his two-volume extensive commentary of Asaṅga's *Compendium of Abhidharma*.

YEAR	EVENTS IN TSONGKHAPA'S LIFE	CULTURAL HISTORICAL EVENTS
1379	Successfully sits for formal debates on the three remaining formal disciplines of academic scholarship: vinaya (monastic discipline), pramāṇa (logic and epistemology), and Abhidharma; he thus becomes a kashipa (master of four disciplines) and formally accepts his first group of students. Following a meditation retreat focused on Sarasvatī, goddess of wisdom and poetry, Tsongkhapa experiences a vision of the goddess and will subsequently be known for his connection to her.	
1380	Studies poetics and Sanskrit grammar with Narthang Sanskritist Namkha Sangpo.	
1381	Receives full ordination vows according to the lineage of Kashmiri paṇḍita Śākyaśrībhadra; begins a four-year sojourn at Tsal Gungthang Monastery, delving into extensive reading of key Indian Buddhist texts in the recently completed canonical collections finalized by Butön.	Drakpa Jangchup retires as Phagdru ruler for religious life; Sönam Drakpa becomes the fourth Phagdru ruler.
1382	Continues with his intensive reading retreat at Tsal Gungthang Monastery.	

YEAR	EVENTS IN TSONGKHAPA'S LIFE	CULTURAL HISTORICAL EVENTS
1383		Fourth Karmapa, Rolpai Dorjé, dies.
1384		Fifth Karmapa, Deshin Shekpa, is born.
1385	Begins writing *The Golden Rosary*, a two-volume exposition of Maitreya's *Ornament*.	Tsongkhapa's childhood teacher Chöjé dies; Miwang Drakpa Gyaltsen becomes the fifth Phagdru ruler; Tsongkhapa's future biographer Khedrup is born.
1386	Continues writing *The Golden Rosary*; composes the official poetic narrative on the life of the recently deceased Phagdru Drakpa Jangchup.	Revered Phagdru patriarch Drakpa Jangchup and Jonang Choklé Namgyal die.
1387	Composes his famed poetic retelling of the story of the bodhisattva Sadāprarudita.	
1388	Completes his *Golden Rosary*, the release of which seals his reputation as a great scholar.	
1389	Teaches seventeen Indian Buddhist texts in a single continuous lecture series.	

YEAR	EVENTS IN TSONGKHAPA'S LIFE	CULTURAL HISTORICAL EVENTS
1390	Reunites with Rendawa in Tsang; meets Lama Umapa, the mystic who will later serve as the medium between Tsongkhapa and his meditation deity Mañjuśrī; composes an open letter, *Queries from a Sincere Heart,* containing a series of probing questions addressed to the meditators of Tibet.	
1391	Visits Butön's Shalu Monastery and, staying until summer 1392, receives from Khyungpo Lhepa the entire transmission of Butön's lineages.	First Dalai Lama, Gendün Drup, is born.
1392	Reunites with Umapa and spends several months with him in retreat, with Umapa serving as a medium for Tsongkhapa's communication with Mañjuśrī; later in the year, Tsongkhapa experiences his first direct vision of Mañjuśrī. At the deity's urging, he departs to the Wölkha Valley for a years-long meditative retreat with his "eight disciples of perfect karma."	Gö Lotsawa Shönu Pal, author of the famed historical work *The Blue Annals*, is born.
1393	Experiences two visions of Maitreya during the Wölkha Valley retreat, leading to his restoration of the Dzingchi Maitreya statue and temple.	

YEAR	EVENTS IN TSONGKHAPA'S LIFE	CULTURAL HISTORICAL EVENTS
1395	Ends his long Wölkha Valley retreat; meets with Lhodrak mystic Namkha Gyaltsen and spends seven months at his hermitage.	
1396	Goes on pilgrimage to Tsari Mountain; gains a powerful conviction in the authority of the Kālacakra tantra; has a vision of goddess Sarasvatī during which she predicts Tsongkhapa's life span will be fifty-seven years.	
1397	Institutes the "Great Scriptural Festival of Nyal"; Gyaltsap formally becomes Tsongkhapa's disciple; Tsongkhapa experiences a breakthrough in his realization of the profound view of emptiness and, in gratitude toward the Buddha, composes the poetic verse "In Praise of Dependent Origination."	
1398	Composes two short instructional texts on lamrim, the second being the famed *Three Principal Elements of the Path*.	Hong Wu's grandson, Zhu Yunwen, becomes second Ming ruler in China, assuming the throne as Jianwen emperor.
1399	Visits Dzingchi Maitreya Temple to lead a fifteen-day prayer festival in honor of the Buddha's miracles at Śrāvastī.	

YEAR	EVENTS IN TSONGKHAPA'S LIFE	CULTURAL HISTORICAL EVENTS
1400	Rendawa and Tsongkhapa spend the winter at Radreng Hermitage.	Drigung Palzin writes a critique of Nyingma views entitled *Clear Differentiation of Dharma and Nondharma*.
1401	Authors the well-known aspiration prayer "Goodness at the Beginning, the Middle, and the End"; at the request of Lochen Kyapchok Palsang and others, begins the composition of his *Great Treatise on the Stages of the Path to Enlightenment*.	Lhodrak mystic Namkha Gyaltsen dies.
1402	Completes his *Great Treatise*; Gungru Gyaltsen Sangpo becomes Tsongkhapa's disciple.	
1403	Authors a commentary on the ethics chapter of Asaṅga's *Bodhisattva Levels* as well as additional commentaries on *Fifty Verses on the Guru* and *Tantric Ethics*.	Yongle becomes the third Ming ruler in China.
1404	Conducts another fifteen-day prayer festival, this time at Radreng, to honor the Buddha's miracles at Śrāvastī; at Mañjuśrī's urging, Tsongkhapa authors his commentary on Nāgabodhi's *Guhyasamājasādhana-vyavasthāli*.	

YEAR	EVENTS IN TSONGKHAPA'S LIFE	CULTURAL HISTORICAL EVENTS
1405	Writes his *Great Treatise on the Stages of Tantra* at the request of Lochen Kyapchok Palsang and Miwang's brother Phagdru Sönam Sangpo.	Taktsang Lotsawa, who would later become famous for critiquing aspects of Tsongkhapa's philosophy, is born.
1406	Khedrup becomes Tsongkhapa's disciple.	
1407	Composes his hermeneutic work *The Essence of True Eloquence*.	Fifth Karmapa, Deshin Shekpa, visits China; eleventh Drigung patriarch Chökyi Gyalpo dies.
1408	Formally declines an invitation from the Yongle emperor to visit China; prepares for the Great Prayer Festival, including initiating renovation of the Jokhang Temple in Lhasa; authors *Ocean of Reasoning*, an extensive commentary on Nāgārjuna's *Treatise on the Middle Way*, at the request of Phagdru ruler Miwang and others.	
1409	Stages the Great Prayer Festival at Lhasa in the first month of the Tibetan New Year; lays the foundation for Ganden Monastery and assigns the task of building it to Dülzin and Gyaltsap.	

YEAR	EVENTS IN TSONGKHAPA'S LIFE	CULTURAL HISTORICAL EVENTS
1410	Returns to Ganden and consecrates the new monastery, which from this point on will be his main base; starts an important phase in his writing focused on advanced Vajrayāna instructions and practice.	Yongle emperor sponsors woodblock printing of the Kangyur.
1411	Authors *Lamp to Illuminate the Five Stages*, an authoritative work on the completion stage of Guhyasamāja tantra, and *Practical Guide to the Five Stages in One Sitting* based on Nāropa's *Lucid Summary of the Five Stages*.	Karmapa Deshin Shekpa returns to Tibet from China.
1412	Receives the sad message of Rendawa's passing.	
1413	Falls ill at Ganden; he and his close disciples undertake numerous healing rituals, and Tsongkhapa's health improves; receives a second formal invitation from the Yongle emperor to visit China and sends his disciple Jamchen Chöjé in his stead.	
1414	Authors his annotated exposition of Guhyasamāja root tantra, based on Candrakīrti's *Clear Lamp*, as well as a summary outline and an analytic exposition of the tantra.	Jamchen Chöjé arrives in Beijing for his first visit to China; sixth Phagdru ruler, Drakpa Jungné, is born.

YEAR	EVENTS IN TSONGKHAPA'S LIFE	CULTURAL HISTORICAL EVENTS
1415	Conducts a teaching festival at Tashi Dhokha Hermitage, with many of central Tibet's great names in attendance, including Phagdru ruler Miwang, the First Dalai Lama Gendün Drup, Gö Lotsawa Shönu Pal, and others; instructs Jamyang Chöjé to establish Drepung Monastery; authors several texts including *Middle-Length Treatise on the Stages of the Path to Enlightenment* and *Milking the Wish-Granting Cow*, an exposition on the generation stage of Cakrasaṃvara tantra.	Fifth Karmapa, Deshin Shekpa, dies.
1416	Authors *Guide Endowed with Three Convictions*, an instruction on the six yogas of Nāropa; lays the foundation for Yangpachen Temple at Ganden; meets Jamchen Chöjé upon his return from China, with the latter bearing gifts for the master, including a woodblock print of the Kangyur.	Jamyang Chöjé founds Drepung Monastery; sixth Karmapa, Thongwa Dhönden, is born; just before his death, Miwang's brother Sönam Sangpo sponsors the production of Tsongkhapa's collected works.
1417	Construction of Yangpachen Tantric Temple at Ganden is completed.	Young Chenga Lodrö Gyaltsen becomes Tsongkhapa's disciple.
1418	Authors *Elucidation of the Intent*, an extensive exposition of Candrakīrti's *Entering the Middle Way*.	

YEAR	EVENTS IN TSONGKHAPA'S LIFE	CULTURAL HISTORICAL EVENTS
1419	Authors his last major work, *Illuminating All the Hidden Meanings*, an exposition of the root tantra of Cakrasaṃvara; experiencing illness and acute pain in his legs, he visits Tölung hot springs; after briefly visiting the newly established Drepung Monastery and paying his final visit to Sera Chöding Hermitage, returns to Ganden. Passes away on the twenty-fifth day of the tenth Tibetan month of the Earth Pig year; remains in the clear-light state for thirteen days, and his body is embalmed and encased inside a stūpa at Ganden Monastery.	Jamchen Chöjé founds Sera Monastery; in the third week following Tsongkhapa's death, Jamyang Khaché composes the celebrated eulogy "Eighty Tsongkhapas," a poetic celebration of Tsongkhapa's life; Gyaltsap succeeds Tsongkhapa as the head of Ganden Monastery and becomes the first Ganden Throne Holder.

Notes

1. Sam Howe Verhovek, "Visiting a Tibetan Monastery," *New York Times*, May 25, 1986.
2. Ippolito Desideri, *Mission to Tibet*, trans. Michael J. Sweet, p. 638.
3. Desideri's notes on Tibetan debate, his annotated topical outline of Tsongkhapa's text, and other extensive notes he took during his study in Tibet can be found at the Jesuit Archives in Rome, under the classification Archivum Romanum Societus Iesu (ARSI) Goa 74. I thank the Jesuit Archives for providing my colleague Donald Lopez and me with access to these works for our book on Desideri entitled *Dispelling the Darkness*.
4. Desideri, *Mission to Tibet*, p. 194.
5. Desideri, *Mission to Tibet*, p. 639.
6. For a contemporary study of Desideri's Tibetan works refuting key concepts of Buddhism, especially the theory of rebirth and the philosophy of emptiness, see Lopez and Jinpa, *Dispelling the Darkness*.
7. Traditional Tibetan histories date the first arrival of Buddhism (in fact, Buddhist texts) in Tibet to the fifth century, during the reign of an earlier king by the name of Lha Thothori Nyentsen.
8. For a succinct history of Tibet's imperial period, seventh to mid-ninth century, see Van Schaik, *Tibet: A History*, ch. 1 and 2, which draws on comparative analysis of the *Old Tibetan Annals* and the *Old Tibetan Chronicle*, two Tibetan historical texts discovered in the Dunhuang caves, and contemporaneous Chinese sources, such as the *Old Tang Annals* and the *New Tang Annals*.
9. In his *New Red Annals* (p. 41), Panchen Sönam Drakpa cites differing opinions among Tibetan historians on the length of this gap in the monastic ordination lineage in central Tibet, with Nelpa Paṇḍita suggesting that it lasted for 111 years, Butön seventy-three years, Panchen's own teacher

Lechen Kunga Gyaltsen ninety-eight years, and Dromtönpa seventy-eight years. Panchen expresses his preference for the final opinion.

10. The dating of Lachen's birth is based on Tseten Shapdrung's *A Short Account of the Life of Lachen Gongpa Rapsel*, p. 187.
11. Matthew Kapstein, *The Tibetans*, p. 91.
12. For a brief account of Atiśa's activities in Tibet and their legacy, see Thupten Jinpa, *The Book of Kadam*.
13. For an English translation of Butön's biography written by his principal disciple Dratsepa Rinchen Namgyal, see David Seyfort Ruegg, *The Life of Bu ston Rinpoché: With the Tibetan Text of the Bu ston rNam thar* (Serie Orientale Roma XXXIV, Roma: Instituto per il Medio ed Estremo Oriente, 1966).
14. For a study of Sakya Paṇḍita's *Gateway to Becoming a Learned* and his role as the gatekeeper of the Dharma in Tibet, see Jonathan Gold, *The Dharma's Gatekeepers*.
15. For an excellent English translation of this important text with explanatory notes, see Jared Douglas Rhoton, trans., *A Clear Differentiation of the Three Codes* (Albany: State University New York Press, 2002).
16. From the point of view of Tibetan tradition, the characterization of Tibetan Buddhism simply as Vajrayāna Buddhism, seen sometimes in contemporary popular writings on Buddhism where only the Chinese tradition is characterized as Mahāyāna Buddhism, is erroneous.
17. For the sake of clarity, it is important to bear in mind the two senses of the terms *sūtra* and *tantra*. In one sense, especially when used alongside titles of specific written works, the terms refer to a specific scripture or text. In contrast, they can also each refer to an entire system or vehicle, such as when used in phrases such as "the Sūtra path," "the Sūtra vehicle," "the path of Tantra," and the "union of Sūtra and Tantra." When used in the second sense, to indicate a vehicle rather than an individual text, I shall capitalize these words.
18. In his testament entitled *Meaningful to Behold* (p. 365) Jangchup Gyaltsen in fact speaks of the need for even the rulers on the local level to remain celibate and become monastics.
19. Quoted in E. D. Hirsch, et al., *The New Dictionary of Cultural Literacy*, Third Edition (Boston: Houghton Mifflin, 2002).
20. Most of these biographies, extant today in Tibetan, were published in modern book format in a four-volume anthology entitled *Anthology of*

Biographies of the Great Tsongkhapa (Beijing: Krung go bod rig pa'i dpe skrun khang, 2015). Since Lobsang Trinlé's extensive biography of Tsongkhapa, *Single Adornment Beautifying the Buddha's Teachings*, had already been published in modern book format (Xinhua: Mtsho sngon mi rigs dpe skrun khang, 1984), it was not included in the 2015 anthology.

21. For a contemporary analysis of Tibetan hagiography and the varieties of "biographies," see Elijah Ary, *Authorized Lives* (Boston: Wisdom Publications, 2015).

22. Briefly stated, here is my methodology. In general, I accord greater credibility to those texts written by Tsongkhapa's contemporaries than to those that appeared later. Within this first category, I take Khedrup's *Entryway of Faith*, effectively the "official" biography, as my basis for establishing a chronology of the major events in Tsongkhapa's life. As much as possible, I seek corroborations from what could be viewed as more independent sources, namely, the writings of those who did not identify themselves as followers of Tsongkhapa's Ganden tradition.

23. Although all sources agree on the month and year of Tsongkhapa's birth, there is some dispute concerning the exact date. In the *Extensive Biography* (p. 99), the author Lobsang Trinlé, known more widely as Gyalwang Chöjé, suggests the twenty-fifth as the likeliest date, while Kharnak Lotsawa (*History of Ganden Tradition*, p. 15) as well as the noted twentieth-century Tibetan scholar and historian Tseten Shapdrung (*Opening the Door of Faith: A Short Biography of Great Tsongkhapa*, p. 170) offer the tenth day of the tenth month as the date of Tsongkhapa's birth. If we accept the latter date, the exact date of Tsongkhapa's birth would be October 23, 1357 (or October 31, 1357, according to an alternative calendar calculation system). The Tibetan calendar system involves harmonizing lunar months with solar years, which requires skipping or doubling days within a month and also adding an extra month every two to three years.

    I thank Tenzin Loden, a contemporary authority on Tibetan astrosciences at the Tibetan Medical Institute, Dharamsala, for drawing my attention to the discrepancies among the various systems that help convert Tibetan calendar dates into Western calendar dates. The conversion system I have used here is based on the calculation of, among others, the noted Kālacakra calendral scholar Edward Henning.

24. Tokden Jampel Gyatso, *Collection of Well-Uttered Insights: A Supplementary Biography of Jetsün Tsongkhapa* (hereafter referred to as *Supplement*), p. 13.

25. Khedrup, *Entryway of Faith*, 81. This last sentence suggests that Khedrup himself had never visited Tsongkhapa's birthplace but had heard about its attributes from others.
26. Most sources speak of six sons and do not mention any sister. However, communication between Tsongkhapa and his aging mother reveals that he did have an elder sister, as he sent his mother and his sister a self-portrait to remember him by (Chahar, *Source of All Goodness*, 34). Lechen Kunga Gyaltsen, in his *Lamp Illuminating the History of Kadam Tradition* (Xinhua: Bod ljongs mi dmangs dpe skrun khang, 2003. p. 674), speaks of "five or six siblings" and provides the names of five: Tsuktor Jam, Cheso, Tsewang Gyal, Kunga Nyingpo (Tsongkhapa), and Loten.
27. The earliest known source of these prophetic dreams Tsongkhapa's parents had is Tokden Jampel Gyatso's *Supplement*, written as a supplement possibly to Khedrup's "official" biography of Tsongkhapa entitled *Entryway of Faith*.
28. Tokden Jampel Gyatso, *Supplement*, p. 13.
29. This story, including the meaning of the word *Kumbum*, is mentioned in the Seventh Dalai Lama Kelsang Gyatso's *Inventory of Kumbum Monastery* (*dkar chag gsal ba'i me long*), Collected Works, vol. *ca*, p. 14b:3. Chahar (*Source of All Goodness*, 33–37) provides a detailed account of how Kumbum Monastery eventually came to be established at the site where drops of blood from Tsongkhapa's afterbirth fell on the ground. Chahar cites *Pearl Garland: Abbatial Successions of Kumbum Monastery* (*sku 'bum gyi gdan rabs mu tig phreng ba*), which, unfortunately, does not appear to be extant today. For a vivid account of life as a young monk at Kumbum Monastery in the 1940s, see Thubten Jigme Norbu, *Tibet Is My Country: The Autobiography of Thubten Jigme Norbu, Brother of the Dalai Lama as Told to Heinrich Harrer* (Boston: Wisdom Publications, 1986).
30. Huc, *Travels in Tartary*.
31. Although during Tibet's imperial period (seventh to the late ninth century) the country had, through two Tibetan emperors' marriages to Chinese princesses, political and military engagements with China, it was the emergence of Mongol Yuan rule in China in the thirteenth century that led to a long period of intertwining political and religious engagements between Tibet, China, and Mongolia. In this complex relationship, it became customary for the ruler of China as well as powerful Mongol leaders to seek high-profile Tibetan lamas as their "imperial priests."

32. This story of Karmapa Rolpai Dorjé's blessing of the young Tsongkhapa is corroborated by the brief biography of the Karmapa found in Pawo Tsuklak Trengwa's *Feast for the Learned: A History of Buddhism in India and Tibet* (p. 964), as well as by Chökyi Jungné's sixteenth-century history of Kamtsang Kagyü tradition entitled *Garland of Countless Moonstone Gems: Biographies of Kamtsang Kagyu Masters* (p. 429), which contains a lengthy biography of Karmapa Rolpai Dorjé. That the latter text was written in the sixteenth century is evident from the fact that, at the time of its writing, the eighth Karmapa, Mikyö Dorjé, was in his youth.
33. This brief biographical sketch of Chöjé Dhöndrup Rinchen is based on that provided in Khedrup's *Entryway of Faith*, pp. 85–87. In his *Abbatial Successions of Jakhyung Monastery* (p. 9), the twentieth-century Tibetan scholar Tseten Shapdrung gives the Earth Ox year of 1349 as the year the monastery was founded by Chöjé Dhöndrup Rinchen.
34. Tseten Shapdrung's *Abbatial Successions of Jakhyung Monastery* (p. 25) reports this story and identifies it as part of an oral tradition.
35. Gungru Gyaltsen Sangpo, *A Commentary on the Realization Narrative*, 215; Nenying Künga Delek, *Doorway to Faith*, p. 347.
36. Tokden, *Supplement*, p. 14.
37. The other three works of Maitreya are *Differentiation of the Middle and Extremes* (*Madhyāntavibhaṅga*), *Differentiation of Phenonmena and Their Nature* (*Dharmadharmatāvibhaṅga*), and *Sublime Continuum* (*Ratnagotravibhāga*).
38. Yeshé Dhöndrup, *Entryway to the Ocean of Pure Faith*, p. 27.
39. Khedrup (*Entryway of Faith*, pp. 89–90) cites all the lines Tsongkhapa could later recall and shared with his students.
40. While Tokden's *Supplement* (p. 15) mentions only the two uncles, Khedrup's *Entryway of Faith* (p. 90) in fact speaks of the young Tsongkhapa being invited by this Drigung official to join him on the long trek to central Tibet.
41. Chahar's *Source of All Goodness* (p. 49) contains the following additional details on Tsongkhapa's departure from Jakhyung Monastery: As the young Tsongkhapa left, Chöjé could not bear the pain of his protégé's departure, so he entered the straw hut that had been built for Tsongkhapa's meditation retreat. After a while, he emerged to see if Tsongkhapa would look back, but he never did. This disappointed the master; he stated then and there that Tsongkhapa would not remember his kindness,

and he asked the monks to throw the hut off the cliff. However, the hut got stuck on a bush and hung off the cliff. It is said that the monks saw a rainbow striking the hut. When the monks reported this incident to the master, he asked them to retrieve the hut, which they did. Chöjé then said that this was a buddha of wisdom. He added that it was not because Lobsang Drakpa (Tsongkhapa) did not remember his teacher's kindness that he did not glance back; rather, it was an indication that he would probably never again in this life look back to his birthplace of Amdo and that he would immerse himself single-pointedly in the Dharma, without any attachment to worldly concerns. This hut came to be known as the Arapacana Meditation Hut; later it was covered with brick and turned into a stūpa, becoming a major object of worship at Jakhyung Monastery.

42. Lechen Kunga Gyaltsen (*History of Kadam Tradition*, completed in 1494) confirms Jampa Ling Monastery in Chamdo being founded by Tsongkhapa's disciple Sherap Sangpo and reports the monastery had around three thousand monks at the time.
43. Khedrup, *Entryway of Faith*, p. 91; Lekpa Sangpo (*Feast of Excellent Tales*, p. 183) in fact speaks of the young Tsongkhapa taking the novitiate ordination at Drigung Thil, in addition to receiving various teachings.
44. Tokden, *Supplement*, p. 15.
45. Khedrup, *Entryway of Faith*, p. 91.
46. *dbus kyi gdan sa chen po drug*. Dungkar Lobsang Trinlé, *Extensive Dungkar Dictionary*, p. 1534. That Tsethang Monastery is not included suggests that it is a pre-fourteenth-century listing system.
47. Although the word *kashipa* literally means "master of four treatises," in its original usage the term is better understood as referring to the master of four disciplines, instead of four texts. Following this original sense, to this day, the Geluk monastic colleges still characterize the subject matter of their scholarship as *zhungchen kapö nga*, the five major disciplines. In the context of using the Tibetan word *ka* (spelled as *bka'*) within the title *kachupa*, however, the word is better understood as referring to a treatise. Hence, *kachupa* would mean "mastery of ten treatises." For an engaging and detailed account on the scholastic curricula of major Tibetan monasteries today, as well as the history of their development, see Dreyfus, *The Sound of Two Hands Clapping*, especially chapters 5 and 6.
48. For example, in describing the curriculum to be pursued at his newly established Tsethang Monastery, Jangchup Gyaltsen (*Testament of Tai*

Situ Jangchup Gyaltsen, p. 363) mentions the four disciplines of classical Indian Buddhist scholarship—pramāṇa (logic and epistemology), Perfection of Wisdom studies, Abhidharma (psychology and metaphysics), and vinaya (monastic discipline and ethics)—as being formally instituted, in addition to the formal study of Hevajra tantra. There is no mention of Madhyamaka philosophy at all as a separate discipline of scholarship.

49. Khedrup, *Entryway of Faith*, p. 91.
50. The *Ornament* is divided into eight chapters, structured around three key themes: (1) the path of the threefold knowledge (chapters 1–3); (2) the four practices by which these paths are cultivated (chapters 4–7); and (3) the resultant state of buddhahood (chapter 8).
51. Two influential Indian commentaries of the *Ornament* are Vimuktisena's (sixth century) *Light on Perfection of Wisdom in Twenty-Five Thousand Lines* (*Āloka*) and Haribhadra's (ca. 770–810) *Clear Meaning* (*Sphuṭārthā*), both exant in Tibetan versions.
52. Khedrup, *Entryway of Faith*, p. 91.
53. Khedrup, *Entryway of Faith*, p. 92.
54. Jamyang Shepa, *Explanation of Tsongkhapa's Biography in Painting*, Collected Works, vol. *nga*, p. 3:a6 (p. 289), and *Anthology of Biographies of the Great Tsongkhapa*, vol. 2, p. 193.
55. This description of drakor is based on Chahar's *Source of All Goodness*, p. 59.
56. Over time, after Tsongkhapa's death, Sangphu would evolve into some eleven separate colleges affiliated with either the Geluk or Sakya schools, with Ratö Monastery being the most well known among the Geluk colleges. For two contemporary studies on Sangphu Monastery, its colleges, and its abbatial successions, see van der Kuijp, "The Monastery of Gsang-Phu Ne'u-thog," and Onodo, "Abbatial Successions."
57. These two earliest works of Tsongkhapa (*dge 'dun nyin shu bsdus pa* and *bsam gzugs kyi zin bris*) are found in *The Collected Works of the Incomparable Lord Tsongkhapa Lobsang Drakpa*, vol. *tsha*, and they are comparable to notes an undergraduate might take to organize their thoughts on a specific topic. The dating of these two texts is based on Chahar (*Source of All Goodness*, p. 58).
58. Two different translations of Butön's *History of Buddhism* exist in English today: *The History of Buddhism in India and Tibet*, trans. E. Obermiller (first published in 1930) and *Butön's History of Buddhism in India and Its*

Spread to Tibet, trans. Lisa Stein and Ngawang Zangpo (Boston: Snow Lion Publications, 2013).

59. Van Schaik, *Tibet* (p. 102), speaks of political problems at Sakya that were the cause of Tsongkhapa's having to make three attempts to take his exams at Sakya.
60. Bodong É Monastery is located in the Lhatse region in Tsang Province, and the monastery's abbatial succession includes Pang Lotsawa Lodrö Tenpa (1276–1342), a luminary of the Tibetan literary tradition. Following its adoption as the base of Bodong Panchen Choklé Namgyal (1376–1451), the monastery became the principal seat of the Bodong lineage of Tibetan Buddhism.
61. Sometime after the fourteenth century, Narthang gained prominence as a major center for printing in central Tibet. Over time, two other major printeries would emerge in Tibet: Dergé and Potala.
62. The details of Tsongkhapa's movements during this period are based on Khedrup, *Entryway of Faith*, pp. 91–93.
63. Khedrup, *Entryway of Faith*, p. 96.
64. Rendawa wrote an open letter listing his major misgivings about the Kālacakra tantra, a letter that elicited enormous excitement as well as rebuttals in Tibet in the early fifteenth century. On this issue, see Jinpa, "Rendawa and the Question of Kālacakra's Uniqueness" in *Essays on the Kālacakra Tantra*.
65. This is not to be confused with the present-day Potala Palace, which was built in the seventeenth century by the Fifth Dalai Lama. Judging by frequent mentions of a Potala in Lhasa in traditional biographies of Tsongkhapa, including Khedrup's *Entryway of Faith*, as well as in Rendawa's biography, it seems there was a monastery or a temple of some sort bearing the same name at the site of the present Potala.
66. Khedrup's *Entryway of Faith* (p. 97) refers to this teacher as Kashipa Loselwa, but Tsongkhapa's own *Record of Teachings Received* lists him as Lodrö Sangpo. Sometime in the fifteenth century, Kyormolung Monastery became converted to Tsongkhapa's Geluk tradition.
67. *gsal stong 'dzin med kyi ngang la thug rtse gcig tu gnas.* Khedrup, *Entryway of Faith*, p. 98. During his early student years in central Tibet, the young Tsongkhapa's main personal practice appeared to be, in addition to his daily recitation of *Chanting the Names of Manjuśrī* and his Vajrabhairava sādhana (both the legacy of his early years with his first teacher, Chöjé),

the Mahāmudrā-type meditation that emphasizes abiding in a nondiscursive state characterized by clarity (*gsal ba*) and emptiness (*stong pa*) and devoid of any specific object (*'dzin med*). Tsongkhapa would come to recognize this type of meditative practice as belonging more to the cultivation of tranquility, albeit focused on the nature of mind, and not representing final meditation on emptiness.

68. Sumpa Yeshé Paljor (*Excellent Wish-Granting Tree*, p. 427) speaks of this "meditation pillar" (*bsam gtan gyi ka ba*) standing inside the main prayer hall of Kyormolung Monastery.
69. This pain in the upper back, which would recur several times later in life, may have been due to some dysfunction in the joints of his thoracic spine. None of the biographies, however, provides any clear description of what this illness is, let alone a diagnosis. This pain would return in an acute form when Tsongkhapa was in his late fifties, making him quite ill for two years.
70. Panchen Sönam Drakpa's *History of Old and New Kadam Traditions* (p. 55) identifies the four earliest students of Tsongkhapa as Tsakho Ngawang Drakpa, Drakpa Lodrö from Kham, Dongtön Yeshé Pal, and Geshé Tönpa.
71. The monastery was later converted to the Shangpa Kagyü tradition of Khyungpo Neljor (d. 1127), who propagated a unique lineage focused on the teachings of the Indian yogini Niguma, believed to be a sister of the famed Nāropa, the main source of instructions of the Tibetan translator Marpa (d. 1097).
72. Khedrup, *Entryway of Faith*, p. 99.
73. Khedrup, *Entryway of Faith*, p. 99. Chahar (*Source of All Goodness*, p. 67) provides a brief description of this practice; a detailed and comprehensive explanation of the practice can be found in *Beautiful Adornment of the Doctrine of Kālacakra* (Collected Works, vol. *tsha*, p. 62b:5) by the Sakya scholar and historian Ngawang Künga Sönam (1597–1659/60), known more widely as Jamgön Amé Shap.
74. English translation of this work, containing both the root text in verse and Tsongkhapa's own commentary, is available in Sparham, *Ocean of Eloquence*.
75. Although Khedrup (*Entryway of Faith*, p. 100) mentions Tsongkhapa receiving a letter from his mother, he does not provide any further details. Chahar (*Source of All Goodness*, p. 68) provides specific personal details.

76. Chahar (*Source of All Goodness*, p. 34) in fact speaks of Tsongkhapa sending two self-portraits, one for his mother and the other for his sister.
77. Tseten Shapdrung (*A Short Story of Je Tsongkhapa's Thangka*, p. 262) offers a detailed eyewitness description of this portrait thangka and argues that the year Tsongkhapa sent it had to be 1378.
78. Khedrup (*Entryway of Faith*, p. 103) writes of this experience as if he were citing verbal communication with Tsongkhapa himself.
79. These two stanzas are found in the colophon of a text Tsongkhapa composed at Nyethang Dewachen, entitled *Staircase for the Clear Mind* (*Blo gsal bgrod pa'i them skas*), which is in volume *tsha* of Collected Works.
80. On a comparative study of this early work of Tsongkhapa as well as his treatment of the topic of twenty persons, see Apple, *Stairway to Nirvana*. "Twenty persons" refers to a system of classifying persons (*saṃghas*) on the four stages toward the attainment of the arhat's state of nirvāṇa: stream enterer, once returner, never returner, and access to arhat state.
81. The entire text of this letter, composed in verse, is found in the *Miscellaneous Writings of Great Tsongkhapa* (Collected Works, vol. *kha*). The letter contains the following colophon (*Miscellaneous Writings*, p. 481): "This letter was sent by Lobsang Drakpa and is accompanied by a yard of white cotton cloth representing my gift. As for detailed news, you would learn it from Geshe Sönam Gyalwa. This was sent from the great learning center of Dewachen on the 27th day of the twelfth month (January 27, 1379)." Neither Tsongkhapa himself nor any of his biographers provides the personal name of this Mongolian prince. However, later Geluk historians and biographers would interpret Tsongkhapa's gift of a white cloth to the Mongolian prince as an auspicious portent of the spreading of Tsongkhapa's Geluk tradition across the Mongol world. See, for example, Lobsang Trinlé, *Extensive Biography*, p. 148.
82. Khedrup, *Entryway of Faith*, p. 103.
83. Judging by the widely accepted statement that Gyaltsap (Tsongkhapa's future successor at Ganden Monastery) was the first *kachupa* (master of ten treatises), we can safely assume that the study of Madhyamaka had become part of the formal monastic curriculum in central Tibet sometime toward the end of the fourteenth century. Later, Tsongkhapa's own Ganden Monastery would become a major center for Madhyamaka scholarship.
84. Khedrup, *Entryway of Faith*, pp. 103–4.

85. Gungru (*Commentary on the Realization Narrative*, p. 223) identifies the other Sanskrit texts as the *Amarakośa* (a famous Sanskrit work on poetic synonyms attributed to the ancient Indian author Amarasiṃha), *Chandoratnakāra* (a Sanskrit work on prosody composed by Ratnākaraśānti), and texts belonging to the genre of "wise sayings" known as *subhaśita* (*legs bshad*). On this last genre, see my introduction to Newman, *The Tibetan Book of Everyday Wisdom*.
86. For a personal account of how this text is studied and used in classical Tibetan literary education, see the introduction of Jinpa and Elsner, *Songs of Spiritual Experience*.
87. This work is found in Tsongkhapa's *Miscellaneous Writings*, pp. 235–92.
88. Khedrup, *Entryway of Faith*, p. 104.
89. Tsethang Monastery was founded in 1351 by Tai Situ Jangchup Gyaltsen, the founder of the Phagdru dynasty. Impressed by the tradition of academic learning based on the Indian Buddhist classics available at Kadam and Sakya monasteries, Jangchup Gyaltsen established Tsethang so that his own Phagdru Kagyu school would have its own center for scholarly studies. It was established to complement Phagdru Kagyü's main monastery Densa Thil, founded by the patriarch of the school, Phagmo Drupa Dorjé Gyalpo (1110–70). Tsethang Monastery is located in the Yarlung Valley, a region pregnant with mythical and historical importance to the origins of the Tibetan nation and its people. Tsethang is around 114 miles to the southeast of Lhasa. Sometime in the eighteenth century, during the Seventh Dalai Lama's time, the monastery became converted to Geluk and was renamed Ganden Chökhor Ling Monastery.
90. Tsongkhapa, *Miscellaneous Writings*, p. 107; for an alternative translation of these lines, see Kilty, *Splendor of an Autumn Moon*, p. 21.
91. Tokden, *Supplement*, p. 17.
92. Khedrup (*Entryway of Faith*, p. 106) lists the names of the other officiating monks at this ordination ceremony.
93. Khedrup, *Entryway of Faith*, p. 106.
94. Khedrup, *Entryway of Faith*, p. 106. In his *Record of Teachings Received* (p. 25b:5), however, Tsongkhapa does not mention receiving any transmission of Sakya lamdré from Drakpa Jangchup but the ceremonial generation of the "engaging aspect" of bodhicitta (*'jug pa sems bskyed*); Khedrup's *Record of Teachings Received* mentions Tsongkhapa having received the instruction on the six yogas of Niguma at that time as well.

95. "In Praise of Dharma Master Drakpa Jangchup" in *Miscellaneous Writings*, pp. 14–16. Judging by a phrase in the colophon of this poem ("composed by the easterner Lobsang Drakpai Pal, a poet who touched the dust under the feet of this Dharma master numerous times"), Tsongkhapa in fact appears to have met the master on several occasions.
96. Unless otherwise stated, all the details on the Phagdru dynasty, including the dates, are based on Panchen Sönam Drakpa's *New Red Annals*, which contains one of the most comprehensive accounts of Phagdru rule in central Tibet.
97. For a contemporary study of the history, architecture, and art of this ancient temple, see Vitali, *Early Temples of Central Tibet*, pp. 1–35.
98. "A Poem in Challenging Composition Style with the Vowel E Only," *Miscellaneous Writings*, p. 470.
99. Neringpa Chimé Rapgyé, "Treasure House of Gems," p. 575.
100. Kunga Gyaltsen, *Meaningful to Behold: Biography of Chenga Sönam Gyaltsen*, Collected Works, vol. *ka*, p. 40b:6 (p. 257).
101. Dan Martin. https://sites.google.com/site/tibetological/gung-thang-dkar-chag.
102. For an English translation of Shang's key work on Mahāmudrā, see Roberts, *Mahāmudra and Related Instructions*, pp. 85–134; for a detailed guide to the practice of Mahāmudrā according to Shang, see pp. 65–82. For Sakya Paṇḍita's specific critique of Shang's Mahāmudrā, see Rhoton, *Clear Differentiation*, p. 141 and n. 71 and the cited secondary literature.
103. The nyungné fasting rite consists of taking a one-day vow of strictly observing the eight precepts of Mahāyāna renewal: abstaining from killing, stealing, sexual activity, lying, or consuming intoxicants; fasting during specified times; abstaining from wearing jewelry; and refraining from sitting or lying on high and fine chairs or beds. The fasting rite can be performed for two days, with the first day as a preliminary when eating only one meal during the day is permitted, and the second day requiring full fasting for twenty-four hours. The nyungné fasting rite could last up to a week, with the eight precepts retaken for the day every morning. Alternatively, the practice could be done over a longer period, from one week and up to three weeks, during which time participants observe silence (other than during the chanting) and have only one meal at midday. Otherwise, avoid both food and drink during this period.
104. For example, Lobsang Trinlé (*Extensive Biography*, p. 167) interprets the

elements of the dream as follows: Climbing the steep, rocky cliff symbolizes climbing toward the nirvanic plane at the top; the smooth white slab represents the purity of Tsongkhapa's mind, in that it is free of the unevenness of the afflictions and the stains of self-centeredness; the brilliance of the blue color symbolizes the attainment of the wisdom that clearly discerns the ultimate and conventional truths; that the flower is attached to a stem indicates the longevity of Tsongkhapa's teaching on this earth; and Tsongkhapa picking up the flower indicates that Tsongkhapa himself would ensure that his teachings remain in the world for a long time, and provides him with an important hand emblem.

105. Khedrup, *Entryway of Faith*, p. 108.

106. Panchen Sönam Drakpa, *New Red Annals*, p. 77. The same source refers to a revolt by some ten regional rulers of the Phagdru domain, an event that came to be referred as "the circling by the ten" (*chu korwa*). According to Taktsang Lotsawa, in *Biography of the Great Bodhisattva Namkha Wöser* (Collected Works, vol. 2, p. 72), this period of strife lasted for three years (*lo gsum gyi bar du*), during which the situation became so dire that the young Phagdru ruler would often sleep in his armor. In any case, the assassination of Dzongchi Drakpa Rinchen must have occurred after 1387, since Tsongkhapa's biographies explicitly mention Tsongkhapa being able to finally accept Dzongchi's long-standing invitation and visit him sometime in 1388.

107. "A Supplication to Dharma Master Drakpa Jangchup," *Miscellaneous Writings*, p. 15. The colophon of this short prayer clearly states that it was composed at the sacred site of the Potala, in Lhasa.

108. The text is some twenty-four long folios in length; its colophon states: "Composed by the easterner Tsongkhapa Lobsang Drakpai Pal at the behest of Miwang Drakpa Gyaltsen." Collected Works, vol. *tsha*, p. 760.

109. "Letter of Advice to the Great Ruler Drakpa Gyaltsen," *Miscellaneous Writings*, p. 483.

110. Lechen (*History of Kadam Tradition*, p. 682) identifies him with Tokden Ngonyalma, a prominent student of Jonang Choklé Namgyal and a major custodian of the tradition's instructions on the Kālacakra tantra. A brief mention of Tokden Ngonyalma is found in George N. Roerich, trans., *The Blue Annals*, p. 779.

111. Khedrup, *Entryway of Faith*, p. 108. In his *Record of Teachings Received*, Tsongkhapa lists many Vajrayāna teachings received from Tokdenpa,

including the guide to the sādhana of Cakrasaṃvara of Ghaṇṭapa lineage, the completion-stage text *Spring Drop* (*dpyid kyi thig le*) of the Kṛṣṇācārya tradition of Cakrasaṃvara, and several important instructions connected with the meditation deity Guhyasamāja.

112. "A Hymn to Tārā," *Miscellaneous Writings*, p. 103.

113. Chenga Lodrö Gyaltsen, "River of Faith: Biography of Tokden Jampel Gyatso," p. 27, and Lechen, *History of Kadam Tradition*, p. 711.

114. Although it is difficult to determine when Tsongkhapa's *Golden Rosary* was committed to woodblock printing, it appears that copies were widely available in central Tibet, even for students. For example, Jamyang Chöjé's biography records that he studied Tsongkhapa's *Golden Rosary* as a young monk at Samyé. Tsangtön, "Lamp Illuminating the Wondrous Story of the Life of Omniscient Jamyang Chöjé Tashi Palden," p. 47.

115. *Golden Rosary*, p. 3a:5. "Mother of the buddhas" is an epithet for the Perfection of Wisdom scriptures. In the opening salutation verses, Tsongkhapa pays homage to his childhood teacher Chöjé as well as to what he refers to as his four teachers (*yongs 'dzin bzhi*) on the Perfection of Wisdom—possibly Yönten Gyatso, Ogyenpa (both of Nyethang Monastery), Nyawön Kunga Pal, and Rendawa.

116. *Mang du thos pa shar tsong kha pa blo bzang grags pa'i dpal.* In the colophon of *The Golden Rosary*, we read: "Composed by the easterner Tsongkhapa Lobsang Drakpai Pal, someone who has read widely and was born at the borders of the Land of Snows." Admiration for *The Golden Rosary* was shared even by some of Tsongkhapa's future critics, such as Taktsang Lotsawa, who would write critically of certain aspects of Tsongkhapa's Madhyamaka view. Speaking of *The Golden Rosary*, Taktsang wrote, "Seeing that, even in youth, the sun of your intellect had / Caused the lotus grove of the root text and *Ornament* to thrive, / The conceit of the night-lotus of my intellect came to fade. / I pray to you, treasury of wisdom profound and vast." Collected Works, vol. 2, p. 161.

117. Admiration for Tsongkhapa's *Golden Rosary* crosses boundaries of sectarian affiliation and time. Over the centuries, it has inspired its own commentaries in the form of annotations, verse summaries, and even large-scale verbatim reproduction. For example, the text known as *General Points of the Perfection of Wisdom* (*shes rab kyi phal rol du phyin pa'i spyi don*) by the famed nineteenth-century Nyingma master Dza Paltrul is composed almost entirely of Tsongkhapa's *Golden Rosary*, produced by

carefully selecting the passages that directly pertain to the exposition of Maitreya's root text and leaving out the glosses on Haribhadra's commentary as well as the more technical aspects of Tsongkhapa's text. In a shorter text, *General Points of the Meditation Stages of the Perfection of Wisdom*, Dza Paltrul in fact acknowledges the source of his exposition to be Tsongkhapa. The longer text, which runs to nearly three hundred folios, however, does not even contain an author's colophon, which suggests that Dza Paltrul might have actually prepared this for his own use and practice, rather than as a freestanding text bearing his name. I thank Donald S. Lopez, Jr., who, having learned this fact from Gareth Sparham, drew my attention to it.

118. Khedrup, *Entryway of Faith*, p. 108; Gungru, *A Commentary on the Realization* Narrative, p. 226.
119. Chan (*Tibet Handbook*, p. 493) describes Sinpori (a village and an ancient monastery by the same name) as directly across from Gongkar Monastery on the other side of the river.
120. Khedrup, *Entryway of Faith*, p. 109.
121. This story is told in some detail in Khedrup's *Entryway of Faith* (pp. 109–11), as well as in Gungru, *Commentary on the Realization* Narrative, pp. 226–27).
122. While Khedrup (*Entryway of Faith*, p. 110) writes of "oral instructions of Milarepa, Marpa, and others," Gungru, *Commentary on the Realization Narrative*, p. 227) explicitly speaks of "oral instructions and life stories of Dakpo Kagyü, such as those of Milarepa and Marpa." Having been exposed to the oral teachings of the Kagyü tradition early, at Drigung Thil where he first landed in central Tibet, and later from the Phagdru patriarch Drakpa Jangchup, Tsongkhapa found these Kagyü teachings to be sources of inspiration throughout his life.
123. Sanskrit titles of these texts are, in their respective order, as follows: *Pramāṇavārttika*, *Abhisamayālaṃkāra*, *Abhidharmasamuccāya*, *Abhidharmakośa*, *Vinayasūtra*, *Mahāyānasūtrālaṃkāra*, *Madhyāntavibhaṅga*, *Dharmadharmatāvibhaṅga*, *Ratnagotravibhāga*, *Mūlamadhyamkakārikā*, *Yuktiṣaṣtikā*, *Śūnyatāsaptati*, *Vigrahāvyavartanī*, *Vaidālyaprakaraṇī*, *Madhyamakāvatāra*, *Catuḥśataka*, and *Bodhicaryāvatāra*. The order on the list of the seventeen Indian root texts is provided here according to Khedrup's *Entryway of Faith*, p. 110. Tokden (*Supplement*, p. 17), on the other hand, says that Tsongkhapa taught "around ten texts" (*po ti bcu tsam*), each one combined

with two to three commentaries, and that, just before embarking on his long intensive meditation retreat, Tsongkhapa taught "twenty-nine texts in a continuous sequence."

124. This is according to Chahar (*Source of All Goodness*, p. 99), who does not, however, provide any information about his source.

125. *Miscellaneous Writings*, p. 19. Sengé Gyaltsen, at whose request this hymn was composed, is probably Khenchen Sengé Gyaltsen, whose short biography is found in Taktsang Lotsawa's works (Collected Works, vol. 2). According to this biography (p. 110), Sengé Gyaltsen was born in the Fire Bird year of 1357, the same year as Tsongkhapa. The biography also contains an interesting story (p. 130) of how Sengé Gyaltsen sought Tsongkhapa's help in persuading Lochen Kyapchok Palsang to assist in the founding of Chökhor Gang Monastery and agree to be its first abbot.

126. Khedrup (*Entryway of Faith*, p. 11) tells this part of Tsongkhapa's story as if he had heard it from the master himself.

127. Khedrup, *Entryway of Faith*, p. 112. Khedrup, in fact, provides a brief account of the life of Umapa, including how his visions went all the way back to his youth.

128. *Miscellaneous Writings*, p. 509. Namkha Gyaltsen was originally a minister at the Phagdru court, who would later (in 1408) be appointed as the governor (*dzong pon*) of Rinpung by the Phagdru ruler Miwang Drakpa Gyaltsen. Pleased by Namkha Gyaltsen's loyalty and service, the Phagdru ruler established Rinpung as a district (*dzong*) within the Phagdru dominion and gave its rulership to Namkha Gyaltsen's family in perpetuity.

129. My dating of Lochen's death is based on a passage found in Taktsang Lotsawa's *Biography of Khen Rinpoché Sengé Gyaltsen* (Collected Works, vol. 2, p. 134), where he identifies the Wood Horse year (1414) as the time when two years have passed since Lochen's death. According to this same biography, Taktsang Lotsawa (p. 111) appeared to have written a biography of Lochen, which, unfortunately, seems lost.

130. Although Tsongkhapa's biographies rarely list Lochen as one of his teachers, some later sources do. If we were to take these sources to be accurate, it was perhaps during this sojourn at Namtsé Deng that Tsongkhapa attended Lochen's teachings.

131. Khedrup, *Entryway of Faith*, p. 113. Only a few of Rendawa's writings appear to have been committed to printing, so most of his writings were for a long time hard to find. Recently, the collected works of Rendawa,

running to ten volumes, have been published in Sichuan by Gangs ljongs bod kyi dpe rnying dpe skrun khang. This modern collection, however, does not contain this commentary on *Ornament of the Pramāṇavārttika*, indicating that the work has been lost. Thanks to Tsongkhapa's careful study of this text with Rendawa, whenever Tsongkhapa later taught Dharmakīrti's text, he would bring in comparative readings of the important Indian commentaries of Devandrabuddhi, Śākyabuddhi, and Prajñākāragupta.

132. Khedrup, *Entryway of Faith*, p. 113.
133. Khedrup, *Entryway of Faith*, p. 114.
134. Khedrup, *Entryway of Faith*, p. 115.
135. Sangyé Tsemo, *Wonders of Excellence: A Biography of Glorious Rendawa*, Collected Works of Rendawa, vol. 1, p. 87.
136. Sangyé, *Wonders of Excellence*, p. 59.
137. These probably were the soldiers returning from the military expedition sent to the Phenpo region early in Miwang Drakpa Gyaltsen's reign, which began in 1385 when Miwang was barely twelve years old. In his *Song of the Spring Queen: A History of Tibet*, the Fifth Dalai Lama, however, refers to two military expeditions sent by Phagdru Drakpa Gyaltsen to Nyangtö. They were triggered because the Nyangtö governor Rapten Kunsang was "a little unskillful in his work," which gave "offense to the High One." For an English translation of this section of the Fifth Dalai Lama's text, see Ahmad, *A History of Tibet by the Fifth Dalai Lama of Tibet*, p. 149.
138. This story, including the exchange between Chökyi Palwa and Tsongkhapa, is found in Khedrup, *Entryway of Faith*, p. 115.
139. Khedrup, *Entryway of Faith*, p. 116.
140. In his *Record of Teachings Received* (p. 9b:1) Tsongkhapa lists several other important Vajrayāna teachings he received at the time from Chökyi Palwa, including the transmission of Candrakīrti's *Clear Lamp*, a commentary on the Guhyasamāja root tantra.
141. *da ni chos kyi bdag po la 'phrod pas 'gyod pa med do.* Khedrup, *Entryway of Faith*, p. 118.
142. Lobsang Trinlé (*Extensive Biography*, pp. 192–97) provides a detailed list of all the tantric teachings Tsongkhapa had received together with their associated instruction lineages. Tsongkhapa's own *Record of Teachings Received* provides the transmission lineage of each of these practices.

143. *rgyal bas gsungs pa'i gdams ngag bdud rtsi'i bcud / snying po'i ro la rang nyid rtse gcig tu / gnas zhing gzhan yang de la 'god 'dod pa'i. Miscellaneous Writings*, p. 170. To appreciate the historical importance of *Queries* within the overall development of Tsongkhapa's thought and mission in Tibet, see Jinpa, "Tsongkhapa's Qualms about Early Tibetan Interpretations of Madhyamaka Philosophy."

144. Pawo, *Feast for the Learned*, p. 1155. Questions were raised as early as the fifteenth century by Jampa Lingpa Sönam Namgyal (who, as a young monk, had received teachings from Tsongkhapa) about Tsongkhapa's authorship of *Queries*. In contrast, most Tibetan scholars consider it to be by Tsongkhapa, albeit from an early period. Accepting it as authentic, the Sakya scholar Shākya Chokden wrote detailed responses to the questions raised by Tsongkhapa, citing virtually the entire text. Although Tsongkhapa's intent was less to refute than to raise critical questions on many of the views of the day, Shākya Chokden took *Queries* to be dismissive of the views and practices of revered earlier Tibetan traditions. Among Tsongkhapa's own followers, *Queries* was recognized as a call for a more self-aware and self-critical approach to the understanding and practice of the Dharma, especially with respect to the view and meditation. Gomchen Ngawang Drakpa (b. 1450), for example, wrote two separate responses to *Queries*, one pertaining to the conduct section and the other to the section on view and meditation. Similarly, Panchen Lobsang Chökyi Gyaltsen (1570–1662) wrote an eloquent versified response to the questions, entitled *Musical Tunes Bringing Joy to Lobsang*, where (p. 10b:1) Panchen takes the text's approach to be a skillful device compassionately employed by Tsongkhapa to teach us. Pema Karpo, the famed Drukpa Kagyü master, too responded to some of Tsongkhapa's questions from *Queries* that he thought could be perceived as being aimed at Kagyü Mahāmudrā. In the last part of his *Conqueror's Treasury: An Explanation of Mahāmudrā: Instruction*, Pema Karpo offers two rebuttals, one to Sakya Paṇḍita and the other to Tsongkhapa's *Queries*.

145. *Jewel Treasury of Wise Sayings*, v. 443; see Newman, *Tibetan Book of Everyday Wisdom*, p. 94.

146. Nāgārjuna, *Treatise on the Middle Way*, 24:11.

147. *Miscellaneous Writings*, p. 171. Shākya Chokden's responses to *Queries* suggest a helpful way to structure Tsongkhapa's text. He organizes his responses in seven main parts, each constituting a specific chapter: (1) crit-

ical responses to questions posed in the preamble, (2) critical responses to questions pertaining to going for refuge, (3) critical responses to questions posed to meditators concerning conduct, (4) differentiating between tranquility and insight, (5) replies to the main section on the view and meditation, (6) replies to questions posed to the scholars though pretending they are for meditators, and (7) replies in summary form. Shākya Chokden's lengthy responses, entitled *Ornament of the Enlightened Intention: Replies to the Queries from a Sincere Heart*, are found in his Collected Works, vol. 23, pp. 297–358.

148. In the concluding section of Gomchen's *Responses to the View and Meditation Sections of "Queries from a Sincere Heart"* (p. 25a:4), he states that because Tsongkhapa's *Queries* convey so many essential points of Buddhist thought and practice, engaging carefully with the text offers a way to enrich both one's understanding and one's practice of the Dharma. I also see important contemporary significance in the questions raised by Tsongkhapa. For example, as Buddhist-derived meditation practices, such as mindfulness, attract interest outside the traditional Buddhist societies, and as scientists, clinical researchers, and educators begin to explore these contemplative techniques as resources to be applied more widely, awareness of the critical questions Tsongkhapa raised about meditation could bring greater clarity to bear on what in science might be called the "key constructs."

149. *Queries from a Sincere Heart* in *Miscellaneous Writings*, pp. 181–82. Gomchen (*Responses to "Queries,"* p. 1a:1) broadly divides the section of *Queries* concerning meditation into three sections: (1) queries pertaining to the union of tranquility and insight; (2) queries pertaining to the threefold attributes of bliss, clarity, and nonconceptuality; and (3) a concluding summary. The first topic is divided further into five subheadings: queries pertaining to the actual union of tranquility and insight, to the distinction between mental laxity and lethargy, to coarse and subtle levels of laxity, to mindfulness and meta-awareness, and to the defining characteristic of a distracted or an undistracted mind.

150. *bde gsal mi rtog pa*. For brief definitions of these three attributes according to the Kagyü Mahāmudrā tradition, see Rangjung Dorjé's "Instructions on the Mahāmudrā Innate Union" in Roberts, *Mahāmudra and Related Instructions*, pp. 161–62.

151. *dmigs bcas sgom par song gi / dmigs med sgom pa ma yin no zer na de la lan ji ltar 'debs*. *Queries from a Sincere Heart*, p. 184.

152. *Queries from a Sincere Heart*, p. 184. The six yogas of Kālacakra, sometimes called the six-branch yoga of Kālacakra completion stage, refer to the six progressive stages in the advanced completion stage of the tantra. The first, the yoga of individual withdrawal (*so sor sdus pa*), is the Kālacakra equivalent of praṇayama (the yoga of winds) aimed at bringing the winds into the central channel. For a detailed explanation on these six stages according to the Kālacakra tantra, see Khedrup Norsang Gyatso, *Ornament of Stainless Light*, trans. Gavin Kilty (Boston: Wisdom Publications, 2004).

153. The second of three texts called *The Stages of Meditation* (*Bhāvanakrama*) is believed to have been written in the aftermath of his defeat of the Chinese Chan monk Hoshang at the debate that took place at Samyé in the late eighth century.

154. Tibetan historians describe a debate between the Indian Buddhist master Kamalaśila and the Chinese monk Hoshang hosted by the Tibetan emperor Trisong Detsen in the eighth century. According to these sources, the debate focused on whether enlightenment is attained through a gradual process of cultivation or whether it can occur as an instantaneous event, with the Indian master propounding the gradualist view and the Chinese monk holding the opposite. From a wider cultural historical perspective, the debate also represented a competition for dominance in Tibet between Indian Buddhism and the Chinese Chan tradition. For a detailed contemporary analysis of the philosophical and soteriological ramifications of this debate, see Ruegg (*Buddha Nature, Mind and the Problem of Gradualism*), especially parts 2–4.

155. Gomchen, *Responses to "Queries,"* (p. 8a:4) reads this discussion about the role of discursive meditation as an important topic emerging from the questions pertaining to the three attributes of bliss, clarity, and nonconceptuality. He divides the section further into four subheadings: (1) queries pertaining to discursive and resting approaches in meditation, (2) queries pertaining to the relation of learning and critical reflection with respect to meditative cultivation, (3) queries regarding the distinction between mental scattering and distraction, and (4) queries as to whether in resting meditation the mind is placed on the object of meditation at all.

156. *thos bsam la ma brten par sgom pa yang dag mi yong bar bshad pa*. *Queries*, p. 185.

157. *klu sgrub kyi lhag mthong dang 'gal bas na de mthar thug gi sgom yin pa dor cig. Queries*, p. 186.
158. This discussion of Rendawa's views is found in his biography *Wonders of Excellence* (p. 56) by his student Sangyé Tsemo.
159. Sangyé, *Wonders of Excellence*, p. 57.
160. Sangyé, *Wonders of Excellence*, p. 57.
161. *deng sang gi man ngag pa rnams la lhag mthong sgom tshul gyi man ngag gtan mi snang*. . . . "Letter to the Dharma Master Lobsang Drakpa Including Expression about the Joy of Solitude," *Miscellaneous Writings*, Collected Works, vol. 3, p. 84.
162. *Miscellaneous Writings*, p. 85.
163. *kho bos ni de lta'i sgom de ha shang gi sgom lugs las khyad par gtan nas ma phyed do. Queries, Miscellaneous Writings,* p. 187.
164. *'on te bden par mi 'dzin pa dang bden med du 'dzin pa gnyis la khyad par yod na khyad par gang yin gsungs shig. Queries*, p. 190.
165. This type of instruction is known also as "introducing the nature of mind" (*sems ngo sprod pa*). Gomchen (*Responses to the View and Meditation Sections*, pp. 19a:2–23b:6) presents a detailed analysis of this section of *Queries*.
166. *rnam rtog thams bcad chos skur ro snyoms yin zer ba 'dug pa. Queries*, p. 193.
167. Khedrup, "Lamp Dispelling Erroneous Paths" (*Miscellaneous Writings*, p. 668), refers to this statement, strongly suggesting that he too accepts the *Queries* to be indeed by Tsongkhapa.
168. *mdor na klu sgrub kyi lta tshul dang 'gal ba'i lta ba ni. Queries*, p. 194.
169. Gomchen (*View and Meditation Sections*, p. 24a:2) identifies the first view as that of the Chinese master Hoshang and the second as "some followers of Shijé lineage." The numbers at the beginning of each set of new positions have been added by the translator to help the reader, based on Gomchen's reading of this section of *Queries*.
170. *rnam rtog ma rig chen po ste*. This is a citation from a sūtra quoted also in Atiśa's *Lamp on the Path to Enlightenment*.
171. Gomchen (*View and Meditation Sections*, p. 25a:1) identifies this as "some followers of Kagyü tradition."
172. Gomchen (*View and Meditation Sections*, p. 26a:2) speaks of some Sakya instructional notes based on teachings of the Indian paṇḍit Vanaratna (who came to Tibet several decades after Tsongkhapa's death) containing views similar to this.
173. *Queries*, pp. 194–96. In his *Lamp Dispelling the Darkness: A Guide to the View*

(*lta khrid mun sel sgron me*), pp. 644–59, Khedrup also lists a number of different views of the Tibetan meditators (*bod kyi bsam gtan pa rnams*) and critically examines them against Tsongkhapa's views on emptiness, often using strikingly similar phraseology as Tsongkhapa's *Queries.*

174. *des na rgyal ba'i bstan pa 'di thos bsam sgom pa gsum ga'i sgo nas 'dzin dgos pa'i rgyu mtshan yang 'di yin no. Queries*, p. 198.

175. *Queries*, p. 199. In his "Lamp Dispelling the Darkness of Erroneous Paths" (*lam ngan mun sel sgron me*), Khedrup also examines the language and meditative approach of some Tibetan instructions and advises his readers, especially the followers of Tsongkhapa, not to dilute their understanding of his teachings on how to cultivate insight on emptiness with approaches that employ such phrases as "uncontrived naturalness" (*ma bcos lhug ma*), "consciousness in its natural state" (*da lta ba'i shes pa so ma*), "whatever thought that may arise gazing at its own face" (*rnam rtog gang shar gyi rang zhal lta ba*), and "remaining in bare awareness" (*rig pa rkyang 'ded*). *Miscellaneous Writings*, Collected Works, vol. *ba*, especially pp. 658–70.

176. *Queries*, p. 201. The phrase "one who is known to be sustained by Guru Mañjuśrī" could be Tsongkhapa's first public acknowledgment of his special connection with the deity Mañjuśrī.

177. For example, the noted contemporary Indo-Tibetan Buddhist studies scholar David S. Ruegg (*Three Studies*, p. 381) suggests that "The *topos* of visionary encounter and teaching may perhaps be understood as implicitly alluding, in India as well as in Tibet, to a felt need for both conservative traditionalism and restorative or renovative interpretation."

178. Sangyé Tsemo, *Biography of Glorious Rendawa*, Collected Works, vol.1, p. 55.

179. See p. 277.

180. "Letter to Lama Umapa in Eastern Tibet," *Miscellaneous Writings*, p. 162.

181. Khedrup provides a brief account of Umapa's life in his *Entryway of Faith*, which probably represents the earliest written source on the life of this mystic. In his *Secret Biography of Tsongkhapa* too, Khedrup offers additional details, including specifics of Tsongkhapa's communication with the mystic. Lekpa Sangpo's *Feast of Excellent Tales* (pp. 485–89) also contains a lengthy section on Tsongkhapa's meetings with Umapa and his communication with Mañjuśrī through Umapa serving as the medium. All three of these texts, Khedrup's two biographies and Lekpa Sangpo's, appear to have been based on a shared source.

182. This Kadam monastery would eventually become the seat of the second most important oracle associated with the Dalai Lama's government. As is the case for many Tibetan monasteries of historical importance, a monastery by the same name exists in India within the Tibetan exile community.
183. This specific detail is found in Khedrup, *Secret Biography of Tsongkhapa*, p. 56.
184. Khedrup, *Entryway of Faith*, p. 124.
185. Khedrup, *Entryway of Faith*, p. 125.
186. Lekpa Sangpo, *Secret Life Stories Not Commonly Known*, p. 517. The "appearance aspect" refers to the conventional truth, while the "emptiness aspect" refers to the ultimate truth. So, essentially, Mañjuśrī is instructing Tsongkhapa not to adopt a standpoint that dismisses the conventional truth; rather, he must take the conventional truth seriously.
187. These details, including Tsongkhapa saying that he did not comprehend what the deity was saying and the deity's further instruction, are found in Khedrup's *Secret Biography of Tsongkhapa* (p. 54), Lekpa Sangpo's *Feast of Excellent Tales* (p. 187), and Gungru's *Commentary on the Realization Narrative* (p. 234).
188. Following the traditional Tibetan perspective, Tsongkhapa assumes the famed second-century philosopher Nāgārjuna to be the same Nāgārjuna who was the author of tantric texts like *The Five Stages* (*Pañcakrama*). Today, modern scholars recognize these to be two different authors. The same situation applies to the tantric authors bearing the names Āryadeva and Candrakīrti.
189. Khedrup, *Secret Biography*, p. 54; Lekpa Sangpo, *Feast of Excellent Tales*, p. 488. The wording in these two texts here is strikingly similar, suggesting their use of a single source.
190. Khedrup, *Secret Biography*, p. 55; Lekpa Sangpo, *Feast of Excellent Tales*, p. 488.
191. These details, including especially the exchanges between Umapa and Mañjuśrī, are found in Lekpa Sangpo, *Feast of Excellent Tales*, p. 490.
192. Khedrup, *Secret Biography*, p. 55; Lekpa Sangpo, *Feast of Excellent Tales*, p. 489.
193. Khedrup, *Secret Biography*, p. 57.
194. Khedrup (*Secret Biography*, p. 57) and Lekpa Sangpo (*Feast of Excellent Tales*, p. 490) both relate this story and identify a few specific instructions

but do not use the phrase "Mañjuśrī cycle of teachings." Tokden's presence at this teaching is confirmed in his biography by Chenga Lodrö Gyaltsen (*Biography of Tokden Jampel Gyatso*, p. 29). The Mañjuśrī cycle of teachings (*'jam dbyangs chos skor*) is a set of empowerments that includes some fourteen different forms of meditation deities. Yeshé Dhöndrup (*Entryway to the Ocean of Pure Faith*, p. 107) provides the entire list of these deities.

195. Chenga Lodrö Gyaltsen (*Biography of Tokden Jampel Gyatso*, p. 29) mentions Tokden practicing a Cakrasaṃvara sādhana based on an oral teaching by Mañjuśrī received through Umapa. Tokden's own *Supplement* (p. 19) contains a brief account of Tsongkhapa's relationship with Umapa, offering some details not found in other sources. Tokden speaks of Tsongkhapa asking Mañjuśrī which of the three—focusing on teaching the great Buddhist classics, giving Vajrayāna teachings including empowerments, or pursuing a life of single-pointed meditation in solitude—would be most beneficial for the Buddha's doctrine in the long term. Tokden also speaks of Tsongkhapa inquiring about the fate of his future birth. He then reports that the deity advised Tsongkhapa to serve the Dharma through teaching both Sūtra and Tantra but not to focus on giving tantric empowerments—for, the deity said, it might shorten Tsongkhapa's life and push him away from genuine attainments. Speaking of the instructions Tsongkhapa received from Mañjuśrī, Tokden concludes, "Given this, it is said that this precious master's tenets are in fact those of Mañjuśrī himself" (*des na rje rin po che 'di'i grub mtha' rnams 'jam dbyangs kyi grub mtha' yin gsung ngo*).

196. Chahar, *Source of All Goodness*, p. 132.

197. *Miscellaneous Writings*, pp. 75–77.

198. This entire instruction can be found in Collected Works, vol. *ba*.

199. Chenga Lodrö Gyaltsen, a student of Tsongkhapa, also provides a succinct summary of Tsongkhapa's guide, which follows the text's division articulated by Tsongkhapa. Chenga's short text is entitled "Guide to the View of the Equivalence of Saṃsāra and Nirvāṇa: An Ear-Whispered Instruction Given by Mañjuśrī to Lama Umapa and to the Precious Master," which is contained in his Collected Works, vol. 1, pp. 55–64.

200. Khedrup, *Secret Biography*, p. 58; Lekpa Sangpo, *Feast of Excellent Stories*, p. 491. According to some later sources, the text that Tsongkhapa wrote down from Mañjuśrī's instruction is, in fact, the eighteen-line instruction found in Tsongkhapa's *Miscellaneous Writings* (pp. 116–17), which most

biographies date to a later vision of the deity that occurred at Gya Sokphu Hermitage in the Dakpo region.

201. *Miscellaneous Writings*, p. 64.

202. Khedrup (*Secret Biography*, p. 58) explicitly states that they were each chosen by the deity to accompany Tsongkhapa on this long intensive retreat.

203. Khedrup (*Entryway of Faith*, p. 126) identifies the time of Tsongkhapa's departure for Wölkha as the "tenth month of the Monkey year when his age was thirty-six" (according to the Tibetan system, which counts the period in utero as year one). The detail about the point to which the group traveled by boat is found in Chenga Lodrö Gyaltsen, *Biography of Tokden Jampel Gyatso*, p. 30.

204. These details about Samten Ling Hermitage are drawn from Kharnak Lotsawa, *History of Ganden Tradition*, p. 184. Kharnak does not provide any information on who the seven meditators were.

205. This description of the hermitage is found in a letter Tsongkhapa wrote from Wölkha to the Phagdru ruler Miwang Drakpa Gyaltsen, *Miscellaneous Writings*, p. 483.

206. *nges med gnas su khyams pa'i rgyal khams pa*. *Miscellaneous Writings*, p. 497.

207. Although not mentioned in any of Tsongkhapa's biographies, this story of the master insisting on following the approach of the early Kadam masters during the retreat is told in some detail in Chenga Lodrö Gyaltsen, *Biography of Tokden Jampel Gyatso*, p. 31.

208. Seven-limb worship is an important devotional practice in Mahāyāna Buddhism. Its best-known early source is the "Vows of Good Conduct," a prayer from the *Flower Ornament Scripture*. Śāntideva's *Bodhicaryāvatāra* (2:1–25 and 3:1–6) also presents this seven-limb practice.

209. Khedrup (*Entryway of Faith*, p. 127) speaks only of Tsongkhapa's fingertips getting cracked due to the repetitive process of pouring grains onto the flat rock base and wiping them off, which is part of the ritual of maṇḍala offering; it is Lobsang Trinlé (*Extensive Biography*, p. 206) who mentions the story about the surface of the flat rock becoming shiny like a mirror.

210. Khedrup, *Secret Biography*, p. 59.

211. *Miscellaneous Writings*, p. 160. Lekpa Sangpo (*Feast of Excellent Tales*, p. 492) mentions Tokden experiencing visions of the deity and states that it is Tokden to whom Tsongkhapa is referring in his letter to Umapa.

212. *Miscellaneous Writings*, pp. 8–9.

213. Khedrup (*Secret Biography*, p. 58) and Lekpa Sangpo (*Feast of Excellent*

Tales, p. 492) mention Tsongkhapa having visions of the thirty-five buddhas associated with the confessional practice known as *tungshak* (literally, "purification of downfalls").

214. Cited in Khedrup, *Entryway of Faith*, p. 127. An English translation of the entire scripture, based primarily on the Chinese version and translated by Thomas Cleary, is available as *The Flower Ornament Scripture* (Boston: Shambhala Publications, 1993).
215. Khedrup, *Entryway of Faith*, p. 127.
216. This verse is cited in both Khedrup's *Entryway of Faith* (p. 59) and Lekpa Sangpo's *Feast of Excellent Tales* (p. 492), suggesting a single source.
217. This story of Garmi and the gift of Maitreya by Lachen is found in Kharnak Lotsawa, *History of Ganden Tradition*, p. 181; Kharnak, however, does not identify his own source.
218. Khedrup, *Entryway of Faith*, p. 128.
219. All of these details are found in Khedrup's *Entryway of Faith*, pp. 128–29.
220. These details, including the reference to the Lhodrak mystic, are from Khedrup, *Entryway of Faith*, pp. 129–30.
221. *Miscellaneous Writings*, pp. 60–61. "Bhadra posture" (in line 3) refers to a sitting posture that resembles the modern posture of sitting on a chair with the feet touching the ground; Tuṣita (line 17) is the heaven where Maitreya, as the future Buddha, is believed to reside at present; the eight worldly concerns (line 29) are gain, loss, pleasure, pain, praise, blame, fame, and disgrace; the threefold activity (final line) refers to study, reflection, and meditative cultivation. The stanza of the prayer running from lines 20 to 23, beginning with the phrase "When you the Buddha's regent," is today chanted as a freestanding popular prayer to Maitreya.
222. See, for example, Desi Sangyé Gyatso's *Yellow Beryl: A History of Ganden Tradition*, pp. 66–67. Desi uses the phrase "what are known as the four great deeds" (*mdzad chen bzhir grags pa*), suggesting that he was drawing from an existing custom.
223. *Miscellaneous Writings*, p. 45; for an English translation of this entire hymn to Maitreya, see Kilty, *Splendor of an Autumn Moon*, pp. 115–49, and Thurman, *Life and Teachings of Tsongkhapa*, pp. 183–91.
224. This praise, running to twenty-five stanzas of four lines each, is found in *Miscellaneous Writings*, pp. 10–14. Jikmé Bang's *Biography of Bodong Choklé Namgyal* (p. 134) speaks of how Rendawa is said to have remarked that Bodong's praise of him was superior in its literary quality, suggesting

some perceived rivalry between him and Tsongkhapa with respect to closeness to Rendawa.

225. This Menlung should not be confused with Menlung Chu Valley at the base of Menlung-Tsé Mountain, located farther to the west in Tibet, where the famous Tibetan poet-saint Milarepa was active.

226. The list of Indian masters provided here is from Khedrup's *Secret Biography* (pp. 59–60); some sources list Bhāviveka instead of Nāgabodhi.

227. Khedrup, *Secret Biography*, p. 60, and Lekpa Sangpo, *Feast of Excellent Tales*, p. 493; the wording in these sources is almost identical, suggesting a single source.

228. Chenga Lodrö Gyaltsen, *Biography of Tokden Jampel Gyatso*, p. 46; this is probably the source for Chahar (*Source of All Goodness*, p. 137) as well. In Tokden's biography, however, the statement is attributed to Sangkyongwa, a student of Tsongkhapa who later founded Nyima Ling Monastery in the Wölkha Valley and was a practitioner of both Tsongkhapa's teachings and the Kagyü lineage (Panchen Sönam Drakpa, *New Red Annals*, p. 60).

229. Khedrup, *Secret Biography*, p. 60, and Lekpa Sangpo, *Feast of Excellent Tales*, p. 493.

230. *Miscellaneous Writings*, p. 116. "Katara" is most probably an acronym, combining the Tibetan letters *ka*, *ta*, and *ra*. Chahar (*Source of All Goodness*, p. 138) gives the following meaning: *ka*, being the first letter in the Tibetan alphabet, simply stands as the opening letter; *ta*, being the last letter of the Sanskrit word *citta* (heart), refers to Tsongkhapa's heart; and *ra*, being the first letter for the Tibetan word *raldri* (sword), stands for sword. "City" here refers to Tsongkhapa's own body. Thus, the first line of this verse means "Tsongkhapa's body had been fed by nectar streaming down a sword."

231. *Miscellaneous Writings*, p. 117. "Sky flowers," and "son of a barren woman" are two of three stock examples of total nonexistence used in the Indian and Tibetan Buddhist texts, the third being the "horn of a rabbit." In identifying Gya Sokphu Hermitage as the place where Tsongkhapa received this eighteen-line instruction, I am following the preamble of this text as recorded in Tsongkhapa's collected works, which reads, "The following is the instruction conferred by Mañjuśrī at that time." A commentary on this instruction is found in the collected works (vol. *ka*) of the eighteenth-century Geluk master Phurchok Ngawang Jampa (1682–1762). In his

"Elucidating the Essential Points" (p. 2b), Phurchok, however, notes that this eighteen-line instruction would be the one that Tsongkhapa received from Mañjuśrī on the rooftop of the Lhasa Jokhang Temple, with Umapa as the medium.

232. *Miscellaneous Writings*, p. 117.

233. This work is found in his *Miscellaneous Writings*, pp. 201–35. Translations of the abridged version of this prayer can be found in Kilty, *Splendor of an Autumn Moon*, pp. 83–95, and Thurman, *Life and Teachings of Tsongkhapa*, pp. 193–98.

234. Lobsang Trinlé (*Extensive Biography*, p. 218) provides this detail concerning the mystic's dream but does not provide his source.

235. Khedrup, *Entryway of Faith*, p. 130.

236. The following details of Tsongkhapa's meeting with Khenchen, as well as the teachings they gave to each other, are based on Jamyang Tenpai Nyima's *Birth Stories of Great Tsongkhapa*, pp. 159–62.

237. Tsongkhapa's own *Record of Teachings Received* (pp. 29b:5–30a:2) lists, in addition to those already mentioned, the following teachings he received from Khenchen: *Mind Training Neutralizing the Peacock's Poison*, *Wheel of Sharp Weapons*, *Stages of the Heroic Mind,* and *Leveling the Conceptions* (four mind-training texts attributed to Atiśa's Indian mind-training teachers). The record also mentions (p. 30a:4) his receiving a "ceremony of generating bodhicitta according to the Mind Only school," suggesting that the Sakya tradition of distinguishing between bodhicitta ceremonies according to the Cittamātra and Madhyamaka schools existed also among Kadam teachers.

238. Jamyang Tenpai Nyima, *Birth Stories of Great Tsongkhapa*, p. 161. The same source speaks of Khenchen consulting his meditation deity Akṣobhya (one of the "four deities of Kadam," the other three being the Buddha, Avalokiteśvara, and Tārā) about Tsongkhapa's view of emptiness. In response, the deity said, "There is no error in the Buddha. This indeed in the flawless view; and, in the context of Highest Yoga tantra as well, there is no view beyond this one. So you should focus on this." Then Khenchen asked the deity, "In that case, is this also the view of Tsonawa?" "That, too, is for generating Nāgārjuna's view; and there is no separation between bodhisattva Manibhadra and Lobsang Drakpa." Later, the bodhisattva Manibhadra and Tsonawa would come to be recognized as Tsongkhapa's former lives.

239. These details about Tsongkhapa and Drupchen's first meeting, including how they saw each other, are found in Drupchen's own "How I Met Jé Tsongkhapa" (Collected Writings of Lhodrak Namkha Gyaltsen, p. 108). Given its importance to the larger narrative of Tsongkhapa, the compilers of Tsongkhapa's writings chose to include this same text in Tsongkhapa's Collected Works as well (vol. *ka*).

240. Drupchen's account, in fact, lists several additional blessing empowerments, including an instructional text entitled *Vajra Garland: Questions and Answers*. "The three lineages of lamrim" probably refers to the lineage of the instructions on the stages of the path stemming from the three Kadam masters: Potowa, Neusurpa, and Gonpawa; Hayagrīva is a horse-headed meditation deity in a wrathful form, especially important for the Nyingma tradition, a lineage with which Drupchen himself appears to be associated.

241. Mitrajogi was an Indian yogin who visited Tibet (at the invitation of Trophu Lotsawa) in the late twelfth century and was particularly revered for a special instruction on Avalokiteśvara practice and the instruction on "The Three Essential Points" (*snying po don gsum*). He was believed by his Tibetan devotees to have attained the power of longevity and, according to legend, was still alive in eastern India.

242. Lhodrak Namkha Gyaltsen, "How I Met Jé Tsongkhapa," p. 109. This exchange, including Drupchen's point about Tsongkhapa possibly becoming the abbot of Bodhgayā, demonstrates the tragic gap in Tibetans' knowledge of Indian history in the late fourteenth century; by this time, there was no functioning Buddhist monastery at Buddhism's holiest site.

243. All the details of this exchange between Drupchen and his meditation deity Vajrapāṇi are found in Lhodrak Namkha Gyaltsen, "How I Met Jé Tsongkhapa," pp. 109–10.

244. These details are found in Lhodrak Namkha Gyaltsen, "How I Met Jé Tsongkhapa," p. 110, as well as in Khedrup, *Entryway of Faith*, p. 131.

245. "Brahmā's Diadem," *Miscellaneous Writings*, p. 52. For alternative translations of these lines, see Kilty, *Splendor of an Autumn Moon*, p. 137, and Thurman, *Life and Teachings of Tsongkhapa*, p. 188.

246. Lhodrak Namkha Gyaltsen, "How I Met Jé Tsongkhapa," p. 110.

247. This is mentioned in Yeshé Dhöndrup (*Entryway to the Ocean of Pure Faith*, p. 141), who gives no information on his own source.

248. "A Supplication to the Lineage Gurus of the Expansive Practice of the Stages of the Path Instruction," *Miscellaneous Writings*, p. 4.
249. *Miscellaneous Writings*, p. 165. Aṭkāvatī (*Changlochen* in Tibetan) is the heaven of Vajrapāṇi.
250. Lhodrak Namkha Gyaltsen, *Garland of Supreme Medicinal Nectar*, Collected Works, vol. 1, p. 290a1. The colophon of this instruction text contains the following intriguing sentence: "This instruction has been sealed and not uttered for up to three years" (p. 593). I am not sure if we can take this statement to suggest that Drupchen penned the instruction a few years after his encounter with Tsongkhapa and then sent the text to him. This may explain why the instruction did not have any lasting effect on Tsongkhapa's own evolving understanding of the view of emptiness, for which he had sought the instruction in the first place.
251. Lhodrak Namkha Gyaltsen, *Garland of Supreme Medicinal Nectar*, p. 595.
252. See, for example, Guru Tashi Chöwang, *Gurta's History of Buddhism*, p. 980. Guru Tashi (pp. 606–11) provides a succinct explanation of Lhodrak Drupchen's unique Vajrapāṇi oral instructions and asserts that the *Garland of Supreme Medicinal Nectar* instruction sent to Tsongkhapa is entirely Dzokchen (*rdzogs chen kho na yin te*).
253. In his historical work *The Blue Annals* (English trans. by Roerich, pp. 200–2), completed in 1479, Gö Shönu Pal provides a brief biography of Longchenpa and mentions that the master wrote various works on Dzogchen. Further research is needed for fuller historical understanding of how and when Longchenpa's writings came to define the principal standpoints of Nyingma Dzogchen views, or whether it is thanks primarily to the eighteenth-century treasure-revealer Jigme Lingpa that Longchenpa's writings came to assume the prominence and importance they enjoy today in the Nyingma tradition.
254. Some sources say that Tsongkhapa paid another visit to Drupchen's teacher Khenchen Chökyap Sangpo after his seven-month stay at Lhodrak Drupchen's hermitage. Lobsang Trinlé (*Extensive Biography*, p. 233) suggests that Tsongkhapa and Khenchen must have actually met on several occasions. Either way, there is no evidence of any additional meetings with Drupchen.
255. Lhodrak Namkha Gyaltsen, *Collected Works*, vol. 1, p. 107.
256. Jamyang Khaché was one of the teachers of Rongtön Sheja Kunrik for

whom the latter would write a praise verse (Collected Works of Rongtön Sheja Kunrik, vol. 1, p. 191).

257. Lhodrak Namkha Gyaltsen, *Collected Works*, vol. 1, p. 94.

258. Khedrup, *Entryway of Faith*, pp. 131–32.

259. *Miscellaneous Writings*, p. 97; for an alternative translation, see Kilty, *Splendor*, p. 71.

260. Numerous pilgrimage guides (*lam yig*) to Tsari exist in Tibetan written by prominent Tibetan masters like Drukpa Pema Karpo, Chökyi Nangwa, and Barwa Gyaltsen of Nyö. For a detailed contemporary study of the sacred Tsari Mountain, see Toni Huber, *The Cult of Pure Crystal Mountain* (New York: Oxford University Press, 1999).

261. Khedrup, *Entryway of Faith*, p. 133.

262. This legend as well as the prayer are found in Lobsang Trinlé (*Extensive Biography*), p. 234. Kecara is a ḍākinī realm associated with the female meditation deity Vajrayoginī.

263. Although Khedrup does not speak of this vision of Maitreya on Mola Pass in either *Entryway of Faith* or the *Secret Biography*, he refers to it in his biographical hymn to Tsongkhapa. The story is told in some detail in Lekpa Sangpo's *Secret Life Stories Not Commonly Known* (p. 526) and repeated in many later biographies of the master.

264. "Prayer Supplicating the Great Master Tsongkhapa by Summarizing His Life in Verses," *Collected Works of Khedrup Jé*, vol. *ba*, p. 353. For an alternative translation, see Thurman, *Life and Teachings of Tsongkhapa*, p. 220.

265. Sucandra (Tib. *zla ba bzang po*) is, according to traditional literature on the origin of the Kālacakra tantra, the king who formally made the request to the Buddha to teach the specific tantra.

266. These details, including Tsongkhapa's dream, are found in Khedrup, *Secret Biography*, p. 63.

267. Khedrup, *Entryway of Faith*, p. 133.

268. These details of Tsongkhapa's vision of Sarasvatī and her warning that the master's life span would be limited to fifty-seven years are found in Khedrup, *Secret Biography*, p. 63.

269. Lekpa Sangpo, *Feast of Excellent Tales*, p. 497; emphasis is mine. "Great Charioteers" (*shing rta chen po*) refer to Nāgārjuna and Asaṅga, who, respectively, set forth the philosophical systems of Madhyamaka and Yogācāra.

270. *de nas bzung ste de ltar mdzad gsung*. Lekpa Sangpo, *Feast of Excellent Tales*, p. 497.

271. Khedrup (*Entryway of Faith*, p. 134) confirms Radrong Monastery to be the place where Gyaltsap came to meet with Tsongkhapa. In the colophon of one of his later works, *How to Undertake the Practice of the Path of the Two Stages of Kālacakra*, Gyaltsap himself speaks of how he had been at the feet of Tsongkhapa for more than two decades. So the dating of Gyaltsap's first becoming Tsongkhapa's student to around 1397 appears to be accurate.

272. Nenying Künga Delek's *Doorway to Faith* (p. 387) seems to be the earliest extant source of the details of Gyaltsap's meeting with Tsongkhapa. In Chahar's *Source of All Goodness*, a lengthy biography of Tsongkhapa written in the nineteenth century, we find more details (p. 158), but the author does not provide his source, likely the lost fifteenth-century biography of Gyaltsap by Tsangtön Künga Gyaltsen.

273. Chahar, *Source of All Goodness*, p. 159. "The lotus under your feet remains firm" is a poetic expression meaning to be well and active. In brief, Gyaltsap is saying that he wished to be with Tsongkhapa until the master's death.

274. Citing Gyaltsap's biography, entitled *Wellspring of Enlightened Qualities* (*Yon tan gyi chu gter*) by the third Drakyap Chungtsang Lobsang Tenpa (1683–1739), this story is told in Yeshé Dhöndrup, *Entryway to the Ocean of Pure Faith*, p. 157. A less colorful version appears in another text, a short biography of Tsongkhapa by the fifteenth-century Nyingma master Neringpa Chimé Rapgyé ("Delighting the Faithful," p. 584).

275. *rtsod bzang mchog gyur dar ma rin chen te*. Sangyé Tsemo, *Biography of Glorious Rendawa*, p. 59.

276. Khedrup, *Entryway of Faith*, p. 135. Khedrup speaks of how, at the time of his writing, this annual multiday Dharma celebration provided the only opportunity for the monks of the monasteries in the Nyal region to participate in a shared Dharma activity.

277. *Golden Rosary*, Collected Works, vol. *tsa*, p. 291b:1 (typeset p. 432). The position, as presented in this citation from *The Golden Rosary*, that nothing is perceived when one realizes emptiness, is at odds with Tsongkhapa's more mature views on emptiness.

278. For an introduction to Dolpopa and his Shentong view (in contemporary language), see Cyrus Stearns, *The Buddha from Dolpo* (Ithaca: Snow Lion

Publications, 1999). English translation of Dolpopa's key text, *Ri chos nges don rgya mtsho*, is available under the title *Mountain Doctrine: Tibet's Fundamental Treatise on Other-Emptiness and the Buddha Matrix*, trans. Jeffrey Hopkins (Ithaca: Snow Lion Publications, 2006).

279. *Golden Rosary*, vol. *tsa*, ch. 1, p. 278b:5 (typeset p. 413).
280. Chapa's most famous work on Madhyamaka philosophy is entitled *Great Summary of the Thought of Three Eastern Madhyamaka Masters* (*dbu ma shar gsum gyi stong thun*).
281. Khedrup, *Secret Biography*, p. 64; Lekpa Sangpo, *Feast of Excellent Tales*, p. 498.
282. Khedrup's *Entryway of Faith* (p. 135) and *Secret Biography* (p. 64) and Lekpa Sangpo's *Feast of Excellent Tales* (p. 498) all mention the reading of Buddhapālita's text as the key to his breakthrough into the view of emptiness. Chahar (*Source of All Goodness*, p. 161) tells a more colorful story of how, the next day, a monk brought Buddhapālita's text as a gift for Tsongkhapa.
283. *Treatise on the Middle Way* (*Mūlamadhyamakakārikā*), 24:14; for an alternative translation, see Sideris and Katsura, *Nagarjuna's Middle Way*, p. 276.
284. Khedrup, *Entryway of Faith*, p. 136.
285. "Hymn to Tsongkhapa," *Miscellaneous Writings*, p. 353; for an alternative translation, see Thurman, *Life and Teachings*, p. 220.
286. *Ocean of Reasoning*, p. 259b:4 (typeset p. 430); for an alternative translation of the passage, see Samten and Garfield (2006), p. 504.
287. "Three Principal Elements of the Path," *Miscellaneous Writings*, p. 30. My translation of this text in its entirety see can be found at http://www.tibetanclassics.org/html-assets/Three%20Principal%20Aspects.pdf.
288. "In Praise of Dependent Origination," vv. 2–4. The entire text of my translation of this praise is available at http:\\www.tibetanclassics.org/html-assets and Kilty, *Splendor*, pp. 217–45, and Thurman, *Life and Teachings*, pp. 95–102.
289. "Dependent Origination," v. 8.
290. "Dependent Origination," vv. 20–21.
291. "Dependent Origination," vv. 35–37.
292. Neither of these texts appears to be extant today. The most well-known extant commentaries on the text are those of the Second Dalai Lama, Changkya Rolpai Dorjé, Tendar Lharam, Palmang Könchok Gyaltsen, and Choné Lama, the last being in fact an interwoven verse commentary.

293. Of these two texts, the first one appears as a freestanding work in volume *pha* of Tsongkhapa's Collected Works, whereas the second text is found in volume *kha*, alongside many other shorter works as part of a collection of *Miscellaneous Writings.*
294. "Essential Points of Mañjuśrī's Path," p. 1a.
295. "Essential Points of Mañjuśrī's Path," p. 2a:1.
296. "Essential Points of Mañjuśrī's Path," p. 2a:3.
297. "Essential Points of Mañjuśrī's Path," p. 2b:3. Sangyé Tsemo, *Biography of Glorious Rendawa* (p. 65) also refers to Tsongkhapa's question to Mañjuśrī about whether Rendawa also had not realized the final view. The author then criticizes some disciples of Tsongkhapa "who are bold but weak in intellect," claiming that Tsongkhapa's view is superior to that of Rendawa because it is the view of Mañjuśrī.
298. "In Response to Master Rendawa's Letter," *Miscellaneous Writings*, p. 154.
299. "Letter to Dharma Master Lobsang Drakpa Including Expression about the Joy of Solitude," Collected Works, vol. 3, p. 78.
300. "Letter to Dharma Master," p. 80.
301. "Letter to Dharma Master," p. 81.
302. Despite the widespread historical recognition of Rendawa's role in the promotion of Madhyamaka philosophy in Tibet, many of his substantive philosophical writings on the subject do not appear to have been printed, in contrast to those of his student Tsongkhapa. Part of the reason for this might have been political. For subsequent Sakyapas who are keen to reassert themselves, especially with respect to their command of the great Indian Buddhist philosophical classics, Rendawa's closeness to Tsongkhapa might have been a cause for caution. On the other hand, members of Tsongkhapa's own community were far too occupied with ensuring the legacy of their own unique teacher, which meant that they felt no loyalty to Rendawa beyond honoring his memory as Tsongkhapa's principal teacher. Thanks to recent efforts in Tibet, however, we now have access to most of his works, compiled in ten volumes in modern book format. My hope is that the publication of his collected works will inspire scholars to undertake a careful study of Rendawa's philosophy of emptiness and how it contrasts with Tsongkhapa's thought on the subject.
303. "Letter to Dharma Master," pp. 82–83.
304. "Letter to Dharma Master," p. 83.
305. "Letter to Dharma Master," p. 83.

306. "Replies to Questions from the Great Spritual Friend Jangchup Lama," *Miscellaneous Writings*, p. 352. In another letter to this monk, this time sent from Ganden, Tsongkhapa refers to Jangchup Lama's contributions to the study of Buddhist classics in the Amdo area, "in the region where once Gongpa Rapsel and his principal disciple Yeshé Gyaltsen made the doctrine greatly flourish" (*Miscellaneous Writings*, p. 473).

307. *Miscellaneous Writings*, p. 353.

308. Khedrup's collected works (vol. *ka*) contain a short response to one Drupa Palwa who had raised some observations about what he perceived to be differences between Rendawa's and Tsongkhapa's views on emptiness. Khedrup does admit a few areas where, on the surface, there are apparent differences between the two, but he asserts that in the final analysis and in their ultimate intent, their views converge. Citing a specific example of such a perceived difference, Khendrup concludes, "on this point, I know both the intention and the tone of teacher and his spiritual son to be the same" (*dgongs pa gcig dang dbyang gcig tu bdag gis rtogs; Miscellaneous Writings*, p. 714). Khedrup's letter suggests that questions were being raised, especially by those who had known both Rendawa and Tsongkhapa, on possible differences between the two masters on the view of emptiness.

309. *bla ma rin po che bka' bzhi pa blo bzang grags pa las springs pa*. *Letters of Master Rendawa*, Collected Works, vol. 3, p. 72.

310. This detail is found in Chahar, *Source of All Goodness* (p. 177), but he does not provide his source.

311. This timeline is from Khedrup, *Entryway of Faith*, p. 137.

312. In the concluding part of this work, Tsongkhapa speaks of how various individuals have asked him to write on the stages of the path but he had not done so until this point. However, "given that you, the sublime one, are different from others, and also you had sent such a forceful letter that also contains other reasons that are most compelling, I have offered a brief presentation shunning elaborations such as correlating the points with scriptural citations and reasoned analysis." *Miscellaneous Writings*, p. 401.

313. *Hundred Thousand Songs of Milarepa* (Tib.), p. 509. For an alternative translation of these lines, see Christopher Stagg's 2016 edition, p. 367. Since *Hundred Thousand Songs of Milarepa*, in its present form, was compiled later by Tsangnyön Heruka (1457–1507), Tsongkhapa must have had at his disposal an earlier compilation of these songs.

314. This detail about Tsongkhapa's reading of Milarepa's songs is found in Jamyang Tenpai Nyima's *Birth Stories of Great Tsongkhapa*, p. 191, and repeated in Lobsang Trinlé, *Extensive Biography*, p. 262.

315. Yeshé Dhöndrup (*Entryway to the Ocean of Pure Faith*, p. 194) cites Lodrö Gyaltsen's biography, written by one Namkha Chösang, which offers such details as how the young monk saw Tsongkhapa as an actual buddha, and how the master in turn affectionately called him "young monk of good karma" (*btsun chung las 'bras pa*). According to the biography, Tsongkhapa later sent the monk and eight others to study at Kyormolung Monastery. This is the bodhisattva Lodrö Gyaltsen who later founded Demothang and Pema Nyiding monasteries; he should not be confused with Chenga Lodrö Gyaltsen of Gyama Rinchen Gang Monastery, who also would become Tsongkhapa's student and would author the famed text *Initial Mind Training Opening the Door of Dharma* (*thog ma'i blo sbyong chos kyi sgo 'byed*).

316. Könchok Jikmé Wangpo, *Garland of Jewels* (p. 40a:2), tells the story of how, during his visit, as the group was crossing a bridge across the Tsangpo River, Tsongkhapa's hat flew off and fell into the river. This made Tsongkhapa remark, "In the valleys of this river here, my teachings will flow like the constant stream of the river." Later, Sangnak Thekchen Ling Monastery would be founded in the region.

317. Lechen, *History of Kadam Tradition*, p. 693. Lobsang Trinlé (*Extensive Biography*, p. 267) states, "It appears that at this teaching at Potala, Rongtön Shākya Gyaltsen and Ngorpa Künsang and others sought to be in the presence of Jé Rinpoché and listened to his teachings." "Ngorpa" here refers to Ngorchen Künga Sangpo, the famed master of the Ngor lineage of the Sakya tradition, who was at the time around seventeen years old.

318. Lechen, *History of Kadam Tradition*, p. 748.

319. These details of Rendawa's reception at Gadong Monastery are found in Sangyé Tsemo's *Biography of Glorious Rendawa*, p. 80, and repeated in some of the lengthier biographies of Tsongkhapa.

320. Sangyé Tsemo, *Biography of Glorious Rendawa*, p. 81; cited also in Könchok Jikmé Wangpo (*Garland of Jewels*, p. 40b:4) and Lobsang Trinlé (*Extensive Biography*, p. 268).

321. Khedrup, *Entryway of Faith*, p. 139.

322. The account of Rendawa's receiving these teachings from Tsongkhapa is found in Nenying, *Doorway to Faith*, p. 391, and cited in Yeshé Dhöndrup, *Entryway to the Ocean of Pure Faith*, p. 200.

323. Khedrup (*Entryway*, p. 139) simply mentions that Tsongkhapa paid a visit to Drigung Thil in the spring and received teachings from its patriarch; the more specific details are found in Könchok Jikmé Wangpo (*Garland of Jewels*), p. 41b:1. A brief biography of Drigung Chökyi Gyalpo in *Lhorong History of Buddhism* (p. 420) identifies him as one of Tsongkhapa's root gurus.

324. This praise is found in his *Miscellaneous Writings*, pp. 24–26.

325. English translations of this prayer can be found in Jinpa and Elsner, *Songs of Spiritual Experience*, pp. 129–33; Kilty, *Splendor*, pp. 193–207; and Thurman, *Life and Teachings*, pp. 87–91.

326. This visit to Taklung Monastery and its date are confirmed in Sangyé Tsemo's *Biography of Glorious Rendawa*, p. 83.

327. Taklung Ngawang Namgyal, *History of Taklung Tradition*, p. 394. This source speaks in fact of Tsongkhapa spending two weeks at the monastery with Taklung Rinpoché and receiving the transmission of the six yogas of Nāropa from him.

328. Tsongkhapa's earlier biographies and Rendawa's biography mention only what they taught. What Lochen taught is found in Könchok Jikmé Wangpo, *Garland of Jewels*, p. 42a:1.

329. These specifics about Karma Könshön challenging Lochen to a debate are found in Pawo Tsuklak Trengwa, *Feast for the Learned*, p. 972, and repeated in Könchok Jikmé Wangpo, *Garland of Jewels*, p. 42a:3.

330. Sangyé Tsemo's *Biography of Glorious Rendawa* (p. 48) does refer to a debate Rendawa had with Karma Könshön concerning the former's critique of the Kālacakra tantra.

331. In his biographies of Khenchen Sengé Gyaltsen (p. 111) and Sempa Chenpo Namkha Wöser (p. 86), Taktsang Lotsawa too uses the phrase "the three Dharma masters of Ü-Tsang" (*dbus gtsang gi chos rje rnam pa gsum*) when referring to Lochen, Rendawa, and Tsongkhapa.

332. This story about the origin of the four-line hymn is found in Drakyap Lobsang Tenpa, *Sun Illuminating Excellent Insights on the Life of Glorious Tsongkhapa Lobsang Drakpa* (p. 667), and repeated in Lobsang Trinlé, *Extensive Biography* (p. 275).

333. Khedrup, *Entryway of Faith*, p. 141.

334. This conversation is recorded in *Biography of Glorious Rendawa*, p.70. In our own time, the American emotion psychologist Paul Ekman has remarked that after spending some time with the Dalai Lama he experi-

enced no episodes of anger for a long while, despite having often struggled with anger in his life. Personal communication at a gathering where the author was present.

335. These details about Tsongkhapa praying in the presence of Atiśa's statue and the subsequent visions are found in Tokden's *Supplement*, p. 20.

336. This story about Tsongkhapa's doubt about writing the section on insight and the vision of Mañjuśrī encouraging him is found in Lekpa Sangpo, *Feast of Excellent Tales*, p. 199.

337. Lekpa Sangpo, *Feast of Excellent Tales*, p. 199. "Twenty types of emptiness" refers to a list differentiating emptiness in terms of its bases, such as inner emptiness (emptiness of the senses), outer emptiness (emptiness of the sense objects), and so on, presented in the Perfection of Wisdom sūtras.

338. Ruegg, Introduction, *The Great Treatise on the Stages of the Path*, vol. 1, p. 23.

339. *Songs of Experience*, v. 7. My translation of the entire text of this verse is available at: http://www.tibetanclassics.org/html-assets/Songs%20of%20Experience.pdf.

340. Ruegg, *The Great Treatise*, vol. 1, p. 19.

341. *How to Apply the Stages of Realizations in Practice,* Collected Works, vol. *cha*, p. 29a:2; and *How to Undertake the Practice of the Path of the Two Stages of Kālacakra*, Collected Works, vol. *ka*, p. 26b:5.

342. For Tsongkhapa's presentation on the combination of these two approaches, see Ruegg, *The Great Treatise*, vol. 3, pp. 57–90.

343. Lekpa Sangpo, *Feast of Excellent Tales*, p. 508.

344. Ruegg, *The Great Treatise*, vol. 1, p. 20. For the benefit of the general reader, I have excluded Tibetan and Sanskrit terms that were in parentheses in the original source.

345. On the issues and arguments concerning the differentiation between the two types of analysis and their respective domains of discourse, see Jinpa (1998) and Jinpa, ch. 2 in *Self, Reality, and Reason in Tibetan Philosophy*.

346. Shamar Chödrak Yeshé, *Biography of Gö Lotsawa Shönu Pal*, p. 516. Tsongkhapa's *Great Treatise* would inspire an entire genre of texts, referred to as *lamrim* or "stages of the path" instructions. The earliest lamrim texts following upon Tsongkhapa's *Great Treatise* are possibly Chenga Lodrö Gyaltsen's four works on the subject, especially his *Essence of Altruism: An Instruction on the Stages of the Path* (contained in Collected Works, vol. 3). For a literature review of lamrim texts inspired by Tsongkhapa's *Great*

Treatise, see Ruegg, *The Great Treatise* (2000). For a translation and contemporary study of the general introductory part of the insight section of *The Great Treatise*, based on four interwoven annotations by later Geluk thinkers, see Napper, *Dependent Arising*.

347. For an alternative translation of these verses, see Tsong-kha-pa, *The Great Treatise*, vol. 3, pp. 368–69. The tenfold activities of Dharma practice are (1) inscribing the words of the Dharma, (2) making offerings to the buddhas, (3) giving to the needy, (4) listening to the Dharma, (5) upholding the Dharma, (6) reading the scriptures, (7) expounding the Dharma, (8) chanting the scriptures, (9) contemplating the meaning of the scriptures, and (10) engaging in the meditative practice of Dharma.
348. An English translation of this work can be found in Tatz, *Asaṅga's Chapter on Ethics*, pp. 94–269, while a translation of Tsongkhapa's text on tantric precepts can be found in Sparham, *Tantric Ethics*.
349. *An Exposition of the Bodhisattva Ethics*, p. 117b:5. For an English translation of these concluding verses, see Tatz, *Asaṅga's Chapter on Ethics*, p. 262.
350. Khedrup, *Entryway of Faith*, p. 141.
351. Khedrup, *Entryway of Faith*, p. 142. Van der Kuijp ("Please Stand Up," p. 253), on the other hand, speaks of Lochen having promptly made a copy of the final, insight, section of *The Great Treatise* and taking this with him.
352. Panchen Sönam Drakpa, *History of Old and New Kadam Traditions*, p. 171.
353. Tsöndrü Sangpo, "A Short Biography of Incomparable Gyaltsen Sangpo," 3b:1. A rare handwritten manuscript of this biography was recently reproduced by Sertsuk Nangten Penying Publishing House, Lhasa, in its *Gungru rgyal mtshan bzang po'i stong thun dang rnam thar* (Lhasa: Ser gtsug nang bstan dpe rnying dpe skrun khang, 2011). The colophon of the text indicates the date of its composition to be the Wood Dog year (1454).
354. Tsöndru Sangpo, "A Short Biography of Incomparable Gyaltsen Sangpo," p. 6a:5.
355. These details, including Tsongkhapa assigning Gyaltsap to write an exposition on the Perfection of Wisdom, are found in Nenying Künga Delek, *Doorway to Faith*, p. 393. Nenying states that he heard about this when he visited Radreng. Nenying, in fact, interprets Tsongkhapa's explicit authorization of Gyaltsap to write the text as foreshadowing the master's selection of Gyaltsap as his future successor.

356. Gyaltsap, *Opening the Door to the Supreme Vehicle: How to Apply the Stages of Realizations*, Collected Works, vol. *ca*. In his colophon, acknowledging his indebtedness to Tsongkhapa, Gyaltsap speaks of how it was from Tsongkhapa that he himself received the instructions on the stages of the path stemming from Atiśa, wherein "the three streams of the stages of the path instructions come to converge."
357. Khedrup, *Entryway of Faith*, p. 394.
358. This specific detail about Tsongkhapa giving his vest to the hermit is found in Könchok Jikmé Wangpo, *Garland of Jewels*, p. 44a:4. Neringpa ("Golden Tree: An Account of Great Tsongkhapa's Disciples," p. 55) provides additional details about a later meeting between Götruk Repa and Tsongkhapa, at Ganden.
359. This work, *Rnam gzhag rim pa'i rnam bshad*, is found in Collected Works, vol. *cha*.
360. Khedrup, *Entryway of Faith*, p. 143.
361. *rdo rje theg pa'i lam gyi rim pa shin tu rgyas pa zhig*. p. 496b:1.
362. English translations of the first three parts of Tsongkhapa's *Great Treatise on Tantra*, undertaken by Jeffrey Hopkins, are found in three volumes, respectively entitled *Tantra in Tibet*, *Deity Yoga*, and *Yoga Tantra*.
363. Cited in various biographies of Tsongkhapa, including Lobsang Trinlé, *Extensive Biography*, p. 630. In some versions of the cited letter, the third line reads, "I have heard of your two treatises, on Perfection and Tantra."
364. Nenying, *Doorway to Faith*, p. 395.
365. Khedrup, *Entryway of Faith*, p. 143. This sādhana, entitled *rdo rje 'jigs byed kyi sgrub thabs bdud las rnam rgyal*, and the rite of burned offering entitled *rdo rje 'jigs byed kyi sbyin bsreg dngos grub rgya mtsho* are found in Collected Works, vols. *tha* and *da*, respectively.
366. On the emergence of woodblock printing in Tibet and Tsongkhapa's role in promoting it, see p. 449, note 530.
367. Khedrup (*Miscellaneous Writings*, p. 619) speaks of a text based on notes from his debate with Bodong scribed by a Ngamring monk by the name of Dönsang Gyaltsen. Bodong's biography too confirms the existence of such a text but asserts that when it was shown to Rendawa—the teacher of Khedrup, Bodong, and Tsongkhapa—the master expressed his sympathy for Bodong's perspectives. (Jikmé Bang, *Biography of Bodong Choklé Namgyal*, p. 192.)

368. The details of Khedrup's dream are recorded in Chöden Rapjor's "Short Biography of the Omniscient Khedrup" (p. 4b:3), a story repeated in subsequent biographies of Khedrup. It seems from its colophon that Chöden Rapjor was a direct student of both Tsongkhapa and Khedrup himself. For an English translation of this earliest short biography of Khedrup, see Ary, *Authorized Lives*, appendix A.

369. Nenying (*Doorway to Faith*, pp. 395–96) states that he heard this story of Khedup's meeting with Tsongkhapa from Jamyang Chöjé, who was present at the meeting.

370. Chöden Rapjor, "Short Biography of the Omniscient Khedrup," p. 5a:1, and repeated in Lobsang Trinlé, *Extensive Biography*, p. 293. Commenting on Tsongkhapa's commendation of Khedrup's ability to see the indivisible union of the guru and meditation deity, Chöden Rapjor remarks (p. 5a:3), "If you logically examine this story, it becomes clear that Tsongkhapa himself admitted being an emanation of Mañjuśrī. What more proof, scriptural or reasoned, do we need than this story?"

371. Khedrup, *Entryway of Faith*, p. 144.

372. This story is told in Tokden's *Supplement* (p. 23) and repeated in Chahar, *Source of All Goodness*, p. 223.

373. Full translation of this work is found in Thurman, *Central Philosophy of Tibet*.

374. For an alternative translation of this sentence, see Thurman, *Central Philosophy*, p. 189.

375. For a collection of essays by contemporary scholars on the Tibetan differentiation between these two subschools of Madhyamaka, see Dreyfus and McClintock, *The Svātantrika-Prāsaṅgika Distinction*.

376. For an English translation of this part of Tsongkhapa's text from his *Essence of True Eloquence*, see Thurman, *Central Philosophy*, pp. 366–75.

377. For a contemporary study of Tsongkhapa's differentiation between the two domains of analysis, see Jinpa, *Self, Reality, and Reason*, especially pp. 42–48.

378. "Nonimplicative negation" (*prasajya*) refers to simple negation and is contrasted with "implicative negation" (*paryudāsa*), the latter implying something in the process of negation. "Buddhist monks do not drink" is an example of the first kind, and here the act of negation does not imply anything else. In contrast, in the statement "Devadatta does not

eat during the day but he hasn't lost any weight," the speaker implies that Devadatta eats at night. For the Mādhyamika, it is critical that the negation involved in the logic of emptiness is the first kind.

379. For an alternative translation, see Thurman, *Central Philosophy*, p. 381. The first part of Candrakīrti's name, Candra, means "moon" in Sanskrit.

380. In my first year as a student at the Shartsé College of Ganden monastic university in southern India, I had the opportunity to memorize *The Essence of True Eloquence*. Chanting it aloud or listening to someone chant it, one can feel the rhythm of its prose and the inherent literary beauty of its composition, despite the density of the subject matter.

381. For an alternative translation of these lines, see Thurman, *Central Philosophy*, pp. 383–84.

382. Jetsün Chökyi Gyaltsen, *Ocean of Faith*, p. 12a:6. According to this source, Yaktön was so impressed by Tsongkhapa's *Essence of True Eloquence* that he wished to go and receive teachings from Tsongkhapa but was dissuaded by some of his own students.

383. A full English translation of this work by Khedrup is available under the title *A Dose of Emptiness* by José Cabezón.

384. Cabeźon, *A Dose of Emptiness*, p. 52.

385. Khedrup's *Great Summary* will be followed, in the late fifteenth century, by the Second Dalai Lama's *Lamp Thoroughly Illuminating the Intent: A Commentary on the Difficult Points of "The Essence of True Eloquence"* (*Drang nges rnam 'byed kyi dka' 'grel rab tu gsal ba'i sgron me*), Collected Works, vol. *nga*. For a scholarly review and annotated translation of selected passages from key Tibetan expositions of this hermeneutics text, see Hopkins *Emptiness in the Mind-Only School* and *Reflections on Reality*.

386. This specific detail about the delegation turning up at Sera Chöding early in the morning is found in Lobsang Trinlé, *Extensive Biography*, p. 296.

387. Khedrup, *Entryway of Faith*, p. 145.

388. According to the conversion system based on the Tibetan Phugpa School of Astro-science I used earlier, this is July 12, 1408. However, if one uses the Tibetan Phugpa Calendar Calculator at www.digitaltibetan.org, the exact date of Tsongkhapa's letter to Yongle should be dated July 21, 1408. While the Yongle emperor's first letter of invitation does not appear to have been preserved, the entire text of Tsongkhapa's response is found in Tsongkhapa's *Miscellaneous Writings*. Lobsang Trinlé (*Extensive Biography*, p. 301) cites Tsongkhapa's letter from an exact copy preserved at

the Potala Palace, which he says contains a listing of gifts that include, among others, something called *gser bra*, the meaning of which he does not know. The version preserved in the *Miscellaneous Writings*, however, does not mention this item.

389. Cited in full in Lobsang Trinlé, *Extensive Biography*, p. 297. In all three lengthy biographies of Tsongkhapa extant today (those of Chahar, Lobsang Trinlé, and Yeshé Dhöndrup) there is confusion about the chronology with respect to the Yongle emperor's invitation to Tsongkhapa. All three sources seem to assume that Tsongkhapa's letter to Yongle, preserved in his *Miscellaneous Writings*, is the response to the only known version of the emperor's letter. It is evident, however, from the colophon of the Yongle emperor's letter that it was written on the "eleventh day of the second month of the eleventh year of Yongle" (*yun lo bcu gcig pa'i lo zla ba gnyis pa'i tshes bcu gcig nyin*), which is 1413. Tsongkhapa's letter to the emperor, on the other hand, is clearly dated the nineteenth of the sixth month of the Tibetan Rat year, which is 1408. The source of this confusion lies perhaps in the assumption on the part of the three biographers that Tsongkhapa received only one formal invitation from the Chinese emperor. Tokden Jampel Gyatso, a close student and longtime attendant to Tsongkhapa, in fact speaks of Tsongkhapa receiving several invitations from the emperor. In any case, the evidence is strong that there were at least two formal invitations extended to Tsongkhapa, one sometime in 1407/8 and the second in 1413.

390. Yeshé Dhöndrup (*Entryway to the Ocean of Pure Faith*, p. 298) mentions these specifics of the format of Yongle's letter and states that he found an exact copy preserved among the texts at the Potala Palace (*gzung sa'i phyag dpe'i khrod na 'dug pa*).

391. For example, in his *Essence of True Eloquence* (p. 53a:3 and Thurman, *Central Philosophy*, p. 264) Tsongkhapa writes, "As I plan to write an exposition of the *Treatise on the Middle Way*, I shall content myself with what I have already said so far and shall not elaborate further." Many of Tsongkhapa's biographers confuse the chronology of *The Essence* and *The Ocean of Reasoning*, taking the latter to be earlier; this prompts Tseten Shapdrung (*Bstan rtsis kun las btus pa*) to erroneously date *Ocean of Reasoning* to 1407 and *Essence* to 1408.

392. For an alternative English translation of these lines, see Samten and Garfield, *Ocean of Reasoning*, p. 8.

393. Sangyé Tsemo, *Biography of Glorious Rendawa*, p. 41.

394. A unique feature of Tsongkhapa's interpretation of Nāgārjuna's philosophy, as read through Candrakīrti, is his careful marriage of the ontology of emptiness with important aspects of epistemology, especially of Dharmakīrti. On detailed analysis of this marriage and the philosophical challenges entailed in the project, see Ruegg, *Three Studies in the History of Indian and Tibetan Madhyamaka Philosophy*, part 1, section 3. Commenting on the innovative perspectives in Tsongkhapa's reading of Candrakīrti on emptiness, a contemporary scholar of Buddhist philosophy suggests that "a fourteenth-century Tibetan philosophy may have been, in certain significant respects, clearer and even much better philosophy than that of the Indian thinkers on which it was based" (Tillemans, *How Do Mādhyamikas Think?*, p. 5).

395. For an alternative rendering of these lines, see Samten and Garfield, *Ocean of Reasoning*, p. 567.

396. Drago Rapjam, *Music of Wondrous Prophecies*, p. 289.

397. The apocryphal text *The Pillar Testament* (p. 233) identifies these points to be her head, shoulders, elbows, hips, knees, the base of her thighs, ankles, and wrists. At each of these points, a temple is said to have been built to keep the demoness pinned to the ground. Interestingly, Nyangrel's *Honey Essence* (p. 228) speaks of the Chinese princess Wencheng seeing the Tibetan plateau in the form of a demoness lying on her back.

398. Vitali, *Early Temples of Central Tibet*, p. 71. Many Tibetan sources, including both *The Pillar Testament* and Nyangrel's *Honey Essence*, speak of the Chinese princess Wencheng's active role in the construction of the Jokhang, on the basis of her supposed knowledge of Chinese geomancy. If true, this would push the date of the temple's construction to sometime after 641, when she arrived in central Tibet. Modern scholars have pointed out that there is no mention of the Nepalese princess in the *Dunhuang Annals* or Nepalese sources and that the exile of the Nepalese prince Narendradeva in central Tibet had ended by 641. This means at least two things: Wencheng probably never met the Nepalese princess, and the construction of the Jokhang must have been completed before 641. See, for example, Vitali, *Early Temples*, p. 72. Among traditional Tibetan sources, Nelpa Paṇḍita's thirteenth-century work *Flower Garland of Ancient Accounts* (p. 26) presents a view similar to that of contemporary historians. He writes, "As for the temples built by the queens, the Nepalese princess

built the Magical Temple (Jokhang), the Chinese princess Wencheng built Ramoché, and Mongsa Tricham (the Tibetan queen) built Draklha."

399. Vitali, *Early Temples*, p. 74.
400. Van Schaik, *Tibet*, p. 5.
401. For an alternative and insightful interpretation of the word *Rasa* and how it changed into *Lhasa*, see Jinpa and Lopez, *Grains of Gold*, p. 93.
402. Vitali, *Early Temples*, p. 77
403. For example, *The Pillar Testament*, pp. 230–31.
404. *The Pillar Testament*, p. 250.
405. Vitali, *Early Temples*, p. 76.
406. Sönam Gyaltsen, *Clear Mirror of History*, p. 165.
407. *gzugs sku 'di la byang chup sems dpa' ni / lo ni nyis brgyar bsnyen bkur byed par 'gyur. The Pillar Testament*, p. 286.
408. Vitali, *Early Temples*, p. 79, citing the Tibetan historian Pawo Tsuklak Trengwa. The Fifth Dalai Lama (*The Catalog of the Magical Temple of Lhasa*, Collected Works, vol. *dza*, p. 14a:4) mentions other important figures associated with the long history of the Jokhang, including the following: the Yatsé king Rilu Mal, who installed the gilded roof atop the chapel of Buddha Śākyamuni; the Yatsé prince Priti Mal and his minister Palden Drak, who installed the gilded roof atop the chapel of Avalokiteśvara; Nyangral Nyima Wöser (twelfth century) and Lhajé Gewa Bum, the latter especially honored for his renovation of the foundation stones and for building the dikes to protect the Jokhang against possible flooding.
409. This is an eleven-headed Avalokiteśvara, a "self-arisen" icon, believed to have appeared by itself without a sculptor. Inside this large statue is another image of the Buddha, which is said to have been miraculously brought from India by Emperor Songtsen himself by sending an apparition monk. In addition to these two facets, according to the legend, when Emperor Songtsen, Princess Bhṛkuṭī, and Princess Wencheng passed away, all three "dissolved" into the heart of this sacred statue, hence the five facets.
410. Vitali, *Early Temples*, p. 78.
411. Khedrup, *Entryway of Faith*, p. 146.
412. These specific details about the beggars living in some of the chapels, and their subsequent relocation, are found in Chahar's *Source of All Goodness* (p. 234) and mentioned in Shakabpa, *Guide to the Central Temple of Lhasa*, p. 20.

413. Richardson, "The Jokhang 'Cathedral' of Lhasa," p. 241.

414. Shakabpa, *Guide to the Central Temple of Lhasa*, p. 20. Drago Rapjam (*Music of Wondrous Prophecies*, p. 289), on the other hand, states that Tokden Genpo Yeshé's (twelfth century) biography mentions a courtyard with forty pillars being added to the temple complex, which suggests that the current khyamra, with ninety pillars, is an expansion of an existing structure.

415. Khedrup, *Entryway of Faith*, p. 146.

416. These three works are found in his *Miscellaneous Writings*, pp. 562–70 and 586–89.

417. Nenying, *Doorway to Faith*, p. 397.

418. *The Catalog of the Great Prayer Festival*, in *Anthology of Biographies*, vol. 1, p. 641. From Khedrup's reference to "the great catalog produced separately" (*Entryway of Faith*, p. 153), it appears that a separate document was created at the time of the prayer festival, listing the names of the sponsors for specific days and the offerings they had made.

419. These details of thc decoration of the Jokhang, its rooftops, and the Barkhor circuit are drawn from "Catalog of the Great Prayer Festival," Khedrup's *Entryway of Faith* (pp. 147–50), and Nenying's *Doorway to Faith* (pp. 398–401).

420. For a scholarly explanation of the date and historical significance of this treaty pillar, see Richardson, "The Jokhang 'Cathedral' of Lhasa," pp. 106–43.

421. Although Tsongkhapa's biographies describe this as horse-headed (*rta mgo ma*), the Fifth Dalai Lama (*The Catalog of Lhasa*, p. 15b:1) states that it is in fact camel-headed. Vitali (*Early Temples*, p. 84n4) asserts that his personal inspection revealed that the cup is in fact camel-headed, not horse-headed. He suggests that this may be one of the three camel-headed cups mentioned in *The King Testament* as having been buried by Songtsen.

422. Khedrup refers to this bodhicitta ceremony in his *Record of Teachings Received*, p. 4b:2.

423. "Prayer Verses Composed for the Creation of *Perfection of Wisdom*, the *King of Meditations*, and Other Scriptures at Nedong," *Miscellaneous Writings*, pp. 576–86. Tsongkhapa also wrote similar dedication verses when a set of the *Perfection of Wisdom in One Hundred Thousand Lines* was created at Taktsé Estate in the Wölkha Valley (*Miscellaneous Writings*, pp. 580–83).

424. Khedrup, *Entryway of Faith*, p. 402.

425. Nenying, *Doorway to Faith*, p. 402.
426. This specific detail is found in Chahar, *Source of All Goodness*, p. 215.
427. See pages 127–30.
428. It is unclear when this tradition of the candidates for the highest geshé degree sitting for their formal examinations began. This question, connected also with the formal adoption of shared academic curricula, titles, and criteria for examination across the major Geluk monasteries, requires further research.
429. Khedrup, *Entryway of Faith*, p. 154.
430. In some versions of the prophecy, the fourth line reads, "Which mountain it is Mañjuśrī will tell." To my knowledge, none of the early biographies of Tsongkhapa written by his immediate students contains this story. The earliest source I have found for this information is Lechen's *History of Kadam Tradition* (p. 697), completed in 1494, where the author cites these prophetic lines.
431. While Khedrup (*Entryway of Faith*, p. 404) and other early biographies mention Tsongkhapa visiting the site, Chahar (*Source of All Goodness*, pp. 261–62) provides specific details, including Tsongkhapa discovering a spring and unearthing a large conch.
432. Chahar, *Source of All Goodness*, p. 260.
433. The legend of Tsongkhapa's discovery of the two objects on Wangkuri Mountain, and of their significance, including their connection to a prophecy, are told in detail in Drago Rapjam, *Music of Wondrous Prophecies* (pp. 294–96), and also mentioned in Ngawang Chökyi Wangchuk's *Hundred and Eight Wondrous Tales* (p. 250), where it is listed as the eighty-fifth wondrous deed of Tsongkhapa. Both of these authors were contemporaries of the Fifth Dalai Lama.
434. Chahar, *Source of All Goodness*, p. 293.
435. Khedrup, *Entryway of Faith*, p. 405.
436. Khedrup, *Entryway of Faith*, p. 154.
437. Chenga himself states that he had been a student of Tsongkhapa since he was nineteen years old, which would mean that he became his student in 1405/6.
438. An English translation of this text is available in Glenn H. Mullin's *Tsongkhapa's Six Yogas of Naropa*.
439. According to Gendün Drup's *Instruction on Mahāyāna Mind Training* (p. 2a:2), one of the teachings Tsongkhapa conducted at the Samten Ling

Hermitage at the time was an extensive instruction on Chekawa's *Seven-Point Mind Training* combined with the eighth chapter of Śāntideva's *Way of the Bodhisattva*. Hortön Namkha Pal was present at this teaching, and it was from him that Gendün Drup himself received the instructions on mind training.

440. Khedrup, *Entryway of Faith*, p. 155.
441. Khedrup, *Secret Biography*, p. 67. The detail about Tsongkhapa being joined by five of his students is mentioned by Yeshé Dhöndrup (*Entryway to the Ocean of Pure Faith*, p. 262), who attributes it to Jamyang Shepa.
442. Chenga Lodrö Gyaltsen, *Biography of Tokden Jampel Gyatso*, p. 43; cited also in Yeshé Dhöndrup, *Entryway to the Ocean of Pure Faith*, p. 262.
443. Khedrup, *Entryway of Faith*, p. 405.
444. Tsongkhapa's eighteen lines, including the colophon dating the composition, are found in his *Miscellaneous Writings*, Collected Works, vol. *kha*.
445. Khedrup (*Secret Biography*, pp. 67–69) cites all eighteen lines and offers a detailed exposition of each line. What I have produced here is a paraphrase of that section from Khedrup's explanation.
446. Khedrup (*Secret Biography*, p. 69) takes this dream Tsongkhapa experienced, from which he wrote down the eighteen lines, to be the "special sign from the meditation deity" (*'dod pa'i mtshan ma*) that Tsongkhapa refers to in his colophon to a latter work on Guhyasamāja, *Practical Guide on the Five Stages of Guhyamsamāja Completion Stage in a Single Sitting*.
447. Lechen, *History of Kadam Tradition*, p. 607.
448. Shamar Chödrak Yeshé, *Biography of Gö Lotsawa Shönu Pal*, p. 495.
449. *'dul ba'i nang khrims dang dgon pa'i bca' khrims.*
450. The rule books of Jampa Ling are contained in *Miscellaneous Writings*, pp. 589–603.
451. Gö Lotsawa Shönu Pal, *The Blue Annals*, p. 113; for an alternative translation of this sentence, see Roerich, *Blue Annals*, p. 83.
452. According to another system, the four are (1) fully ordained monks and nuns, (2) novices, (3) probationary nuns, and (4) lay practitioners.
453. The colophon of this text states that it was compiled in Wölkha, so it could be dated possibly around 1409 when Tsongkhapa was in the area while the construction of Ganden Monastery was in progress.
454. *klog pa thos bsam gyi 'khor lo / spong ba bsam gtan gyi 'khor lo / bya ba las kyi 'khor lo.*
455. Tsongkhapa's edited versions of the two explanatory tantras are found in

his Collected Works, vol. *ca*. What he did was to create what he considered to be a clean, reliable version of the tantras rather than producing an edition recording all the variant readings, as is the case in producing "diplomatic editions." The only annotation system in use by Tibetans at the time was interlinear annotation, whereby the notes are inserted into the body of the text in a smaller font, either directly after a key word or below, with dots indicating the part of the main text to which the note is connnected.

456. *Miscellaneous Writings*, p. 477. The receipt of this letter and the gift of the Maitreya statue are confirmed by Karmapa's biography found in Chökyi Jungne's *Garland of Countless Moonstone Gems*, p. 550.

457. An authoritative translation of this important work by Gavin Kilty is available as part of The Library of Tibetan Classics series, under the title *Lamp to Illuminate the Five Stages* (Boston: Wisdom Publications, 2017).

458. On the transmission of the Guhyasamāja tantra in India and Tibet, as outlined in Tsongkhapa's *Lamp*, see Kilty, *Lamp to Illuminate*, chapters 5 and 6. Gö Khukpa Lhatsé's key work, *Great Summary on Guhyasamāja* (*Gsang 'dus stong thun*), is referred to extensively in Tsongkhapa's writings on the tantra.

459. *Collected Works*, vol. *nya*, p. 62b:5.

460. Kilty, *Lamp to Illuminate*, p. 562.

461. Kilty, *Lamp to Illuminate*, p. 566. Tsongkhapa uses the same epithet to refer to himself in *A Practical Guide to the Five Stages in One Sitting*, as well as his commentaries on the two explanatory tantras, *Caturdevīpariprccha* and *Vajrajñānasamuccaya*.

462. *Lucid Summary of the Five Stages*, v. 1bc, as cited in Tsongkhapa's *Practical Guide on the Five Stages of Guhyasamāja Completion Stage in a Single Sitting*, p. 5b:2.

463. The use of this tripartite framework became so widespread that later Tibetan authors would employ it even to present the systems of various Indian philosophies, including those of the non-Buddhist schools.

464. "Notes on 'A Lucid Summary of the Five Stages'" (*rim lnga bsdus pa'i zin bris*), Collected Works, vol. *cha*.

465. "Notes on 'A Lucid Summary of the Fives Stages,'" p. 1a:1.

466. *A Practical Guide to the Five Stages in One Sitting*, Collected Works, vol. *nya*, p. 2b:1.

467. This short text is found in Tsongkhapa's *Miscellaneous Writings*, pp. 447–57.
468. For an alternative translation of this passage, see Kilty, *Lamp to Illuminate*, p. 109.
469. See, for example, Rhoton, *Clear Differentiation*, p. 129 (Tibetan language edition p. 3:255).
470. Kilty, *Lamp to Illuminate*, p. 108; translation slightly modified.
471. Kilty, *Lamp to Illuminate*, p. 104.
472. Kilty (*Lamp to Illuminate*, p. 105) translates this passage as "the melting bodhicitta brought on by the blazing caṇḍālī ignited by the force of the winds entering the dhūtī from the practice of penetrating the vital points of the channel cakras in the body."
473. Kilty, *Lamp to Illuminate*, p. 107.
474. For a succint contemporary presentation on the place of sexual desire and sexual bliss in Buddhist thought in general and in tantra in particular, see the Afterword in Lopez and Jinpa, *Treatise on Passion*.
475. Kilty, *Lamp to Illuminate*, p. 68.
476. Kilty, *Lamp to Illuminate*, pp. 125–28.
477. *Five Stages in One Sitting*, Collected Works, vol. *nya*, p. 23b:4.
478. This translation is based on Kilty, *Lamp to Illuminate*, p. 251, with minor modifications.
479. Kilty, *Lamp to Illuminate*, p. 103.
480. Khedrup's collected works, vol. *pa*, contains a short text entitled, "Explanation of Some of Tsongkhapa's Oral Instruction by Relating Them with the Two Guides, the *Lamp* and *One Sitting*" (*rje'i zhal shes 'ga' zhig gsal sgron dang gdan rdzogs dang sbyar te bshad pa*).
481. This work is contained in Khedrup's collected works, vol. *ma*. On the complicated relationship between this work and other texts found in Tsongkhapa's collected works, see note 566.
482. Khedrup, *Entryway of Faith*, p. 156.
483. "An Uncommon Oral Instruction from Lord Mañjuśrī's Teaching Scribed by Tsongkhapa and Sent to Master Rendawa," Collected Works, vol. *na*, p. 8a:4.
484. The currently extant *Biography of Glorious Rendawa* (p. 108) mentions only that a portion of Rendawa's ashes were sent to Tsongkhapa, but Yeshé Dhöndrup (*Entryway to the Ocean of Pure Faith*, p. 274) cites another biography (possibly a lost one) with details connected with the statue.

485. This dream is recorded in Khedrup's *Secret Biography*, pp. 69–70.
486. Khedrup, *Entryway of Faith*, p. 157.
487. Neringpa, *Golden Tree*, p. 543.
488. While Khedrup's *Entryway of Faith* (p. 158) speaks only of Tsongkhapa's health improving as a result of the healing rites, the specific details of these rites and the visions he experienced are found in *Secret Biography*, pp. 71–72.
489. For Tsongkhapa's letter to the Yongle emperor and the emperor's earlier formal invitation, see p. 229–32.
490. Khedrup, *Secret Biography*, p. 72; Lekpa Sangpo, *Feast of Excellent Tales*, p. 506.
491. Khedrup, *Secret Biography*, p. 72; Lekpa Sangpo, *Feast of Excellent Tales*, p. 506. Lekpa Sangpo records another dream Tokden had around this time, in which he saw a tall white stūpa, said to be that of Tsongkhapa, surrounded by six smaller ones. Tokden would later share this dream with Tsongkhapa.
492. Lekpa Sangpo, *Feast of Excellent Tales*, states, "From the fifth day of the sixth month of the Horse year (1414) the master's ill health was cleared."
493. Tsongkhapa's colophon to his *Annotations* (p. 519b:2) speaks of how there had been "three stages" (*rim pa gsum*) in finalizing the Tibetan translation of Candrakīrti's *Clear Lamp*: first was the translation of the text by Lochen Rinchen Sangpo; this was then revised by Gö Khukpa Lhatsé with help of the Indian paṇḍita Jñānākāra; finally, Gö himself undertook another revision with the help of another Indian paṇḍita, Kṛṣṇa Samadhivajra. Tsongkhapa states that he collected all of Gö's explanations of this final revised translation of Candrakīrti's text and made some further editorial corrections himself.
494. Many biographies of Tsongkhapa erroneously date the composition of his interlinear annotations on the Guhyasamāja root tantra and its commentary by Candrakīrti to the period after the summer teaching festival at Tashi Dhokha. Panchen Sönam Drakpa (*History of Old and New Kadam Traditions*, p. 52) points out that this error is due to a passage in Khedrup's *Entryway of Faith* (p. 158) that may have been read to imply that the work was authored after the Tashi Dhokha teaching festival.
495. Gö Lotsawa Shönu Pal, *The Blue Annals*, vol. 1, p. 444; for an alternative translation of this passage, see Roerich, *Blue Annals*, p. 366.
496. That the Tashi Dhokha teaching festival took place in the summer of

1415 is confirmed by other independent sources, such as the biographies of Gendün Drup and Gö Lotsawa Shönu Pal, both of whom first met Tsongkhapa at the teaching, and by the biography of Jampa Lingpa by Jangchup Namgyal Gelek (p. 9a:2). The biography of Miwang's younger brother Chenga Sönam Gyaltsen, who became a close disciple of Tsongkhapa, also mentions his attendance at this teaching. Gö Lotsawa speaks of how Tsongkhapa, when teaching his hermeneutic work, *The Essence of True Eloquence*, remarked that there exists a specific hermeneutic approach from the perspective of Maitreya's *Ratnagotravibhāga* that is consonant with the principles he had outlined in his text. "Given that the attending students lacked the appropriate karmic receptivity," Gö Lotsawa continues, "when such words were uttered, not even a single person came forward to make a maṇḍala offering and request for this to be taught. For my own part, I was able to gain great insights appropriate to my own capacity." (Shamar Chödrak Yeshé, *Biography of Gö Lotsawa Shönu Pal*, p. 473.) Years later, Gö Lotsawa himself would write a lengthy work on Maitreya's *Ratnagotravibhāga*.

497. Lechen, *History of Kadam Tradition*, p. 703.
498. Nenying, who was himself a student of Gendün Drup, describes this first encounter in his *Doorway to Faith*, p. 412.
499. Yeshé Dhöndrup, *Entryway to the Ocean of Pure Faith*, p. 277.
500. Lechen (*History of Kadam Tradition*, p. 760) mentions how senior monks at Narthang, where Gendün Drup was based at the time, told the young Gendün Drup that Ganden Monastery was the best place to deepen one's command of Madhyamaka and pramāṇa. Similarly, Taktsang Lotsawa's autobiography (p. 24) indicates that during his student years he studied Madhyamaka primarily with Jamyang Chöjé based on Tsongkhapa's writings.
501. Yeshé Dhöndrup (*Entryway to the Ocean of Pure Faith,* p. 278), lists Ngorchen as well.
502. Shamar Chödrak Yeshé, *Biography of Gö Lotsawa Shönu Pal*, p. 464.
503. Jangchup Namgyal Gelek, *Biography of Jampa Lingpa*, p. 9b:1.
504. Panchen Sönam Drakpa, *History of Old and New Kadam Traditions*, p. 110. Tsangtön Kunga Gyaltsen's "Life of Omniscient Jamyang Chöjé Tashi Palden" (p. 70) speaks of a different dream connected with the founding of Drepung; cited in Yeshé Dhöndrup, *Entryway to the Ocean of Pure Faith*, p. 275, as well. This biography of Jamyang Chöjé erroneously identifies

the year Tsongkhapa advised Jamyang Chöjé to found Drepung while at Tashi Dhokha Hermitage to be that of the Water Snake (1413).

505. Yeshé Dhöndrup (*Entryway to the Ocean of Pure Faith*, p. 278) identifies locations for four of these statues: in front of the Avalokiteśvara icon in the Jokhang Temple, inside the Drepung prayer hall, at Tashi Lhünpo Monastery, and at Ganden Monastery. The *Biography of Jampa Lingpa* (p. 9b:2), on the other hand, speaks of young Jampa Lingpa drawing, on a wooden plank on the back of Tsongkhapa's throne at Tashi Dhokha, a beautiful portrait of Tsongkhapa, which later became an important object of admiration and worship.

506. Khedrup, *Entryway of Faith*, p. 158.

507. The dating of the composition of this medium-length version of *Treatise on the Stages of the Path* is based on Yeshé Dhöndrup, *Entryway to the Ocean of Pure Faith*, p. 281. English translations of the insight or emptiness section of this text can be found in Thurman, *Life and Teachings*, pp. 103–69, and Hopkins, *Tsong-kha-pa's Final Exposition of Wisdom*.

508. Asaṅga, *Śrāvaka Levels*, Tengyur, vol. 73, p. 381.

509. *Middle-Length Treatise on the Stages of the Path to Enlightenment*, Collected Works, vol. *pha*, p. 164a:1.

510. Ibid., p. 165a:1. According to Chenga Lodrö Gyaltsen ("Ultimate Path of the Ear-Whispered Transmission: A Guide to the Middle View Transcending All Extremes," p. 39), some of Tsongkhapa's immediate disciples appeared to have held the view that meditative practice that involves nonmentation is nothing but a concoction by unlearned Tibetan meditators. Citing both *The Great Treatise* and the *Middle-Length Treatise on the Stages of the Path*, Chenga states emphatically that Tsongkhapa in fact accepts a legitimate tranquility practice that involves simple abiding in a state of mere nonconceptuality (*sems mi rtog pa tsam*). The nature and status of nonconceptual meditation would remain an important issue for debate within Tsongkhapa's Geluk tradition, with some equating it with the discredited views of the Chinese monk Hoshang, while others, like Tokden Jampel Gyatso (1356–1428), Chenga Lodrö Gyaltsen (1402–72), Khedrup Norsang Gyatso (1423–1513), Panchen Lobsang Chökyi Gyaltsen (1570–1662), Changkya Rolpai Dorjé (1717–86), and Tendar Lharam (1759–1831) advocated a nuanced perspective like that outlined in Tsongkhapa's *Middle-Length Treatise on the Stages of the Path*.

511. This verse is by the Indian master Amoghavajra and is cited in Tsongkhapa's *Milking the Wish-Granting Cow*, p. 16a:1. Tsongkhapa provides (pp. 15a:1–16a:2) some specific details on Lūipa's life (his name spelled also as Lūyipa or Lūhipa), including his parents' names and the fact that he was from the Swat Valley region of modern-day Pakistan.

512. This sādhana, entitled *Bcom ldan 'das dpal 'khor lo bde mchog gi mngon par rtogs pa'i rgya cher bshad pa 'dod pa 'jo ba,* is contained in Collected Works, vol. *ta*. Khedrup (*Entryway of Faith*, p. 412) simply provides a list of major tantric texts Tsongkhapa composed following his return to Ganden Monastery from the Tashi Dhokha rainy-season retreat. He does not provide any details on the sequence of the writing of these texts.

513. Both of these sādhanas are contained in Collected Works, vol. *ta*.

514. For an alternative translation, see Kilty, *Lamp to Illuminate*, p. 113.

515. *Sheaves of Attainments*, Collected Works, vol. *dza*, p. 45a:5.

516. *Sheaves of Attainments*, Collected Works, vol. *dza*, p. 2a:2.

517. *Lū hi pa'i lugs kyi rdzogs rim rnal 'byor chen po'i khrid kyi rim pa mdor bsdu pa*. The text is contained in Collected Works, vol. *dza*.

518. In the opening section of his text, Tsongkhapa provides some details of the life of Ghaṇṭapa, probably drawn from Abhayadatta's *Lives of Eighty-Four Mahāsiddhas*.

519. These two works, entitled *Dril bu pa'i lugs kyi lus dkyil gyi mngon rtogs dgongs pa rab gsal* and *Lus dkyil dbang chog rin po che'i bang mdzod*, respectively, are contained in Collected Works, vol. *tha*.

520. *Lus dkyil dbang chog rin po che'i bang mdzod*, Collected Works, vol. *tha*, p. 28b:3.

521. *mang du thos pa'i dge slong 'khor lo sdom pa'i rnal 'byor pa shar tsong kha pa blo bzang grags pa'i dpal*. This work is contained in Collected Works, vol. *tha*.

522. An English translation of this work is available in Mullin's *Tsongkhapa's Six Yogas of Naropa*.

523. Kunga Gyaltsen, *Meaningful to Behold*, Collected Works, vol. *ka*, p. 40b:5 (p. 257).

524. Chenga Sönam Gyaltsen, *Garland of Lapis Lazuli: Dispelling Misunderstandings Concerning Kagyu Thought*, Collected Works, vol. *kha*, p. 82b:3 (p. 164).

525. Collected Works, vol. *ta*, p. 65a:3.

526. Chenga Sönam Gyaltsen, *A Thousand Light Rays Illuminating Great Bliss: A Guide to the Six Yogas of Nāropa*, Collected Works, vol. *kha*, p. 3b:5 (p. 199).

527. Chenga Sönam Gyaltsen, *Garland of Lapis Lazuli*, p. 83b:1 (p. 166).

528. Khedrup, *Entryway of Faith*, p. 414.

529. Ngawang Jamyang Nyima's "The Liberating Story of How Jamchen Chöjé Shākya Yeshé Went to the Chinese Palace on Behalf of Great Tsongkhapa" actually states, "Having reached Sera in central Tibet, he met with the precious master" (p. 6b:1), suggesting that Tsongkhapa was at the time (in 1416) at Sera Chöding Hermitage. However, since all the biographies of Tsongkhapa are unanimous in maintaining that Tsongkhapa did not descend Ganden Mountain between the fall of 1415 and the fall of 1419, it must have been at Ganden where Jamchen Chöjé met with Tsongkhapa upon returning from China. This short biography of Jamchen Chöjé does not mention his bringing the gift of the printed Kangyur, but it is mentioned in later sources, such as Yeshé Dhöndrup (*Entryway to the Ocean of Pure Faith,* p. 331), who says this Kangyur is housed at Sera Monastery.

530. For a brief history of Tsongkhapa's role in promoting woodblock printing in Tibet, and how his works were probably the first printed texts in Tibet, see Jackson, "The Earliest Printing of Tsong-kha-pa's Works."

531. Yeshe Dhöndrup, *Entryway to the Ocean of Pure Faith*, p. 284.

532. Yeshe Dhöndup, *Entryway to the Ocean of Pure Faith*, p. 289.

533. Khedrup, *Entryway of Faith*, p. 415. The Tibetan texts give the height as "seventeen *mtho*s when measured at the back," *mtho* being the measure of the space covered from the tip of the thumb to the tip of the ring finger when the two are fully extended (approximately eight and one-half inches).

534. Khedrup, *Entryway of Faith*, p. 416. Tokden (*Supplement*, p. 25) speaks of how, when the large statue of the meditation deity Vajrabhairava was being sculpted, his central face emerged as if naturally, and also of how when the three-dimensional maṇḍalas were being created, the three principal deities—Vajradhātu, Akṣobhya, and Cakrasaṃvara—emerged as if naturally.

535. Cited in Yeshe Dhöndrup, *Entryway to the Ocean of Pure Faith*, p. 287.

536. Tokden, *Supplement*, p. 26.

537. *Miscellaneous Writings*, p. 531.

538. Tokden, *Supplement*, p. 26.

539. Khedrup, *Entryway of Faith*, p. 162.

540. Gyama Rinchen Gang Monastery was founded in the twelfth century by Shönu Drakpa (1090–1171), a disciple of the famed Kadam master

Neusurpa. The monastery was rebuilt in 1181 by the founder's nephew, Sangye Wötön, also known as Wötön Rinpoché, a renowned scholar during his lifetime. The Kashmiri paṇḍita Śākyaśribhadra is said to have visited the monastery twice at the invitation of Wötön Rinpoché.

541. Lodrö Jikmé Gyaltsen, *Opening the Door of Faith: A Biography of Chenga Lodrö Gyaltsen*, p. 2.

542. Hortön Namkha Pal, *Rays of Sun: A Mind-Training Guide*, p. 2b:1. English translation of this text is available under the title *Mind Training Like the Rays of the Sun*, translated by Brian Beresford (Dharamsala: Library of Tibetan Works & Archives, 1992).

543. This is possibly the text referred to by the twentieth-century Geluk author and teacher Mugé Samten as "Jangsem Radrengwa's *Stream of Bodhicitta*" (*Biography of Jikmé Trinlé Gyatso*, Collected Works, vol. 1, p. 24). Mugé lists this text among many other works on which Jikmé Trinlé Gyatso had received teachings, suggesting that it was extant in the nineteenth century. Despite my efforts, I have not been able to locate it.

544. Panchen Sönam Drakpa, *History of Old and New Kadam Traditions*, p. 52.

545. This work is contained in Collected Works, vol. *na*.

546. Rendawa, "Jewel Garland: An Open Letter Addressed to the Upholders of the Dharma Concerning Critical Examination of Kālacakra Tantra," especially pp. 116–20.

547. The listing of these questions is based on Taktsang Lotsawa's *Thousand Lights of Reasoning: A Rebuttal* (*Rtsod lan lung dang rigs pa'i 'od stong*), his response to Rendawa's uncertainties about Kālacakra. For a detailed discussion of Rendawa's critique of Kālacakra, see Jinpa, "Rendawa and the Question."

548. *A Memorandum on Clear Differentiation of the Difficult Points of Stainless Light* (*Stong phrag bcu gnyis pa dri ma med pa'i 'od kyi dka' ba'i gnas rnam par 'byed pa brjed byang*), Collected Works, vol. *na*, p. 14a:1.

549. Ibid., p. 13b:4; Tsongkhapa also provides a specific treatment of the nature of the fourth empowerment in Kālacakra in his *Great Exposition of Tantra*, Collected Works, vol. *ga*, pp. 310b:6–313b:6.

550. *Great Exposition of Tantra*, p. 312b.

551. *Great Exposition of Tantra*, p. 440a.

552. Gö Lotsawa Shönu Pal, *The Blue Annals*, p. 931; for an alternative translation, see Roerich, *Blue Annals*, p. 795.

553. This dating is based on Yeshé Dhöndrup, *Great Exposition of Tantra*, p. 296.

554. Both of these texts, the sādhana and the rites of empowerment, are contained in Collected Works, vol. *tha*.

555. Panchen Yeshé Tsemo's *Biography of Gendün Drup* (p. 13b:3) mentions how around this time, in the fall of 1418, Gendün Drup visited Tsongkhapa at Ganden. After receiving teachings on lamrim and the master's exposition of the root tantra of Cakrasaṃvara, Gendün Drup returned to his home monastery, Sangphu.

556. Khedrup, *Entryway of Faith*, p. 162. See also Jackson, "The Earliest Printing."

557. Lekpa Sangpo (*Feast of Excellent Tales*, p. 509) speaks of various signs indicative of the presence of this Dharma protector around Tsongkhapa, including experience of its presence by some of Tsongkhapa's attendants.

558. *Miscellaneous Writings*, p. 113.

559. It is evident from the colophon of Lochen's text that it was completed in 1399 (the Earth Rabbit year), making it quite possibly the first known Tibetan commentary on Candrakīrti's *Entering the Middle Way*. Rendawa's text, however, does not specify the year of its composition, so it is difficult to determine when it was written. That Tsongkhapa was aware of Rendawa's commentary can be inferred from occasional references to Rendawa's interpretation of specific passages of *Entering the Middle Way* in Tsongkhapa's *Elucidation of the Intent*.

560. Tsongkhapa, *Elucidation of the Intent: A Thorough Exposition of "Entering the Middle Way,"* translated by Thupten Jinpa (Library of Tibetan Classics; forthcoming).

561. Perhaps the earliest reader on *Elucidation of the Intent* was the one by Lodrö Rinchen Sengé, a direct disciple of Tsongkhapa and the founder of Sera Jé College of Sera Monastery. This was followed by the Second Dalai Lama's *Adornment of the Clear Elucidation of the Intent: An Exposition of Entering the Middle Way*; Jetsün Chökyi Gyaltsen's *Presentation of the General Points on Madhyamaka* (*Dbu ma'i spyi don*); and Panchen Sönam Drakpa's *General Points* (*spyi don*) and *Analysis* (*mtha' dpyod*), which were followed by numerous other similar "textbooks" (*yig cha*) on Madhyamaka that used Tsongkhapa's *Elucidation* as the basis.

562. Chahar, *Source of All Goodness*, p. 310.

563. Jamyang Shepa, *Garland of Cintamani Gems*, p. 525; Yeshé Dhöndrup, *Entryway to the Ocean of Pure Faith*, p. 296; Chahar, *Source of All Goodness*, p. 310.

564. Gö Lotsawa Shönu Pal, *The Blue Annals*, p. 471; for an alternative translation of this passage, see Roerich, *Blue Annals*, p. 389.
565. Entitled *Moonlight Illuminating the Essential Points*, this work is contained in Khedrup's Collected Works, vol. *ka*.
566. There is another set of notes on Tsongkhapa's oral instructions, entitled *The Cycle of Short Instructional Pieces on Guhyasamāja Tantra* (*Gsang ba 'dus pa'i man ngag yig chung*), contained in Collected Works, vol. *dza*, which features almost all the texts found in *Door-Frame Essential Instructions* (*Zhal bzhes gnad kyi them yig*). This suggests a complex relationship among the three collections of notes: *Door-Frame Essential Instructions* and *The Cycle of Short Instructional Pieces* (both contained in Tsongkhapa's Collected Works), and Khedrup's *Twenty-One Short Pieces on Guhyasamāja*, which is contained in Khedrup's Collected Works, vol. *ma*.
567. *Cycle of Short Instructional Pieces on Guhyasamāja*, Collected Works, vol. *dza*, pp. 41b:2–43a:6.
568. This text on the transference of consciousness, running to twenty-nine long folios, is contained in Collected Works, vol. *da*.
569. An English translation of this important Indian Buddhist classic is available in James Blumenthal, *The Ornament of the Middle Way: A Study of the Madhyamaka Thought of Shantarakshita* (Ithaca: Snow Lion Publications, 2004).
570. *Notes on "Ornament of the Middle Way,"* Collected Works, vol. *ba*, p. 1b:3.
571. Khedrup, *Entryway of Faith*, p. 176.
572. Khedrup, *Entryway of Faith*, p. 176.
573. Khedrup (*Entryway of Faith*, p. 176) mentions Tsongkhapa being brought on a palanquin (*do li*).
574. Khedrup, *Entryway of Faith*, p. 176.
575. Khedrup, *Entryway of Faith*, p. 176.
576. Tsangtön Kunga Gyaltsen, "Life of Omniscient Jamyang Chöjé Tashi Palden," p. 92.
577. Khedrup, *Entryway of Faith*, p. 177. Jamyang Chöjé's biography (Gyaltsen, "Life of Omniscient," p. 91) also lists these teachings conducted at Drepung during this visit.
578. All of these details surrounding Tsongkhapa's decision to leave Drepung are found in Khedrup's *Entryway of Faith*, p. 177.
579. These details are recorded by Khedrup's *Entryway of Faith*, p. 78.
580. In his *Sun Nourishing the Dharma Lotus: A History of Buddhism* (p. 353),

Drukpa Pema Karpo speaks of Tsongkhapa holding a ritual skull cup in the air and asking for a volunteer who would drink from it. He writes, "As no one dared to volunteer, Sherap Sengé took the cup. Although Khedrup is said to have mocked [Sherap Sengé] for doing so, it was from Sherap Sengé that a tantric monastery first emerged in Tsang, and from this emerged the Upper and Lower Tantric colleges. All of these [monasteries] are true upholders of Marpa's lineage."

581. Chahar, *Source of All Goodness*, p. 330. Panchen Sönam Drakpa (*History of Old and New Kadam Traditions*, p. 98) also mentions Sherap Sengé volunteering to be the custodian of Tsongkhapa's tradition of the study and practice of Guhyasamāja. Khedrup (*Entryway of Faith*, p. 178), on the other hand, simply mentions Tsongkhapa giving an instruction to set up monastic communities to continue with the study and practice of Guhyasamāja and Cakrasaṃvara, without mentioning Sherap Sengé. Yeshé Dhöndrup (*Entryway to the Ocean of Pure Faith*, p. 332) states that according to Sherap Sengé's biography, written by Dungkar Tsangyang Drukdra, it was at Ganden that Sherap Sengé offered his pledge to be the custodian of Tsongkhapa's tantric traditions.
582. Khedrup, *Entryway of Faith*, p. 178.
583. These exchanges are reported by Chahar (*Source of All Goodness*, p. 331), who was probably drawing on a biography of Sherap Sengé that is no longer extant.
584. These details are found in Chahar (*Source of All Goodness*, p. 331), who unfortunately does not provide his source.
585. According to the colophon of a third text, based on notes taken from the discourse on *Spring Drop*, Tsongkhapa appears to have given this teaching at two different hermitages (*dgon gnas gnyis su*). This third text claims to have been produced from merging the notes taken by senior disciples and correlating these with the scriptural sources. *Notes on How to Engage in the Meditations of the Spring Drop Completion Stage*, Collected Works, vol. *dza*.
586. Lechen, *History of Kadam Tradition*, p. 758.
587. These details are found in Khedrup, *Entryway of Faith*, p. 179.
588. Khedrup, *Entryway of Faith*, p. 179.
589. For example, Lobsang Trinlé, *Extensive Biography*, p. 573.
590. These details are found in Khedrup, *Entryway of Faith*, pp. 179–80.
591. Khedrup, *Entryway of Faith*, p. 180.
592. Khedrup, *Entryway of Faith*, p. 180.

593. Chahar, *Source of All Goodness*, p. 334; however, he does not provide his own source.

594. Khedrup, *Entryway of Faith*, p. 181. Inner offering (*nang mchod*) is an important ritual within tantric meditation, which uses a liquid substance like alcohol or black tea inside a skull cup. The ritual involves imaginatively generating from within emptiness a large human skull cup placed upon a tripod supported by a blazing triangle of fire stirred by a wind from beneath. Within this skull cup "five types of meat" and "five types of nectar" are imagined being boiled, the fusion of which is purified with dissolution of the three syllables, OṂ AH HŪṂ, respectively symbolizing the essence of enlightened body, speech, and mind. It is called "inner offering" because all the substances used in this visualization belong to sentient creatures. In contrast, outer offering (*phyi mchod*) refers to rites of offering in which the substances visualized are not part of sentient beings.

595. Khedrup, *Entryway of Faith*, p. 181.

596. This description is from Tsongkhapa's attendant Lekpa Sangpo, as described in his *Feast of Excellent Tales*, p. 510.

597. Khedrup, *Entryway of Faith*, p. 181.

598. In the verse colophon of his "Eighty Tsongkhapas: A Biographical Hymn to Great Tsongkhapa," Jamyang Khaché writes, "This was written on the fifteenth day of the month, / Which fell on the third week following / The great master's departure from this world. . . ." Yeshé Dhöndrup (*Entryway to the Ocean of Pure Faith*, p. 343) erroneously dates the composition of this hymn to the fifth week after Tsongkhapa's passing.

599. The Sanskrit letter *a* being a negative particle, in Mahāyāna Buddhism the letter is often used as a symbol for emptiness, the ultimate nature of reality. Thus, "the meaning of *a*" refers to emptiness.

600. "Eighty Tsongkhapas: A Biographical Hymn to the Great Tsongkhapa," in *Anthology of Biographies*, vol. 1, pp. 601–2. Jamyang Khaché's personal name is Jamyang Sönam Pal.

601. Khedrup, *Entryway of Faith*, p. 186.

602. Khedrup (*Entryway of Faith*, p. 184) speaks of special signs lasting up to forty-nine days and how, while the master was "equipoised in the dharmakāya state, there appeared a halo of rainbow-colored light in front of Tsongkhapa's face." Khedrup does not, however, explicitly say how long Tsongkhapa remained in the clear-light dharmakāya state. My

estimation of thirteen days for Tsongkhapa's thukdam period is based on the account of the master's own attendant Lekpa Sangpo. Thukdam refers to an intriguing phenomenon in which the body of the deceased remains without decomposition for multiple days. In our contemporary time, Kyapjé Ling Rinpoché, who was the senior tutor to the present Dalai Lama and also the ninety-seventh holder of Tsongkhapa's throne, remained in thukdam for thirteen days following his passing in December 1983.

603. Lekpa Sangpo, *Feast of Excellent Tales*, p. 511.
604. Khedrup, *Entryway of Faith*, p. 187.
605. *Miscellaneous Writings*, p. 361.
606. Details from Khedrup, *Entryway of Faith*, pp. 187–88.
607. Khedrup, *Entryway of Faith*, p. 189.
608. Khedrup, *Entryway of Faith*, p. 189; Ngawang Jamyang Nyima, "The Liberating Story of How Jamchen Chöjé Shākya Yeshé Went to the Chinese Palace on Behalf of Great Tsongkhapa," p. 7b:2.
609. Pawo Tsuklak Trengwa, *Feast for the Learned*, p. 1155.
610. Shākya Chokden, *Views Held by Sakya Masters and Their Immediate Heirs*, Collected Works, vol. *'a*, p. 96.
611. Panchen Sönam Drakpa, *New Red Annals*, p. 95. See also Jackson, "The Earliest Printing."
612. Pöntsang Tsewang Gyal, *Lhorong History of Kagyü Tradition*, p. 392. Writing in 1446 (the Fire Tiger year), the author notes, "Having produced all of master's [Tsongkhapa's] sacred collected works, he had performed expansive deeds of Dharma giving." It is not clear whether the word *produced* (*bzhengs pa*) means commissioning the texts to woodblock printing or simply producing handwritten volumes. Taktsang Lotsawa's *Biography of the Great Bodhisattva Namkha Wöser* (p. 94) also mentions Namkha Wöser producing (*bzhengs pa*) "the entire collected works of Butön as well as of the great Tsongkhapa, and half of Rendawa's writings" to be housed in the newly constructed temple at Chökhor Gang Monastery.
613. Yeshé Dhöndrup (*Entryway to the Ocean of Pure Faith*, p. 355) states that Sherap Sengé's biography (no longer extant) mentions how he proofread the entire collection for this project of publishing the master's writings. Unfortunately, we do not have any idea how many volumes this first collection contained or what its catalog looked like, let alone do we possess

a copy of this collection. A careful study is required to determine when and how the established set of Tsongkhapa's collected works (in eighteen or nineteen volumes) came to be finalized.

614. For an English translation of this autobiographical poem, see Thurman, *Life and Teachings*, pp. 35–51.
615. *Miscellaneous Writings*, p. 121; for an alternative translation, see Thurman, *Life and Teachings*, p. 36.
616. Lekpa Sangpo, *Feast of Excellent Tales*, p. 514.
617. The first recorded use of the term *secret biography* to characterize the esoteric dimension of someone's life, especially relating to visionary experiences, appears in the writings of Lhodrak Namkha Gyaltsen, the mystic from Lhodrak whom Tsongkhapa met in 1395 (see chapter 7). After Tsongkhapa's, the best-known secret biographies are those of the Fifth Dalai Lama (*Secret Visions of the Great Fifth Dalai Lama*), Tsangyang Gyatso (the Sixth Dalai Lama), Jonang Taranatha, and Pema Lingpa.
618. Tokden Jampel Gyatso, *Wondrous Tales: A Secret Biography*, p. 10.
619. My hesitation is based on a statement in this short biography: Speaking of Tsongkhapa's devotion and affection for his childhood teacher Chöjé, Tokden writes (*Supplement*, p. 14) that whenever Tsongkhapa "would utter the name of his teacher [Chöjé] he would fold his palms together and tears would fill his eyes. And, even to this day, he observes, without lapse, the anniversary of the teacher's passing." Tokden's use of present tense here is unmistakable. Toward the end of the text (p. 24), however, one finds the following passage: "There are so many inconceivable events in the life [of the master], such as the ones I have just mentioned. As for these, you should look at the one composed by Changra Kachuwa (Khedrup)." One possibility is that Tokden began writing Tsongkhapa's short biography while the master was still alive and finalized it after his death. Another possibility is that the explicit reference to Khedrup's *Secret Biography* is a later insertion by an editor and Tokden meant his short biography as a supplement not to Khedrup's "official" biography but to his own earlier *Secret Biography of Great Tsongkhapa*. General convention among Tsongkhapa's biographers is to treat Tokden's as a supplement to Khedrup's official biography of Tsongkhapa.
620. In the opening verses of his secret biography, Lekpa Sangpo writes, "As for the excellent tales / shareable commonly with everyone, / in relation to your life, / I have striven to declare these elsewhere. / Once again,

however, there is the treasure / of secrets greater than secrets, / tales of wonder unexcelled, / which even the mighty ones cannot outdo. / This nectar stream poured with joy / from the vase that is your mouth / had been scooped up in my mind's hands. / I shall now offer the chance / to taste this nectar to the fortunate ones / who are firm in faith, / the few who have embraced the conduct / of devotion to mentors of the supreme vehicle. / O fortunate ones adorned with beauty of faith, / those earnest with eyes in fixed gaze like an animal, / grab this ornament that will adorn your ears." Lekpa Sangpo, *Excellent Feast of Tales*, p. 515.

621. There appear to have been at least two other lengthy biographies of Tsongkhapa written by the master's immediate disciples. Neringpa ("Golden Tree," p. 556), for example, mentions an extensive biography of Tsongkhapa written by Jamyang Khaché, the author of the eulogy "Eighty Tsongkhapas." Similarly, Thuken Chökyi Nyima (*Crystal Mirror of Philosophical Systems*, p. 90) speaks of another lengthy biography of Tsongkhapa, authored by Joden Sönam Lhundrup, a direct disciple of Tsongkhapa. To the best of my knowledge, neither of these two works is extant today.

622. Segal, *Myth*, p. 6.

623. On Dromtönpa's former life stories, see Thupten Jinpa, "Introduction," in *The Book of Kadam* (Boston: Wisdom Publications, 2008), and part 2, containing translations of four selected stories from the collection.

624. Jamyang Khaché, "Eighty Tsongkhapas: A Biographical Hymn to Great Tsongkhapa," v. 20. The hymn mentions Tsongkhapa receiving a blessing from master Atiśa in a dream during his youth (v. 11); his initial communication with Mañjuśrī through Umapa (v. 25); his own vision of the deity (v. 26); his vision of Mañjuśrī surrounded by the great Indian Buddhist masters that occurred at Gya Sokphu Hermitage (vv. 31–33); his meeting Drupchen and receiving instructions from Vajrapāṇi through the mystic (v. 38); Vajrapāṇi's prophecy that Tsongkhapa would have seven special students (v. 58); and so on.

625. Khedrup, *Entryway of Faith*, p. 183. Later, in a biographical hymn to Tsongkhapa, he makes the same statement about Tsongkhapa's attainment of buddhahood during the intermediate state.

626. This is the prophecy made by Drupchen channeling the meditation deity Vajrapāṇi.

627. Khedrup, *Entryway of Faith*, p. 183.

628. English translation of this hymn can be found in Thurman, *Life and Teachings*, pp. 43–51.
629. All four of these texts are found in the *Anthology of Biographies*, vol. 1.
630. Khedrup Norsang Gyatso, *A Short Account of Great Tsongkhapa and His Disciples*, p. 326. Interestingly, all of these epithets appear to have been taken by Norsang Gyatso from the colophon of Khedrup's *Great Summary on Emptiness*, except that in Khedrup's version, instead of "emanation of Mañjuśrī" he has "heart son of Mañjuśrī" (for alternative translations of these epithets of Tsongkhapa in Khedrup's colophon, see Cabezón, *A Dose of Emptiness*, p. 388. Ary (*Authorized Lives*, pp. 15–22) suggests that it was only around the seventeenth century that the Geluk tradition began characterizing Tsongkhapa as identical with or an emanation of Mañjuśrī. Textual evidence demonstrates this conjecture to be incorrect. To begin with, Tsongkhapa's successor and principal disciple Gyaltsap explicitly uses the epithet "Precious master who is identical with Mañjuśrī, the All-Knowing Glorious Lobsang Drakpa" in the long colophon of his influential work *The Core Ornament: An Exposition of "Ornament of Clear Realizations"* (*Rnam bshad snying po rgyan*). Similarly, in the opening of his "Explaining Some of the Master's Oral Teachings by Relating Them to the *Lamp* and *One Sitting*" (*Rje'i zhal shes 'ga' zhig gsal sgron dang gdan rdzogs dang sbyar nas bshad pa*, p. 1a), Khedrup pays homage to his "sublime guru who is indivisible from Mañjuśrī." Thus, it is not surprising to see Khedrup Norsang Gyatso, a hugely important fifteenth-century figure in the tradition, listing "emanation of Mañjuśrī" as an important epithet of Tsongkhapa.
631. Cited in Nenying, *Doorway to Faith*, p. 404. This passage is translated on p. 345.
632. Lechen, *History of Kadam Tradition*, p. 695; the passage cited is from the chapter of *The Book of Kadam* entitled "Vajra Songs of Immortality."
633. "Propitiation of Dharma Protector Dorjé Drakden," in Collected Works of Gendün Gyatso, vol. *cha*, p. 184. Shapkar Tsokdruk Rangdrol (1781–1851) also cites this verse from the Second Dalai Lama in his *Magical Volume on Padmasambhava* (*O rgyan sprul pa'i glegs bam*, Collected Works, vol. 7, p. 326), and underscores the identification of Padmasambhava with Atiśa and Tsongkhapa. The phrase "five-hundreth" (*lnga brgya*) in the context of "the crown jewel of this five hundredth" alludes to the widespread belief that the Buddha's teaching will last for ten sets of five hundred years.

634. Cited in Panchen Sönam Drakpa, *History of Old and New Kadam Traditions*, p. 54. The passage is found in *Lamp Illuminating Prophecies Concerning the Future* (p. 52), a collection of prophecies attributed to Padmasambhava.

635. Chapter 41 of this work is devoted entirely to prophecies about Tsongkhapa and cites from such varied sources as *The Pillar Testament* (*ka chems ka khol ma*), *The Book of Kadam* (*bka' gdams glegs bam*), the writing of the woman mystic Machik Lapdrön, and several terma texts, with explanatory commentaries on the cited verses.

636. An alternative name of Ganden Monastery, used often by Tsongkhapa himself, is Geden Monastery. "The meeting points of Dri and Den" refers, possibly, to a site between Drigung and Densa Thil.

637. Cited in Kharnak Lotsawa, *History of Ganden Tradition*, p. 5. (Although almost all the prophecies cited in Kharnak are found also in the slightly earlier work Ngawang Chödrak Gyatso's *Poetic Narrative on the Life of Jé Tsongkhapa*. I have chosen Kharnak's *History of Ganden Tradition* as my source here, as it is more well known.) This sūtra, entitled *Mdo sde gdams ngag 'bog pa'i rgyal po*, does not exist in the Tibetan canonical collection of the Kangyur. According to the seventeenth-century Tibetan scholar Drakyap Lobsang Tenpa (*Sun Illuminating Excellent Insights*, p. 611), this sūtra is said to have forty-two chapters; the prophecy on Tsongkhapa is located in the final chapter. Citing oral tradition stemming from Jamyang Shepa, the author asserts that this sūtra also contains prophecies of other Tibetan figures, such as the great Drigung master Kyobpa Jikten Gönpo.

638. Kharnak Lotsawa, *History of Ganden Tradition*, p. 6.

639. The first set of lines Kharnak cites from the tantra is found in Kangyur, rgyud, vol. *ma*, p. 326a:2.

640. Cited in Kharnak's *History of Ganden Tradition*, p. 8.

641. *Clear Words* (*Prasanapada*), Tengyur, vol. 60, p. 660, cites from *Laṅkāvatāra Sūtra* and *Dhamamega Sūtra*.

642. *The Pillar Testament*, p. 287. "Changing the face of the Buddha" is a reference to Tsongkhapa's restoration of the Buddha image at Jokhang Temple, which involved offering a fresh layer of gold paint and adorning the image with a jeweled crown.

643. Kharnak, *History of Ganden Tradition*, pp. 11–12.

644. Cited in Kharnak, *History of Ganden Tradition*, p. 12.

645. Cited in Ngawang Gelek Gyaltsen, *A Chat Concerning Prophecies of Jetsün*

Lobsang Drakpa (completed in 1658), in *Anthology of Biographies*, vol. 2, p. 61.

646. Cited in Ngawang Gelek Gyaltsen, *Anthology of Biographies*, p. 60.

647. In his *White Crystal Mirror: A Catalog of the Magical Temple of Lhasa* (p. 39), Ngawang Lobsang Gyatso, the Fifth Dalai Lama, writes, "There are in many authoritative treasure texts, such as those of Ratna Lingpa and Dorjé Lingpa, extremely elevated praises of master Tsongkhapa. By producing a negative prophecy, Depa Nangtsewa only showed himself to be a fake treasure revealer." A more detailed critique of this "false" prophecy can be found in Ngawang Gelek Gyaltsen's *A Chat Concerning Prophecies of Jetsün Lobsang Drakpa* and Drago Rapjam's (seventeenth century) *Music of Wondrous Prophecies*. Both of these texts are featured in the second volume of the *Anthology of Biographies*.

648. Volume *ga* of Gendün Gyatso's collected works contains a cycle of meditation deity sādhanas, including one on Padmasambhava and one on Hayagrīva, the horse-headed deity popular in the Nyingma tradition.

649. Desi Sangyé Gyatso, *Yellow Beryl*, p. 14.

650. Sumpa Yeshé Paljor, *Excellent Wish-Granting Tree*, p. 482.

651. Thuken (Geshe Lhundrup Sopa et al., *Crystal Mirror*, p. 90) refers to a passage in a now-lost biography of Tsongkhapa by one of his immediate disciples, Joden Sönam Lhundrup, where, in response to a question about the authenticity of the Dzokchen view, Tsongkhapa is reported to have said, "Yes, it is pure, but adulterations fabricated by later ignoramuses have entered into it." Thuken also states (p. 91) that his own teacher, Changkya Rolpai Dorjé, spoke of a similar story found in another biography of Tsongkhapa, written by Lhula Kachupa. Neringpa ("Delighting the Faithful," p. 593) asserts that he himself had seen a guide on Dzokchen, as well as one on the six yogas of Niguma, composed by Tsongkhapa himself. My own sense is that at this point there is simply no adequate textual evidence on the basis of which to make any determination of Tsongkhapa's actual views on Dzokchen. See also chapter 7 on the intriguing oral instruction Tsongkhapa received from the Lhodrak mystic Namkha Gyaltsen, entitled *Garland of Medicinal Nectar*, containing strikingly Dzokchen-sounding terminology.

652. This voluminous biography of Tsongkhapa has been translated into German and is available under the title *Das Leben Lamastischen Heiligen Tsongkhapa Blo-Bzaṅ-Grags-Pa (1357–1419)* (Rudolf Kaschewsky, 1971).

653. Lobsang Trinlé, *Extensive Biography*, pp. 57–58. I have not reconstructed the Sanskrit of the names of number 2 (Möpa Raptu Gawa) and number 26 (Saten), whose names are spelled, respectively, in Tibetan as Mos pa rab tu dga' ba and Sa brtan.

654. Chöden Rapjor, "Short Biography of the Omniscient Khedrup," in Collected Works of Khedrup Jé, vol. *ka*. Chöden Rapjor was a close disciple of Khedrup but had also received teachings from Tsongkhapa.

655. These five different visions of Tsongkhapa experienced by Khedrup are recorded by Chöden Rapjor in his "Short Biography of the Omniscient Khedrup," Collected Works, vol. *ka*, pp. 122–32.

656. This work is featured in the second volume of *Anthology of Biographies*, and its colophon states it was written at Gephel Monastery in the fourth Tibetan month of the Water Bird year (1513).

657. This work, which is found in Jamyang Shepa's Collected Works, vol. *nga*, is featured also in the second volume of *Anthology of Biographies*.

658. A custom at the major Geluk monastic universities is for the student to make offerings of tea, meals, and so on to the entire community sometime in the year of his formal sitting for the geshe examination. Depending on one's resources, a student can also offer something more enduring to the monastery, such as a statue, a sponsored publication, a work of art, and so on. When I was graduating from the Shartsé College of Ganden Monastery in 1989, I raised funds from my friends to have an entire set of fifteen thangkas on the life of Tsongkhapa commissioned.

659. *Geluk* is in fact an abbreviation of Geden Ringluk, literally, "the tradition of the virtuous ones." There appears to be a consensus among modern scholars of Tibetan Buddhism that the term *Geluk* has to be of later origin. On this view, the followers of Tsongkhapa initially were known as *Gadenpa*, literally, "followers of [the traditions of] Ganden Monastery," while the revised name *Geluk* may imply a sectarian sense of superiority—of being more authentic, virtuous, or pure than other orders. But textual evidence suggests that, in fact, the name *Geden* was used interchangeably with *Ganden* from an early stage, in terms like *Geden Mountain* (*ri bo dge lden*), *Gedenpa* (those from Geden), and *tenets of Sa Ge* (*Sa* referring to Sakya and *Ge* to Geluk). For example, the colophons of some of Tsongkhapa's own major writings completed at Ganden, such as *Elucidation of the Intent*, and also the writings of Gyaltsap contain the term *Geden Mountain*. Similar phraseology is found also in the writings

of Gö Shönu Pal, Jampa Lingpa, Jangdak Namgyal Draksang, Neringpa, and Ngorchen Kunga Sangpo.

660. The five are Shaluwa Lekpai Gyaltsen (1375–1450), Lodrö Chökyong (1389–1463), Baso Chökyi Gyaltsen (1402–73), Lodrö Tenpa (1402–76), and Mönlam Palwa (1414–91). Except for the last, all were direct disciples of Tsongkhapa.

661. See p. 318.

662. In his autobiography (p. 28), Taktsang Lotsawa refers to these three—Lochen, Sengé Gyaltsen, and Namkha Wöser—as "the trio of father and sons of Chökhor Gang Monastery" (p. 37). Sengé Gyaltsen was revered as an emanation of Dromtönpa.

663. According to Neringpa ("Golden Shoot: A Supplement to the Account of Great Tsongkhapa's Disciples," p. 564), Markham Drakpa Sangpo (also known as Khyenrap Wangchuk) founded monasteries in the northern regions of central Tibet, where he established a tradition that honors both Sakya and Geluk texts and lineages. There were other eminent figures in that same region—notably Künkhyen Namkha Sönam, the great Chöje Namsö, Chöje Namyewa, and Chöje Söyewa—who upheld a tradition that did not distinguish between Sakya and Geluk lineages.

664. Kharnak Lotsawa (*History of Ganden Tradition*) provides a comprehensive account of how Tsongkhapa's tradition came to spread to different parts of Tibet, including providing the names of monasteries that were newly founded or converted from existing ones by Tsongkhapa's students. This list of Geluk monasteries was further updated by Desi Sangyé Gyatso in his *Yellow Beryl* and in Sumpa Yeshé Paljor's *Excellent Wish-Granting Tree*.

665. Cited in Könchok Jikmé Wangpo, *Garland of Jewels*, p. 65b:6.

666. *Biography of Taktsang Lotsawa*, Collected Works, vol. 2, p. 22.

667. Collected Works of Shamar Chödrak Yeshé, vol. 6, p. 435. *Garlands of Countless Moonstone Gems* (p. 569) also mentions the third Shamarpa, Chöpal Yeshé, receiving transmissions of such Geden texts as Tsongkhapa's *Five Stages in One Sitting* and *Lamp to Illuminate the Five Stages*.

668. Shamar Chödrak Yeshe, *Biography of Gö Lotsawa Shönu Pal*, Collected Works of Shamar Chödrak Yeshé, vol. 1, p. 561.

669. Kunga Gyaltsen, *Meaningful to Behold*, Collected Works of Chenga Sönam Gyaltsen, vol. *ka*, p. 61b:1.

670. Chenga Sönam Gyaltsen, *A Thousand Light Rays Illuminating Great Bliss*, Collected Works, vol. *kha*, p. 192.

671. Chenga, *A Thousand Light Rays*, p. 192.

672. Cited in Panchen Sönam Drakpa, *History of Old and New Kadam Traditions*, p. 132. Although Tsöndru Sangpo's "Short Biography of Incomparable Gyaltsen Sangpo" does not mention this incident, it appears that Gungru did not consider himself a student of Khedrup. His biography (p. 8b:6) lists six main teachers, naming them as, in addition to his main teacher Tsongkhapa, Gyaltsap, Dülzin, Bodhisattva (possibly Radrengwa Shākya Yeshe), Rinpoché Gyalwa, and Chösangwa.

673. "In Response to a Letter from Tripiṭaka Holder Sangyé Palwa," *Miscellaneous Writings*, p. 515.

674. *rje thams cad mkhyen pa tsong kha pa chen po'i bka' brgyud 'dzin par 'dod pa rnams kyis ni. Miscellaneous Writings*, p. 683. Ary (*Authorized Lives*, p. 51) makes the somewhat outrageous claim that "Khedrup himself did not even consider Tsongkhapa to be his most important teacher." He cites a letter Khedrup wrote in which he speaks of his three principal teachers, a list that does not include Tsongkhapa. This letter, written as a response to a series of seven questions posed by one Sangyé Rinchen, has clear indications that it was written when Khedrup was in his youth. One important clue comes in his response to the fourth question, about whether or not *tathāgatagarbha* (buddha essence) actually exists naturally within sentient beings. Khedrup's response is telling. He answers the question exactly along the lines of Sakya Paṇḍita, who maintained that the concept of *garbha* (essence) is figurative and the scriptures that present the concept must be considered not definitive (*Miscellaneous Writings*, p. 693). In Khedrup's later writings, such as *Great Summary on Emptiness*, he would adopt Tsongkhapa's position on the question, wherein the scriptures that present tathāgatagarbha are in fact recognized as being definitive. Thus, the fact that Khedrup did not consider Tsongkhapa to be one of his principal teachers when he was writing that letter does not in any way prove that he never came to regard the master thus.

675. "Letter to Shenyen Sherap Sangpo," *Miscellaneous Writings*, p. 456.

676. Khedrup in fact wrote a scathing critique of Ngorchen's *Extensive Explanation of Hevajra Sādhana* (*Kye rdo rje'i sgrub thabs rgyas par bshad pa*). Entitled *The Meteoroid Wheel-Weapon: A Rebuttal*, Khedrup's text is a response to what he regarded as Ngorchen's criticism of aspects of Tsongkhapa's tantric works.

677. According to Panchen Sönam Drakpa (*New Red Annals*, p. 96), Ngorpa is

said to have told the Rinpung ruler Norbu Sangpo that he would give the ruler some requested transmissions if Norbu Sangpo would fulfill three wishes, to the effect that (1) all Gelukpas within the Rinpung domain be converted to Sakya; (2) Gendün Drup's construction of Tashi Lhünpo Monastery be prevented; and (3) substantial material gifts be made to the newly established Ngor Monastery. In response, Norbu Sangpo is reported to have said that, in general, forcible sectarian conversion should never be attempted, and that if he were to prevent the construction of Tashi Lhünpo, it would bring great disrepute to the Rinpung family. Regardless of the truth of the specifics, it was widely known that Ngorpa did try to undermine the project of constructing Tashi Lhünpo Monastery, prompting Gendün Drup to write a sad poem lamenting the rising sectarian tone in Tibet.

678. According to Neringpa (*Golden Tree*, p. 549), following Gorampa's visit to the monastery founded in Ngamring by Shönu Gyalchok, the sectarian feelings of the monks began to rise, resulting in the ending of the tradition, which the monastery's founder had instituted, of chanting prayers composed by Tsongkhapa, including his hymn to Maitreya and the aspirational prayer "Goodness at the Beginning, the Middle, and the End." Elsewhere, Neringpa ("Golden Shoot," p. 566) speaks of how Jangdak Namgyal Draksang advised the monks of Ngamring Monastery and Sangden Monastery not to be caught up in Sakya-Geluk sectarianism.

679. Goram Sönam Sengé, *Distinguishing the Views on Emptiness*; Cabezón and Dhargyay, *Freedom from Extremes*, p. 201.

680. Shamar Chödrak Yeshé, "Responses to Neuring Rinpoché's Questions," Collected Works, vol. 6, p. 485.

681. Ngorpa raised critical questions on aspects of Tsongkhapa's Vajrayāna writings that he felt were in conflict with the Sakya tradition's understanding of the Hevajra tantra. Khedrup, Tsongkhapa's biographer and student, wrote a lengthy rebuttal of Ngorpa, entitled *The Meteoroid Wheel-Weapon* (*Gnam lcags 'khor lo*).

682. "A Response to Sasang Lotsawa Ngawang's Objections," *Miscellaneous Writings*, p. 356.

683. Shākya Chokden, *Ocean of Wondrous Faith: A Biography of the Omniscient Lord and Teacher Rongtön Shākya Gyaltsen*, p. 21b:7.

684. This work is found in his Collected Works, vol. 6, pp. 570–703. Until a comprehensive study of Rongtön's writings against Tsongkhapa's works

has been undertaken, it will remain difficult to discern what specific aspects of Tsongkhapa's views Rongtön actually critiqued.

685. Although a student of Jamyang Chöjé and other prominent members of Tsongkhapa's Geluk tradition, Taktsang saw himself primarily as a disciple of Lochen Kyapchok Palsang, who, in fact, died when Taktsang was very young. Taktsang apparently wrote a biography of Lochen that is no longer extant, and he identified strongly with Lochen's Chökhor Ling Monastery.

686. The entirety of Taktsang's critique of Tsongkhapa's Madhyamaka is found in the former's doxographical work *Establishing the Freedom from Conceptual Elaborations on the Basis of Understanding All Philosophical Systems* (*Grub mtha' 'kun shes nas mtha' bral grub pa*), Collected Works, vol. 1, pp. 265–86. For a contemporary study on Taktsang's critiques of Tsongkhapa's Madhyamaka and a subsequent rebuttal by Panchen Lobsang Chökyi Gyaltsen, see Cabezón, "On Sgra pa shes rab rin chen pa'i rtsod lan of Paṇ chen blo bzang chos rgyan."

687. "Presenting the Attributes of Revered Lobsang Drakpa," Collected Works, vol. 2, p. 163. Taktsang's primary motive in criticizing specific aspects of Tsongkhapa's Madhyamaka appeared to be his wish to defend Lochen Kyapchok Palsang's Madhyamaka writings against Tsongkhapa's influential interpretations.

688. For a translation of Gorampa's critiques of Tsongkhapa's Madhyamaka, see Cabezón and Dhargyay, *Freedom from Extremes*. That Tsongkhapa's most vocal critics came from the Sakya school and not Kagyü, the other Tibetan tradition dominant at the time, reveals the complicated reality of Tsongkhapa's own personal relationship with these two schools. As we saw throughout this biography, Tsongkhapa developed and maintained close personal connections with important monasteries as well as personalities within the Kagyü traditions. In contrast, except for his close personal relationship with his teacher Rendawa, Tsongkhapa does not appear to have established significant relationships with any important Sakya institutions. In fact, at the beginning of the fifteenth century, once Tsongkhapa established Ganden Monastery, many monastics, including those belonging to Sakya monasteries, appeared to have flocked to join Tsongkhapa's growing community. Clearly, the primary reasons behind the critiques of Tsongkhapa's views were genuinely doctrinal and philosophical, but we cannot rule out social and political motives as well.

689. A succinct presentation of the two views and their sources, as understood by Shākya Chokden, can be found in his *Discourse Explaining the Origin of Madhyamaka (Dbu ma'i byung tshul bshad pa)*, Collected Works, vol. 4. For a translation of this work, see Komarovski, *Three Texts on Madhyamaka*, pp. 1–36.
690. Shākya Chokden, *Views Held by Sakya Masters and Their Immediate Heirs*, Collected Works, vol. 23, p. 94.
691. Mikyö Dorjé, "In Praise of Five Great Learned Ones Who Appeared Later in the Land of Snows Who Composed Extensive Treatises," Collected Works, vol. 2, p. 205. The other four "later" Tibetan masters for whom the Karmapa wrote praises are Sakya Paṇḍita, Dolpopa Sherap Gyaltsen, Butön, and Shongtön Lotsawa. In his colophon, the Karmapa refers to himself as "someone who has a faith in the master [Tsongkhapa] that cannot be swayed by others" (*rje nyid la gzhan dkrir med pa'i dad pa can*).
692. "In Praise of Lord Tsongkhapa Lobsang Drakpa," Collected Works, vol. *tha*, p. 108. Elsewhere, Pema Karpo writes, "O Tsongkhapa, unrivaled by anyone; / Though there are pretentious scholars who compete with you, / Seeing that you alone remain unrivaled, / I, Pema Karpo, shall not compete but praise you." Cited in Yeshé Dhöndrup, *Entryway to the Ocean of Pure Faith*, p. 414. See note 633 for an explanation of the meaning behind the term "five-hundredth."
693. Fifth Dalai Lama, "A Commentary on Miktsema Prayer Thoroughly Elucidating the Meaning of Words," Collected Works, vol. *na*, p. 4a:6.
694. Taklung Ngawang Namgyal, *History of Taklung Tradition*, p. 393.
695. By identifying "three principal disciples," I am following possibly the earliest listing of Tsongkhapa's students, found in Neringpa's *Golden Tree*, p. 543, where he refers to them as "the three precious ones" (*rin po che rnam pa gsum*). Lechen's *History of Kadam Tradition* (p. 706), completed in 1494, lists Gyaltsap and Dülzin as the "two principal spiritual sons" (*sras kyi thu bo gnyis*), a system followed also by Panchen Sönam Drakpa in his *History of Old and New Kadam Traditions*. The latter, however, lists Khedrup as "the sole inner heart son" (*nang thugs kyi sras gcig*). An alternative system of ranking, which has become the received position today, identifies Gyaltsap and Khedrup, the two immediate successors to the abbotship of Ganden Monastery, as "the two chief spiritual heirs" (*sras kyi thu bo gnyis*). On the question of identifying Tsongkhapa's "chief spiritual heir" (*sras kyi thu bo*), see Ary, *Authorized Lives*, pp. 47–58.

696. The names of these monasteries established by Tsongkhapa's students in various parts of Tibet are drawn from Kharnak Lotsawa's *History of Ganden Tradition*, cross-checked against two later sources: Desi's *Yellow Beryl* and Sumpa Yeshé Paljor's *Excellent Wish-Granting Tree.*

697. "A Letter to Jang Lama," *Miscellaneous Writings*, p. 502.

698. Two remarkable historical works of the early sixteenth and early seventeenth century, Panchen Sönam Drakpa's *History of Old and New Kadam Traditions* (composed in 1529) and Kharnak Lotsawa's *History of Ganden Tradition* (completed in 1630), contain extensive lists of monasteries belonging to Tsongkhapa's tradition that had been established in different parts of Tibet. The information on Geluk monasteries from these two sources was later updated in Desi Sangyé Gyatso's *Yellow Beryl* (completed in 1693) and Sumpa Yeshé Paljor's *Excellent Wish-Granting Tree* (completed in 1748) thus providing a comprehensive list of most Geluk monasteries existing in the mid-eighteenth century.

699. The historian Sumpa Yeshé Paljor, known for his partisan Geluk views, writes (with some exaggeration), "These days, here in the Amdo region, apart from the Geluk tradition no other tradition exists. Thus, the region remains extremely pure when it comes to view and practice, and, free from disagreements concerning how to uphold the Dharma, the land enjoys great auspiciousness." *Excellent Wish-Granting Tree*, p. 691.

700. Although Madhyamaka was not part of the formal curriculum during Tsongkhapa's student years, it became so before the end of the fourteenth century. This focus on formal and systematic study of "five disciplines" remains the core of classical monastic education to this day, especially in Tsongkhapa's Geluk monasteries.

Bibliography

NOTE: I have distinguished between two formats of Tibetan printed texts: the traditional xylograph woodblock prints (which have folio numbers with sides *a* and *b*) and modern typeset editions in book format. Scanned texts from the library of the Tibetan Buddhist Resources Center are labeled according to their work numbers, e.g., TBRC W*. Unless otherwise stated, Tsongkhapa's collected writings, as well as those of his two immediate disciples, Gyaltsap and Khedrup, used in this volume are from the Kumbum edition—a woodblock edition of 19 volumes, listed just below as *Collected Works of the Incomparable Lord Tsongkhapa Lobsang Drakpa*. To provide a sense of the size of the Tibetan texts, the titles of those works that are of book-length have been italicized

Tibetan and Indian Works

Works by Tsongkhapa (1357–1419)

COLLECTED WORKS OF THE INCOMPARABLE LORD TSONGKHAPA LOBSANG DRAKPA

———. *An Annotated Commentary Clearly Elucidating the Words and Meaning of "The Clear Lamp," The Great Exposition of the Guhyasamāja Tantra* (*Dpal gsang ba 'dus pa'i rgya cher bshad pa sgron ma gsal ba'i tshig don ji bzin 'byed pa'i mchan gyi yang grel*). Collected Works. Vol. *pa*.

———. *Door-Frame Instructions: Essential Oral Instructions* (*Zhal shes gnad kyi them yig*). Collected Works. Vol. *nya*, 645–94.

———. *Elucidation of the Intent: A Thorough Exposition of "Entering the Middle Way"* (*Dbu ma la 'jug pa'i rnam bshad dgongs pa rab gsal*). Collected Works. Vol. *ma*, 1–605. (English translation by Thupten Jinpa; Boston: Wisdom Publications, forthcoming.)

———. *Essence of True Eloquence: Distinguishing the Provisional and the Definitive Meaning* (*Drang ba dang nges pa'i don rnam par 'byed pa legs bshad snying po*). Collected Works. Vol. *pha*, 441–687. (English translation in Thurman 1984.)

———. "Essential Points of Mañjuśrī's Path Sent as a Scroll to Master Rendawa" (*Rje btsun 'jam pa'i dbyangs kyi lam gyi gnad rje red mda' ba la shog dril du phul ba*). Collected Works. Vol. *pha*, 729–39.

———. "Explaining without Distortion the Intention of the Conquerors on the Difficult Points of Tranquillity and Insight" (*Zhi lhag gnyis kyi dka' ba'i gnas la rgyal ba'i dgongs pa phyin ci ma log par bshad pa*). Collected Works. Vol. *pha*, 719–27.

———. *Gateway to Enter the Seven Works of Dharmakīrti Dispelling the Darkness of the Mind of Those Who Are Interested* (*Sde bdun la 'jug pa'i sgo don gnyer yid kyi mun sel*). Collected Works. Vol. *tsha*, 713–60.

———. *Golden Rosary of Excellent Utterances: Extensive Exposition of "Ornament of Realization" As Well as Its Commentary* (*Shes rab kyi pha rol du phyin pa mngon par rtogs pa'i rgyan 'grel pa dang bcas pa rgyas par bshad pa legs bshad gser gyi phreng ba*). Collected Works. Vols. *tsa* and *tsha*.

———. *Great Treatise on the Stages of the Path to Enlightenment* (*Byang chub lam rim chen mo*). Collected Works. Vol. *pa*. (English translation in Tsong-kha-pa 2000–2004.)

———. *Great Treatise on the Stages of the Path of Tantra* (*Sngags rim chen mo*). Collected Works, Vol. *ga*.

———. *A Guide to the Six Yogas of Nāropa Endowed with Three Convictions* (*Na ro chos drug gi khrid yig yid ches gsum ldan*). Collected Works. Vol. *ta*, 395–525. (English translation in Mullin 1996.)

———. "Guide to the View on Equality of Samsara and Nirvana" (*Srid zhi mnyaṁ nyid kyi lta khrid*). Collected Works. Vol. *ba*, 761–811.

———. *Lamp to Illuminate the Five Stages of Glorious Guhyasamāja Tantra* (*Dpal gsang ba 'dus pa'i man ngag rim pa lnga rab tu gsal ba'i sgron me*). Collected Works. Vol. *ja*, 1–681. (English translation in Kilty 2017.)

———. *The Main Path to Enlightenment: An Exposition of the Bodhisattva's Ethics* (*Byang chub sems dpa'i tshul khrims kyi rnam bshad byang chub gzhung lam*). Collected Works. Vol. *ka*, 563–798. (English translation in Tatz 1986.)

——. "Meeting with Lhodrak Drupchen and the Gift of a Tooth to Khedrup Jé" (*Lho brag grub chen dang mjal tshul dang mkhas grub rje la tshems gnang skor*). Collected Works. Vol. *ka*, 223–32. Anthology of Biographies of the Great Tsongkhapa. Vol. 1, 284–89.

——. *A Memorandum on Clear Differentiation of the Difficult Points of Stainless Light* (*Stong phrag bcu gnyis pa dri ma med pa'i 'od kyi dka' ba'i gnas rnam par 'byed pa brjed byang*). Collected Works. Vol. *na*, 1–216.

——. *Middle-Length Treatise on the Stages of the Path to Enlightenment* (*Byang chub lam rim 'bring po*). Collected Works. Vol. *pha*, 1–439.

——. *Milking the Wish-Granting Cow: Extensive Exposition of the Sādhana of Glorious Cakrasaṃvara* (*Dpal 'khor lo sdom pa'i mngon par rtogs pa rgya cher bshad pa'dod pa 'jo ba*). Collected Works. Vol. *ta*, 1–393.

——. *Miscellaneous Writings of Great Tsongkhapa*. Collected Works. Vol. *kha*, 1–631. (See bibliography of works listed under *Miscellaneous Writings*)

——. "Notes on 'A Lucid Summary of the Five Stages'" (*Rim lnga bsdus pa'i zin bris*). Collected Works. Vol. *cha*, 483–531.

——. "Notes on Eight Difficult Points of the *Treatise on the Middle Way*" (*Rtsa ba shes rab kyi dka' gnad brgyad kyi zin bris*). Collected Works. Vol. *ba*, 585–619. (English translation in Ruegg 2002.)

—— *Notes on the Vinaya text*, Root Lines on Vinaya (*'dul ba mdo rtsa ba'i zin bris*). Collected Works. Vol. *kha*, 633–859.

——. *Ocean of Reasoning: An Exposition of "Treatise on the Middle Way"* (*Rtsa ba shes rab kyi rnam bshad ṭik chen rigs pa'i rgya mtsho*). Collected Works. Vol. *ba*, 1–583. (English translation in Samten and Garfield 2006.)

——. *Opening the Eyes to View the Hidden Meaning* (*Sbas don lta ba'i mig 'byed*). Collected Works. Vol. *tha*, 221–93.

——. *Practical Guide on the Five Stages of Guhyamsamāja Completion Stage in a Single Sitting* (*Dpal gsang ba 'dus pa'i rdzogs rim rim lnga gdan rdzogs gi dmar khrid*). Collected Works. Vol. *nya*, 813–957.

——. *Record of Teachings Received* (*Gsan yig*). Collected Works. Vol. *ka*, 247–310.

——. *Sheaves of Attainment: A Guide to the Completion Stage of Cakrasaṃvara According to the Lūipa Tradition* (*Rnal 'byor gyi dbang phyug lui pa'i lugs kyi bde mchog gi rdzogs rim dngos grub snye ma*). Collected Works. Vol. *dza*.

——. *Short Instructional Pieces on Guhyasamāja Tantra* (*Gsang ba 'dus pa'i man ngag yig chung*). Collected Works. Vol. *dza*, 591–721.

——. "Staircase for the Clear Mind" (*Blo gsal bgrod pa'i them skas*). Collected Works. Vol. *tsha*, 827–911.

——. "Treasury of Jewels: A Rite of Initiation of Ghaṇṭapa Cakrasaṃvara Body Maṇḍala" (*Dril bu lus dkyil gyi dbang chog rin po che'i bang mdzod*). Collected Works. Vol. *tha*, 163–219.

——. "An Uncommon Oral Instruction from Lord Mañjuśri's Teaching Scribed by Tsongkhapa and Sent to Master Rendawa" (*Rje btsun 'jam pa'i dbyangs kyi gsung rje bstun tsong kha pas yi ger mdzad nas rje red mda' bar phul ba*). Collected Works. Vol. *na*, 217–31.

MISCELLANEOUS WRITINGS OF GREAT TSONGKHAPA

——. "Brahmā's Diadem: A Hymn to Lord Maitreya through Lamentation" (*Rje btsun byams pa mgon po la smre sngags kyi sgo nas bstod pa tshangs pa'i cod paṇ*). *Miscellaneous Writings*, 45–55. (English translations in Thurman 1982 and Kilty 2001.)

——. "A Brief Presentation of the Stages of the Path" (*Lam gyi rim pa mdo tsam du bstan pa*). *Miscellaneous Writings*, 380–403.

——. "A Hymn to Lord Mañjuśrī Entitled 'Ocean of Clouds of Praise Bringing Joy to Mañjuśrī'" (*Rje btsun 'jam pa'i dbyangs la bstod pa 'jam dbyangs mnyes par byed pa'i bstod sprin rgya mtsho*). *Miscellaneous Writings*, 63–75. (English translation in Kilty 2001.)

——. "A Hymn to Tārā." *Miscellaneous Writings*, 102–4.

——. "Hymn to Yama King Kālarūpa in His Inner Aspect: Crushing the Forces of Demons" (*Gshin rje gshed chos kyi rgyal po la nang sgrub kyi sgo nas bstod pa bdud dpung phe mar 'thag pa*). *Miscellaneous Writings*, 113–15.

——. "In Praise of Goddess Vijayā Achieving Immortality" (*Rnam rgyal ma'i bstod pa 'chi med grub pa*). *Miscellaneous Writings*, 97–102. (English translation in Kilty 2001.)

——. "In Praise of Great Rendawa" (*Red mda' ba chen po la bstod pa*). *Miscellaneous Writings*, 9–13.

——. "In Praise of Jamgön Sakya Paṇḍita" (*'Jam mgon sa skya paṇ ḍi ta la bstod pa*). *Miscellaneous Writings*, 19–21.

——. "In Praise of Master Drakpa Jangchup" (*Chos rje grags pa byang chub bzang po'i bstod pa*). *Miscellaneous Writings*, 16–19.

——. "In Praise of the Buddha for His Teaching of Dependent Origination" (*Ston pa la rten cing 'brel bar byung bar gsungs pa las brtsams te bstod pa legs bshad snying po*) a.k.a. "In Praise of Dependent Origination" (*Rten 'brel bstod pa*). *Miscellaneous Writings*, 30–36. (English translation in Thurman 1982; Kilty

2001; and by Jinpa at http://www.tibetanclassics.org/html-assets/In%20 Praise%20of%20Dependent%20Origination.pdf.)

——. "In Response to Jang Lama's Letter" (*Jang bla ma la'i zhu yig gi lan du gnang ba*). *Miscellaneous Writings*, 472–73.

——. "In Response to Master Rendawa's Letter" (*Rje red mda' ba'i gsung lan*). *Miscellaneous Writings*, 144–59.

——. "Invoking Sarasvatī, Singing Her Praise, and Supplicating Her" (*Sgra dbyangs lha mo dbyangs can ma spyan drangs nas bstod cing gsol ba 'debs pa*). *Miscellaneous Writings*, 106–7.

——. "Lamp Illuminating the Precious Jewels: A Hymn to Lord Maitreya" (*Rje btsun byams pa mgon po la bstod pa rin po che gsal ba'i sgron me*). *Miscellaneous Writings*, 55–60.

——. "Letter of Advice to the Great Ruler Drakpa Gyaltsen" (*Mi dbang chen po grags pa rgyal mtshan zhes grags pa la gstam tu bya ba'i 'phrin yig*). *Miscellaneous Writings*, 481–87.

——. "Letter to a Mongol Prince" (*Gong ma hor rgyal bu'i mi'i dbang po'i drung du phul ba*). *Miscellaneous Writings*, 480–81.

——. "Letter to Karmapa Deshin Shekpa" (*Karma pa de bzhin gshegs pa la phul ba*). *Miscellaneous Writings*, 476–79.

——. "Letter to Lama Umapa in Eastern Tibet" (*Bla ma dbu ma pa la khams su phul ba*). *Miscellaneous Writings*, 159–63.

——. "Letter to Rinpung Namkha Gyaltsen from Rong Chölung" (*Rin spungs pa dpon nam mkha' rgyal mtshan la rong chos lung nas springs pa*). *Miscellaneous Writings*, 509–10.

——. "Letter to the Yongle Emperor of the Ming Court" (*Gong ma tā ming rgyal por phul ba'i chap shog*). *Miscellaneous Writings*, 622–24.

——. "Letter to Vajrapāṇi Lhodrak Khenchen" (*Lho brag mkhan chen phyag rdor ba la phul ba*). *Miscellaneous Writings*, 163–67.

——. "Letter to Yönten Gyatso When Leaving for Wölkha" (*'Ol khar byon dus yon tan rgya mtsho la gdams pa*). *Miscellaneous Writings*, 497–98.

——. "Liturgical Texts Compiled for the Great Lhasa Prayer Festival" (*Lha sar smon lam chen mo'i dus su rje tsong kha nyid kyis khrigs su 'debs pa*). *Miscellaneous Writings*, 562–70.

——. *Mount Meru of Blessings: A Poetic Narrative on the Life of the Great Bodhisattva Drakpa Jangchup* (*Spyan snga grags pa byang chub dpal bzang po'i rtogs brjod snyan dngags byin rlabs kyi lhun po*). *Miscellaneous Writings*, 291–338.

——. "Notes Written by Second Vajradhara Himself at Wölkha Samten Ling Hermitage on the Unusual Visions He Experienced at the Site" (*'Ol kha bsam gtan gling du gnas der ngo mtshar ba'i ltas khyad par can gzigs pa dag rdo rje 'chang gnyis pa rang nyid kyis brjed byang du mdzad pa*). *Miscellaneous Writings*, 120.

——. "A Poem in Challenging Composition Style with Vowel E Only" (*E yig dbyangs nges pa'i bya dka' ba'i rtsom*). *Miscellaneous Writings*, 470–71.

——. *Poetic Narrative on the Story of Bodhisattva Sadāprarudita* (*Byang chub sems dpa'i rtag tu ngu'i rtogs pa brjod pa*). *Miscellaneous Writings*, 236–91.

——. "A Prayer to the Lineage Gurus of Immediate Transmission" (*Byin brlabs nye brgyud kyi bla ma rnams la gsol ba 'debs pa*). *Miscellaneous Writings*, 8–9.

——. "A Prayer to the Lineage Gurus of the Expansive Practice Transmission of the Stages of the Path Instruction" (*Byang chub lam gyi rim pa'i rgya chen spyod pa'i brgyud pa la gsol ba 'debs pa*). *Miscellaneous Writings*, 2–8.

——. "Prayers for Goodness in the Beginning, the Middle, and the End" (*Thog mtha' bar gsum du dge ba'i smon lam*). *Miscellaneous Writings*, 570–74. (English translation in Jinpa and Elsner 2000.)

——. "Queries from a Sincere Heart" (*Dri ba lhag bsal rab dkar*). *Miscellaneous Writings*, 170–201.

——. "Realization Narrative" (*Rtogs brjod 'dun legs ma*). *Miscellaneous Writings*, 120–27. (English translation in Thurman 1982.)

——. "Replies to Questions from the Great Spiritual Friend Jangchup Lama" (*Bshes gnyen chen po byang chub bla ma'i dris lan*). *Miscellaneous Writings*, 341–56.

——. "A Reply to Tsakho Ngawang Drakpa's Letter Speaking about the Establishment of Monastic Institutions in Gyalrong" (*Shar gyal mo rong du sngon med pa'i rab tu byung ba'i sde khyad par can btsugs nas springs yig byung ba'i lan*). *Miscellaneous Writings*, 457–62.

——. "A Response to Sasang Lotsawa Ngawang's Objections" (*Sa bzang lo tsa ba ngag dbang gis brgal rtag gi yi ge phul ba'i lan*). *Miscellaneous Writings*, 356–73.

——. "A Short Practice Taught by Lord Mañjuśrī" (*Rje btsun 'jam pa'i dbyangs kyis gsungs pa'i nyams len mdor bsdus*). *Miscellaneous Writings*, 116–17.

——. "Songs of Experience on the Stages of the Path" (*Lam rim nyams mgur*). *Miscellaneous Writings*, 127–33. (English translation by Thupten Jinpa at http://www.tibetanclassics.org/html-assets/Songs%20of%20Experience.pdf).

——. "Supplication to Dzingchi Maitreya" (*Rdzing phyi'i byams pa la gsol 'debs*). *Miscellaneous Writings*, 60–61.

——. "Three Principal Elements of the Path" (*Lam gyi gtso bo rnam pa gsum*). *Miscellaneous Writings*, 463–65. English translation by Thupten Jinpa at http://www.tibetanclassics.org/html-assets/Three%20Principal%20Aspects.pdf.

Other Tibetan and Indian Works

Anthology of Biographies of the Great Tsongkhapa. Typeset edition. 4 vols. Beijing: Krun go bod rig pa dpe skrun khang, 2015.

Asaṅga (fourth century). *Śrāvaka Levels* (*Śrāvakabhūmi*; *Nyan thos kyi sa*). Tengyur. Beijing: Comparative edition. Vol. 73, 3–485.

Candrakīrti (seventh century). *Clear Words* (*Prasannapada*; *Tshig gsal*). Tengyur. Beijing: Comparative edition. Vol. 60, 3–483.

"Catalog of the Great Lhasa Prayer Festival" (*Lha sa smon lam chen mo mgo tshugs pa'i dkar chag*). Anthology of Biographies of the Great Tsongkhapa. Vol. 1, 613–43.

Chahar Lobsang Tsultrim (1740–1810). *Source of All Goodness: A Biography of Great Tsongkhapa Presented in Easy-to-Understand Terms* (*Rje thams bcad mkhyen pa tsong kha pa chen po'i rnam thar go sla bar brjod pa bde legs kun gyi 'byung gnas*). Anthology of Biographies of the Great Tsongkhapa. Vol. 3, 1–506.

Chenga Lodrö Gyaltsen (1402–72). "Guide to the View of the Equivalence of Saṃsāra and Nirvāṇa: An Ear-Whispered Instruction Given by Mañjuśrī to Lama Umapa and to the Precious Master" (*Srid zhi mnyam nyid kyi lta khrid snyan brgyud rje btsun 'jam dbyangs kyis bla ma dbu ma dang rje rin po che gnyis la gnang ba*). Collected Works of Chenga Lodrö Gyaltsen. Typeset edition. Lhasa: Ser gtsug nang bstan dpe rnying 'tshol bsdu phyogs sgrig khang, 2010. Vol. 1, 55–64.

——. "River of Faith: Biography of Tokden Jampel Gyatso" (*Rje bstun 'jam dpal rgya mtsho'i rnam thar dad pa'i chu rgyun*). Collected Works of Chenga Lodrö Gyaltsen. Vol. 2, 26–52.

——. "Ultimate Path of the Ear-Whispered Transmission: A Guide to the Middle View Transcending All Extremes" (*Mtha' bral dbu ma'i lta khrid kyi snyan brgyud zab lam mthar thug*). Collected Works of Chenga Lodrö Gyaltsen. Vol. 3, 28–54.

Chenga Sönam Gyaltsen (1386–1434). *Garland of Lapis Lazuli: Dispelling Misunderstandings Concerning Kagyu Thought* (*Bka' brgyud kyi dgongs par log par rtogs pa sel bar byed pa bai durya'i phreng ba*). Collected Works of Chenga

Sönam Gyaltsen. Lhasa: Reprinted as part of 'Bri gung chos mdzod chen mo, 2004. Vol. *kha*, 92–186.

——. *A Thousand Light Rays Illuminating Great Bliss: A Guide to the Six Yogas of Nāropa* (*Dpal na ro'i chos drugs gi khrid yig bde chen gsal ba'i 'od zer stong ldan*). Collected Works of Chenga Sönam Gyaltsen. Vol. *kha*, 187–527.

——. *A Thousand Lights Opening the Eyes: History of the Precious Kagyu Tradition* (*Bka' brgyud rin po che'i chos 'byung mig 'byed 'od stong*). Collected Works of Chenga Sönam Gyaltsen. Vol. *ka*, 1–180.

Chöden Rapjor (fifteenth century). "Short Biography of the Omniscient Khedrup" (*Mkhas grub thams bcad mkhyen pa'i rnam thar mdor bsdus*). Collected Works of Khedrup Gelek Palsang. Vol. *ka*, 109–34. (English translation in Ary 2015.)

Chökyi Jungné (sixteenth century). *Garland of Countless Moonstone Gems: Biographies of Kamtsang Kagyu Masters* (*Skam tshang bka' brgyud kyi rnam par thar pa rab 'byams nor bu zla ba shel gyi phreng ba*). Typeset edition. Kunming: Yunan Nationalities Press, 1998.

Desi Sangyé Gyatso (1653–1705). *Yellow Beryl: A History of Ganden Tradition* (*Dga' ldan chos 'byung bai ḍūrya ser po*). Typeset edition. Xining: Krung go bod kyi shes rig dpe skrun khang, 1989.

Drago Rapjam (seventeenth century). *Music of Wondrous Prophecies: A Biography of the Dharma King Great Tsongkhapa* (*Chos kyi rgyal po tsong kha pa chen po'i rnam par thar pa ngo mtshar lung bstan gyi rol mo*). Anthology of Biographies of the Great Tsongkhapa. Vol. 2, 265–328.

Drakyap Lobsang Tenpa (seventeenth century). *Sun Illuminating Excellent Insights on the Life of Glorious Tsongkhapa Lobsang Drakpa* (*Tsong kha pa blo bzang grags pa'i dpal gyi rnam par thar pa legs bshad nyin mor byed pa*). Anthology of Biographies of the Great Tsongkhapa. Vol. 2, 619–700.

Drati Rinchen Dhöndrup (seventeenth century). "Short Biography of the Dharma Master Jamchen Chöjé Shākya Yeshé" (*Byams chen chos kyi rje shākya ye shes kyi rnam par thar pa mdor bsdus*). Collected Works of Drati Rinchen Dhöndrup. Typeset edition. Lhasa: Ser gtsug nang bstan dpe rnying 'tshol bsdu phyogs sgrig khang, 2010, 293–97.

Drukpa Pema Karpo (1527–92). *Conqueror's Treasury: An Explanation of Mahāmudrā Instruction* (*Phyag rgya chen po'i man ngag gi bshad sbyar rgyal ba'i gan mdzod*). Collected Works of Kunkhyen Pema Karpo. Darjeeling: Kagyu Sung rab nyams gso khang, 1973–74. Vol. *zha*, 7–370.

——. "In Praise of Lord Tsongkhapa Lobsang Drakpa" (*Rje tsong kha pa blo *bzang grags pa la bstod pa*). Collected Works of Kunkhyen Pema Karpo. Vol. *tha*, 107–9.

——. *Sun Nourishing the Dharma Lotus: A History of Buddhism* (*Chos 'byung bstan pa'i pad ma rgyas pa'i nyin byed*). Typeset edition. Xinhua: Bod ljongs bod yig dpe rnying dpe skrun khang, 1992.

Dungkar Lobsang Trinlé (1927–97). *Extensive Dungkar Dictionary* (*Dung dkar tshig mdzod chen mo*). Beijing: China Tibetology Publishing House, 2002.

Gendun Drup (first Dalai Lama) (1391–1474). *An Instruction on Mahāyāna Mind Training* (*Thegs pa chen po blo sbyong gi gdams pa*). Collected Works of Gendun Drup. Tashi Lhunpo woodblock print; scanned TBRC W24769. Vol. 6, 505–612.

Gendun Gyatso (second Dalai Lama) (1476–1542). "Propitiation of Dharma Protector Dorjé Drakden" (*Bstan skyong rdo rje grags ldan la mchod gtor 'bul tshul*). Collected Works of Second Dalai Lama Dge 'Dun Rgya Mtsho. Dharamsala: Library of Tibetan Works & Archives, 2006. Vol. *cha*.

Gö Lotsawa Shönu Pal (1392–1481). *The Blue Annals* (*Deb ther sngon po*). 2 vols. Typeset edition. Sichuan: Nationalities Press, 1984. (English translation in Roerich 1949.)

Gomchen Ngawang Drakpa (1418–96). *Garland of Attainments for the Learned: Responses to "Queries from a Sincere Heart"* (*Lhag bsam rab dkar gyi dris lan dngos grub 'phreng ba mkhas pa'i rgyan*). Collected Works of Gomchen Ngawang Drakpa. Delhi: Ngawang Sopa, 1980. Vol. 2, 392–441.

——. *Responses to the View and Meditation Sections of "Queries from a Sincere Heart"* (*Lhag bsam rab dkar gyi lta sgom dris lan*). Collected Works of Gomchen Ngawang Drakpa. Vol. 2, 443–506.

Goram Sönam Sengé (1429–89). *Distinguishing the Views on Emptiness: Moonlight Illuminating the Essential Points of the Supreme Vehicle* (*Lta ba'i shen 'byed theg mchog gnad kyi zla zer*). Collected Works of Goram Sönam Sengé. Bir, India: Yashodhara Publications, 1995. Vol. 5, 417–510. (English translation in Cabeźon and Dhargyay 2006.)

Gungru Gyaltsen Sangpo (1384–1450). *Great Summary* (*Stong thun*). In *Gung ru rgyal mtshan bzang po'i stong thun dang rnam thar*. Typeset edition. Lhasa: Ser gtsug nang bstan dpe rnying 'tshol bsdu phyogs sgrig khang, 2011.

——. *Lamp of Well-Uttered Insights: A Commentary on Realization Narrative* (*Rtogs brjod 'dun legs ma'i 'grel pa legs par bshad pa'i sgron me*). Anthology of Biographies of the Great Tsongkhapa. Vol. 1, 198–283.

Guru Tashi Chöwang (nineteenth century). *Gurta's History of Buddhism* (*Gur bkra'i chos 'byung*). Typeset edition. Xinhua: Nationalities Press, 1990.

Gyaltsap Dharma Rinchen (1364–1432). *Heart Ornament: An Exposition of the "Clear Meaning" Commmentary on "Ornament of Realizations"* (*Bstan bcos mngon rtogs rgyan gyi 'grel pa don gsal ba'i rnam bshad snying po rgyan*). Collected Works of Gyaltsap Dharma Rinchen (Kumbum woodblock print). Vol. *kha*.

——. *How to Undertake the Practice of the Path of the Two Stages of Kālacakra* (*Dpal dus kyi 'khor lo'i lam rim pa gnyis ji ltar nyams su len pa'i tshul*). Collected Works of Gyaltsap Dharma Rinchen. Vol. *ka*.

——. *Opening the Door to the Supreme Vehicle: How to Apply the Stages of Realizations in Practice* (*Mngon par rtogs pa'i rim pa nyams su len tshul theg mchog sgo 'byed*). Collected Works of Gyaltsap Dharma Rinchen. Vol. *ca*, 1–124.

Hortön Namkha Pal (1373–1447). *Rays of Sun: A Mind-Training Guide* (*Blo sbyong nyi ma'i 'od zer*). Woodblock print, Lhasa (n.d.); TBRC W15448. (English translation in Beresford 1992.)

Jamyang Chöjé Tashi Palden (1379–1449). "Secret Biography of Lord Master Lobsang Drakpa: A Poem of Supplication" (*Rje btsun bla ma blo bzang grags pa'i dpal gyi gsang ba'i rnam thar gsol 'debs*). Anthology of Biographies of the Great Tsongkhapa. Vol. 1, 192–97. (English translation in Thurman 1982.)

Jamyang Khaché (fourteenth/fifteenth century). "Eighty Tsongkhapas: A Biographical Hymn to Great Tsongkhapa" (*Rje btsun tsong kha pa chen po'i rnam thar bstod pa tsong kha brgyad cu ma*). Anthology of Biographies of the Great Tsongkhapa. Vol. 1, 594–603.

Jamyang Shepa (1648–1722). *Garland of Cintamani Gems: Biography of Great Tsongkhapa in Two Hundred and Five Paintings* (*Rje btsun tsong kha pa chen po'i rnam thar ras bris kyi nyis brgya lnga pa tsinta maṇi'i phreng ba*). Anthology of Biographies of the Great Tsongkhapa. Vol. 2, 489–530.

Jamyang Tenpai Nyima (a.k.a. Ngari Lhatsun) (sixteenth century). *Birth Stories of Great Tsongkhapa: Thousand Lights Opening the Lotus Grove of Faith for the Fortunate Ones* (*Shar tsong kha pa chen po blo bzang grags pa'i dpal gyi rnam thar skal ldan dad pa'i pad tshal rgyas pa'i 'od stong*) (1571). Anthology of Biographies of the Great Tsongkhapa. Vol. 2, 148–206.

Jangchup Gyaltsen (1302–64). *Testament of Tai Situ Jangchup Gyaltsen: Meaningful to Behold* (*Ta'i si tu byang chub rgyal mtshan gyi bka' chems mthong ba don ldan*) in *Rlang gi po ti se ru rgyas pa*. Typeset edition. Xinhua: Bod ljongs mi dmangs dpe skrun khang, 1986.

Jangchup Namgyal Gelek (fifteenth century). *Biography of Jampa Lingpa: A*

Wondrous Garland (*Byams pa gling pa chen po'i rnam par thar pa ngo mtshar phreng ba*). Scanned from handwritten dbu med manuscript. TBRC W26621.

Jetsun Chökyi Gyaltsen (1459–1544). *Ocean of Faith: A Biography of the Omniscient Khedrup Gelek Palsang* (*Mkhas grub thams bcad mkhyen pa dge legs dpal bzang gi rnam thar dad pa'i rol mtsho*). Collected Works of Khedrup Gelek Palsang. Kumbum woodblock print. Vol. *ka*, 1–77. (English translation in Ary 2015.)

Jikmé Bang (fifteenth century). *Biography of Bodong Choklé Namgyal* (*Bo dong pan chen gyi rnam thar*) (1453). Typeset edition. Xinhua: Bod ljongs bod yig dpe rnying dpe skrun khang, 1991.

Kelsang Gyatso (seventh Dalai Lama) (1708–1757). *Inventory of Kumbum Monastery* (*Sku 'bum gyi dkar chag*). Collected Works of Seventh Dalai Lama. Gangtok: Reproduced from Drepung blocks by Lama Dhöndrup Sangye, 1975. Vol. *ca*, 1–42.

Khardo Söpa Gyatso (1672–1749). "Precious Garland of Prophecies: A Side Ornament to the Biography of Great Tsongkhapa" (*Rgyal ba tsong kha pa chen po'i rnam par thar pa'i zur rgyan lung bstan gyi phreng ba*). Anthology of Biographies of the Great Tsongkhapa. Vol. 2, 329–56.

Kharnak Lotsawa (seventeenth century). *History of Ganden Tradition: Wish-Granting Tree Delighting the Learned Ones* (*Dga' ldan chos byung dpag bsam sdong po mkhas pa dga' byed*) (1630). Typeset edition. Lhasa: Ser gtsug nang bstan dpe rnying 'tshol bsdu phyogs sgrig khang, n.d. TBRC W1KG25150.

Khedrup Gelek Palsang (1385–1438). "Biographical Poem Supplicating the Great Lord Tsongkhapa" (*Rje btsun tsong kha pa chen po'i rnam par thar pa mdo tsam brjod pa'i sgo nas gsol ba 'debs pa*). *Miscellaneous Writings*. Collected Works of Khedrup Gelek Palsang. Kumbum woodblock print. Vol. *ba*, 351–56. (English translation in Thurman 1982.)

——. *Entryway of Faith: The Wondrous Biography of the Lord Teacher Tsongkhapa* (*Rje btsun bla ma tsong kha pa chen po'i rnam thar dad pa'i 'jug ngogs*). Collected Works of Jé Tsongkhapa. Vol. *ka*. Anthology of Biographies of the Great Tsongkhapa. Vol. 1, 78–191.

——. "Explaining Some of the Master's Oral Teachings by Relating Them to the *Lamp* and *Five Stages in One Sitting*" (*Rje'i zhal shes 'ga' zhig gsal sgron dang gdan rdzogs dang sbyar nas bshad pa*). Collected Works of Khedrup Gelek Palsang. Vol. *pa*, 769–95.

——. *A Great Summary on Emptiness Opening the Eyes of the Fortunate Ones* (*Stong *thun skal bzang mig 'byed*). Collected Works of Khedrup Gelek Palsang. Vol. *kha*, 1–543. (English translation in Cabezón 1992.)

———. "In Response to Lama Drupa Pal Who Discerns Some Difference between the Teacher and His Son with Respect to Cultivating the View" (*Bla ma sgrub pa dpal las rje yab sras lta ba skyong ba'i gnad la bzhed pa mi 'dra ba'i go tshul 'ga' zhig la 'di 'dra 'dug pa ji ltar yin zhes pa'i lan*). Collected Works of Khedrup Gelek Palsang. Vol. *ba*, 713–17.

———. "Lamp Dispelling the Darkness of Erroneous Paths" (*Lam ngan mun sel sgron me*). *Miscellaneous Writings*, 636–89.

———. *Lamp Dispelling the Darkness: A Guide to the View* (*Lta khrid mun sel sgron me*). Collected Works of Khedrup Gelek Palsang. Vol. *nga*, 631–83.

———. *Miscellaneous Writings of the Omniscient Khedrup* (*Mkhas grub thams bcad mkhyen pa'i gsung thor bu*). Collected Works of Khedrup Gelek Palsang. Vol. *ba*, 345–752.

———. "Praise to Gyaltsap Jé" (*Rgyal tshab rje la bstod pa*). *Miscellaneous Writings*, 361–65.

———. *Record of Teachings Received by the Omniscient Khedrup Gelek Palsang* (*Mkhas grub thams cad mkhyen pa'i gsan yig*). Collected Works of Khedrup Gelek Palsang. Vol. *ka*, 143–231.

———. "A Reply to a Letter from Tripiṭaka Holder Sangyé Palwa" (*Sde snod 'dzin pa sangs rgyas dpal pa'i phrin lan*). *Miscellaneous Writings*, 462–518.

———. "A Response to Geshé Konting Goshri" (*Bshes gnyen kon ting go shri'i rtsom lan*). *Miscellaneous Writings*, 596–635.

———. *Secret Biography of Tsongkhapa: Cluster of Precious Gems* (*Gsang ba'i rnam thar dngos grub kyi snye ma*). Collected Works of Jé Tsongkhapa, vol. *ka*. Anthology of Biographies of the Great Tsongkhapa. Vol. 1, 51–77.

Khedrup Norsang Gyatso (1423–1513). *A Short Account of Great Tsongkhapa and His Disciples* (*Rje btsun tsong kha pa chen po dang de nyid la slob ma ji ltar byung tshul mdo tsam brjod pa*) (1491). Anthology of Biographies of the Great Tsongkhapa. Vol. 1, 326–43.

Könchok Chödrak (1646–1718). *Loud Summer Thunder: A Commentary on Tsongkhapa's Praise Entitled "Song of the Spring Queen"* (*'Jam mgon chos kyi rgyal po'i bstod pa dpyid kyi rgyal mo'i glu dbyangs kyi 'grel pa dbyar gyi rnga gsang*). Anthology of Biographies of the Great Tsongkhapa. Vol. 2, 106–47.

Könchok Jikmé Wangpo (1728–91). *Garland of Jewels: History of Ganden Tradition* (*Dga' ldan chos 'byung nor bu'i phreng ba*); incomplete. Collected

Works of Könchok Jikmé Wangpo (Tashi Khyil woodblock print). Vol. *ca*, 529–697.

Kunga Gyaltsen (fifteenth century). *Meaningful to Behold: Biography of Chenga Sönam Gyaltsen* (*Spyan snga bsod nams rgyal mtshan gyi rnam thar mthong ba don ldan*). Collected Works of Chenga Sönam Gyaltsen. Vol. *ka*, 181–342.

Lamp Illuminating Prophecies Concerning the Future (*Ma 'ong lung bstan gsal ba'i sgron me*). Attributed to Padmasambhava and revealed as treasure texts. Leh: Reproduced from the original manuscript by Thondup Tashi, 1973. TBRC W1KG22374.

Lechen Kunga Gyaltsen (1432–1506). *Lamp Illuminating the History of Kadam Tradition* (*Bka' gdams chos 'byung gsal ba'i sgron me*) (1494). Typeset edition. Xinhua: Bod ljongs mi dmangs dpe skrun khang, 2003.

———. *Twelve Wondrous Deeds of the Omniscient Gendun Drup* (*Thams bcad mkhyen pa'i rnam thar ngo mtshar mdzad pa bcu gnis*) (1497). Collected Works of Gendun Drup. Vol. 5, 129–78.

Lekpa Sangpo (fourteenth/fifteenth century). *Feast of Excellent Tales* (*Rmad 'byung gtam gyi dga' ston*). Anthology of Biographies of the Great Tsongkhapa. Vol. 1, 482–514.

———. *Secret Life Stories Not Commonly Known* (*Kun gyis thun mong du ma gyur pa'i gsang ba'i rnam thar*). Anthology of Biographies of the Great Tsongkhapa. Vol. 1, 515–40.

Lhodrak Namkha Gyaltsen (1321–1401). *Garland of Supreme Medicinal Nectar: Responses to Queries* (*Zhus lan sman mchog bdud rtsi'i phreng ba*). Collected Works of Lhodrak Namkha Gyaltsen. Thimphu: Reproduced from a rare manuscript by Kunsang Topgey, 1985, 581–602. Also in Collected Works of Tsongkhapa. Vol. *ka*. (English translation in Thurman 1982.)

———. "How I Met Jé Tsongkhapa." In *Secret Biography Dispelling the Darkness of Misconceptions* (*Gsang ba'i rnam thar log rtog mun sel*). Collected Works of Lhodrak Namkha Gyalsen, 107–10.

———. *Secret Biography Dispelling the Darkness of Misconceptions* (*Gsang ba'i rnam thar log rtog mun sel*). Collected Works of Lhodrak Namkha Gyaltsen, 93–110.

Lobsang Trinlé (nineteenth century). *Single Adornment Beautifying the Buddha's Teachings: Biography of Great Jé Tsongkhapa* (*Rje tsong kha pa chen po'i rnam thar thub bstan mdzes pa'i rgyan gcig*) a.k.a. *Extensive Biography of Jé Tsongkhapa* (*Rje tsong kha pa'i rnam thar chen mo*) (1845). Typeset edition. Xinhua: Mtsho sngon mi rigs dpe skrun khang, 1984.

Lodrö Jikmé Gyaltsen (fifteenth century). *Opening the Door of Faith: A Biography of Chenga Lodrö Gyaltsen* (*Span snga blo gros rgyal mtshan gyi rnam thar dad pa'i sgo 'byed*). Collected Works of Chenga Lodrö Gyaltsen. Vol. 2, 1–25. Typeset edition. Lhasa: Ser gtsug nang bstan nang bstan dpe rnying 'tshol bsdu khang, 2010.

Mikyö Dorjé, Karmapa (1507–54). "In Praise of Five Great Learned Ones Who Appeared Later in the Land of Snows Who Composed Extensive Treatises" (*Gangs can phyis byon pa'i mkhas pa chen po bstan bcos rgyas mar mdzad pa'i dam pa lnga la bstod pa*). Collected Works of Karmapa Mikyö Dorjé. Lhasa: dPal brtsegs dpe rnying bod kyi dpe skrun khang, 2004. Vol. 2, 205–7.

Mönlam Pal (fifteenth century). *Biography of Gö Lotsawa Shönu Pal* (*'Gos lo gzhon nu dpal gyi rnam thar*). Scanned from handwritten dbu med manuscript. TBRC W26618.

Mugé Samten Gyatso (1914–93). *Biography of Master Jikme Trinlé Gyatso* (*Rje 'jigs med phrin las rgya mtsho'i rnam par thar pa*). Collected Works of Mugé Samten Gyatso. Typeset edition. Sichuan: Nationalities Press, 2009. Vol. 1, 1–260.

Nāgārjuna (second century). *Treatise on the Middle Way* (*Mūlamadhyamakakārikā*; *Dbu ma rtsa ba shes rab*). Tengyur. Comparative edition. Vol. 57, 3–46.

Namkha Wöser (sixth century). *Explanation of Tsongkhapa's Biography in Painting* (*Rje btsun tsong kha pa chen po'i rnam thar ras bris su byas pa'i rnam bshad*) (1513). Anthology of Biographies of the Great Tsongkhapa. Vol. 2, 1–40.

Nāropa (ca. eleventh century). "Lucid Summary of the Five Stages" (*Pañcakrama-saṃgraha-prakāśa*; *Rim pa lnga bsdus pa gsal ba*). Tengyur. Comparative edition. Vol. 41, 1747–51.

Nelpa Paṇḍita (thirteenth century). *Flower Garland of Ancient Accounts* (*Sngon gyi gtam me tog gi phreng ba*) (1283). In *Bod kyi lo rgyus deb ther khag lnga*. Typeset edition. Xinhua: Bod ljongs mi dmangs dpe rnying dpe skrun khang, 1990.

Nenying Kunga Delek (1446–96). *Doorway to Faith: A Biography of Conqueror Lobsang Drakpa* (*Rgyal ba blo bzang grags pa'i rnam par thar pa dad pa'i 'jug ngogs*) (1492). Anthology of Biographies of the Great Tsongkhapa. Vol. 1, 344–412.

Neringpa Chimé Rapgyé (fifteenth century). "Delighting the Faithful: An Account of How Tsongkhapa Engaged in Teaching, Debate, and Composition" (*Rje tsong kha pas 'chad rtsod rtsom gsum mdzad tshul gyi rnam thar dad ldan dga' byed*); incomplete. Anthology of Biographies of the Great Tsongkhapa. Vol. 1, 582–93.

——. "Golden Shoot: A Supplement to the Account of Great Tsongkhapa's Disciples" (*Rje tsong kha pa chen por bu chen byon tshul gyi kha skong gser gyi myu gu*); incomplete. Anthology of Biographies of the Great Tsongkhapa. Vol. 1, 563–67.

——. "Golden Tree: An Account of Great Tsongkhapa's Disciples" (*Rje tsong kha pa chen por bu chen byon tshul gyi rnam thar gser gyi mchọd stong*) (1470). Anthology of Biographies of the Great Tsongkhapa. Vol. 1, 541–62.

——. "Treasure House of Gems: How the Qualties of Being Learned, Disciplined, and Kind Were Present in Great Tsongkhapa" (*Rje tsong kha pa chen po la mkhas btsun bzang gsum gyi yon tan mnga' tshul rnam thar nor bu'i bang mdzod*) (1470). Anthology of Biographies of the Great Tsongkhapa. Vol. 1, 568–81.

Ngawang Chödrak Gyatso (sixteenth century). *A Cluster of Flowers Adorning the Buddha's Doctrine: Poetic Narrative on the Life of Jé Tsongkhapa* (*Rje tsong kha pa chen po'i rtogs brjod thub bstan rin po che'i rgyan med tog gi chun po*) (1560). Typeset edition. Beijing: Nationalities Press, 2015.

Ngawang Chökyi Wangchuk (1606–1652). *Hundred and Eight Wondrous Tales: A Biography of Omniscient Lobsang Drakpa in Brief Summaries* (*Thams bcad mkhyen pa blo bzang grags pa'i rnam par thar pa nyung ngur bsdus pa ngo mtshar ba'i gtam rgya rtsa brgyad pa*). Anthology of Biographies of the Great Tsongkhapa. Vol. 2, 207–64.

Ngawang Gelek Gyaltsen (seventeenth century). *Meteoroid Wheel-Weapon Destroying the Distorted Talk Concerning Prophecies about Lord Lobsang Drakpa* (*Rje btsun blo bzang grags pa'i lung bstan la brtsams pa'i 'bel gtam log rtog 'joms pa'i rnam cags 'khor lo*) (1645). Anthology of Biographies of the Great Tsongkhapa. Vol. 2, 54–72.

Ngawang Jamyang Nyima (dates unknown). "The Liberating Story of How Jamchen Chöjé Shākya Yeshé Went to the Chinese Palace on Behalf of Great Tsongkhapa" (*Byams chen chos rje shā kya ye shes de nyid rje tsong kha pa chen po'i sku tshab tu rgya nag pho brang du phebs tshul gyi rnam thar*). Scanned from a photocopy of unknown origin. TBRC W25577.

Ngawang Kunga Sönam (1597–1659). *Beautiful Adornment of the Doctrine of Kālacakra*. Collected Works of Ngawang Kunga Sönam. Vol. *tsha*. Kathmandu: Sa skya rgyal yongs gsung rab slob gnyer khang, 2000. TBRC W29307.

Ngawang Lobsang Gyatso (Fifth Dalai Lama) (1617–82). "A Commentary on Miktsema Prayer Thoroughly Elucidating the Meaning of the Words as Well as Associated Practices" (*Dmigs brtse ma'i ṭikka nyams len dang 'brel ba tshig don rab gsal*). Collected Works of Fifth Dalai Lama. Reproduced from Lhasa Shöl woodblock print. Gangtok: Sikkim Research Institute of Tibetology, 1991–95. Vol. *na*, 471–91.

———. *Song of the Spring Queen: A History of Tibet* (*Bod kyi deb ther dpyid kyi rgyal mo'i glu dbyangs*). Typeset edition. Beijing: Nationalities Press, 1980. (English translation in Ahmad 1995.)

———. *White Crystal Mirror: The Catalog of the Magical Temple of Lhasa* (*Lha ldan sprul pa'i gtsug lag khang gi dkar chag shel dkar me long*). Typeset edition. Xinhua: Bod ljongs mi dmangs dpe skrung khang, 1987.

Nyangrel Nyima Wöser (1124–92). *Honey Essence: History of Buddhism in Tibet* (*Chos 'byung me tog snying po sbrang rtsi'i bcud*). Typeset edition. Xinhua: Bod ljongs mi dmangs dpe skrun khang, 1988.

Palmang Könchok Gyaltsen (1764–1853). *Great Heavenly Drum: Abbatial Successions of Tashi Khyil Monastery* (*Bkra shis 'khyil gyi gdan rabs lha'i rnga chen*). Typeset edition. Kansu: Nationalities Press, 1987.

Panchen Delek Nyima (sixteenth century). *Captivating the Scholar's Mind: Biography of the Omniscient Khedrup* (*Mkhas grub thams bcad mkhyen pa'i rnam thar mkhas pa'i yid 'phrog*). Collected Works of Khedrup Gelek Palsang. Vol. *ka*, 79–108.

Panchen Lobsang Chökyi Gyaltsen (1570–1662). "Door Sign of a Treasure House: Brief Life Stories of the Masters of the Precious Lineage of the Profound Path of the Geden Tradition" (*Dge ldan bka' brgyud rin po che'i zab lam brgyud pa'i rnam par thar pa mdor bsdus gter gyi kha byang*). Collected Works of Panchen Lobsang Chögyen. New Delhi: Reproduced from the Tashi Lhunpo blocks by Mongolia Lama Guru Deva, 1973. Vol. *ka*, 563–83.

———. *Musical Tunes Bringing Joy to Lobsang: Responses to "Queries from a Sincere Heart"* (*Dri ba lhag bsam rab dkar gyi dris lan blo bzang blo bzang bzhad pa'i sgra dbyangs*). Collected Works of Panchen Lobsang Chögyen. Vol. *nga*, 537–58.

Panchen Sönam Drakpa (1478–1554). *History of Old and New Kadam Traditions: Beautiful Adornment of the Mind* (*Bka' gdams gsar rnying gi chos 'byung yid kyi mdzes rgyan*) (1529). Typeset edition. Lhasa: Bod ljongs bod yig dpe rnying dpe skrun khang, 2001.

———. *The New Red Annals: A History of Tibet* (*Rgyal rabs deb dmar gsar pa*) a.k.a. *Magical Key: A History* (*Rgyal rabs 'phrul gyi lde mig*) (1538). Typeset edition. Xinhua: Bod ljongs mi dmangs dpe skrun khang, 1989.

Panchen Yeshé Tsemo (b. 1433). *Wondrous Garland of Jewels: A Biography of* the Omniscient Gendun Drup (*Thams bcad mkhyen pa dge 'dun grub dpal bzang po'i rnam thar rmad byung nor bu'i phreng ba*) (1494). Collected Works of Gendun Drup. Vol. 5, 1–128.

Pawo Tsuklak Trengwa (1504–66). *Feast for the Learned: A History of Buddhism in India and Tibet* (*Chos 'byung mkhas pa'i dga' ston*). 2 vols. (with continuous pagination) (1564). Typeset edition. Beijing: Nationalities Press, 1986.

Phurchok Ngawang Jampa (1682–1762). "Elucidating the Essential Points: A Brief Commentary of Lord Mañjuśrī's Instruction Given Directly to Tsongkhapa" (*'Jam dpal dbyangs kyis rje bla ma la gnang ba'i gdams pa'i ṭikka mdor bsdus gnad don gsal ba*). Collected Works of Phurchok Ngawang Jampa. New Delhi: Reproduced from the Phurbuchok Hermitage block prints by Ngawang Sopa, 1973. Vol. *ka*, 230–46.

The Pillar Testament (*Ka chems ka khol ma*). Attributed to Songtsen Gampo. Typeset edition. Kansu: Nationalities Press, 1989.

Rangjung Dorjé, Karmapa (1284–1339). "Instructions on the Mahāmudrā Innate Union" (*Phyag rgya chen po lhan cig skyes sbyor gyi khrid yig*). In *Mnyam med bka' brgyud lugs kyi phyag rgya chen po dang 'brel ba'i chos skor*. Delhi: Institute of Tibetan Classics, 2008. (English translation in Roberts 2011.)

Rendawa Shönu Lodrö (1349–1412). "Jewel Garland: An Open Letter Addressed to the Upholders of the Dharma Concerning Critical Examination of Kālacakra Tantra" (*Dus kyi 'khor lo'i dpyad pa las brtsams te bstan 'dzin rnams la springs pa nor bu'i phreng ba*). Collected Works of Master Rendawa. Typeset edition. Sichuan: Bod yig dpe rnying bsdu sgrig khang, 2015. Vol. 1, 113–29.

——. "Letter to Dharma Master Lobsang Drakpa Including Expression about the Joy of Solitude" (*Chos rje blo bzang grags pa la gnang ba'i springs yig dben pa la dga' ba'i gtam dang bcas pa*). Collected Works of Master Rendawa. Vol. 3, 78–89.

——. "A Letter to Precious Teacher Kashipa Lobsang Drakpa" (*Bla ma rin po che bka' bzhi pa blo bzang grags pa la springs pa*). *Miscellaneous Writings*, Collected Works of Master Rendawa. Vol. 3, 71–74.

——. *Miscellaneous Writings* (*Gsung thor bu'i skor*). Collected Works of Master Rendawa. Vol. 3, 4–272.

Rongtön Sheja Kunrik (1367–1449). *Presentation of the Difficult Points of [Nāgārjuna's] Madhyamaka Analytic Corpus* (*Dbu ma rigs tshogs kyi dka' ba'i gnad bstan pa*). Collected Works of Rongtön Sheja Kunrik. 10 vols. Typeset edition. Sichuan: Nationalities Press, 2008, 570–703.

Sakya Paṇḍita (1182–1251). *Clear Differentiation of the Three Codes* (*Sdom gsum rab dbye*). Collected Works of Sakya Paṇḍita. Typeset edition Beijing: Krung go'i bod rig pa'i dpe skrun khang, 2007. Vol. 2, 1–91. (English translation in Rhoton 2002.)

——. *Treasury of Reasoning* (*Tshad ma rigs pa'i gter*). Collected Works of Sakya Paṇḍita. Vol. 3, 1–46.

——. *Treasury of Wise Sayings* (*Legs par bshad pa rin po che'i gter*). Collected Works of Sakya Paṇḍita. Vol. 1, 196–239. (English translation in Newman 2018.)

Sangyé Tsemo (fifteenth century). *Wonders of Excellence: A Biography of Glorious Rendawa* (*Dpal ldan red mda' ba'i rnam thar ngo mtshar smad 'byung*). Collected Works of Rendawa. Typeset edition. Sichuan: Bod yig dpe rnying bsdu sgrig khang, 2015. Vol. 1, 24–112.

Shakabpa Wangchuk Deden (1907–89). *Guide to the Central Temple of Lhasa* (*Lha ldan rva sa 'phrul snang gtsug lag khang gi dkar chag*). Kalimpong: Shakabpa House, 1982.

Shākya Chokden (1428–1507). *A Discourse Explaining the Origin of Madhyamaka* (*Dbu ma'i byung tshul bshad pa*). Collected Works of Shākya Chokden. Thimphu: Kunsang Topgey, 1975. Vol. 4, 209–40.

——. *Ocean of Wondrous Faith: A Biography of the Omniscient Lord and Teacher Rongtön Shākya Gyaltsen* (*Rje btsun thams bcad mkhyen pa bshes gnyen rong ston sha kya rgyal mtshan gyi rnam thar ngo mtshar dad pa'i rol mtsho*). Collected Works of Shākya Chokden. Vol. 16, 299–378.

——. *Ornament of the Enlightened Intention: Replies to the Queries from a Sincere Heart* (*Dri ba lhag bsam rab dkar gyi lan rgyal ba'i dgongs rgyan*). Collected Works of Shākya Chokden. Vol. 23, 297–358.

——. *Views Held by Sakya Masters and Their Immediate Heirs* (*Sa skya rje btsun sku mched kyi lta ba'i bzhed tshul*). Collected Works of Shākya Chokden. Vol. 23, 71–104.

Shamar Chödrak Yeshé (1453–1526). *Biography of Gö Lotsawa Shönu Pal: Wish-Granting Tree of Delightful Excellent Qualities* (*Dpal ldan bla ma dam pa mkhan chen thams bcad mkhyen pa gzhon nu dpal gyi rnam par thar pa yon tan rin po chen mchog tu dgyes pa'i ljon pa*) (1493). Collected Works of Shamar Chödrak Yeshé. Typeset edition. Lhasa: Krung go'i bod rig pa'i dpe skrun khang, 2009. Vol. 1, 459–564.

——. "Biography of the Precious Realized Adept Chökyi Pal Yeshé [Third

Shamarpa]" (*Rtogs ldan rin po che chos kyi dpal ye shes kyi rnam thar*) (1508). Collected Works of Shamar Chödrak Yeshé. Vol. 1, 430–49.

——. "Responses to Neuring Rinpoché's Questions" (*Neu rings rin po che'i dris lan*) (1512). Collected Works of Shamar Chödrak Yeshé. Vol. 6, 483–86.

Shang Tsöndru Drakpa (1123–93). *Ultimate Supreme Path of Mahāmudrā* (*Phya rgya chen po lam bzang mthar thug*). In *Mnyam med bka' brgyud kyi lugs kyi phyag rgya chen po dang 'brel ba'i chos skor*. Delhi: Institute of Tibetan Classics, 2008. (English translation in Roberts 2011.)

Shapkar Tsokdruk Rangdrol (1781–1851). *Magical Volume on Padmasambhava* (*O rgyan sprul pa'i glegs bam*). Collected Works of Shapkar Tsokdruk Rangdrol. Typeset edition. Xining: Mtsho sngon mi rigs dpe skrun khang, 2002. Vol. 7, 215–440.

Sönam Gyaltsen (1312–75). *Clear Mirror of History* (*Rgyal rabs gsal ba'i me long*) (1368) Typeset edition. Beijing: Nationalities Press, 2002.

Sumpa Yeshé Paljor (1704–88). *Excellent Wish-Granting Tree: A History of Buddhism* (*Chos 'byung dpag bsal ljon bzang*) (1748). Typeset edition. Kansu: Nationalities Press, 1992.

Taklung Ngawang Namgyal (1571–1626). *Ocean of Wonders: A History of Buddhism* (*Chos 'byung ngo mtshar rgya mtsho*) a.k.a. *History of Taklung Tradition* (*Stag lung chos 'byung*) (1609). Typeset edition. Xinhua: Bod ljongs bod yig dpe rnying dpe skrun khang, 1992.

Taktsang Lotsawa (1405–77). *Biography of Khen Rinpoché Sengé Gyaltsen* (*Mkhan rin po che seng ge rgyal mtshan gyi rnam thar*). Collected Works of Taktsang Lotsawa Sherap Rinchen. Typeset edition. Beijing: Krung go'i bod rig pa dpe skrun khang, 2007. Vol. 2, 106–44.

——. *Biography of the Great Bodhisattva Namkha Wöser* (*Sems dpa' chen po nam mkha' 'od zer gyi rnam thar*). Collected Works of Taktsang Lotsawa Sherap Rinchen. Vol. 2, 64–105.

——. *Biography of the Great Translator Sherap Rinchen* (*Lo chen thams bcad mkhyen pa shes rab rin chen dpal bzang po'i rnam par thar pa*) (1470). Collected Works of Taktsang Lotsawa Sherap Rinchen. Vol. 2, 1–52.

——. "Briefly Expressing the Attributes of Lord Lobsang Drakpa" (*Rje btsun blo bzang grags pa'i ngang tshul mdo tsam du brjod pa*). Collected Works of Taktsang Lotsawa Sherap Rinchen. Vol. 3, 161–63.

Tatsak Tsewang Gyal (fifteenth century). *Lho Rong History of Kagyu Tradition*

(*Lho rong chos 'byung*) (1446). Typeset edition. Xinhua: Bod ljongs bod yig dpe rnying dpe skrun khang, 1994.

Thuken Chökyi Nyima (1737–1802). *Crystal Mirror of Philosophical Systems* (*Grub mtha' shel gyi me long*). Typeset edition. Kansu: Nationalities Press, 1984. (English translation in Geshe Sopa et al. 2009.)

Tokden Jampel Gyatso (1356–1428). "Collection of Well-Uttered Insights: A Supplementary Biography of Jetsun Tsongkhapa's Biography" (*Rje btsun tsong kha pa'i rnam thar zur 'debs legs bshad kun 'dus*). Collected Works of Jé Tsongkhapa. Vol. *ka*. Anthology of Biographies of the Great Tsongkhapa. Vol. 1, 11–28.

———. "Wondrous Tales: Extremely Secret Aspects of the Life of the Incomparable Dharma Lord Lobsang Drakpa" (*Chos kyi rje blo bzang grags pa'i rnam thar shin tu gsang ba rmad du byung ba'i gtam*). Anthology of Biographies of the Great Tsongkhapa. Vol. 1, 7–10.

Tsangnyön Heruka (1452–1507). *Hundred Thousand Songs of Milarepa* (*Rje btsun mi la ras pa'i mgur 'bum*). Xinhua: Mtsho sngon mi rigs dpe skrun khang, 1981. (English translation in Stagg 2016.)

Tsangtön Kunga Gyaltsen (fifteenth century). "Lamp Illuminating the Wondrous Story of the Life of Omniscient Jamyang Chöjé Tashi Palden" (*Thams bcad mkhyen pa 'jams dbyangs chos rje bkra shis dpal ldan pa'i zhal snga nas kyi rnam par thar pa ngo mtshar rmad du byung ba'i gtam rab tu gsal ba'i sgron me*). In *Biographies of the Successive Abbots of Glorious Drepung Monastery* (*Dpal ldan 'bras spung gi gdan rabs rim byon gyi rnam thar*). Scanned from modern book format. TBRC W3CN6943.

Tseten Shapdrung (1910–85). *Abbatial Successions of Jakhyung Monastery* (*Bya khyung dgon pa'i gdan rabs*). Collected Works of Tseten Shapdrung. Typeset edition. Beijing: Nationalities Press, 2007. Vol. 1, 1–168.

———. *Compendium of Chronologies* (*Bstan rtsis kun las btus pa*). Xinhua: Mtsho sngon mi rigs dpe skrun khang, 1982.

———. *Opening the Door of Faith: A Short Biography of Great Tsongkhapa* (*Rnam thar chu thigs tsam bkod pa dad pa'i sgo 'byed*). Collected Works of Tseten Shapdrung. Vol. 1, 169–84.

———. *A Short Account of the Life of Lachen Gongpa Rapsel* (*Bla chen dgongs pa rab gsal gyi rnam par thar pa mdo tsam brjod pa*). Collected Works of Tseten Shapdrung. Vol. 1, 185–204.

———. "A Short Story of Jé Tsongkhapa's Thangka, the Principal Icon of Jang Lama's Khadi Ka Monastery" (*Byang bla ma chos kyi rgyal po'i gdan sa kha di ka'i dgon pa'i rten gtso rje rtsa thang gzhan phan chen mo'i lo rgyus mdor bsdus*). Collected Works of Tseten Shapdrung. Vol. 1, 403–12.

Tsöndru Sangpo (fifteenth century). "A Short Biography of Incomparable Gyaltsen Sangpo" (*Mtshungs med chos kyi rje thams cad mkhyen pa rgyal mtshan bzang po dpal bzang po'i rnam thar mdor bsdus*) (1454). Photo image of handwritten manuscript as well as modern typeset edition. In *Gung ru rgyal mtshan bzang po'i stong thun dang rnam thar*. Typeset edition. Lhasa: Ser gtsug nang bstan dpe rnying 'tshol bsdu khang, 2011.

Yeshé Dhöndrup (1792–1855). *Entryway to the Ocean of Pure Faith: The Wondrous Life of Great Lord Tsongkhapa* (*Rje btsun tsong kha pa chen po'i ngo mtshar rmad du byung ba'i rnam par thar pa rnam dkar dad pa rgya mtshor rol pa'i 'jug ngogs*) (1843). Anthology of Biographies of the Great Tsongkhapa. Vol. 4.

Secondary Literature

Ahmad, Zahiruddhin, trans. 1995. *A History of Tibet by the Fifth Dalai Lama of Tibet*. Bloomington: Indiana University Press.

Apple, James B. 2009. *Stairway to Nirvana: A Study of the Twenty Saṃghas Based on the Works of Tsongkkhapa*. Albany: State University of New York Press.

Ary, Elijah. 2015. *Authorized Lives*. Boston: Wisdom Publications.

Beresford, Brian, trans. 1992. *Mind Training Like the Rays of the Sun*. Dharamsala: Library of Tibetan Works & Archives.

Cabezón, José Ignacio. 1992. *A Dose of Emptiness: An Annotated Translation of the sTong thun chen mo of mKhas grub dGe legs dpal bzang*. Albany: State University of New York Press.

——. 1995. "On Sgra pa shes rab rin chen pa'i rtsod lan of Paṇ chen blo bzang chos rgyan." *Études Asiatiques* 69, no. 4: 643–69.

——, and Geshe Lobsang Dhargyay. 2006. *Freedom from Extremes: Gorampa's "Distinguishing the Views" and the Polemics of Emptiness*. Boston: Wisdom Publications.

Chan, Victor. 1994. *Tibet Handbook: A Pilgrimage Guide*. Chico: Moon Publications.

Desideri, Ippolito. 2010. *Mission to Tibet: The Extraordinary Eighteenth-Century Account of Father Ippolito Desideri*. Translated by Michael J. Sweet. Boston: Wisdom Publications.

Dreyfus, Georges B. 2003. *The Sound of Two Hands Clapping: The Education of a Tibetan Buddhist Monk*. Berkeley: University of California Press.

——, and Sarah McClintock, eds. 2003. *The Svātantrika-Prāsaṅgika Distinction: How Much Difference Does a Difference Make?* Boston: Wisdom Publications.

Geshe Lhundrup Sopa et al., trans. 2009. *Crystal Mirror of Philosophical Systems.* By Thuken Chökyi Nyima. Boston: Wisdom Publications.

Gold, Jonathan. 2007. *The Dharma's Gatekeepers: Sakya Paṇḍita on Buddhist Scholarship in Tibet.* Albany: State University of New York Press.

Hirsch, E. D., et al. 2002. *The New Dictionary of Cultural Literacy.* Third edition. Boston: Houghton Mifflin.

Hopkins, Jeffrey. 1999. *Emptiness in the Mind-Only School of Buddhism: Dynamic Responses to Dzong-ka-ba's* The Essence of Eloquence: Volume 1. Berkeley: University of California Press.

——. 2002. *Reflections on Reality: Dynamic Responses to Dzong-ka-ba's* The Essence of Eloquence: Volume 2. Berkeley: University of California Press.

——. 2008. *Tsong-kha-pa's Final Exposition of Wisdom.* Ithaca: Snow Lion Publications.

Huc, Evariste. 1852. *Travels in Tartary. Thibet and China During the Years 1844–5–6.* Translated by W. Haslitt. London: Office of the National Illustrated Library.

Jackson, David. 1990. "The Earliest Printing of Tsong-kha-pa's Works: The Old Dga' ldan Editions." In *Reflections on Tibetan Culture: Essays in Memory of Turrell V. Wylie.* Edited by Laurence Epstein and Richard F. Sherburne. Studies in Asian Thought and Religion, vol. 12. Hamburg: Universität Hamburg: 107–16.

Jinpa, Thupten. 1998. "Delineating Reason's Scope for Negation: Tsongkhapa's Contribution to Madhyamaka Dialectical Method." *Journal of Indian Philosophy* 26: 275–308.

——. 1999. "Tsongkhapa's Qualms about Early Tibetan Interpretations of Madhyamaka Philosophy." *The Tibet Journal* 24, no. 2 (Summer): 1–28.

——. 2002. *Self, Reality, and Reason in Tibetan Philosophy: Tsongkhapa's Quest for the Middle Way.* London: Routledge Curzon.

——. 2008. "Introduction." In *The Book of Kadam: The Core Texts.* Boston: Wisdom Publications.

——. 2009. "Rendawa and the Question of Kālacakra's Uniqueness." In *As Long as Space Endures.* Edited by Edward A. Arnold. Ithaca: Snow Lion Publications.

——, trans. Forthcoming. Tsongkhapa. *Elucidation of the Intent: An Extentive*

Exposition of Candrakīrti's "Entering the Middle Way." Library of Tibetan Classics. Vol. 19. Boston: Wisdom Publications.
—— and Jaś Elsner, trans. 2000. *Songs of Spiritual Experience: Tibetan Poems of Insight and Awakening*. Boston: Shambhala Publications.
—— and Donald S. Lopez, trans. 2014. *Grains of Gold: Tales of a Cosmopolitan Traveler.* By Gendun Chopel. Chicago: University of Chicago.
Kapstein, Matthew. 2006. *The Tibetans*. Oxford: Blackwell Publishing.
Kilty, Gavin, trans. 2001. *The Splendor of an Autumn Moon: The Devotional Verse of Tsongkhapa*. Boston: Wisdom Publications.
——, trans. 2017. *Lamp to Illuminate the Five Stages*. By Tsongkhapa. Boston: Wisdom Publications.
Komarovski, Yaroslav, trans. 2000. *Three Texts on Madhyamaka*. By Shakya Chokden. Dharamsala: Library of Tibetan Works & Archives.
Lopez, Donald S., and Thupten Jinpa, trans. 2017. *Dispelling the Darkness: A Jesuit's Quest for the Soul of Tibet*. Cambridge: Harvard University Press.
——. 2018. "Afterword." In *Treatise on Passion: A Tibetan Guide to Love & Sex*. By Gendun Chopel. Chicago: University of Chicago Press.
Martin, Dan. https://sites.google.com/site/tibetological/gung-thang-dkar-chag.
Mullin, Glenn H., trans. 1996. *Tsongkhapa's Six Yogas of Naropa*. Ithaca: Snow Lion Publications.
Napper, Elizabeth. 1989. *Dependent Arising: A Tibetan Buddhist Interpretation on Mādhyamika Philosophy*. Boston: Wisdom Publications.
Newman, Beth, trans. 2018. *The Tibetan Book of Everyday Wisdom*. Boston: Wisdom Publications.
Onodo, Shunzo. 1990. "Abbatial Successions of the Colleges of gSang phu sNe'u thog Monastery." *Bulletin of the National Museum of Ethnology* 15, no. 4: 149–71.
Rhoton, Jared Douglas, trans. 2002. *A Clear Differentiation of the Three Codes*. Albany: State University New York Press.
Richardon, H. E. 1985. *A Corpus of Early Tibetan Inscriptions*. London: Royal Asiatic Society.
Richardson, Hugh. 1998. "The Jokhang 'Cathedral' of Lhasa." In *High Peaks, Pure Earth: Collected Writings on Tibetan History and Culture*. London: Serindia Publications.
Roberts, Peter Alan, trans. 2011. *Mahāmudra and Related Instructions*. Boston: Wisdom Publications.

Roerich, George N., trans. 1949. *The Blue Annals.* Delhi: Motilal Banarsidass.

Ruegg, David Seyfort. 1966. *The Life of Bu ston Rinpoché: With the Tibetan Text of the Bu ston rNam thar.* Serie Orientale Roma XXXIV. Rome: Instituto per il Medio ed Estremo Oriente.

——. 1989. *Buddha-Nature, Mind and the Problem of Gradualism in a Comparative Perspective: On the Transmission and Reception of Buddhism in India and Tibet.* London: School of Oriental and African Studies.

——. 2000. *Three Studies in the History of Indian and Tibetan Madhyamaka Philosophy: Studies in Indian and Tibetan Madhyamaka Thought Part 1.* Vienna: Arbeitskeis für Tibetische und Buddhistische Studien Universitat Wein.

——. 2000. "Introduction." In *The Great Treatise on the Stages of the Path,* Volume 1. Translated by The Lamrim Chenmo Translation Committee. Ithaca: Snow Lion Publications.

——. 2002. *Studies in Indian and Tibetan Madhyamaka Thought Part 2.* Vienna: Arbeitskeis für Tibetische und Buddhistische Studien Universitat Wein.

——. 2004. "The Indian and Indic in Tibetan Cultural History, and Tsong-kha-pa's Achievement as a Scholar and Thinker: An Essay on the Concepts of 'Buddhism in Tibet' and 'Tibetan Buddhism.' *Journal of Indian Philosophy* 32: 321–43. Republished in David Seyfort Ruegg, *The Buddhist Philosophy of the Middle* (Boston: Wisdom Publications, 2010), 375–98.

Samten, Geshe Ngawang, and Jay Garfield, trans. 2006. *Ocean of Reasoning: A Great Commentary on Nāgārjuna's Mūlamadhyamakakārikā.* By Tsongkhapa. New York: Oxford University Press.

Śāntideva. 1996. *Bodhicaryāvatāra.* Translated by Kate Crosby and Andrew Skilton. Oxford: Oxford University Press.

Segal, Robert A. 2006. *Myth: A Very Brief Introduction.* New York: Oxford University Press.

Sideris, Mark, and Shōyū Katsura, trans. 2013. *Nāgārjuna's Middle Way.* Boston: Wisdom Publications.

Sparham, Gareth, trans. 1993. *Ocean of Eloquence: Tsongkhapa's Commentary on the Yogācāra Doctrine of Mind.* Albany: State University of New York Press.

——, trans. 2005. *Tantric Ethics: An Explanation of the Precepts for Buddhist Vajrayāna Practice.* Boston: Wisdom Publications.

Stagg, Christopher, trans. 2016. *The Hundred Thousand Songs of Milarepa: A New Translation.* By Tsangnyön Heruka. Boulder: Shambhala Publications.

Tatz, Mark, trans. 1986. *Asaṅga's Chapter on Ethics with the Commentary of Tsong-*

khapa, The Basic Path to Awakening, The Complete Path. Lewiston, NY: The Edwin Mellen Press.

Thurman, Robert A. F., ed. 1982. *Life and Teachings of Tsongkhapa*. Dharamsala: Library of Tibetan Works & Archives; Boston: Wisdom Publications, 2018.

——. 1984. *Central Philosophy of Tibet*. New Jersey: Princeton University Press.

Tillemans, Tom. 2016. *How Do Mādhyamikas Think?* Boston: Wisdom Publications.

Tsong-kha-pa. 2000–2004. *The Great Treatise on the Stages of the Path to Enlightenment*. Translated by The Lamrim Chenmo Translation Committee. 3 vols. Ithaca: Snow Lion Publications.

van der Kuijp, Leonard. 1987. "The Monastery of Gsang-phu Ne'u-thog and Its Abbatial Succession from ca. 1073 to 1250." *Berliner Indologische Studien* 3: 103–27.

——. 2015. "May the 'Original' *Lam rim chen mo* Please Stand Up: A Note on Its Indigenous Textual Criticism." In *The Illuminating Mirror: Tibetan Studies in Honour of Per K. Sørensen on the Occasion of His 65th Birthday*. Edited by Olaf Czaja and Guntram Hazod, 253–68. Wiesbaden: Dr. Ludwig Reichert Verlag.

Van Schaik, Sam. 2011. *Tibet: A History*. London: Yale University Press.

Verhovek, Sam Howe. "Visiting a Tibetan Monastery." *New York Times*, May 25, 1986.

Vitali, Roberto. 1990. *Early Temples of Central Tibet*. London: Serindia Publications.

Index

LIVES OF THE MASTERS

"Since the time of Buddha Shakyamuni himself, Buddhists have been accustomed to recollect the lives of great teachers and practitioners as a source of inspiration from which we may still learn. The Lives of the Masters series continues this noble tradition, recounting the stories, wisdom, and experience of many accomplished Buddhists over the last 2,500 years. I am sure readers will find the accounts in this series inspirational and encouraging."

—His Holiness the Dalai Lama

"The lives of the most important Buddhist masters in history written by the very best of scholars in elegant and accessible prose—who could ask for more?"

—José Cabezón, *Professor of Tibetan Buddhist Studies University of California Santa Barbara*

BOOKS IN THE SERIES

Atiśa Dīpaṃkara: Illuminator of the Awakened Mind
Gendun Chopel: Tibet's Modern Visionary
Tsongkhapa: A Buddha in the Land of Snows

Please visit www.shambhala.com for more information on forthcoming titles.